W9-BUF-412

THE OPEN DECISION

THE OPEN

THE OPEN DECISION

THE CONTEMPORARY AMERICAN NOVEL
AND ITS INTELLECTUAL BACKGROUND

BY *Jerry H. Bryant*

CALIFORNIA STATE COLLEGE · HAYWARD

New York Fp THE FREE PRESS

COLLIER-MACMILLAN LIMITED · LONDON

A Division of The Macmillan Company

Printed in the United States of America

The Free Press
A Division of The Macmillan Company
866 Third Avenue, New York, New York 10022

Collier-Macmillan Canada Ltd., Toronto, Ontario

Library of Congress Catalog Card Number: 79–128473

printing number
1 2 3 4 5 6 7 8 9 10

For the Folks

PREFACE

ALL STATEMENTS of fact and fancy in this book, except when quoted or paraphrased, are mine, and I accept full responsibility for them. However, many people helped me come to them: many of my students, especially those in The Lower Mission Improvement Society; many of my colleagues and friends, especially Professors Edward Clay, J. E. Conner, Norman S. Grabo, Eugene Mayers, Marian Whitehead, and Dr. John Edward Talley, all of whom have read parts of this book in various forms; Robert C. Albrecht, who read the whole manuscript; and Beverly McDaid, who almost finished the typescript on time. Others helped me, but to name them would lengthen these acknowledgments interminably. They know I am grateful.

I thank California State College, Hayward, for a paid leave of absence of one quarter, which allowed me to complete the first main draft.

J. H. B.

CREDITS AND ACKNOWLEDGMENTS

I THANK the *Arizona Quarterly* and the *South Atlantic Quarterly* for allowing me to use parts of my articles first published by them respectively: "The Last of the Social Protest Writers" (Winter, 1963), copyright by *Arizona Quarterly;* "The Hopeful Stoicism of William Styron" (Autumn, 1963), copyright by Duke University Press. I wish also to thank the following individuals and publishers for allowing me to quote from the following works:

Saul Bellow, *The Adventures of Augie March;* Viking Press, 1953; reprinted with permission of Viking Press, copyright 1953 by Saul Bellow.

Albert Einstein and Leopold Infeld, *The Evolution of Physics;* Simon and Schuster, 1938; reprinted with permission of Mr. Arthur Donigan.

James Jones, *From Here to Eternity,* Charles Scribner's sons, 1951; reprinted with permission of Charles Scribner's Sons and William Collins Sons & Co., Ltd.

Norman Mailer, *The Naked and the Dead,* Rinehart & Co., 1948; reprinted with permission by Mr. Scott Meredith.

Irwin Shaw, *The Young Lions,* Random House, 1948; reprinted with permission of Random House, Inc., copyright 1948 by Irwin Shaw.

Alexander Trocchi, *Cain's Book,* copyright © 1960, by Grove Press, Inc.; reprinted with permission of Grove Press.

Alfred North Whitehead, *Process and Reality,* reprinted with permission of The Macmillan Company from *Process and Reality* by Alfred North Whitehead. Copyright 1929 by The Macmillan Company; renewed 1957 by Evelyn Whitehead. Permission also from Cambridge University Press.

CONTENTS

ONE

INTRODUCTION

Contemporary American fiction, that is, American fiction that has appeared since the Second World War, has received enormous attention. Books, learned and popular articles, reviews, collections of interviews with authors, courses in our colleges—all have subjected the recent American novel to unprecedented scrutiny. In general, this outpouring of criticism and interpretation has been beneficial and illuminating, not only for the reader but for the writer as well. Specific critical works, however, have been limited in the breadth of their reference and in the number of writers discussed in them. Most of these works are an essay about one author, a unified study of four or five authors, or a set of disconnected essays about authors and themes. Seldom has there been any attempt to formulate, in one work, the broad issues of the modern intellectual climate, or any effort to place our novels in terms of such a formulation.

In *The Open Decision,* I have tried to survey a much larger number of novels than one ordinarily finds treated in a single study. I recognize that such an attempt is in danger of oversimplification and superficiality. But although something may be lost in depth, a great deal can be gained by treating many diverse novels against the background of a single theme. I seek the broad picture, even though at times it may be blurred, rather than the narrow focus that reveals every detail, every pore and blemish in a single face. With one or two exceptions, such as Irwin Shaw and John P. Marquand, the novelists treated here published their first works during or after World War II.

I have also tried to formulate the principal moral and philosophical issues which preoccupy our age and which constitute the assumptions of our novelists. Most criticism has been limited to the influence of Existentialism upon the contemporary American novelist. I have tried to construct the logic of the larger intellectual climate to be found in present-day physics, philosophy, sociology, psychology, and other disciplines of study. This climate is unified by a particular view of reality, and one of this book's main assumptions is that this view of reality forms the foundation of contemporary morality and that the novels studied herein examine that foundation and dramatize the dilemmas of that morality.

Some critics—though by no means all—have complained about the portrait of man that has been drawn by the contemporary American novelist. It shows, some say, an ignominious insect, cowering and helpless without his old God; or it shows an aimless, purposeless victim of biological and social forces over which he has no control; or it shows a sensitive creature too delicate for this world, plunged in a melancholy gloom of "alienation," "estrangement," "*angst*," "despair." Certainly no one can deny that these words and this criticism do have some validity. Contemporary literature does seem to depict man in, to use the commonplace, a "crisis of identity." But to go no further is to distort the facts. Such criticism implies that the human being can have value only when he can refer to some antecedent absolute which confers upon man his purpose and his meaning. Lacking a belief in deity, the argument goes, man can only subside into the hopelessness that comes from being alone in the universe, trapped in absurdity and purposelessness. That the contemporary American novel does frequently depict loneliness and hopelessness is true. What I argue against is the judgment that that picture is to be interpreted as an expression of pessimism and disgust with the human condition. On the contrary, it can be—it must be, if the evidence is to be honored—interpreted as affirming the human condition.

The ground for this interpretation is to be found in the intellectual construct which forms one of the basic approaches to human life taken in the twentieth century. To name that construct, I have borrowed a phrase from Max Scheler, the noted but seldom translated German phenomenologist whose main work was composed in the 1920's. I mean by that phrase something broader than Scheler meant by it. "Man is a creature," writes Scheler, "whose very essence is the open decision."[1] The phrase "the open decision" is the starting point for my definition of the contemporary intellectual construct that affirms the worth, the glory, of the human being in a world bereft of God, in a world whose "ancestral order," as Walter Lippmann put it, has been dissolved by the "acids of modernity." This phrase and this construct imply that to be human is our highest good. They state that to be human is to be open to possibilities, to be condemned (as Sartre says) to choose from those possibilities, and to suffer the consequences of those choices. They suggest that to be human is to be aware of this freedom and, paradoxically, the limitations which it imposes. A man becomes most human, says Scheler in *Man's Place in Nature,* when he separates himself from the imperatives of his environment and becomes "self-conscious." Only animals fail to make the separation, and thus they are driven, willy-nilly, by instinct. They lack the consciousness to acknowledge their open possibilities. The human being says "No" to nature, to the lower drives and the world in which these drives are most comfortable, and in doing so he sublimates them and appropriates their energy for the activities of his essential being. When he says "No," man commits himself, says Scheler, to the spirit of his essential individuality and thus combines his life forces—the instinctual drives and the "pure spirit"—into an instrument for the realization of his full human possibilities, the intense and creative awareness of his existence.

When man says "No," he affirms his own existence by differentiating himself from what Edmund Husserl, Scheler's German teacher and the founder of modern phenomenology, called the "stream of existence," by pointing to himself as an intelligible and self-recognizable creature. This man, acutely aware and open, is also "hopeless," in the sense that he cannot appeal his condition to some higher court. He is condemned to exist within the limitations imposed. But in that existence he is absolute in himself, the center of his universe, the originator of his actions, and the creator of his identity and purpose. In him lies reality and in reality lies value. As he becomes more vividly aware, he becomes more "real." He stands out against the world, intensely aware of his past, of the moment to which that past brings him, and of the community in which he has his existence. He *is* "estranged" and "alienated." He *does* feel "*angst*" and "despair." He is inescapably isolated. By its nature the community would suppress his individuality, the ground of his identity. In his being as a living creature he is limited by inevitable death. But these conditions of man's existence, although they are the cause of pain and anxiety and loneliness, are also the foundation of a high intensity of individual satisfaction, and that is the value of human life in the philosophy of the "open decision," the value that I try to identify in Part I. That is the value presupposed in the work of the contemporary American novelist, which I try to demonstrate in Parts II and III. The value of human life, in the absence of value conferred by a transcendent deity, is not necessarily serene and restful happiness; it is the intensity with which the individual knows he is alive and feels growth, change, imminent death. "Man," writes Karl Jaspers, Scheler's better-known contemporary and intellectual fellow,

> torn from the sheltering substantiality of stable conditions and cast into the apparatus of mass-life, deprived of his faith by the loss of religion, is devoting more decisive thought to the nature of his own being. Thus it is that there have arisen the typical philosophical ideas adequate to our own epoch. No longer does the revealed Deity upon whom all is dependent come first, and no longer the world that exists around us; what comes first is man. . . .[2]

The typical frame of these "typical philosophical ideas" Jaspers refers to is illustrated in the work of Ludwig Wittgenstein, a logical positivist and analytical philosopher belonging successively to schools of thought toward which Jaspers was a sworn enemy. In his early association with the Vienna Circle, Wittgenstein concluded that the only way to investigate a given language is through a meta-language, a kind of metaphorical deity that transcends the language under investigation. A generation later, however, Wittgenstein reversed his opinion, for the concept of the meta-language leads to analytical methods of infinite regress. One simply cannot discover a meta-language, just as one cannot discover God—at least by any acceptable logical or empirical methods. Wittgenstein instead postulated the idea of a "language-game," which is, as he says, just like a children's game. Its limitations are imposed by the common agreement of those who play the particular game rather than from something inherent, Godlike, in the language itself. The movements or activities of the participants have meaning, are understandable, only in terms of the rules and aims of the game. The question is, writes Wittgenstein, "not one of explaining a language-game by means of our experiences, but of noting a language game."[3] The contemporary American novelist writes within the limits of the language-game of our era, named in the phrase "open decision," and entailing all that the phrase implies. Interpretation of this fiction is not a matter of explaining why the novelist writes as he does, but of noting the language-game he plays and the movements he makes according to it.

The contemporary American novelist, schooled in this game from the time he is able to think, constructs actions whose intelligibility and meaningfulness are illuminated when associated with the rules of construction. The problems of human life that preoccupy these novelists arise from the assumptions basic to the game. Thus, the focus of attention of almost every novelist treated in this book is upon two related things: first, the way in which the individual human being can become more himself; and second, the obstacles to that achievement. The game embodied in the "open decision" presupposes that self-identity is founded upon a high degree of consciousness. The tragedy of the human condition is that consciousness can never be absolute, knowledge can never be total. Satisfaction lies, paradoxically, in the discovery and the acceptance of the freedom to conceive dreams and the limitations life places upon us in the realization of those dreams. Every victory of human consciousness contains some element of defeat. It is this ambiguity that gives the novels of our time their air of apparent pessimism. It is difficult for us to see in the ending of Norman Mailer's *The Naked and the Dead,* Bernard Malamud's *The Fixer,* or Saul Bellow's *Herzog* any ground for affirming the human condition. Mailer's Sergeant Croft is denied success in his attempt to climb Mt. Anaka; Malamud's Yakov Bok remains in the hands of a bigoted Russian state; and Herzog seems to surrender to helplessness as he reclines upon a dirty bed in his home in the Berkshire Hills. But all of them arrive at a higher consciousness that sheds light upon the human condition, its limits and its possibilities. Croft, on the tantalizing verge of absolute knowledge, discovers not only limits to his own appetites for such power, but his comradeship with other human beings. Yakov Bok discovers that he need not be what the state would force him to be. And Herzog discovers that he can no longer cushion his sensitive feelings in romanticism, childhood, and "total explanation."

What these writers and their contemporaries regard as important to the mid-twentieth-century human being grows out of the assumptions of our twentieth-century language game—the "open decision." It constitutes the perceptual patterns according to which our novelists grant priority to issues. They recognize the thirst for the absolute; they assume that the absolute is beyond the human's grasp; in their novels they dramatize this conflict and conclude affirmatively that our highest satisfaction is to be achieved within the limits of our condition as given, though they admit with some regret that not all that we can conceive of can be actualized. They tacitly assume that reality self-evidently embodies the highest good, and that the highest reality lies in a consciousness which reveals its very limitations. The game is "won" when such consciousness is achieved.

This game did not come into being suddenly, nor is it totally unique to our age. But it is not important to my purpose to trace its genesis or show its corollaries in previous eras. I am interested only in its content, not its historical origins. Because that content was codified in its present form during the first three decades of the twentieth century, a large number of the documents I discuss were written during that period. I do not, however, exclude material from earlier or later years. Much will be omitted. Some will object to the authors and documents that I use to describe the "open decision," or to the fact that I do not use other authors and documents. I do not claim to be exhaustive. I do hope that my selectiveness will be adequately descriptive.

1

PHYSICAL REALITY

To ask "What is the 'open decision'?" is to ask "What is the human being?" The answer to this single question lies partly in the twentieth-century view of physical reality, for any conception of human nature has roots in the prevailing conception of physical nature. This chapter examines the basic modern view of physical reality as it is formulated by twentieth-century physicists. It is important to do this, not because every author discussed in Parts II and III is a student of modern science, fully informed about relativity theory, quantum mechanics, and the uncertainty principle—though many, including Kurt Vonnegut, John Barth, and Thomas Pynchon, are —but because the discoveries of modern science are so pervasive a part of our world-view. No present-day author can escape his debt to that view. I do not, therefore, discuss the findings of modern physics to establish that they *determined* the attitude found in the "open decision," but to point up the ubiquity of that attitude and to articulate some of the basic propositions of our contemporary language-game. This chapter thus forms part of the basis for my discussion of the contemporary American novel in Parts II and III. I should also note in this introductory paragraph that it is said almost universally that science caused the dissolution of what are taken to have been the comfortable beliefs of our ancestors. It would be more accurate to say that science as we think of it has not been a cause of change, but simply one of change's manifestations.

Modern physics tells us things, not only about the nature of the world in itself, but also our relationship to it. It is with that relationship that our novelists are basically concerned. Indeed, the

For Notes to Chapter 1, see pages 397–398.

days have long passed since men considered that the two could be treated separately. The relationship between the observer and the "reality" observed has always been a factor in scientific theory, especially in post-Renaissance science. Bacon, discussing the Idols, argues that men's dependence upon Aristotelianism and Scholasticism blinded them to what is "really" there in the world. Locke was concerned with the inadequacy of our senses to discern the "truth" about the nature of things. For all the similarities, there is an important difference between the modern view and that of Bacon and Locke or Galileo and Newton. We do not claim to "know" physical reality in the same sense as Galileo and Newton "knew" it. The classical physicist, inheriting Newton's assumptions, concludes that once he knows all the relationships between physical bodies, his knowledge will be absolutely complete. Herman von Helmholtz writes in the mid-nineteenth century:

> . . . we discover the problem of physical material science to be to refer natural phenomena back to unchangeable attractive and repulsive forces whose intensity depends wholly upon distance. The solubility of this problem is the condition of the comprehensibility of nature. And [science's] vocation will be ended as soon as the reduction of the natural phenomena to simple forces is complete and the proof given that this is the only reduction of which the phenomena are capable.[1]

The modern physicist finds the problem a little more difficult. Not only does matter in itself defy von Helmholtz's final explanation; the nature of things has set a gap in our relationship with matter which seems impossible to bridge. What this means is that, as Alfred North Whitehead says, "all explanation must end in an ultimate arbitrariness."[2] How are these notions reflected in our conception of physical reality?

What is real for the ordinary person in his everyday life is irrelevant to the physicist. It is useful to regard the desk before me as "real"; it holds my typewriter and piles of paper. What can it mean to me that the "thing" serving me is not ultimate and irreducible? For the physicist, however, this is crucial. Though he might not put it this way, what is "real" for him is the elementary particle, the irreducible entity that is the ultimate constituent of matter. And we must remember that in the "open decision" the "real" is the ground of value. Traditionally, this ultimate constituent, this "reality," has been explained by the classical atomic theory prominent in western cultural history. At the bottom of this explanation lies the idea of substance, the idea that these particle-atoms are, in Newton's words, "solid, massy, hard, impenetrable, moveable," so hard "as never to wear or break in pieces." The conviction that such entities exist provided a certain amount of comfort to the classical physicist and the intellectual climate he helped establish. The staying power of the classical atom resembles God's own immutability. The atom, in this view, makes nature "lasting." Change, says Newton, adumbrating von Helmholtz, is "to be placed only in the various Separations and new Associations and Motions of these permanent particles; compound Bodies being apt to break, not in the midst of solid Particles, but where these particles are laid together, and only touch a few Points."[3]

For classical physics, writes John Dewey, "reality in order to be solid and firm must consist of those fixed immutable things which philosophy called Substances. Changes could be *known* only if they could be somehow reduced to recombinations of original unchanging things."[4] The things themselves do not undergo changes. The particle is not "internally" influenced by the world it appears in. Only its motion and position can, in this view, be affected, and that is a matter of external relations only. By the middle of the nineteenth century, physicists were sure that the classical atomic theory held the final truth about the nature of matter. Here is James Clerk Maxwell on the subject:

> The formation of the atom is . . . an event not belonging to that order of nature under which we live. It is an operation of a kind which is not, as far as we are aware, going on on earth, or in the sun or the stars, either now or since those bodies began to be formed. It must be referred to the epoch, not of the formation of the earth or of the solar system, but of the establishment of the existing order of nature, and till not only these worlds and systems, but the very order of nature itself is dissolved, we have no reason to expect the occurrence of any operation of a similar kind.[5]

We know now that this is not an exact representation of the material reality that has come to light in the late nineteenth and early twentieth centuries through scientific experimentation. Radium atoms are destroyed and plutonium atoms can be created. We also know that what the classical physicist took as an irreducible massy substance is a system of smaller units: electrons, protons, mesons, neutrinos (the list goes on and on). Nor is it simply a matter of the classical physicist's failure to go far enough. Neither the word *atom* nor *elementary particle* refers to anything like the traditional Newtonian atom. The modern elementary particle has no substance in the classical sense. It does not lend itself to clear representation, to descriptions by words or pictures. The physicist talks about it mathematically, but mathematics does not say anything about the nature of the thing in itself, its reason for acting as it does, or its reason for being in the first place. The laws of the atom and its parts, furthermore, are not Newton's laws of motion which were said to apply to the classical atom; they are the laws of quantum.

The quantum theory was first postulated to explain heat radiation in black bodies. According to classical mechanics, radiant and light energy emitted from a body is wavelike, taking the form of a kind of continuous ray. But studies in the late nineteenth century of the radiating alpha-, beta-, and gamma-rays revealed data that conflicted with this assumption. In 1900, Max Planck inaugurated quantum physics by theorizing that the energy emitted from a heated black body was not a ray but a series of discrete bursts—quanta.[6] The size of the quantum "packet" emitted depends, says Planck, upon the frequency of emission multiplied by a very small number designated by *h*. This is Planck's "constant," probably one of the most fundamental discoveries of modern physics.

The discontinuousness of a natural event is in direct contradiction to some of the most basic assumptions of classical physics, but in 1905 Einstein confirmed Planck's findings. In his explanation of the "photoelectric effect," Einstein extended the quantum interpretation of radiant energy from heat to light and x-rays. When a "ray" of light falls upon a metal surface, Einstein said, electrons are liberated in the form of photoelectrons. This effect is the result of the interactions between quanta of light—photons—and the electrons of the metallic atoms, in which the photons communicate their energy to the electrons in individual bursts rather than in streams or waves. Einstein's proposition raised a basic paradox: sometimes light—as well as matter—acts like a wave, sometimes like a particle. More than that, his proposition was another phase in our education in the relationship between the observer and the thing observed. We were learning the tremendous extent of our ignorance, at least as seen from the viewpoint of classical physics, about matter itself and our ability to "know" it.

And in 1905, the year that Einstein published his paper on the photoelectric effect, there was a good deal more to be learned about our ignorance. And we learned it. Physicists trained in the classical view began, step by step, to dismantle that view. In 1899, J. J. Thomson discovered the electron. He postulated that electrons were spread through the atom like raisins in a pudding. A decade later Ernest Rutherford constructed a different model of the atom, expressing it as a tiny solar system, with a very small massy nucleus, around which satellite electrons whirled. Both models, however, were based upon the laws of classical physics, laws which were assumed to be applicable to micro- as well as macroscopic bodies. According to these laws, any orbiting body that loses its energy must succumb to the gravitational pull of the parent body and fall into that body. If the electron really does orbit the atomic nucleus, then something is wrong with the laws. Electrons lose energy in the process of radiation. But in changing their energy levels they do not fall into the nucleus. The atom does not collapse after every radiation. Its system remains more or less stable. How could this be explained if the classical laws of physics were to retain their validity?

Niels Bohr sought the answer by going beyond Rutherford, but maintaining the essentially mechanical explanation of classical physics. Rutherford had said that the electrons move in fixed orbits about the nucleus and emit energy while in those orbits. Bohr suggested that a single electron had many possible orbits available to it, though in the course of its lifetime it need not occupy all the orbits possible. It does, however, occasionally leap from one orbit to another; and it does so whenever it changes its energy level. The change of orbit is marked by the emission of a quantum of energy. It does not fall into the nucleus upon its loss of energy, or get caught between orbits; it simply shifts orbits. In George Gamow's metaphor, Bohr's electron behaves like an automobile transmission, which can be put into any one gear at a single time but not in two gears at once or in between gears. Significantly, the result of this explanation was the discovery that the energy change undergone by an electron moving from one orbit to another "turned out to be exactly equal to the quantum constant *h* used by Planck."[7]

Bohr used the quantum theory to serve Rutherford's classical picture of orbits and centers and particles capable of being specifically located in time and space. He took the behavior of the electron within the atom to be explainable in terms of the quantum action. Something happens to the elementary particle which shows it to be far different from the Newtonian atom. It undergoes internal changes as it loses energy, and those internal changes seem to affect its externally observable behavior—at least so Bohr postulated. But Bohr's hypothesis did not explain why the electron occupies only some orbits rather than one or all available to it, why there is no radiation of the electron in orbit, why there is a relationship between the frequency of radiation and the electron's energy rather than between the intensity of radiation and the electron's energy. If the behavior of the electron could not be explained by regarding it as a particle operating under the laws of Newton, how could it be explained?

The problem was that the electron was still being regarded as a particle analogous to the old atom and to planets and stars and other bodies. It was expected to have a definite location at a definite time, to have an identity in the sense that a Newtonian atom or the moon has identity. Such identity depends upon our ability to use words like "it," "here," "there" in talking about the electron. The implication is that identity is associated with objectivity—that is, with a thing's being observable as it is in itself. But the electron eluded this kind of identification.

In 1924, Louis de Broglie sought to break the impasse, making what David Park has called "the most fruitful abstract assumption that anybody had made in twentieth-century physics." That assumption carried modern physics further away from its classical forbears and picked up the implications in Einstein's theory of the photoelectric effect: ". . . if light is a wave field with aspects of a particle, then the uniformity of nature suggests that particles, that is, matter, must therefore have aspects of a wave field."[8] It is with this theory that the modern understanding of physical reality in itself begins. Unfortunately, we can approach that understanding only through an analogy and not through direct observation of the entity itself.

The questions for the moment are: What is the electron doing while it is in "orbit"? What happens when it changes orbits? De Broglie's answer is "wave mechanics." If an electron has the properties of waves, we can understand it by examining the nature of waves.

Einstein uses this analogy to explain wave behavior: If we take a flexible rubber tube in our hand and move the end up and down, we create a wave that moves along the body of the tube to the other end. If the other end is free, the wave will move along without any interference and will dissipate at the free end. If the other end is fixed, the first wave will hit the fixed end and bounce back toward our hand. If we create another wave, it will move, as did the first one, toward the fixed end of the tube. As it travels it will meet wave number one. The returning wave "interferes" with the outgoing wave. The result of this interference is a "standing wave." It "stands" between the two fixed ends—"nodes"—of the rubber tube, and has the shape of the arc in a child's jump rope when it is held at both ends and rotated. If we think of the electron as having the properties of waves, this analogy suggests what the electron is doing while it is in orbit. The standing wave is analogous to the electron's orbit. So long as its standing wave is characterized by two nodes, the electron will occupy a two-node orbit. A different standing wave can be produced by changing the number of nodes. Fix the middle of the rubber tube and we have three nodes: one at both ends and one in the center. The standing wave created by interference in this case is pictorialized by two arcs, one between each set of two nodes. In this picture, one arc rises above the axis running through the three nodes, and the other arc drops below it. The rubber tube is analogous to the electron and its aspect as a wave, and the standing wave—to repeat—is analogous to the electron's orbit. To say that the electron changes orbit is to say that it changes its standing wave.

The possible number of standing waves that might appear in the rubber tube—or the electron—is as large as the possible number of nodes. But there is nothing to force the tube—or the electron—to form all of the standing waves possible. Also, in any standing wave there can be no fractional number of nodes or arcs, hence no half-waves or "almost" orbits. Three nodes in the rubber tube give a two-arc standing wave, four nodes a three-arc standing wave, and so forth. As Einstein says, "The sentence, 'the number of nodes in a standing wave is 3.576,' is pure nonsense."[9] If the electron has wave properties, it cannot be composed of a standing wave made of 3½ nodes; by analogy, it cannot occupy more than one orbit at a time and cannot fall between orbits.

Wave mechanics provides a useful mathematical apparatus for dealing with the atomic electron. But it does not help us to conceptualize this ultimate constituent of matter. It does not tell us what the electron "is." To do that we have to "see" it, and that brings the whole problem to a head. If we must see the electron to satisfy our demands about its nature, about its very existence, then we are sentenced to eternal dissatisfaction, for the electron does not allow itself to be seen in the same way the classical elementary particle allowed itself to be seen. This essentially is the content of Werner Heisenberg's "uncertainty principle," a proposition which caps some three decades of atomic research and which administers the *coup de grâce* to the hope that classical physics could be used to explain the modern atom.

As Heisenberg says, the uncertainty principle states that we cannot

> determine accurately *both* the position and the direction and speed of a particle *at the same instant.* If we determine experimentally its exact position at any moment, its movement is disturbed to such a degree by that very experiment that we shall then be unable to find it at all. And conversely, if we are able to measure exactly the velocity of a particle, the picture of its position becomes totally blurred.[10]

In order to locate the particle and measure its speed, we must, as suggested earlier, "see" it; and to see it we need to throw light upon it. Light is made up, the assumption is, of "photons," entities which, like electrons, have wave-particle duality. When light's photons hit an electron there is an exchange of energy in which a quantum of energy—as Einstein has explained—in the form of a photoelectron is liberated. The difficulty lies in this interaction between the photon, by which we want to "see," and the electron. If the photon has a relatively short wave length, is fairly "bright," it will have the impact of a particle upon the electron. The exchange of energy will be relatively great and under the impact of the interaction, the electron will be thrown off its course. The short-wave photon will trigger a short-wave energy change in the electron, which will make it act in this moment like a particle. The electron's velocity and direction will be disturbed, but its position as a particle will be determined with considerable accuracy. If we wish to reduce the disturbance to the electron's velocity, we increase the photon's wavelength. The long-wave photon will take a longer period of time to transfer its energy to the electron and the impact, less sudden, will not be as great. The electron will not be so severely jarred from its course and its velocity may then be more precisely measured. But what has been achieved in the accuracy of measuring the electron's velocity is accompanied by a loss in accuracy in locating it as a particle. The photon is "dimmer" and the interaction is more like that between two waves rather than two particles. We "see" something more like a blur than a well-defined particle.

The relationships between the imprecisions in determining the location of the electron when we emphasize the measurement of velocity, and vice versa, are "uncertainty relationships." If we want to reduce simultaneously the imprecision of both factors, we still have to accept a minimum of imprecision, or uncertainty, in both factors. Compared with the more precise measurements of classical physics, this gives us only a probability of the location and the velocity of the electron, which takes into account the minimum error. This "probability function" refers to what Heisenberg calls our "deficiency of knowledge" about the "real" speed and "real" location of the electron during observation, "real" here used as the classical physicist would use it. What the probability function does give us is the probable speed and location of the electron, and numbers for predicting the probable speed and location of the "same" electron at a later time. The "uncertainty relations," on the other hand, express what is mathematically a discrepancy between what we expect to find, according to classical physics, and what we have been able to find so far. As Heisenberg says, the paradox of the uncertainty principle "starts from the fact that we describe our experiments in the terms of classical physics and at the same time from the knowledge that these concepts do not fit nature accurately. The tension between these two starting points is the root of the statistical character of quantum theory."[11] The exciting thing about the concept of the uncertainty principle is that it reveals the profound significance of Planck's constant. The product of the errors given by the measurement of position and speed simultaneously—that is, the minimum deficiency of our knowledge about the electron—is not less than Planck's constant divided by the mass of the entity being measured. Planck's constant is a mathematical way of saying that in atomic physics we can go no further than this point in objectifying nature, in extracting from nature the picture that classical physics has led us to expect.

For those who feel that we are explaining nature adequately and satisfactorily only when we can make definite statements about definite substances—for instance, the Newtonian atom—the uncertainty principle is simply unacceptable. As Einstein puts it,

> If, according to classical mechanics, we know the position and velocity of a given material point and also what external forces are acting, we can predict, from the mechanical laws, the whole of its future path. The sentence: 'The material point has such-and-such a position and velocity at such-and-such an instant,' has a definite meaning in classical mechanics. If this statement were to lose its sense, our argument about foretelling the future path would fail.[12]

The validity of the statement Einstein refers to seems so self-evident that to contradict it would result only in meaninglessness. Surely, even though we cannot measure it precisely, there is something there that the word *electron* (substitute *proton, neutrino, meson,* and so forth) refers to that corresponds in itself to our picture of a *thing,* an entity that has a certain objective permanence and occupies space. This is, in a sense, what meaning is for us in the physical world. Indeed, Heisenberg himself seems to hold out the possibility that the electron does have a kind of being that would satisfy the expectations of common sense (of classical physics): "The error in the experiment does—at least to some extent—not represent a property of the electron but a deficiency in our knowledge of the electron."[13] But as younger physicists who have grown up with the paradox of the uncertainty principle mature, they find less difficulty in thinking of the electron in itself as being paradoxical. David Park writes that the indeterminacy of the electron is "the exact reflection of a universal property of nature."[14] It has also been said that "the lack of definiteness is not due to inexact observation; what is meant is that certain quantities are of such a nature as to forbid sharp numerical evaluation."[15] When this idea is recorded in college physics textbooks, we know that it has received a kind of final sanction. Eric Rogers puts the whole problem with admirable clarity in his book *Physics for the Inquiring Mind.* The assumption that our ideas about the macro-world are also applicable to the micro-world of "electrons, nuclei, [and] quanta," he writes, gives us

> a view of Nature revealed in terms of that assumption. (If we ask, "How angry is the storm," the reply for a thunderstorm is, "Very angry." Yet we should be unwise to let that answer prove that storms have tempers.) Whatever the micro-world really is—and that "really" may be itself a macro-man's mistake—it is not a world of waves or particles. Forced into a wave description by a wave question, it gives a wave answer, and a complaint of particle ignorance. Or, asked a particle question, it gives a particle answer with wave ignorance. It is not Nature that pulls down a curtain over particle facts when we ask a wave question. It is our questioning that forces a non-wave-non-particle electron into an uncomfortable wave form, or an equally artificial particle shape. In fact, one uses a wave picture "to describe accurately, not the *electron,* but the *state of one's knowledge about the electron.*"[16]

We are brought back to the earlier proposition that modern physics is not quite a study of matter in itself, but of the complex relationship between the observer and the reality observed. In the view represented by Rogers' statement, physics does not give us empirical information about the ultimate constituents of material reality in itself. What does it mean, then, to talk about material reality? If we cannot cognize it in itself, can we say anything significant or useful about it? To put the question this way is to hide a basic assumption, which, if kept hidden, distorts the entire situation. The assumption is that to be real, reality must be objective. That is, it must have an ultimate identity wholly perceivable by an observer. This assumption is what John Dewey calls the "spectator theory of knowledge."[17] The observer looks; what he sees is an object; it is the "real." What it discloses to us is the "truth" about itself. Plato said that what our senses deliver to us about the material world is opinion. True knowledge is the rational apprehension of ideas. Cognition objectifies. For example, the sensation of heat upon the flesh is felt, experienced in that one unique feeling only by the subject who feels it. The nature of heat is something that is cognized or apprehended, generalized and objectified. What is cognized, said Plato, is the real. What is experienced in a fleeting sensation by a subject is less real. The real, as an object, has duration. Appearance, rendered to us subjectively by our senses, is impermanent. This is the spectator theory of knowledge.

Modern physics says that we cannot objectify material reality so as to encompass it in total explanation. No picture that we use to try to visualize it, no words we devise to describe it can duplicate or completely clarify that individual action of the electron. It is of such a character that it does not in itself completely correspond to our knowledge of it. We may say, in view of this notion, that the "real" eludes our attempt to objectify it completely. If we use the word *reality* to refer to the thing in itself which we cannot cognize as an object, we must think of that referent as a subject whose "reality" can be fully "known" only to itself, where "known" does not mean "cognized" but "experienced." To represent that "reality" to our cognition we are forced into using words that denote the impossibility of cognizing it: *uncertain, ambiguous, ambivalent, paradoxical, contradictory.* These words simply reveal the difference between the nature of our understanding, which operates on objects, by definition, and the nature of the subjective reality of, for example, the electron, whose only objective existence is in the effects observed. That is, as Bertrand Russell says, "The electron is known by its 'effects.'" But effects, as he points out, in modern physics are not the warrant of some identifiable entity—in the old sense—being there. That is, effects disclose only themselves. The effects can be examined, but, as Russell says, "what occurs within the electron (if anything occurs there) it is absolutely impossible to know. . . ."[18]

Russell makes the important distinction between the "old" and "new" views of matter. The old view, that of substance, thought of "a piece of matter" as having duration and occupying identifiable positions in space and time. The new view thinks of a piece of matter as an event. "An event does not persist and move, like the traditional piece of matter; it merely exists for a little moment then ceases. A piece of matter will thus be resolved into a series of events. . . . The whole series of these events makes up the whole history of the particle, and the particle is regarded as *being* its history, not some metaphysical entity to which events happen." This implies that a "real" physical entity has a subjective existence that is characterized by an internal experience. If we say, for example, an electron has "mass," we also say that it has energy, for, according to relativity theory, *mass* and *energy* refer to the same phenomenon. An observer might measure the electron's mass, objectifying it. But what the observer measures "has no physical significance as a property of the body," of the thing in itself. What Russell calls the body's "proper mass" is "not dependent upon the observer." This proper mass "is a genuine property of the body . . . [and] it represents, so to speak, the energy which the body expends internally, as opposed to that which it displays to the outer world."[19]

As Russell puts it, physical reality implies a center. A candle placed before a mirror is more real than its image reflected in the mirror. Take away the mirror, and light rays emanating from the candle remain. We can still see the candle. Take away the candle and the mirror image vanishes too. "This makes us say that the light-rays which make the image are only reflected at the surface of the mirror, and do not really come from a point behind it, but from the 'real' object." Events belonging to the candle's light—two people looking at the candle, for example—though different, are related to the same center. Light emanates from it in all directions, not just a few, as with the mirror image. The real thing, therefore, is the center of its world, and there are as many "world-centers" as there are real events. Though such events "are" not objects, our relationship with them is at least partly objective. That is, we cannot "know" them, in the sense of experience, as they "know" themselves—cannot, as Russell says, get at their "intrinsic nature . . . except when they happen to be events in our own lives."[20]

Physics thus suggests one of the reasons for the sense of separateness between men; that separateness characterizes our basic relationship with the world. Physics also suggests reasons for the despair and alienation so common to many descriptions of the modern temper. Actually, however, modern man, like his ancestors, has taken his contemporary conception of physical reality as a model for thinking of himself and postulating new values. Russell's notion is that reality lies in a subject that is not completely objectifiable. I will deal with this proposition at greater length in other chapters, but it is important to show at this point its connection with the contemporary American novel. The previous discussion has demonstrated three major changes introduced into the conception of physical reality by modern science: the changefulness of the basic particle, the ambiguity of the "particle's" wave-particle nature, and the impossibility of ever completely objectifying or knowing that basic "reality." If these are the characteristics of reality, then man must embrace them if he is to achieve his highest good. As I will say in Chapter 2 of this Part, what holds in the modern mind for the electron, by analogy holds for the human being. Change, ambiguity, and subjectivity (in a sense, these are synonyms) thus become ways of defining human reality. Novelist after novelist examines these features, and expresses almost universal frustration at being deprived of the old stability of metaphysical reality, but in most cases finds in these characteristics a ground for affirmation and even optimism. Ralph Ellison's *Invisible Man* chronicles the journey of its narrator from a condition of supposed completeness and absolute stability and changelessness—like the eighteenth-century atom—to a recognition that human reality is ultimately unknowable, always changeable, and open to possibility. The hero does not lament over this condition. He becomes convinced that living it is the only way to find freedom and to achieve the highest good. Saul Bellow's Augie March believes that his goal is to find "rest" and final stability, but he, too, discovers that his own identity is ambiguous, subject always to change, and that restlessness is his lot. And James Baldwin, in *Another Country,* celebrates growth and change as those attributes by which the human being, sacred in his subjectivity and individuality, fulfills his nature.

More than this, the subatomic particles of quantum physics are internally changed in their relationships with other particles. Analogously, the human being at his best, is internally affected when his associations with other human beings are open, sincere, and genuine. It is this conception of human nature that we find underlying the high value contemporary novelists, like James Purdy, J. D. Salinger, James Baldwin, place on love. Those who can love—for example, the "hero" of the novelists of World War II—are vulnerable to pain, but they are also the ones who achieve the highest awareness of themselves and the fulfillment of their potential.

For now, the subject is physics and what its practitioners can know of material reality. "As regards events which do not form part of our own lives," says Russell, "physics tells us the pattern of them, but is quite unable to tell us what they are like in themselves."[21] At this point, we are carried down a new path, the path of relativity. One of the outcomes of quantum theory and the uncertainty principle is that the heart of material reality is subjective, which means that we cannot fully objectify it for our complete cognition, but can only apply words to it that indicate its elusiveness. Relativity theory takes us into the opposite consideration, the consideration of what we can know. "In the theory of relativity," writes Russell, "we are concerned with *structure,* not with the material of which the structure is composed."[22]

In the "open decision," the absolute is in the subjective individual experience, not in a transcendent order conferred upon our world by an antecedent force. The contemporary American novelist sometimes tacitly, sometimes explicitly, makes the same assumption. In science, the corollary to this proposition is the theory of relativity which, analogous to the new conceptions of the atom, modifies (in some cases overthrows) the old convictions about the absoluteness and the reality of the objective. That is, in relativity the world is always viewed from the standpoint of a single observer or instrument. Just as there is no meta-language for Wittgenstein, so there is no meta-observer or meta-system for Einstein, and so no final and complete observation of all reality. The observer in relativity theory has an analogy in the "open decision"—the existing subject. In principle, each subject is the center of his world, viewing it uniquely, seeking to order it, and conferring value upon it. From this standpoint, the subjective self is the locus of reality and of value. It is this principle which underlies most of the themes in the novels I discuss: the themes of the individual versus authority, of self-knowledge and self-ignorance, of rebellion against forces (natural or human) that would violate the integrity of the subject. I shall try to demonstrate this connection more fully and convincingly by turning to a discussion of the nature of relativity and its difference from the physical views which preceded it.

The theory of relativity does not apply to things as they are in themselves, but to the laws which govern the way things behave with each other and to the laws which govern our perceptions of things. It shows another aspect of our relationship with the world, of our conception of reality and of our own nature. At the center of relativity is Einstein's proposition that, in Max Born's words, "concepts and statements which are not empirically verifiable should have no place in a physical theory."[23] The special and the general theories of relativity were advanced because unverifiable assumptions had been detected in traditional physical theory. Newton formulated his laws of motion on the assumption that space and time are separate and absolute. Space, he said, "is everywhere uniform and immobile," and time "in itself and without relation to anything external flows at a uniform rate."[24] Time and space, in this view, comprise a giant measuring grid for all of the universe. Take away all other bodies but, say, the earth, and one can still measure the distance the earth travels and the velocity of its motion by the universal scale. Even space without bodies is conceivably measurable. Universal space and time form a meta-coordinate system in which all measuring rods have the same scale and all clocks have the same rhythm. Within this system bodies may be said to occupy one position at one time. The identification of that position and the body's speed are independent of the observer. This also means that events may be said to occur simultaneously.

Newton's successors formulated two other propositions: (1) that light moves through space at a constant speed relative to absolute space and time; and (2) that it is propagated by the ether, a lighter-than-air substance which was thought to permeate the universe and was said to be at absolute rest. This view postulates subcoordinate systems whose observers operate in relation to both the meta-coordinate system and to other observers in other subsystems. When these systems are in uniform motion relative to each other, goes the traditional argument, observers in them will measure the same event with different numbers. The "true" measurement is that made by the standards of absolute time and space in which the ether stands at absolute rest.

This attitude is usually illustrated by a crude analogy between a slow-moving action of a piece of matter and the allegedly fastest thing in the universe—light. A person floating in a boat on a river toward a bridge at five miles an hour throws a ball at the bridge.

The speed of the ball is twenty miles an hour relative to the boat. The observer on the boat will clock the ball at twenty miles an hour. An observer on the river bank, however, can see that the boat is moving at five miles an hour relative to the bank. From his viewpoint the speed of the ball is twenty-five miles an hour, for it picks up the additional five-miles-an-hour velocity of the boat. For the "same" event the observers in two different coordinate systems have different figures. The sameness of the event is meaningful only in terms of the meta-coordinate system of absolute time and space. The clocks and measuring rods used in the reference system of the boat are the same ones used by the man on the bank, for the length of an inch and the duration of a minute, once they are set in the meta-system, are assumed to be the same relative to absolute time and space and hence the same in all subsystems. In a universe where absolute time and space take precedence over all other systems, only the numbers will change in the transfer of the description of a physical event from one system to another. The equations by which the numerical descriptions are changed were established by Galileo and are called the Galilean transformations (sometimes classical transformations). They are formulated on the assumption that time and space are separate, that the coordinates of a graph used to represent the event refer to pure distance, and that the factor of time is not one of the coordinates but is, so to speak, added later. By means of these equations, a hypothetical observer at rest in the ether of space can determine the way in which the numbers will change from one system to another. More than that, he can tell what the "real" speed of the ball is. According to this reasoning, the speed of light will be constant relative to the ether, but different relative to observers in two different reference systems. "Different" is intelligible here because of the absolute reference system of universal space and time, against which all motion can be hypothetically measured. The difference will depend upon the speed of the light's source through the ether. Experiment should be able to verify the existence of the ether and measure the speed of the earth through it without reference to any other heavenly body. As James Jeans explains it, the experiment might go like this: As the earth moves, an experimenter shoots a beam of light in front of it in the direction of its motion towards a mirror in space. An observer in the ether would measure the beam of light at 186,300 miles per second relative to his position of absolute rest in space. An observer on earth would find that the velocity of light as it traveled to the mirror and back again is slightly less. The reason for this is that as the beam of light travels to and from the mirror, from the earth and back to it, the earth also moves. The distance travelled by the light in one second to and from the mirror, therefore, is 186,300 miles minus x miles which the earth moves in the meantime. The earth will thus clock the trip of the light beam at 186,300−x miles per second. The x stands for the distance the earth travels through the ether in that one second, arrived at on the assumption that the light beam's speed, the number of miles it travels in one second, is constant relative to the ether. If the earth were at rest in the ether and hence in space, the journey out and back would lose or gain no time. The measurement of light's speed would be the same as for the hypothetical observer in the ether.[25]

There were several attempts at just such an experiment during the nineteenth century, but none gave the expected results. It was as if the earth was at rest in the ether, for no time difference between the two beams of light ever could be detected. As with the atom, so with space. The traditional assumptions could not account for experimental evidence. In 1905, Einstein published a paper on electromagnetism which contained the special theory of relativity and which revoked the basic assumptions of classical physics. It says that time and space are relative, not absolute. That is, there is no coordinate system whose measurements of time and space take precedence over any other system. It also says that "the velocity of light *in vacuo* is the same in all CS [coordinate systems] moving uniformly, relative to each other." Classical physicists assumed that the velocity of one system relative to another system would produce differences in the numbers by which measurements are represented. Chaos was avoided by referring to universal time and space. Einstein's theory makes the same assumption, except that it rejects universal time and space. Motion, say both theories, has some effect upon physical measurement in coordinate systems. How, then, can observers in different systems get the same measurement for the speed of light? Einstein's answer seems to be in complete disagreement with common sense. ". . . if the velocity of light is the same in all CS, then moving rods must change their length, moving clocks must change their rhythm, and the laws governing these changes are rigorously determined."[26] The trouble with such a statement is that it is formulated in words more appropriate to classical than to relativity physics. The words *same* and *change* imply a transcendent standard according to which a measurement is the "same" or according to which it "changes." It also suggests that something happens to the clocks and rods in themselves. Neither of these implications is quite accurate.

The problem lies in the way observers in, say, system A see things as compared with the way observers in system B, in motion relative to A, see things. An observer on the boat, in the earlier example, will, according to the special theory, express the speed of the ball thrown from the boat with the same numbers as will the observer on the bank. Yet each would assume that the measuring instruments of the other are inaccurate, that the other's clocks run "faster" or "slower," that the other's rods are "longer" or "shorter." The comparison here is strictly a matter between the two observers. Russell writes that "Distances in space, like periods of time, are in general not objective physical facts, but partly dependent upon the observer." Clocks and rods measure their own time and length accurately, from the standpoint of the observer using them in his system. But the clocks and rods of system A cannot measure time and length in system B if the latter is moving very rapidly at great distances relative to A. The instruments of two earthly observers, one in China and one in America, will seem pretty much the same when the observers compare notes. Those same instruments, used to measure subatomic particles in the laboratory, will also suggest that the particles seem "to increase in mass with rapid motion." But those instruments belong to the earth rather than to the particles. From the particles' viewpoint, their mass "remains constant, and it is we who suddenly grow thin or corpulent."[27] Relative motion, therefore, does not affect observer A's measuring system, but rather the way his instruments measure events in system B. Three feet still make a yard and sixty seconds a minute in both systems. But if A were in motion relative to B, his yard and his minute would appear different from those of B. It cannot be said, however, that, lacking an absolute standard, either is more "right" than the other. What does remain constant are the laws governing the changes. The basis of those laws is not the Galilean transformations but the Lorentz transformations. The product of late nineteenth-century mathematics, the Lorentz transformations incorporate time into the space coordinates and they establish that the differences in the appearances between two observations are reciprocal. That is, the measurements by A of events in system B will differ from B's measurement of those events in precisely the same ratio as the measurements by B of events in system A differ from the measurements by A of those events. Such reciprocity gives results much different from those of classical physics. If B travels past A at, say, three-fifths the speed of light, everything in A will seem shorter to B than it does to A. What A takes as a circular dinner plate, B will see as an oval. Similarly, A will regard what are round plates to B as oval to himself. Time, too, is affected. A will see that B's cigar lasts twice as long as his own; vice versa for B. The answers they get in their measurements are not about intrinsic properties of things in themselves but about the way they see things. In this sense, the observer is the center of his world and his measurements depend upon the conventions of his instruments, establishing an analogy with the concept of the electron or a candle—all subjects—as "world-centers."

Einstein not only rejected the notion of absolute time and space, substituting the Lorentz for the Galilean transformations, he also discarded the idea of the ether as a meaningful factor in physical theory because it could not be verified, and he destroyed the concept of "simultaneity" in doing so. According to the special theory, we cannot say that two events occur simultaneously, for simultaneity cannot be verified. What observer A will regard to have been two simultaneous events, observer B will regard as having happened at different times. The perception depends upon the observer's motion relative to the events. The same thing applies to single events. What A thinks of as the past, B may see as the present or the future.

The special theory applies only to systems in uniform motion relative to each other, motion in which neither speeds up nor slows down. What of those systems which are in nonuniform motion relative to each other? Einstein deals with them under the umbrella of the general theory of relativity, which formulates laws which "hold for every body of reference, whatever may be its state of motion."[28] Like the special theory, the general theory undercuts one of the basic assumptions of classical physics: the principle of gravity that postulates action at a distance, the notion that bodies exert force upon each other according to their mass and the distance between them. In this view, bodies move toward or away from each other because they are "attracted" or "repulsed." Einstein's first rule in the search for a substitute for the concept of action at a distance is the "principle of equivalence," the proposition that no observer can distinguish between the effects of classical gravity and acceleration. Say a ball is suspended in the center of a rocket ship's interior. It remains suspended as the rocket ship rises away from the earth with a velocity identical to that of the ball. Let the rocket accelerate and the ball appears to drop to the ship's floor. An observer inside the ship without access to an external reference point to reveal his acceleration might attribute the ball's behavior to an attraction in the rocket ship's floor. An observer outside the ship who sees it accelerate relative to the ball attributes the ball's behavior to acceleration. What law will express that behavior without reference to either classical gravity or acceleration that will be acceptable to all systems? The answer is in the formulas growing out of the principle of equivalence, which produce a different way of conceiving the physical character of the macro-world.

The formulas of the equivalence principle emphasize changing relationships between bodies rather than the position of bodies. They are "structure laws describing the changes in the gravitational field,"[29] rather than laws describing the simultaneous positions of objects and their attraction upon each other. These "structure laws" give us the two difficult concepts of space-time and the curvature of space-time. The coordinates of space-time by which the behavior of a body is measured depend upon the observer, but the way those coordinates operate is governed by laws applicable in all systems. "The general principle of relativity," says Einstein, "requires that all these [systems] can be used as reference-bodies with equal right and equal success in the formulation of the general laws of nature; the laws themselves must be quite independent of the choice of [system]."[30] It is as if space-time is a continuum and the observer chooses the coordinates to apply to the particular part of that continuum under observation.

There is no space-time without bodies, and there are no bodies without relative motion. In the vicinity of moving bodies, space-time is curved. The behavior of bodies is to be explained, not by saying that they are affected from a distance by other bodies, but by saying that space-time is curved. The life of a body in space-time is expressed in its "world-line"—its geodesic, defined as the shortest distance between two points. In Euclidean geometry a geodesic is a straight line, its coordinates given by the plane along which the geodesic moves. In relativity physics, a body's geodesic is usually some form of curve, especially when the coordinates entail very great distances. For example, coordinates chosen to express the geodesic of a person moving over the earth would produce, if the area were small enough, a path approximating very closely a Euclidean straight line. Coordinates representing the solar system would produce a curved geodesic. In each case, the laws governing the coordinates are the same.

How does all this relate to the "open decision" and to the novelists writing in terms of the "open decision?" I said earlier that the theory of relativity does not examine what things are in themselves but the structure of our knowledge of things. "Measurements of distances and times," writes Bertrand Russell, "do not directly reveal properties of the things measured, but relations of the things to the measurer. What observation can tell us about the physical world is therefore more abstract than we have hitherto believed."[31] Does this mean that we are trapped in an inescapable solipsism, can never know completely things in themselves as they "really" are, but only get answers in terms of the question asked? In a sense, the answer is yes. The "objects" we observe are, in this view, abstract representations of "real" subjects. Man's understanding, as I have already said, is sentenced to separation from that physical world which it seeks constantly to know. To those for whom the only acceptable condition lies in the total explanations of classical physics, this new attitude brings pessimism and despair. For others, this attitude offers an exciting and an affirmative conception of the human being and of his relationship to his world. It suggests an unprecedented freedom and openness in both physical reality and, by analogy, human reality.

The assumption that reality does not completely disclose itself to an observer does not mean that there is no reality. "The physicist," writes Arthur Eddington, "so long as he thinks like a physicist, has a definite belief in a real world outside him." It is true that different observers from different viewpoints see things differently. From one viewpoint a plate looks round, from another, oval. Neither view has a legitimate claim to being the "right" one. This does not mean that there is no "real" plate, but simply that observers' objectifications of the plate do not exhaust its reality. To assume that one viewpoint contains absolute explanation is to close both the possibilities of the physical reality observed and the human reality observing. "Reality," says Eddington, "is only obtained [i.e., cognized or objectified by the understanding] when all conceivable points of view have been combined."[32] But to do this one would have to be God. The relativistic viewpoint attempts to correct for our not being God and urges us to open ourselves to as wide a range of views as our limitations will permit us, to avoid imprisoning ourselves any more than we are already imprisoned. In doing so, the physicist assumes that our abstractions will correspond ever more closely to the thing in itself, and the observer will free himself more and more from the prejudice and distortion of unexamined traditional viewpoints. Einstein writes:

> Physical concepts are free creations of the human mind, and are not, however it may seem, uniquely determined by the external world. In our endeavor to understand reality we are somewhat like a man trying to understand the mechanism of a closed watch. He sees the face and the moving hands, even hears its ticking, but he has no way of opening the case. If he is ingenious he may form some picture of a mechanism which could be responsible for all the things he observes, but he may never be quite sure his picture is the only one which could explain his observations. He will never be able to compare his picture with the real mechanism and he cannot even imagine the possibility of the meaning of such a comparison. But he certainly believes that, as his knowledge increases, his picture of reality will become simpler and simpler and will explain a wider and wider range of his sensuous impressions. He may also believe in the existence of the ideal limit of knowledge and that it is approached by the human mind. He may call this ideal limit the objective truth.[33]

David Bohm puts the view even more explicitly:

> We may compare the structure of the totality of natural law to an object with a very large number (in reality infinite) of sides, having facets within facets, facets reflecting facets, facets consisting of mosaics of facets, etc. To know what the object is, then, we must have a large number of different kinds of views and cross-sections. Each view or cross-section then contributes to our understanding of many aspects of the object. The relationships between the views are, however, equally important, for they serve to correct the errors which arise as a result of regarding one or a limited number of views as a complete representation of the whole object; and they also indicate qualitatively new properties not apparent in the separate views (as two plane views of a scene taken from different angles permit us to infer its three-dimensional character). We see, then, that while each view and cross-section may vary depending on our relationship to the object, we can obtain a closer and closer approximation to a concept of the real nature of the object by considering more and more views and cross-sections and their relationships. This concept, then, becomes less and less dependent on our own relationship to the object as the number of views and cross-sections is increased.[34]

There is in these statements a sense of both freedom and humility. They suggest an attitude that has freed itself from assumptions derived from a single or a few viewpoints. Such freedom is desirable because it not only brings us closer to a cognition of "true" reality, but puts the human observer in the way of gaining a more accurate understanding of himself and his place in the world. This conception of physical reality and our relationship to it has important implications for other areas of human behavior, from metaphysics to ethics, from social theory to psychology. It is at the heart of the "open decision," and to be found in all planes of contemporary thought. For example, Northrop Frye, a literary critic and not a physicist, writes words that ring familiarly against those of Einstein and Bohm. The freedom from a single viewpoint Frye calls "transvaluation," which is "the ability to look at contemporary social values with the detachment of one who is able to compare them in some degree with the infinite vision of possibilities presented by culture. One who possesses such a standard of transvaluation is in a state of intellectual freedom. One who does not possess it is a creature of whatever social values get to him first: he has only the compulsions of habit, indoctrination, and prejudice." Similarly, he bases his principle of literary criticism upon the argument that "no set of critical standards derived from only one mode can ever assimilate the whole truth about poetry."[35]

In the nature of things there will always be a gap between the world in itself and the abstract model by which the human understanding pictures that world. There is an advantage in this, however, that is of profound importance to the human being, because the principle applies to him as well as to physical reality. The advantage is that the gap preserves the integrity of the individual subject, human or nonhuman. If no observer can ever completely objectify reality, that reality possesses a radical freedom and independence.

Our understanding is not isolated from the world. Its line of communication is the abstract model which it draws up on the basis of its points of view. Our present viewpoint teaches us not to mistake the model for the thing in itself; it also teaches us that we can have better relationships with physical reality when our model, constructed in freedom and honesty, corresponds more and more closely with the world we want it to represent. Models, says one English physicist, do not merely picture for us some aspect of physical reality derived from experiment and empirical observation. They suggest other new aspects which have not turned up in experiment and they help explain things which might have gone unexplained without the models. By the use of a model, "we try to investigate the further properties we expect [the parts of reality we are investigating] to have, and if we are correct in our expectations we shall conclude that the model, at least as far as we have gone, is a description of reality and not an illusion arising from our previous partial knowledge." Of course the model does not satisfy all of our expectations, but "if we were forbidden to talk in terms of models at all, we should have no expectations at all, and we should then be imprisoned forever inside the range of our existing experiments."[36]

What we conclude from modern physics, then, is that the ultimate constituents of physical reality in themselves are not ultimately and completely knowable to an observer. We may approach an ideal limit of knowledge through our abstractions and models, whose construction is governed by our freedom from the assumption that any one or few points of view give a total explanation. And though those models fall short of complete correspondence to the world in itself, they are the means by which man fulfills his need to cognize. Moreover, both atomic and relativity theory establish suppositions about human reality: that it, too, is indeterminate as an object; that its reality is its subjective experience; and that it can know itself best when it keeps itself free of traditional closed viewpoints.

This human reality is the subject of the next chapter. For now it will suffice to point out that many of these conclusions, besides constituting the tacit assumptions of, are overtly embodied in the contemporary American novel. The notion that the observer is the "world-center" is expressed explicitly in Thomas Berger's *Little Big Man* (1964). When the old Indian Chief, Lodge Skins, is about to die, he climbs to a high plateau. The narrator, Jack Crabb, gains a new insight into the human condition as he watches the old man perform the death ritual. The pale blue sky appears as an enclosed dome, but Jack takes pains to emphasize that it is not enclosed, "it was open and unlimited," very much like Einstein's unbounded universe. But besides this focus upon the vastness of the universe and its openness, there is a reference to the "world-center," the unifier of the world, and to the movement of that center which is at the heart of relativity. "I was there in movement," says Jack, "yet at the center of the world, where all is self-explanatory merely because it *is*." Though the subject moves, he remains at the center of his world and views that world according to the laws of his reference system.

The concept of the "world-center" appeared in novels written earlier in the twentieth century as the "central intelligence" or the "center of consciousness," principally in the work of Henry James, James Joyce, and William Faulkner. They used it to give their reporting of events and feelings a more valid psychological reality, filtering those reports through the mind of the single observer rather than through a meta-observer, that is, an omniscient observer. This technique rendered the "world-center" more important than the content of the subject's observations, and emphasized the process of observation. The contemporary American novelist is less concerned with relativity as technique than with relativity as a moral and intellectual foundation for value. Because it reflects a "truth" about what these novelists take to be reality, it is represented as a desirable state of being. Those characters who delude themselves that the abstraction they derive from their limited world-center represents an absolute truth are presented as deficient. The form this subject usually takes is that of a conflict between abstractions and existence, between models and subjective experience. Frankie Addams, in Carson McCullers' *Member of the Wedding,* and Alma Mason, in James Purdy's *The Nephew,* both suffer from the illusion that the view they derive from their center of observation represents an absolute picture of an objective reality. Neither Frankie nor Alma has taken up the relativistic viewpoint that would free them from unnecessary distortion of their world, and they suffer profoundly when their experience does not conform to their abstraction. Both, partly through love, and partly through merely the force of life, are freed from their old bonds and find a more open existence, founded on an implied recognition that no one world-center takes precedence over any other and that no one viewpoint, even though it may unify the world of its viewer, discloses total explanation. To learn that, for McCullers and Purdy, destroys one's innocence but opens the way for a more intense satisfaction.

I have moved from the emphasis upon the observer as the world-center to its corollary—the deficiency of the models derived from that center of observation and the need to admit as many viewpoints as possible in order to approach nearer to reality. These novelists do not, any more than the physicists, recommend an abandonment of building models simply because those models are ultimately deficient. As Dr. Hesse says, models help us find things in reality that we could not find without them. If our novelists did not believe that, there would be little justification for writing their novels. The novel is a kind of model of reality that liberates the intelligence from the bounds of its centrality so that it may glimpse the world from other viewpoints and come to a more profound insight into the world as it is. And liberation from a limited viewpoint is, in the "open decision," the *sine qua non* of human fulfillment. As a theme, this assumption appears frequently. Thomas Pynchon's *V.* and Alexander Trocchi's *Cain's Book,* for example, explore, in widely differing ways, the polar opposites of relying too heavily upon abstract models to find reality and rejecting such models altogether. Neither course is feasible. Ironically, it is through a model—the novel—that we have this demonstrated to us. Both Trocchi and Pynchon, like most of the other novelists, are highly self-conscious of the novel as an abstract construct that examines a condition that never yields itself up completely as itself. Its function is to break bonds and to reveal new viewpoints, just as the theory of relativity broke the bonds of the concepts of absolute time and space and simultaneity.

2

HUMAN REALITY

OUR ATTEMPT to define the "open decision" and its corollary of the human being leads us now to metaphysics. Alfred North Whitehead says that metaphysics—or "speculative philosophy"—is "a coherent, logical, necessary system of general ideas in terms of which every element of our experience can be interpreted."[1] Speculative philosophy has not been a popular activity in twentieth-century philosophy. Whitehead, however, has filled the vacuum like a giant, with great success though frequently with exasperating obscurity. I turn to him for a general explanation of "reality," the propositions of which I will often use in this discussion of the "open decision." Whitehead calls his metaphysics the "philosophy of organism," and the ultimate real thing it seeks to explain is the "actual entity."[2] It includes an explanation of the ultimate constituent of physical reality discussed in the last chapter:

> . . . the general principles of physics are exactly what we should expect as a specific exemplification of the metaphysics required by the philosophy of organism . . . this metaphysical description of the simplest elements in the constitution of actual entities agrees absolutely with the general principles according to which the notions of modern physics are framed.[3]

He shows his closeness to Einstein's preoccupation with structure laws when he says that the lectures making up his main metaphysical work, *Process and Reality,* are dominated by "relatedness" rather than "quality."[4]

The philosophy of organism is not limited in its application to the science of physics: "The partially successful philosophic gen-

For Notes to Chapter 2, see pages 398–399.

eralization will, if derived from physics, find applications in the fields of experience beyond physics. It will enlighten observation in those remote fields, so that general principles can be discerned as in process of illustration. . . ."[5] I am suggesting in this chapter that there is a meaningful connection between the conception of physical reality expressed by modern physics and the conception of the human being expressed by other modern thinkers. Indeed, Whitehead states explicitly that the reality represented in the words "actual entity" is fundamentally—metaphysically—the same in the physical and the human experience: "An occasion of experience which includes a human mentality is an extreme instance, at one end of the scale, of those happenings which constitute nature." The "human experience [contains] factors which also enter into the descriptions of less specialized natural occurrences."[6] Max Scheler writes in the same vein, "The physiological and psychic processes of life are strictly identical in an ontological sense."[7] The reasons for this correspondence should become clear in the course of the discussion. The metaphysical principles that explain the basic features of physical reality also explain the basic features of human reality. Human reality may be thought of as what Russell calls a "world-center," a real thing with its own subjective integrity, but elusive and ambiguous when one seeks to objectify it.

In expressing these principles, Whitehead illustrates one of the main points of the previous chapter, the disparity between the intellect and its object, between the conceptual and the particular. Metaphysics, says Whitehead, attempts to fit each specific moment of "practice" or experience into a scheme of general statements and categories. The tool of the philosopher in this task is language, the means by which men express what they generally agree upon in their experience. Language, however, and the generalizations it embodies must always fall short of ultimate agreement with the totality of particular experience: ". . . no language can be anything but elliptical, requiring a leap of imagination to understand its meaning in its relevance to immediate experience . . . no verbal statement is the adequate expression of a proposition." Traditionally, Whitehead argues, philosophy has overstated its validity. It has committed the "fallacy of misplaced concreteness," accepting statements about real things made in terms of single categories or limited points of view as totally explanatory. It has also sought to establish unequivocally clear premises and deduce from them a system of thought. Philosophy, however, must avoid the single point of view; and correlatively, it must accept the notion that in the nature of things, premises are initially "ill-defined and ambiguous." "In philosophical discussion, the merest hint of dogmatic certainty as to finality of statement is an exhibition of folly."[8] The implication of these statements is that the appearance of certainty in statements does not warrant certainty about a thing in itself, but only about the fact that a statement has been made. If, furthermore, reality is in itself "ill-defined and ambiguous"—as the uncertainty principle suggests—then statements about it must take this into consideration.

The disparity between the particular and the general is one of the main elements in the cult of despair that many say informs the contemporary attitude. That disparity, however, need not lead to nihilism. Philosophy becomes the effective link between the particular and the general when men understand the distinction between the two. To philosophize is to see that there is a coherence between particular events. Our senses thus function as a ground for philosophical speculation, abstracting from the motion of elementary particles the "things" of our sensuous experience. There is a "simplicity" about the table before me when I view it from my standpoint that is not present when seen from the view of a molecular or atomic physicist. Not to simplify—or philosophize—is to obscure such simplicity. Nor must we confine ourselves to only one stage of abstraction or simplification, for that would obscure other general truths that link the table as a thing with its molecules as things. Philosophy combines sensitivity to particulars with a generalizing "breadth of thought." In doing so it serves "an ultimate claim of existence." This reasoning leads Whitehead to a statement that is one of the fundamental features of my definition of the "open decision" and to my discussion of the contemporary American novel: "The two sides of the organism require a reconciliation in which emotional experiences illustrate a conceptual justification, and conceptual experiences find an emotional illustration."[9] In Chapter 1, I noted that because conceptual models failed to account absolutely for subjective existence is no reason not to construct them. That proposition is here deepened and enriched. For fulfillment, the organism—that is, the human being—must fuse the particular moment with that conceptual thought which tells us that we have discovered a "meaning." To lose oneself in the "insistent particularity of emotion" is to immobilize the human potential for satisfaction and, as Bellow's Herzog says, to fall asleep in the "thick embrace" of "reality." To assume that only conceptual thought discloses reality is to empty the human experience of rich and incommunicable emotion. Unless these opposites are fused, says Whitehead, one becomes gripped in a "life-tedium."

It is precisely this life-tedium in which so many of the characters of the contemporary American novelist languish, and from which they either escape, or perish. For example, Benny Profane, in Pynchon's *V.*, is so devoted to the particular that he deprives himself of the illumination of the general. In the end, with the lights of Malta's main city having been mysteriously but symbolically extinguished, he runs to the dark sea and there dies. The characters of John Barth—especially Ebenezer Cook, in *The Sot-Weed Factor,* and George Giles, in *Giles Goat-Boy*—are, on the other hand, so bound to abstractions that they cannot see the world of particular events, and both have to undergo agonizing initiation into the fusion of the conceptual and the emotional. Ebenezer "marries" the emotional—or existential—in the form of disease-ridden Joan Toast, and George Giles short-fuses a huge computer (whose sole function is to make abstract distinctions) by "coupling" with Anastasia Stoker and rejecting the absolute control of the intellect. The value here lies in the existing subject, the ambiguous, nonobjectifiable "world-center" that is defined by its ambiguity, living in a world where the fusion of thought and feeling, though limiting, provides the highest satisfaction. The affirmation in the contemporary American novel comes with the embrace of that satisfaction as worthy in itself. This is also Whitehead's affirmation, and to him I return. What exactly is Whitehead's notion of the "world-center?"

I noted in Chapter 1 that modern physics rejects the classical conception of an atom as a substance to which things happen but which does not change in itself. Whitehead calls the doctrine of substance the root of materialistic physics and points out that classical physics "has proved to be . . . mistaken."[10] Equally mistaken is the shift of that same doctrine to the explanation of protons and electrons. Yet, in "all philosophic theory there is an ultimate." The problem has been that too many philosophers have assumed that "ultimate" to be God or "The Absolute," possessing a "final, 'eminent' reality, beyond that ascribed to any of its accidents,"[11] of which the classical atom is an analogue. If this is mistaken—and Whitehead says it is—what can more accurately, and ultimately, describe things as they are? Whitehead's answer, of course, is the philosophy of organism.

In the philosophy of organism the ultimate is not a changeless substance with an " 'eminent' reality." It is a "creativity" that, apart from its accidents, "is devoid of actuality." This is the same view that Russell takes: a particle *is* its history of events, "not some metaphysical entity to which events happen." Thus, into the world of protons and electrons, says Whitehead, come the "mysterious quanta of energy," arising apparently from the protons and electrons. Their nature is vibratory, rhythmic. "Thus there is every reason to believe that rhythmic periods cannot be dissociated from the protonic and electronic entities." That is, the quantum vibrations are not something that happens to irreducible protons and electrons; they *are* those entities. Whitehead is quick to apply this proposition to the human being: "It is said that 'men are rational,' " with the implication that this rationality is man's substance in the same way that the atom's massiness and hardness are its substance. "This," argues Whitehead, "is palpably false: [men] are only intermittently rational—merely liable to rationality. The intellect of Socrates is intermittent: he occasionally sleeps and he can be drugged or stunned."[12] There is, thus, a discontinuousness in human reality, a rhythm in the core of his being, that obeys the general laws that also apply to physical reality. It is relevant here to point out that the same theory is expressed by Jean-Paul Sartre, who asserts that a man "is" the "ensemble of his acts."

This rhythmic entity is Whitehead's "actual entity," and there is nothing more "real" than it. All actual entities are generically similar; there is, thus, only one kind of reality. This is the "ontological principle" that makes it possible to talk about physical reality and human reality in the same terms. It is also the principle that repudiates one of the basic assumptions of western intellectual history—that God is different in kind from our world and is the cause of our world. In the philosophy of organism, God is an actual entity (to be explained later). And all actual entities are self-creative—"causally independent." Most importantly, the actual entity is an individual subject. In the philosophy of organism, these words are actually redundant when used together, for an individual is a subject and a subject is an individual. But both words must be emphasized. The "sole reality of the Universe," declares Whitehead, is made up of "individual things"—that is, of actual entities. These entities are subjective in that they exist as process, and their process is unique to them, cannot be totally objectified or experienced by any other actual entity, a proposition consistent with the physical description of elementary particles. These entities experience "feelings" and "emotions," words which Whitehead calls "technical terms," but which he uses in ways analogous to their application to the human being. Indeed, Whitehead says that "The basis of experience is emotional,"[13] and every actual entity has a life defined by the way it feels or has emotions, by the "form" of its "inner life." Different actual entities have different forms, but the inner life—the reality—of an electron is generically similar to the inner life of a human mentality. Both fall under the same metaphysical principles. What is said of physical reality applies metaphysically to the human reality.

Whitehead defines *feeling* as "the term used for the basic generic operation of passing from the objectivity of the data to the subjectivity of the actual entity in question."[14] This rather imposing statement simply means that feeling is the actual entity's absorption into its own life of the world about it. "Feelings are vectors," says Whitehead, "for they feel what is *there* and transform it into what is *here*."[15] The act by which this transformation is effected Whitehead calls *prehension*. It is the means by which the actual entity creates itself; it is, in effect, the life process, the basic mode of "real" experience.

An illustration of prehension must wait upon the establishment of one or two other premises. The actual entity is an event of the present moment. No actual entity can prehend any other actual entity. That is, no subject can absorb into its own life the life of another subject. This preserves, in the reality of our world, the integrity of every subject, and recalls the same point made in Chapter 1. What is the datum, then, that the actual entity prehends if it is not another actual entity? The answer introduces the subject-object relationship that figured so importantly in Chapter 1. The data available for prehension are objects, which Whitehead defines as "already-constituted" actual entities, which have ceased to live and become available to life as objects. A. H. Johnson, in his book *Whitehead's Theory of Reality,* furnishes an example of these generalizations: ". . . when a student (a subject) comes across a theory (datum) which appeals to him as a profound truth, he pounces [prehends] on [*sic*] it with delight (subjective form) and henceforth it is a part of his very being."[16] The experience of appropriating the theory, in this example, is the actual entity. The theory was once an actual entity in its own right when its author "prehended" it from someone else or from a previous state of thought. It ceased to be a feeling when, say, it was written down. It then became available to another subject as an object.

In this way the past becomes the present in an actual entity. When the human being "feels" a datum of the past, he "enjoys this emotion both objectively, as belonging to the past, and also formally as continued in the present." A person who experiences Plato's doctrine of Ideas, knowing it originated in a time distant from his own, experiences it with historical perspective as well as with the immediate intensity of feeling. In this way, the past is recapitulated in the present through the experience of the existing actual entity. In physical reality, one form in which the actual entity appears is the quantum event. A series of such events makes up, say, an electron or proton. These "particles" are "routes" of successive events. Each event prehends from its forerunner the data that makes up its own subjective form. The act of prehension is the "transition of things, one to another" mentioned earlier. In the vocabulary of Chapter 1, the quantum event is the standing wave of the electron. The change in the standing wave is the transition from one quantum event to the next, during which event A dies and becomes an "already-constituted" entity and event B prehends what is now A's objectivity. So long as event A is a subject, constituted of its prehensions, it is not available as a datum. It is busy as a process of becoming. That is its life. When it completes its process and ceases to prehend data, it becomes a datum serving other actual entities. The "sole reality" of the universe is made up of these prehensions, these acts of appropriation. The universe is thus a constantly changing pattern of relationships between the experiences of actual entities. "The present moment is constituted by the influx [prehension] of *the other* into that self-identity which is the continued life of the immediate past within the immediacy of the present."[17]

This brings up two issues: causal independence and the continuity of nature. The actual entity, to repeat, is an individual subject. Whitehead calls it ultimate reality. It is, therefore, preceded by no more ultimate cause—by anything more real—but is itself *causa sui*. It is "finally responsible" for how it lives and feels, for what it prehends. No actual entity has in its own past any other actual entity operating as an "efficient cause" of its existence. This final responsibility for its own creation is causal independence, and it is the ground for one of the fundamental characteristics of reality—"freedom within the universe."[18] "The freedom inherent in the universe is constituted by this element of self-causation."[19]

The act of prehension, causal independence, final responsibility—all emphasize the individuality of the actual entity. They reflect the discontinuousness of the world and they partly constitute the "doctrine of absolute individuality"—the doctrine, as I suggested earlier, which some moderns have interpreted as the source of pessimism and despair. But also implied in the act of prehension is the continuity of nature. That is, the philosophy of organism does not suppose a universe of absolutely isolated entities and it does not disregard the efficacy of history and the past. Though the actual entity is self-creative and causally independent of its environment, there is a continuity between the prehending subject and its predecessors. Though subjects cannot appropriate each other, they can appropriate the already-constituted actual entities, which were once subjects themselves. As objects, the already-constituted entities are not identical with the subjects they once were, but when a new subject prehends one of these objects, it establishes a continuity between old and new. In this way, Whitehead fuses the paradoxical states of continuity and discontinuity, which provides a metaphysical explanation of the wave-particle duality—a foundation for regarding the elementary particle as a fusion of waveness and particleness that eludes our categories of perception and understanding. Whitehead calls this concept of continuity the "Doctrine of the Conformation of Feeling." It means that the definitively characteristic feeling of one existent conforms, after that existent dies, with the feeling of the following existent. The second subject prehends an object with a feeling that belongs only to itself, maintaining a conformity with but modifying the original in an individual act of prehension.

An explanation of the Doctrine of the Conformation of Feeling is also an explanation of the process of prehension and the nature of the actual entity's existence. Whitehead illustrates the doctrine with an example of a man experiencing anger. A stretch of anger is made up of a series of discrete actual entities, in the same way that an electron is made up of a series of discrete quantum events. The separate moments of a stretch of anger contribute to each other. Moment A spends itself and becomes an objective datum from which moment B creates itself through prehension. Moment B reenacts the subject of moment A when A has been objectified. B takes A's original subjective form into its own subjective process as an object. The transaction is neither a pure repetition of the original subject nor merely a representation of it. B's experience of objective A's feeling is unique to B. Yet, by means of the reenactment, "The anger is continuous throughout the successive occasions of experience. This continuity of subjective form is the initial sympathy of B for A. It is the primary ground for the continuity of nature."[20]

The existence of the actual entity is made up of its absorption of data into its subjective experience. The data are possibilities from which the actual entity can choose; for example, as I have said, the number of standing waves that might enter into one phase of an electron's life is very high. But the actual entity is not required by necessity to prehend all the possibilities open to it. The selections that it does make constitute its identity; it creates itself by choosing from the data available to it. The basis upon which the actual entity chooses one alternative rather than another is, in Whitehead's words, the "subjective aim." Thus, the actual entity develops toward a particular end in creating itself. It is, then, a "process of becoming." This facet of its character distinguishes it from the "real" things of previous theory. The Platonic Idea, the Aristotelian Form, the Christian God—these are absolutes whose "existence" is a self-identity of eternal duration. They are perfection, the actualization of all potential. To speak of them "becoming" is a contradiction in terms. They *are.* Analogously, in this traditional view, the atom is self-identical and undergoes no internal change.

Man, too, has an essence—a soul—which has the status of being rather than becoming. The "essence" of the actual entity, on the other hand, is not *being* in the classical sense, but becoming. It is open to the data before it and decides which of those data it will become. It is, in this sense, the "open decision." This aspect of the actual entity's nature is emphasized by what, from the standpoint of the old view, would be a paradox. When its "aim" is achieved, the actual entity perishes. When it ceases to prehend data in the construction of itself it is no longer a living subject. It becomes the objective "already-constituted" entity referred to above. Death and discontinuity interpenetrate with life and continuity. Each, it seems, implies the other. And the sole reality of the universe, for Whitehead, is the becoming of the individual actual entities of which it is comprised.

The terms "being" and "becoming" recall Henderson's conversation with the African chief Dahfu in Bellow's *Henderson the Rain King.* Henderson laments the fact that Dahfu seems to be a "Be-er," at rest, and that he, Henderson, is merely a "becomer." All of Bellow's characters are touched in some degree with the same unsatisfied appetite to find an ultimate equilibrium. But in keeping with the thought of his time, as I am trying to represent it through Whitehead, Bellow prohibits his people from achieving that equilibrium, that state of motionlessness that would grant them final sanctuary. Augie March, Henderson, Herzog, perhaps even Tommie Wilhelm in *Seize the Day,* learn that their life is defined as "becoming," and the implication is that here lies value, for when the human being—just as Whitehead's actual entity—ceases to "become" he ceases to live. And life, as defined in the "open decision," is tacitly assumed to be the highest good. To achieve that good in all its ambiguity and shortcomings, one must embrace, as Bellow says, "the condition *as given*" (my italics).

It is at this point, also, in Whitehead's philosophy that we come to a statement of the nature of human value, of the highest good. The actual entity seizes data from the world around it to achieve its subjective aim. The "reward" of that achievement, so to speak, is nothing more specific than "satisfaction." The character of that satisfaction is central to one of the main points I am trying to make. Satisfaction, says Whitehead, "is the attainment of something individual to the entity in question."[21] The form of the entity's life—

the way that it grasps its world—is unique to each actual entity, even while it sustains the continuity of nature. This is the basis for value, for defining the preferred situation. "The good," says Aristotle, "is that at which all things aim."[22] This statement applies to the notion of good implicit in Whitehead's metaphysics, and it applies to the notion of good in the "open decision," the attainment of a high intensity of individual satisfaction. The value of the actual entity—which, it must be emphasized, includes the human being—is, says Whitehead, in its being an end in itself, a being which is for its own sake.

A high intensity of individual satisfaction is achieved in proportion to the amount of freedom the actual entity has, and the amount of freedom depends, at least in part, on the actual entity's environment. Whitehead speaks of various kinds of environment. The kind relevant to this discussion is what Whitehead calls a "society," which is a group of actual entities " 'ordered' among themselves by virtue of a particular 'ideal' character dominating each of the individual component actual entities."[23] The existence of a society is dependent upon its members. In keeping with the Doctrine of the Conformation of Feeling, each subject passes on its feeling of the "ideal" social character to the next subject. The members of the society thus cooperate in perpetuating the characteristic social order, producing a recognizable similarity between the members who, "by reason of their common character . . . impose upon other members . . . the conditions which lead to that likeness." The freedom of the actual entity, therefore, is not absolute. It does not guarantee unlimited actualization or fulfillment: "No actual entity can rise beyond what the actual world as datum from its standpoint —*its* actual world—allows it to be."[24] Thus, the role of a society in providing for a high intensity of individual satisfaction is crucial.

The best society, implies Whitehead—that society which provides the greatest amount of effective freedom—is one which combines a reasonable longevity and order with the encouragement of individual originality, upon which satisfaction relies. A society that endures for more than a "reasonable" time is usually characterized by a high degree of conformity among its members and a low degree of originality. It reflects "a reign of acquiescence," in which the appropriation of data merely anticipates the "preservation of types of order and of patterns of feeling already dominant in the inheritance." It is empty of "ideal novelty." An example of such a society—a "nonliving" society—is a rock, whose actual entities are rigidly bound to a small range of data and to a physical past. The nonliving society is deficient in alternatives and contrasts. Its rigidity maintains a high degree of order through conformity but prevents growth and inhibits individual satisfaction.

A living society, on the other hand, possesses a lower degree of order and endurance but a higher degree of hospitality to novelty and originality; when we provide for alternatives, we have a recognizable basis for choosing. Such a society establishes the possibility of a high intensity of individual satisfaction, which is the definitive characteristic of life: "In so far as the mental spontaneities of occasions do not thwart each other, but are directed to a common objective amid varying circumstances, there is life."[25]

The importance of the society in the attainment of the preferred situation implies one of the fundamental features of the actual entity's satisfaction. A high intensity of individual satisfaction is not attained by absolute selfishness or self-centeredness. If satisfaction depends upon what the actual entity can draw from its society, reciprocally it depends upon what it contributes to the society. For the human actual entity this secures a long-cherished value—a sense of responsibility to others, a respect for the value of others: "One sees oneself as a unit in a complex social organization of cooperating members. You come to realize that what is of value in your life will be preserved [as objective data for other subjects], and that there are elements of value in the lives of others." Thus, part of one actual entity's satisfaction is in the efficacy with which it makes itself available to other members of the society in their own development toward satisfaction. The achievement of satisfaction, as already mentioned, is simultaneously the moment of death. But that " 'perishing' is the assumption of a rôle in a transcendent future. . . ." Indeed, it is the only way that development can occur: "Thus perishing is the initiation of becoming. How the past perishes is how the future becomes."[26] The satisfaction of one individual depends upon the satisfaction of others. This is the metaphysical basis for morality:

> Morality of outlook is inseparably conjoined with generality of outlook. The antithesis between the general good and the individual

> interest can be abolished only when the individual is such that its interest is the general good, thus exemplifying the loss of minor intensities in order to find them again with finer composition in a wider sweep of interest.[27]

This social relationship is always part of the denotation of *intensity of individual satisfaction.* Conflicts between actual entities implying excessive self-interest contribute to disorder in the society, and disorder reduces the possibility of a high intensity of individual satisfaction. Without a minimum of common purpose, there is no life. An atom whose component actual entities are deprived of orderly data will disintegrate. The schizophrenic person, unable to unify the overwhelming variety of possibilities he is confronted with, fails to fashion a single self, a recognizable identity or society, and so contributes to the thwarting of his own satisfaction and even helps bring his own destruction. "Any tendency," says Whitehead, "to a high-grade multiple personality would be self-destructive by the antagonism of divergent aims. In other words, such multiple personality is destructive of the very essence of life, which is conformation of purpose."[28]

With this said, however, we must return to a previous point. Conformation of purpose must not harden into the "tyranny" of the nonliving society, which repudiates novelty and originality and freedom. Life is the balance between order or plan (embodied in the conformation of purpose among individual actual entities making up a society) and freedom (which arises from the presence of a wide range of alternative possibilities). It is in this balance, another aspect of the fusion of emotion and intellect already discussed, that the highest degree of satisfaction is to be found. The society best designed to provide this balance is the one whose "ideal character" lies in the value placed on novelty and originality. In such a society the ordering force entails the individual freedom of each actual entity. It provides contrasts, but not conflicts. The nearer a society approaches this character, the nearer it comes to the ideal level of intense individual satisfaction. The nonliving society, as mentioned earlier, falls far below the ideal. At the other end of the scale come human political states, whose patterns fall under the same metaphysical explanations as do rock societies. The totalitarian state—Nazi Germany, for example—has analogues with the nonliving society. It closes possibilities, forces a conformity of purpose upon its citizens so rigid that it snuffs out any intensity of individual satisfaction. It carries order too far—so far, indeed, that it claims the need to execute millions of its own members. Its dominant ideal is destructive of life.

The metaphysical underpinnings of this relationship between the individual and his society form one of the main bases of the novels I treat in the three chapters of Part II. The war novelist depicts a society whose military hierarchy is bent upon forcing the individual out of his spontaneous existence into preordained paths. The business novelist warns against the smothering qualities either of the large industrial corporation or of the intrusive government that would thwart individual initiative. The "hip" novelist admonishes his heroes to break away from a middle-class world that demands too much conformity. Yet, also in keeping with the principles I have outlined, these writers celebrate, not isolation from society, but the necessity of living in one and the benefits that might be derived from it. Sergeant Croft, that cold loner in *The Naked and the Dead,* acknowledges that he could not have climbed Mt. Anaka alone, and among the squad of men he commands there emerges a camaraderie from which they all take some strength. Ayn Rand's mythical characters in *Atlas Shrugged* flee what Rand calls a totalitarian government and build a society whose defining principle is private initiative. And William Burroughs preaches that the cooperative, a social system providing for a high degree of contrast simultaneously with a high degree of social responsibility, is the foundation of freedom and growth—in short, life. Implied in this whole subject is the ever-present ambiguity which I will take up later in connection with Freud's *Civilization and Its Discontents:* the fact that society both limits and liberates. Croft, for example, might have reached the summit of Mt. Anaka alone, had he not been burdened with the resistance of his men. At the same time, he *could not* have done it alone, for "those mountains would have eroded the courage of any man." For now, however, we must return to metaphysics.

The human society most likely to produce actual entities whose satisfaction is intense is the one whose structure, as so many of our novels attest, is based upon freedom and alternatives. The data available to each individual for prehension arise from other indi-

actual entity which unifies it." This is precisely what is implied in the theory of relativity. ". . . apart from the experiences of subjects there is nothing, nothing, nothing, bare nothingness."[32]

Whitehead's philosophy of organism seems to reinforce Nietzsche's proposition that God is dead. Yet, Whitehead postulates a God. Unlike the Christian—transcendant force of completed perfection, interested in our world but not of it—Whitehead's God is generically similar to the actual entities making up reality, in accordance with the "ontological principle." In fact, God is the ultimate actual entity, the never-finished becoming of nature's process. He is the "primordial" entity from which all other entities prehend their data. At the same time, paradoxically, he is the ultimate subjective aim, containing all possibilities. By prehending some of these possibilities, every ordinary actual entity prehends some of God. And in having a subjective aim themselves, every ordinary actual entity exemplifies God. Each actual entity fulfills itself by realizing its subjective aim: the completion of its possibilities. God, too, is an actual entity in the process of achieving its aim. God's aim is partially carried out in the action of every ordinary actual entity. He has a stake, therefore, in their success. God does not perish, because his process is never completed. Thus God will never disappear or become an object. He will simply be the various epochs that constitute his reality.

Whitehead's metaphysics has not received broad support from his contemporaries and successors in metaphysics and philosophy. Today, though, he seems to be getting more and more serious attention. And in my view, his general statements about reality provide the most cogent guidelines in talking about the world view embodied in the "open decision." Those general statements, as I have already said, apply to both physical and human reality. I want to emphasize, too, that what the human being values today relates very closely to the modern conception of the "true" and the "real." That truth and reality, as described in the philosophy of organism, lies in the individual subjective experience. Various degrees of value appear in the various degrees of intensity with which that experience is individualized. The word *individual* here denotes several characteristics: self-creativity, freedom ("causal independence"), limitation (that is, the individual dies and he is limited by the data available to him in his society). When these words are used to refer to human reality in particular, they mean that the human being is free to choose data from the world around him—free in the sense that no one can make the choice for him, not in the sense that he has the power to actualize any subjective aim he might conceive. Because he is free, he—and only he—can be responsible for what he is. Individual satisfaction occurs in its highest intensity with human consciousness. It is this metaphysical principle that underlies the preoccupation in the contemporary American novel with the interior character of the human individual and causes our novelists to see the issues in terms of individual satisfaction as it may be gained within the conditions of the "open decision." It is in consciousness that the sense of self, with all its contradictions and limitations, achieves its most vivid state. In order more explicitly to establish the grounds upon which the novels discussed in Parts II and III are built, I turn now to the metaphysics of that consciousness as formulated by a group of thinkers who called themselves phenomenologists and who constructed the statements that form the basis of modern Existentialism.

The writers I discuss in this section focus upon the human being and his definitive feature: consciousness. They are concerned with his freedom, his aims, the natural limitations placed upon those aims, and his conflict and harmony with the world into which he emerges. Their work contains, sometimes explicitly, sometimes implicitly, a set of positive values by which men might guide their conduct and achieve a high intensity of individual satisfaction. A discussion of that work brings us closer to a full definition of the "open decision."

The human consciousness spoken of by the phenomenologist is analogous to Whitehead's actual entity. It is the "absolute reality" of the human being, beyond which there is nothing; it is the irreducible of individual human existence. The phenomenologist seeks first to isolate this existent and then describe it. Phenomenology is thus a method, a metaphysics, and a ground for ethics all rolled into one. The method was first devised by Edmund Husserl. Its main principle recalls the relativism of Einstein and the cross-sectional view of reality of David Bohm—freedom from traditional preconceptions, from single points of view, from "those confusions which are too deeply rooted in us, as born dogmatists."[33] The more one is freed from these confusions the more conscious he is. And the more conscious he is, the nearer he approaches his "true" nature. Ethically, the implication is that it is "better" to be conscious than not. Thus the method implies something about the metaphysical nature of human reality as well as its ethics.

The first prejudice we must lay aside in the search for true consciousness, says Husserl, is that which derives from traditional natural science. His is, therefore, "a *phenomenology of consciousness,* as opposed to a *natural science about consciousness.*" A natural science of consciousness would be behavioral psychology. Such a science is invalid, argues Husserl, because it operates under presuppositions and is thereby limited as to what it can experimentally discover. Psychology, in using the procedures of natural science, attempts to apply methods to a subject which does not lend itself to those methods. The nature of consciousness is simply obscured by such investigation, for it "almost inevitably means to reify consciousness." In other words, consciousness, like Whitehead's actual entity and like the elementary particle of the uncertainty principle, is not thing-like, not graspable in the sense that the classical atom or the "rational" human being is graspable. Consciousness is an elusive *process* which cannot be captured as itself, which cannot be fully objectified. One needs, therefore, a method of investigation which "follows the nature of things to be investigated and not our prejudices and preconceptions."[34]

Science would miss the essence of the entity to be discovered—consciousness. This must be investigated according to its own nature. Consciousness must investigate itself. It cannot perceive itself as it perceives the physical, for it is "not experienced as something which appears; it is 'vital experience' and vital experience viewed in reflexion, it appears as itself through itself. . . ."[35] It is relevant to point out that Husserl's conception of consciousness as "vital experience" resembles Wordsworth's conception of poetry: where Husserl says "vital experience viewed in reflexion," Wordsworth says "emotion recollected in tranquillity." Whitehead's comments about Wordsworth are even more pertinent, for they link his metaphysics with Husserl's phenomenology. Whitehead notes that

Wordsworth found something in nature "that failed to receive expression in science"—a unity, a feeling, a presence in surrounding things. Wordsworth's poetry, as a kind of "vital experience," "expresses the concrete facts of our apprehension, facts which are distorted in scientific analysis."[36] Similarly, Husserl maintained that consciousness is a reality which, if truth and accuracy are to be served, must be approached by the investigator free of the limiting presuppositions of natural science.

The means by which Husserl seeks to rid the mind of those presuppositions is what he calls the "eidetic" reduction—"eidetic" because it tries to clear away all obstructions in order to reveal "pure" consciousness ("eidos"). This, clearly, is a return to the old Cartesian method of "doubt." By this means, we overcome the limitations set up in our investigations of nature—psychologically or scientifically—and thus arrive at "the free outlook upon transcendentally purified phenomena." The important step in this reductive process is the isolation of "pure" consciousness from empirical consciousness, which is the servant of natural science and which embodies one of our principal prejudices. Empirical consciousness, says Husserl, limits our experience to the "natural standpoint," to the perceptions of "concrete" things in the "real natural" world. Such perception does not give "true Being," but only a "*mere 'this,'*" which is the object of natural science. What we perceive from this standpoint is a "spatial thing," a cluster of perspectives appearing as something intelligible and self-identical. These perspectives are "subjective modes of appearing" to the consciousness while the "thing-in-itself" remains unchanged. When one walks around a table, for example, the perspectives are altered as they are perceived from different positions by the observer, but the table, in itself, remains unchanged. When empirical consciousness experiences these perspectives it does so as a "unity of apprehension," as "one identical thing." That apprehension, however, is not the absolute total of the concrete thing's possible perspectives. It is the "ideal possibility" of transforming the sensory data, the perspectives, into intelligible "determinate, ordered, continuous perceptual patterns." Husserl expresses phenomenologically one of the points made in Chapter 1: the empirical consciousness of natural science is not consciousness of the absolute actual entity in itself. It is the consciousness of particular features abstracted from things in themselves that tell us those things are in space. This intelligibility is what arises from the "natural standpoint"—useful for some kinds of investigation, but distorting for others. The role of this empirical consciousness is to produce perceptual patterns of perspectives "with ever-increasing completeness, from endlessly new points of view, and with ever-richer determinations," leading us, as Einstein and David Bohm have suggested, ever closer to the identification of the perspectives with the thing in itself.[37]

Such an identification, however, is only a mental construct, for the perceived phenomenon is by definition a disclosure of relative perspectives, the perception of which is a flow of awareness resembling the history of a feeling embodied in Whitehead's Doctrine of the Conformation of Feeling. ". . . the perceptual," says Husserl, "now is ever passing over into the adjacent consciousness of the just-past, a new now simultaneously gleams forth, and so on." Things are given to the empirical consciousness not in themselves but in these "modes of appearing." Consequently, perception always entails "a certain *inadequacy*." During the continuum of perception experienced by the empirical consciousness, perspectives come into and go out of clear focus. If, for example, we observe a bridge of several spans, the portions at the edges of our vision will be less clear than those at the center of our vision. When we shift our view to the less clear portion, it becomes clearer while the other diminishes in clarity. If we change our perspectives in order to take in more of the bridge, our whole vision becomes less clear. This is simply a statement about the gap between knowledge and object that was discussed in Chapter 1. Indeed, Husserl seems specifically to foreshadow Heisenberg's uncertainty principle: "In principle a margin of determinable [cf. the role of Planck's constant in Heisenberg's theory] indeterminacy always remains over, however far we go along our empirical way, and however extended the continua of actual perceptions of the same thing we may have treasured. No God can alter this in any way. . . ."[38]

Empirical consciousness does tell us that we are immersed in a "stream of experience," which we regard from the natural standpoint, that is, objectively. We know that we are in that stream. At the same time we *know* that we know. We have, in other words, a consciousness of empirical consciousness. This more radical consciousness is what Husserl calls *eidos*—"transcendental consciousness." And this is what he sets out to examine, to find what is "immanent in *it*." The means for isolating this eidos for study is, as I have noted, the phenomenological reduction. We take all of our prejudices, presuppositions, and dogmas—all the traditional categories of our apprehension of the world (which are mainly "scientific")—"bracket" them, and set them aside. This bracketing leaves the consciousness of consciousness, which "in itself has a being of its own" and which is absolutely unique in its nature. This is the human form of Whitehead's actual entity. The study of it is what Husserl calls "the philosophy of the Beginning," the basis of which is that absolute individuality of which Whitehead wrote. This study, says Husserl,

> leads eventually to the point that I, who am here reflecting upon myself, become conscious that under a consistent and exclusive focusing of experience upon that which is purely inward . . . I possess in myself an essential individuality, self-contained. . . .[39]

What do we see when we have bracketed and set aside all that is not pure consciousness? On what grounds does Husserl assign to this consciousness the conditions of ultimate Being and absolute reality? The perspectives of things disclosed in empirical consciousness have the form of appearances, not of the "real" things in themselves. Those perspectives give no warrant of the existence of the things from which they apparently arise. Moreover, those perspectives do not rise in the perceiving subject. When the subject moves away from empirical consciousness to consciousness of itself, a different kind of perception appears—"immanent perception." That is, the content of this pure consciousness arises from the subject. The immanence of this content in the subject guarantees its "*Existenz*" in a way the content of empirical consciousness cannot be guaranteed. The consciousness of immanent perception does not see itself "out there," but as an "I" looking "out there." We see ourselves as an identity that is different from the stream of experience in which we are immersed, grasping ourselves as the "pure subject" of that identity. Since the existence of this self, argues Husserl, is given immanently, it is "in principle, undeniable." Thus does Husserl return, with perhaps a slightly new twist, to the old Cartesian argument:

> In every way . . . it is clear that everything which is there for me in the world of things is on grounds of principle *only a presumptive reality;* that *I myself,* on the contrary, for whom it is there (excluding that which is imputed to the thing-world "by me"), I myself or my experience in its actuality am *absolute* Reality . . . given through a positing that is unconditioned and simply indissoluble.

The eidos, like Whitehead's actual entity, is both the center and the unifier of the universe. Its "privileged position," however, holds only for itself and its related stream of experience. Its standpoint is only its own. It does not occupy a position at absolute rest relative to the rest of the universe. From these postulates arises one of the important features of the "open decision." The intelligibility and the meaning of the world are functions of the eidos. Since the eidos is not dependent upon any other source than itself for what it perceives, it is the source of its own meaning. Meaning in this sense is the immanent perception by the eidos of itself, not the objectification of natural perspectives. One must see, says Husserl, that the world's "being" lies "in a certain 'meaning' which presupposes absolute consciousness as the field from which the meaning is derived. . . ."[40]

Through reflection, the eidos thus emerges from the world around it as a separate identity. As it becomes less and less submerged in the stream of experience, it becomes a more and more "disinterested spectator" and gives "a progressively more complete and explicit view of the objective world" that it is conscious of.[41] Freedom from the stream of experience allows it to take up more vantage points, which makes it more aware and less constricted by the compulsion that assumes there is only one way of doing or seeing things. It takes up Bohm's cross-sectional view and occupies the state of "intellectual freedom" described by Northrop Frye. Such awareness is the condition for a high intensity of individual satisfaction. The eidos comes to comprehend its value as "a field for the free consummation of the conscious processes of one and the same pure Ego."[42] As it identifies itself as something separate, it simultaneously affirms its experiences in the stream of life as its own. Without the consciousness of that separate identity, there can be no very acute sense of existence. That alienation from nature to which many thinkers have reacted with despair here is named as the basis for human value and satisfaction. As the sense of one's individual uniqueness becomes greater, the intensity of satisfaction increases.

Martin Heidegger follows Husserl's general pattern of thought, but where Husserl concentrates on the phenomenological method, Heidegger puts more emphasis upon the examination of being itself. Though he regards his major philosophical work, *Being and Time,* as preliminary to a metaphysics for all being, he is concerned principally with human being. His word for that "state" is *Dasein,* and when it is translated literally it recalls Husserl's conception of the eidos as being aware of itself in the stream of experience. Dasein—literally, "being there"—is a kind of basic consciousness, a sense of the presence of things and the awareness of a self which has that sense. This self, as Heidegger describes it, is not some preexistent atomic subject that undergoes no internal change and has no internal relations with the world. It is an entity which is given duration by its awareness that because it recognizes a world, it is possible to refer to itself as a unity that views that world. In doing so, it is, as Werner Brock paraphrases Heidegger, a "process of happening." With this phrase we can see that Dasein is another way of expressing one of the major assumptions of the "open decision"—that "being" or "existence" is not static atomism, but subjective process. In Heidegger's view, the definitive characteristic of that process is the consciousness of "being there," as I have said. Dasein is such that it puts questions about its nature as "there-ness." It is defined, says Heidegger, "by the fact that, in its very Being, that Being is an *issue* for it."[43]

Dasein is similar to Whitehead's actual entity and Husserl's eidos. It is a process which happens in the world, and it appears in two fundamental aspects: the "authentic" and the "inauthentic." Authentic Dasein is essentially the consciousness of oneself arising out of the flow of time. The more vivid that consciousness becomes, the greater the good attained—the higher the intensity of individual satisfaction. Vividness increases or diminishes with the increase or diminishment of the sense of self within time. That sense is basically of a future about which Dasein, in its most authentic state, will "care." Indeed, authentic Dasein *is* care; that is, in its fundamental attention to its being, it has what Werner Brock calls "concern" for its future. It is appropriate here to recall Whitehead. The actual entity's basic experience, he writes, is characterized by "the Quaker word 'concern'. . . . The occasion as subject has a 'concern' for the object."[44] Whitehead's actual entity exists as prehensions of subjects within its vicinity. What we might call the "tone" of that existence is concern for the material it prehends. Similarly, Heidegger's Dasein is "concerned" for what it becomes in its life as a process of happening.

Like Whitehead's actual entity, Dasein has an "aim" toward the future. In its effort to realize that aim it chooses data for itself, certain ways of feeling and being. That data it must draw from a past, and its choices, free of antecedent causes, express the fact that it considers those data "worth repeating." Reflecting Whitehead's Doctrine of the Conformation of Feeling, Heidegger says that Dasein serves its own intensity of individual consciousness by making its own choices from the past on the basis of its concern for the future. In its authentic aspect, Dasein's choice and selection are acts of originality, made so by its vivid consciousness that past existence possesses potentialities worth repeating and that its choices of those potentialities are its own and no one else's. Dasein's consciousness of itself as a historical being, with a past and a future, protects it from slavery to the past for the sake of the past. It produces a respect for the integrity of the self, a respect which emphasizes its intelligibility and its duration from the past to the future. A diminishment of consciousness means a diminishment of freedom, and either a totally slavish dependency upon the past simply because it *is* the past, or an indifference to it altogether. Either of these states is "inauthenticity."

Inauthenticity is a "fallenness" into the "they" of the everyday world, a submergence in the stream of experience. In this state the consciousness of the self diminishes. Dasein hides in anonymity, binding itself, for example, to the strictures of its society, becoming those strictures as if it had no choices—like the actual entity in the nonliving society. Submerged inauthentically in the world, Dasein loses its concern for the future, becomes indifferent to the "repetitions" of the past, and thereby loses its identity in duration. It loses its sense both of self and the time out of which the self arises. In this state, as E. L. Allen says, we "invent specious arguments to prove that all is as it should be, till we become estranged from ourselves, entangled and lost."[45] One becomes bound to the collective, the "they." Dasein becomes blind, not "caring." There is little question that authentic existence, with its high intensity of self-awareness, embodies a higher good than does inauthentic existence. Yet, Dasein is defined by the presence of both inauthenticity and authenticity. Part of its nature is to be, in some degree, inauthentic.[46]

Heidegger says that temporality is the condition of Dasein, that Dasein is a seizing of certain data from the past in order to fulfill an aim toward the future. If this is the case, then the general nature of the future also figures into the definition of Dasein. Dasein's temporality implies a horizon, a limit. Its horizon is its own death, which is the disappearance of the sense of self in time. Death is therefore part of Dasein's future, a potential for what it might some day "be." The paradox is that this potential is for "not being." When it is realized, Dasein becomes a "whole." At that point, Dasein has no more future, no more possibilities, and so it ceases to be itself—as Whitehead's actual entity "perishes" as it achieves its subjective aim. Dasein cannot experience its wholeness as Dasein, for that wholeness is not part of its nature. To reject death is to reject Dasein's nature. Inauthentic Dasein is such rejection. It takes place in the state of fallenness, wherein Dasein either thinks it will escape death or it will assume an "indifferent tranquillity . . . in view of the 'fact' that 'one' dies."[47] Peter L. Berger writes,

> To exist authentically is to live in full awareness of the unique, irreplaceable and incomparable quality of one's individuality. By contrast, inauthentic existence is to lose oneself in the anonymity of the ["they"], surrendering one's uniqueness to the socially constituted abstractions. This is especially important in the way one faces death. The truth of the matter is that it is always one single, solitary individual who dies. But society comforts the bereaved and those who are to die themselves by subsuming each death under general categories that appear to assuage its horror. A man dies, and we say "Well, we all have to go someday." This "we all" is an exact rendition of the ["they"]—it is everybody and thus nobody, and by putting ourselves under its generality we hide from ourselves the inevitable fact that we too shall die, singly and solitarily.[48]

Not until Dasein is certain of its own being can it "enjoy" the absolute certainty and acceptance of its own death. For Heidegger, this certainty implies a guarantee of being. And that guarantee entails a high intensity of satisfaction.

Concern for death as the horizon of Dasein's temporality is fundamental to the vividness with which Dasein experiences its emergence from the stream of existence. One of the features of that vividness is "dread"—*angst,* the experience of being aware of one's own potential for not being; it is the subjective *experience* of Nothingness, not merely its apprehension, that gives the word an intelligibility for the human being. Authentic Dasein is partly defined by its experience of Nothingness. The dread it feels is not dread of "something" in the world, but of an indefinite condition which cannot be described precisely or formulated exactly. Only when Dasein grasps the dark and absolute potentiality of not being and experiences dread can it be called authentic. The irony is that the very thing that makes it human also both reveals and constitutes its doom.

Bounded by death, Dasein's nature is to recognize itself as a being with a personal horizon—its own death—and to exist as a projection of itself into the future. That it projects itself into the future as it emerges out of the past implies that there is something it can be which it is not now. The Care that guides Dasein's choices of "repetitions" "calls" to Dasein to be itself as this negative thing, this something which it "is" not yet. This call is "Conscience," which exhorts Dasein to avoid losing itself in the "they"—the "one like many." Without Conscience Dasein is vulnerable to the proposition that the collective is the sphere in which being is known, for in the collective one is safe. But the price of that safety is the vivid sense of self. Conscience, combined with Dread, calls Dasein into that authentic world in which all is strange and unsafe, but which belongs to the unique individual self. Conscience is also a catalyst in Dasein's time-bound self-creativity. It reveals to Dasein that it is "guilty," that it is not now something which it can be. This recalls Dasein's character as a historical being, defined by its ability to look forward toward something which it is not in the present. The guilt that Heidegger speaks of is not a sense of shame or sin, but the force that moves Dasein to do or feel. It shows that Dasein has a kind of privation in its own being. The presence of a sense of guilt as Heidegger defines it suggests that Dasein is free of the collective's presuppositions, that it chooses its being itself in its own unique way. In that freedom, it becomes responsible for what it is and what it will be. To remain deaf to Care's call, submerged in the "they," is to be inauthentic. Authentic Dasein hears the call of Conscience and resolves to rise as an individual self in a world of "they's." Doing so entails genuine action, which combines the spontaneity of freedom and openness with the responsibility of planning and decision.

Resoluteness contributes to the intensity of the awareness of one's self as an identifiable entity; it contributes to Dasein's authenticity. But authenticity in the form of action—or any form—does not imply self-isolation, an emphasis which recalls the social character of Whitehead's actual entity. "The 'resolve,'" as Brock writes, "is characterized as the 'authentic self-Being,' which means not a Dasein isolated from the world, but 'Being-authentically-in-the-world.'"[49] Dasein—"being there"—is conditioned by its world. Its process of existence transpires as part of the community. Its identity is created through its own independence as well as through the world that it enacts in its "repetitions." Its individual satisfaction includes both an awareness of the self and of the world from which that self arises.

The values implied in the work of Husserl and Heidegger are to be found in their conception of human reality—the self awareness of its identity in the midst of the world. Freedom is the condition of the most intense awareness of this identity—freedom from the presuppositions and prejudices of the past (as in Husserl's "empirical consciousness"), from the dulling of consciousness in "theyness." The attainment of the eidetic reduction and authenticity is characterized by this freedom, but it is also characterized by affirmation of the limits of human existence. If the human being is defined as having the absolute possibility of death, then individual satisfaction can only be inhibited by a refusal to entertain this possibility, to grasp its unique and altogether real application to the individual subject. The paradox that the good of self-consciousness discloses human limits does not seem to trouble Husserl or Heidegger. Jean-Paul Sartre, however, finds that paradox disturbing, sees it as the ground of man's futility. The incompleteness of man's being, which means that his existence is a process moving toward completeness, dooms him to frustration. Even so, Sartre illuminates the metaphysics of the "open decision" as it is formulated by Husserl and Heidegger.

Being, says Sartre, has two aspects. They are, in Sartre's well-known terms, *en-soi* and *pour-soi,* generally translated as "in-itself" and "for-itself." In-itself is the whole fabric of raw materiality which lies unchanged by perception. Husserl calls it the "medium of dormant actuality."[50] It can never be more than itself. It strives to fulfill no possibilities because it has none. Having no future, in-itself has no freedom to be something which it is not now, as Heidegger put it. The for-itself is consciousness, that to which the in-itself is partially revealed. Whatever is not consciousness is in-itself. For-itself does not exist without in-itself because it is the "revelation of the In-itself,"[51] which is to say that it is the consciousness of being in the world. But the main characteristic of in-itself is that it never reveals itself "completely" to consciousness. Its being "does not exist *only* in so far as it appears."[52] The form in which in-itself appears to for-itself is a phenomenon, but it also possesses a "transphenomenal being," which "is itself in itself." It spills beyond the perspectives experienced by the consciousness. With this doctrine of "transphenomenality" we are brought back to the uncertainty principle and the statements of Whitehead and Husserl.

The for-itself is similar to Heidegger's Dasein in that its being is an "issue" for it. In-itself is not aware of being itself. For-itself sees that it is not in-itself. This is an act of "nihilation" and through it the for-itself attains self-awareness. It sees that in not being in-itself, it is Nothingness. Sartre invents a quaint metaphor to describe this awareness: for-itself is a hole in being, a figure of speech which captures the sense of feeling surrounded by a world that is so strong in Heidegger. As that hole in being—that Nothingness—for-itself is "lack," and what it lacks is the full completeness of the in-itself. In the form of this lack, the for-itself has possibilities surpassing itself toward some future condition. The preferred condition at which it aims is the in-itself. It is always trying to "fill up the hole" of its nothingness and thereby become completely correspondent with in-itself, seeking the "repose" of complete identification with the in-itself. "Thus human reality," says Sartre, "is the desire of being-in-itself."[53] The in-itself has some of the characteristics formerly ascribed to God: a complete self-sufficiency, a nature that requires nothing more than it is. Thus, Sartre can say that man—for-itself—"fundamentally is the desire to be God," to be the completed realization of his possibilities without losing his own character as a for-itself.

For-itself projects itself into the future toward the preferred situation of repose, the closure of possibilities. The agent of that projection is consciousness, that which can conceive of a state of affairs other than the one existing in the present. For-itself, like the actual entity, is composed of its "project," which is the pursuit of the state of affairs conceived of. The selection of a particular "project" for surpassing the present toward the future and the implementation of that project through bodily acts and thoughts bring about a rupture with the given. If it conceived of no future embodied in some other state of affairs, for-itself would be a completed whole, without possibilities, and no longer a for-itself. Because it can break with the given, it is free—free to choose from its possibilities. Implicit in that freedom, however, is the absurdity that there is no reason to choose one possibility or project over another.

The longing of for-itself to fill its lack is fruitless. It is impossible for the consciousness to become identical with the world of full being, for then it would lose its identity as consciousness. For-itself cannot achieve the repose it seeks. For this reason, Sartre says, the human being is a "useless passion"—"by nature an unhappy consciousness with no possibility of surpassing its unhappy state."[54] Part of the structure of the human being is to be unable to achieve the preferred condition of total identification with "God"—in-itself. In its emergence as a self-aware identity, for-itself learns that its nature is to desire what it cannot have. This contradiction does not, however, make it impossible to have values and to live affirmatively. There is an implied value in the condition which postulates an unapproachable ideal and guarantees for itself only the unhappy recognition that the ideal is unattainable. Only the authentic human reality perceives his situation, and throughout his writings, Sartre, sometimes tacitly, sometimes explicitly, assumes with Heidegger that authenticity is more desirable than inauthenticity. The reality of the human being is too often sacrificed for an inauthentic "happiness." The character of this happiness—similar to the dulling familiarity of Heidegger's "they"—is signaled by Sartre's term *mauvais fois:* bad faith. This is the illusion that the for-itself can achieve its desire of becoming in-itself without losing its identity as for-itself; it is the illusion that existence and being are fully accounted for by the perspectives one perceives of the object. Bad faith mistakes the part for the whole, the abstract for the concrete totality. A person is in bad faith when he assumes that he fully accounts for himself by saying that he "is" a teacher, a waiter, a plumber. Reality does not admit such total explanations. The for-itself, says Sartre, is by definition perpetually open to its own possibilities for the future; the in-itself is always more than its phenomenal manifestation to consciousness.

Sartre gives us some examples of bad faith in his novel *Nausea.* Roquentin, the protagonist, has discovered that existence is a sweet, sticky, cloying mass without form or purpose. This is the in-itself. The bourgeoisie of Bouville, the little French town which is the setting of the story, do not permit themselves knowledge of this existence. They cast a veil of recognizable order, rationality, and purpose over it and take the veil for reality. They are in a state of "fallenness." Like the fallen, the Bouvillois, says Roquentin, "aren't afraid. They feel at home." They are in bad faith because they think their explanations represent completely and accurately the "real" world. At lunch, Roquentin becomes disgusted with his friend, the "Self-taught Man," who describes his love of humanity and the way in which that love has saved him from despair. As an example, he nods with loving eyes at a young couple in the café. Angry at his hypocrisy, Roquentin tells him that his love is not for the young couple who are actually there in the café as unique and individual subjects, but for the "Youth of the Man, the Love of Man and Woman, the Human Voice."[55] The Self-taught Man has deluded himself that he reacts to the existent when in reality he reacts only to the safer "general idea" of abstractions, which in themselves have no existence and do not surpass themselves toward a future.

The very term *bad faith* implies a value. It is somehow "better" not to be in bad faith than to be in it. Bad faith rejects human life and its paradoxical nature, which is simultaneously "to be what it is not and not to be what it is."[56] Human life is also freedom and responsibility for oneself. Bad faith looks for shelter from this hard condition by claiming that the self must do what "they" do, that, for example, the rules of society absolutely determine one's inner nature. It assumes to be necessary what is voluntary. Yet, it is not as if bad faith is something the human being takes up or lays down. The human being is defined by the fact that he is always more or less in bad faith, is always more or less in a state of inauthenticity. It is the measure of his paradoxical nature. Bad faith reflects the conscious effort to fill the hole in being. It is not possible for the human being to be completely free of bad faith. At the same time, it is not possible for the human being to be completely sheltered from freedom and responsibility. Human morality and value lie in the degree of consciousness men have of their predicament. The higher the degree of consciousness, the more men seek freedom, even though it carries with it a certain amount of unhappiness. It is in this search that men live significantly: ". . . the ultimate meaning of the acts of honest men is the quest for freedom as such."[57] If the highest intensity of individual satisfaction occurs in the human condition, then it entails paradox and contradictoriness, the affirmation of a nature in which incompleteness and unhappiness are inherent.

THE IMPLEMENTATION OF FREEDOM

I HAVE TRIED in Chapters 1 and 2 to establish the empirical and the metaphysical bases of the contemporary view of human reality. The view articulated by the modern physicist and by Whitehead, Husserl, Heidegger, and Sartre is also the view of the contemporary American novelist. That view carries with it an explanation of reality which satisfies the novelist because it seems to account for the truth of things. That truth lies in the individual human existent. Thus our novels are organized around the issue of individual integrity; that is the pre-eminent issue in terms of which our novelists view the world. Beneath the action and the characters lies the logical construction of the "open decision," which derives from the conception that, metaphysically, absolute reality is in the human individual. If this is so, it follows that, to achieve the maximal good of such a reality, it is desirable to "be" as human as possible, which means to be as individual as possible. According to our metaphysics individuality implies ambiguity, process, growth, death, and love of other individuals. It also implies, paradoxically, that human beings seek to resolve ambiguity, to abandon process for stasis, to grow *to* a point in order to stop at absolute rest, to flee from inescapable personal death, and to escape the terrible burden of loving others. These tense issues constitute the main motifs of the novels treated in this book. The conflicts that give the novels their suspense and interest are embedded in the modern conception of the individual. And the resolutions advanced by our novelists derive from this same concept:

For Notes to Chapter 3, see pages 400–401.

That is, the individual, according to our metaphysics, is composed of contradictory elements. Satisfaction depends upon their fusion, not upon the victory of any one over the rest. The success of such a fusion in turn depends wholly upon one's freedom to transcend the limitations of the various poles, and this brings us back to Sartre's statements at the end of the last chapter.

Sartre's emphasis upon freedom reflects one of the basic presuppositions of the "open decision." Freedom is the basis of value, for a choice made freely is more individual—hence more valuable—than one made under compulsion. Compulsive choice limits the individual's alternatives and binds him to a rigid past, just as Whitehead's "non-living" society binds the actual entity to severely limited possibilities. Freedom entails a range of alternatives, an awareness of the capacity to choose and the motives for choosing, and the recognition that the consequences of choice are unpredictable. Such freedom is the *sine qua non* of the self's individuality and creativity. The Pioneer American sociologist Charles H. Cooley writes,

> Where suggestions are numerous and conflicting [Whitehead would say "contrasting"] we feel the need to choose; to make these choices is the function of the will, and the result of them is a step in the progress of life, an act of freedom or creation . . . but where suggestion is single, as with religious dogma in ages of faith, we are very much at its mercy. We do not perceive these limitations, because there is no point of vantage from which we can observe and measure the general state of thought; there is nothing to compare it with. Only when it begins to change, when competing suggestions enter our minds and we get new points of view from which we can look back upon it, do we begin to notice its power over us.[1]

There is an unpredictableness of the consequences of our free choices, and it is another imperative of our conception of freedom. Without a meta-system of value we can have no assurance that our choice is "right" or effective. Our ignorance makes our freedom, as Marjorie Grene describes it, "dreadful." The twentieth century is full of studies showing that men have occasionally found it impossible to deal with any freedom from absolute systems, such as Christianity, and have sought to surrender their freedom to substitute systems—such as political totalitarianism. Yet, it is just that "dreadful" freedom which characterizes the human condition at the height of its painful consciousness. Freedom, indeed, *is* consciousness.

The contemporary American novelist, as I have suggested, both tacitly and overtly assumes the intrinsic value of freedom and identifies it with consciousness. Such freedom and such consciousness, I have said, are the prerequisites for fusing the contradictory poles of the human individual in order to achieve satisfaction—the vivid awareness of oneself in a world of limits, of ambiguities, of possibilities. The question for the novelist, as well as for the social commentator, then becomes, What are the conditions under which the individual can most successfully exercise his freedom in choosing from his alternatives those which will be most valuable for achieving satisfaction? A character dominated by "bad faith" (like Alma Mason in *The Nephew*), an obsessive neurotic compulsion (like Cass Kinsolving in *Set This House on Fire*), or social tyranny (like so many in the war novel, the business novel, and the "hip" novel) are thwarted in their drive for satisfaction, because in the reduction of their freedom—that is, their consciousness—their individuality is diminished. In order to deal more effectively with the answers examined by the novelist, I turn now to the answers set forth in the intellectual background from which he draws. These divide broadly into two classes: (1) the social, in which the emphasis is upon the organization of society as a means of securing man's freedom; and (2) the psychological, in which the emphasis is upon the individual's private experience and self, either in defiance of or freedom from organized society.

The social answer stresses the reciprocal effect that the individual and society have upon each other. This way of formulating the issue, although relevant to all of the novels discussed later, is most immediately important to the war and business novels of our period. The extreme expression of this attitude is in Cooley's statement that " 'society' and 'individuals' do not denote separable phenomena, but are simply collective and distributive aspects of the same thing. . . ."[2] Similarly, John Dewey asserts that there is no such thing as a pure individual or a pure society; they both imply each other. It is therefore, this argument goes, of prime importance that society have the principles of freedom built into it, for then both society and the individual benefit. The strongest, most forceful, and most stable societies, says Dewey, are those whose "members can function to the limit of their capacities," those which use "the diversity of individual capacities in initiative, planning, foresight, vigor, and endurance."[3] This attitude recalls Whitehead's conception of a society as both an extension and a condition of the actual entity's existence, and Heidegger's notion of Dasein as being-in-the-world. It does shift the emphasis away from metaphysics to action in the world. When the American war and business novelists examine this issue they emphasize the dangers of any society that is not founded on the principle of freedom. Such societies produce ignominious cowards, like Roth in *The Naked and the Dead,* or egomaniacal generals like Mallon in Ned Calmer's *The Strange Land.* The values I note here are implied in the negative social pictures drawn by our novelists. Some novelists, however, like Irwin Shaw (see page 148), lay out specifically the features of a society described by the writers treated in this chapter.

There is a radical connection between the philosophical principles of freedom as articulated by scientists like David Bohm and writers like Sartre, and the sociological approach to the human condition. It can be seen clearly in the theory of Max Weber. The social sciences, he says, are empirical sciences, and their students must come to the subject divested of the stultifying limitations of folklore and solidified opinions handed down by tradition. Social scientists are not the promoters of any particular moral standard; they do not "provide binding norms and ideals from which directives for immediate practical activity can be derived." That would be a failure to "measure the general state of thought," as Cooley says. The sociological task, according to Weber, is to bring the individual to a higher state of consciousness of his relationship to the values by which he behaves, to show the individual that his choices imply "the espousal of certain virtues" and that "choice itself is his own responsibility." Society's governing principle must be a tolerance for reactions against some of its own most cherished notions. To a judge who would deny the right of an anarchist to teach law because anarchy begins by denying law's validity, Weber answers: "An anarchist can surely be a good legal scholar. And if he is such, then indeed the Archimedean point of his convictions, which is outside the conventions and presuppositions which are so self-evident to us, can equip him to perceive problems in the fundamental postulates of legal theory which escape those who take them for granted."[4]

Karl Mannheim lays out a social program based upon Weber's theoretical statements. Like Weber, Mannheim says that the end of society is to provide the individual with a wide range of possibilities and the freedom to choose from that range. Without his freedom and his possibilities, the human being loses his humanness and becomes a creature of habit, compulsively obeying his traditional folkways as though there were no other way to think or act. He becomes imprisoned by bad faith and fails to attain Frye's "intellectual freedom."

In *Ideology and Utopia,* first written in 1929, then revised and expanded in 1936 for its English translation, Mannheim explains those forces that hinder the achievement of individual satisfaction and the means by which they can be overcome. Individual satisfaction, says Mannheim, is impaired by either a free-swinging individualistic anarchy or the excessive regimentation of totalitarianism. In the first extreme, the data are not adequately ordered to allow efficient self-creativity; in the second, the data are too restricted to provide an adequate range for self-creativity. To avoid either of these extremes, one must transcend them. The basic tool for such transcendence is the "sociology of knowledge."[5] This is a habit of thought or a frame of mind rather than a particular philosophy or set of values, and its features are familiar. It assumes a detached vantage point in order to make clear that all knowledge is rooted in the "social texture," that all knowing comes from one's own world rather than from a separate and antecedent world. The "sociology of knowledge" is a method of overcoming all particularistic views of reality and thereby bringing the individual into what Cooley, in another context, has called a "saner relation" with his world. It embraces all thought styles and attempts to understand as many alternatives as the conscious mind may entertain. Thus, Mannheim does not search for permanent specific truths fixed by an antecedent reality, but for a *way* of making society an efficient source of freedom and data for the self-creating human being.

The great threats to the autonomy of the human being are those modes of thought which Mannheim calls "ideology" and "utopia." Ideology seeks to maintain the *status quo* on the grounds that it is absolute truth, and in doing so, ideology serves contemporary vested interests. Utopian thought constructs an ideal situation which can be brought into being only by totally shattering the *status quo*. Both habits of mind lead to a particularistic view of reality—to a "false consciousness," as Mannheim calls it—which distorts evidence and fails to take account of new factors which might require a modification of conduct. "False consciousness" is a form of bad faith and inauthenticity, in which the individual deludes himself into thinking that a certain single set of laws or standards is the only possible set. It prohibits the free pursuit of genuine meaning and is similar to the dependence on the past which characterizes Whitehead's nonliving society.

By means of the "sociology of knowledge" the individual may avoid the limitations inherent in ideology and utopia. It leads him to see that his values are formed by his social situation and that his society is in turn affected by his values; that human social experience is a complex web of interreactions between various thought styles, individuals, and society, no one of which can properly be given priority. Such awareness confers upon him the true freedom to choose. If he remains ignorant and unaware, he remains a slave to the unexamined extremes of ideology or utopia, to the blind compulsive forces which are more proper to mechanical instinct than to purposeful humanity. Mannheim, in other words, would move the determining factors of our conduct from the unconscious to the conscious where they can take part in real choice. When we do this, says Mannheim, "we are more and more thrown back upon our true self and, whereas formerly we were the servants of necessity, we now find it possible to unite consciously with forces with which we are in thorough agreement."[6]

The ideal state—the preferred situation—is that in which the individual enjoys the free exercise of choice within a wide range of alternatives. That state, Mannheim declares in *Man and Society*, can be brought into being through social planning. Planning, however, raises a danger which Mannheim recognizes:

> Is not an ideally planned society a prison, a straight-jacket, even compared with the almost intolerable life led by many classes in an unplanned society? In the latter the people may be threatened with insecurity, but the individual is still (potentially at least) a free agent and can cope with his difficulties himself. Does not the continual

development of social technique lead to the complete enslavement of the individual?[7]

His answer to this question, of course, is that correct planning not only does not deprive the individual of his independence; it makes him more free. Correct planning is that which is freely entered into by the individual made alert to himself and his motives through the sociology of knowledge. It will create or perpetuate a social structure which insures the very freedom which allowed the plan to come about. It is true that a planned society does require a kind of conformity which anarchic individualism might find oppressive. But the conformity of a planned society is freely and consciously chosen. Planning, therefore, must arrange for the individual to be induced to conform, to desire to conform, to prefer the proper conformity in order to win those advantages which anarchy does not provide. In the planned society, the citizen's guide is the sociology of knowledge, which delivers into his possession a wide range of alternatives, allowing him to choose with a clear view of the source and the possible consequences of his choice. The planned society, as Mannheim sees it, need be neither totalitarian nor mechanistic. It is a venture in which all its members actively choose to cooperate.

Planning is planning for something. It implies certain purposes and projected ends. Mannheim says that if the project is to have meaning it must be founded upon a "hierarchy of basic aims." If there is no ultimate reality except that of the individual, however, how is the planner to construct such a hierarchy? The answer lies in the principles of pragmatism: the hierarchy is to be worked out by "practical experience." To assist him, the planner may draw on several basic universal virtues "which are essential to the maintenance of a planned society . . . co-operation, brotherly help, and decency."[8] Mannheim elects not to define these words, but he declares that the ideals they stand for must be actualized if the planned society is to succeed.

Because government in a planned society is crucial, it is important that the proper sort be chosen. For Mannheim the proper sort is parliamentary, for it divides the power of the government among its several branches, preventing the domination of any one branch. It allows conflicts to arise between groups, provides grounds for compromise, and encourages warring factions to work out their disagreements freely. It makes possible the simultaneous play of hate and love, anger and approval, channeling emotion rather than stifling it, and avoiding the sense of helpless frustration that encourages dictatorial manipulation.

Mannheim does not provide directions for dealing with those groups who refuse to cooperate and who reject the concept of the sociology of knowledge for their own uncompromising absolutes. We do not discover, therefore, how the society he envisions comes into being. Nor does he answer a fundamental question: Who is going to name the program of aims and virtues? Beneath his theory lies a tacit, pleasant, but questionable assumption: that private interest will voluntarily give way to public, that the planners will be disinterested men, and that people will eschew jealousy, ambition, greed. What is important for us is the consensus that Mannheim's ideas embody. Recall, for example, Whitehead's metaphysical axiom that participation in a well-ordered society produces the highest intensity of individual satisfaction, when "well-ordered" does not mean totalitarian but planned for freedom.

Yet, whatever disavowals the social planner makes, his aims and his methods provoke suspicions. Some of Mannheim's statements about freedom suggest something less than he promises: "From now on men will find a higher form of freedom in allowing many aspects of their individual lives to be determined by the social order laid down by the group, provided that it is an order which they themselves have chosen." Through "skillful guidance," the individual will be allowed "every opportunity for making his own decisions."[9] The use of words like "skillful guidance," "induce," "technique" leans uncomfortably toward operant conditioning. We are given visions of the deployment of immense power in the hands of a few. The freedom spoken of is the freedom to choose the mode of conduct we have been conditioned to desire by a social structure which has a vested interest in our making the "right" choice. It is considerations like these that make Karl Jaspers regard the social structure as a sinister "apparatus," characterized by "mass-life," and threatening the "real self" of every human being. Similarly, Freud writes of civilization's "discontents," cautioning against those tremendous demands that society makes on man's spontaneity and individuality, demands enforced, not through some tyrannical police organization with brass knuckles and billy clubs, but the subtle internalization of the rightness of those demands. In this way, the social law is administered through individual conscience, and the human being is faced with the constant threat of being reduced to an automaton.

The paradox that the individual seems unable to live with society or without it is widely noted and makes up one of the commonplaces of the "open decision." The harmony and contentment foreseen by the social planner, in this view, are not aims achievable within man's condition. Reinhold Niebuhr writes that "the sociologists, as a class, understand the modern social problem even less than the educators. They usually interpret social conflict as the result of a clash between different kinds of 'behavior patterns,' which can be eliminated if the contending parties will only allow the social scientist to furnish them with a new and more perfect pattern which will do justice to the needs of both parties." What they do not realize, says Niebuhr, is that conflict is inevitable, that reason does not guide men's decisions or fairness their choices. By definition society means struggle between opposing power blocs and conflict between "politics and ethics." Politics is the operating principle of the collective ethics of the individual. These conflicting principles exist side by side in our world. Indeed, our world is defined by their simultaneous presence. Each sphere pursues its own laws: "Society must strive for justice even if it is forced to use means, such as self-assertion, resistance, coercion and perhaps resentment, which cannot gain the moral sanction of the most sensitive moral spirit. The individual must strive to realise his life by losing and finding himself in something greater than himself."[10]

When the war novelists and business novelists take up this theme, they are successful in capturing the pathos inherent in these contradictions. James Jones's Robert E. Lee Prewitt, for example, a kind of Billy Budd, has a deep allegiance to the Army apparatus. He prides himself on being a thirty-year man. But his integrity, just as Niebuhr suggests, moves him to commit actions which inevitably bring him into conflict with the organization he loves, and, tragically, he is destroyed by that organization for the very acts that gain the reader's sympathy and admiration. In many of the business novels, the most admirable characters are those who achieve success in the business corporation, but simultaneously realize with regret that they have sold to the apparatus some of their best and most spontaneous qualities.

But the clash between the individual and his society—between the self and its limits—is the condition of our existence, perhaps even the warrant that we are alive. In this view, we are most human when we are most conscious of the clash. Thus, Jaspers would enlist the human being in his "existence-philosophy," through which the authentic self may struggle to maintain his integrity by rejecting the "authoritative forms" of the apparatus while at the same time living among them. He must not, that is, withdraw from society. If he is to have any satisfaction at all, he must "live at harmony with the powers of this world without being absorbed by them." It is only by remaining within the framework of the apparatus that the self can realize meaning and purpose in his life, for they come only through social ties—not "coercive ties," but those "ties freely comprehended" and assumed.[11] Through such ties, the individual voluntarily takes up commitments to others and by doing so accomplishes what Niebuhr suggests. He realizes "his life by losing and finding himself in something greater than himself." In the end, the solution to the problem of the individual and society lies in their fusion, not in a reconciliation in which one or the other ceases to be itself. Echoing Jaspers and Niebuhr, R. W. McIver declares that the extreme individualism that regards all government "as the enemy of liberty" is as dangerous to individual fulfillment as the extreme collectivism which claims that "only in the state are we at one with ourselves and the world." These views, he says, confound society with the state, and he points out that clear-headedness chooses neither extreme, but does "justice to both sides." "We must accept the individuality of the unit, we must seek the individual as the bearer and inheritor of human values, and on the other hand we must see the unity as that which sustains, incorporates and promotes all human values."[12] Whitehead's metaphysics continues to be confirmed. And, it is true, so frequently in the contemporary American novel, we feel more the poignancy inherent in the nature of things—the inescapable battle between the self and the organization—than a zealous rejection of society as such, even in its worst forms. This does not mean that the individual is a helpless victim. How does he, then, help himself? The answer lies in that now-familiar attribute: expanded consciousness.

This answer, like the one I have just discussed, is applicable to all of the novels I discuss, but it is especially relevant to those dealt with in the last chapter.

To avert the dangers of the planned state, to fuse the extremes of our world and ourselves, and to attain a high intensity of individual satisfaction require a high degree of consciousness. The psychological question of self-fulfillment concentrates upon the individual rather than the structure of his society. For example, Freud would say that though the inhibition of self-fulfillment may be triggered by the clash between society and the individual, the problem to which he addresses himself lies somewhere in the person's own psyche, and it appears as a neurosis. The main aim of psychoanalysis is the dissolution of the neurosis, the expansion of consciousness which will reveal the authentic self and the motives by which it operates, and the liberation of the self. Psychoanalysis does not transform the individual into something different, any more than the embracing of the contradictions. It should, however, change the subject's attitude toward his condition and thereby modify the quality of his existence. The validity of psychoanalysis is tied to a human personality structure which Freud formulated partly from observation and partly from intuition, a structure which in its general outlines and implications coincides with the conception of the individual as it is expressed in the "open decision." Thus, my discussion of the psychological means of achieving a high intensity of individual satisfaction through freedom adds to a definition of the "open decision." Though the main features of Freud's personality theory are well known, I have decided to describe them once again as a means of demonstrating the way in which that theory reflects and contributes to the world view I am trying to establish. Lionel Trilling has said that the central characteristic of the background from which twentieth-century writing emerges is the celebration of the unconscious, especially as it appears in Fraser's *The Golden Bough* and Freud's psychology. I am emphasizing the value placed by modern thought upon consciousness.

Freud analysed the human psyche into the id, the ego, and the super-ego. The id, as Calvin Hall says, is "the true psychic reality

. . . the primary subjective reality, the inner world that exists before the individual has had experience of the external world."[13] It need hardly be pointed out that this "primary subjective reality" is the psychological parallel to the elementary particle, Whitehead's actual entity, Husserl's eidos, and Heidegger's Dasein. Freud reflects the modern preoccupation with the individual existent as the primordial reality. The id is the ground for any future development; it is therefore everything. The ego and super-ego are simply modifications of this primary structure. The subjectivity and primordiality of the id make it, as I say, analogous to Whitehead's actual entity. As the actual entity is comprised of its prehensions of data, so the id is made up of instincts, "unconscious wish-impulses,"[14] which direct the id's appetite for data. The instincts operate according to the "pleasure principle"—self-gratification—seeking to dispel the discomfort that arises from the tension of an unfulfilled wish. The pure id, one might say, exists as the embryo in the womb. Here no wish goes unfulfilled, at least ideally, for the womb is designed to anticipate every unconscious desire and to satisfy it before the tension of unfulfillment appears. In the womb, the id's external world is more or less identical with itself and denies it nothing. It is thus unaware of being a self.

With birth, the id is cast into an environment which places severe limitations upon the fulfillment of its wishes. The appearance of an external world which does not exactly correspond with the id's desires creates the state of consciousness. Though Freud does not put it in quite these terms, consciousness is, as Whitehead and Heidegger might say, the perception of the contrast between the id's world and the external world. The result of this perception is the ego. Whatever is conscious in the id is the ego, though ego is not synonymous with consciousness, as will become important later. The ego is the function by which the id transacts business with the external world. In this role, the ego judges the extent to which the desires of the id can be fulfilled by the external world: ". . . the ego seeks to bring the influence of the external world to bear upon the id and its tendencies, and endeavours to substitute the reality principle for the pleasure principle which reigns unrestrictedly in the id. For the ego, perception plays the part which in the id falls to instinct."[15] The ego works by interposing "the processes of thinking" between the origin of the id's wish-impulses and the attempt to gratify them; this delays any action which the id might initiate and which might be destructively precipitate. If the id expresses desires which cannot be satisfied by the external world or which cannot be satisfied without some resultant pain, the ego must either rechannel that desire—sublimate it—or repress it.

The ego administers the reality principle as a kind of agent of the law-giving super-ego. Usually, says Freud, "the ego carries out repressions in the service and at the behest of its super-ego." He also calls the super-ego the "ego ideal," the image of itself which the ego seeks to actualize. Like the ego, the super-ego is a modification of the id, growing out of the confrontation between the id's wish-impulses by the reality of the external world. It develops during the struggle of the individual with the Oedipus complex. The triumph of the reality principle over the Oedipus complex results in an adequate super-ego. As a baby, when the id is most powerful, the boy instinctively acquires a wish-impulse for his mother, "which originally related to the mother's breast." The boy deals with his father "by identifying himself with him."[16] As he grows older and his wishes become more specific, he desires his mother and becomes hostile to his father as the obstacle of the gratification of his wish. When in the process of maturing it comes time to dissolve the complex, the boy must take up another "object-choice," for reality prohibits the gratification of the original wish. Though the new "object-choice" may be second best, it is better than nothing, and nothing is what the boy would get if he persisted in pursuing his infantile desire. In making the shift he is helped along by a renewed identification with his father. The result of the rechanneling of his desire—a sublimation—is an object-affection for his mother and a disappearance of the hostility for his father. This simple pattern is complicated by the bisexual nature of all humans. The boy may also take up a feminine attitude toward the father, trying to gain his affections through seductiveness, and become correspondingly hostile to his mother. The Oedipal complex is characterized by this ambivalence.

The complex can be dissolved or repressed if the boy successfully identifies with his father. In this case a positive "subject-relation" will be maintained with the mother which will simultaneously replace the feminine relation the boy had with his father under the influence of his bisexuality. Successful repression is made possible by the emergence of the super-ego. In the early stages of life, when the wish-impulses dominate, the parents are the obstacles to the gratification of the id's desires, and thus are agents of the real world, placing limits on the potential success of the id's desires. Eventually, the id must be persuaded first that the original wish cannot, indeed *ought* not, be gratified, and second that the only solution to this unavoidable impasse is to take that second-best object-choice which can and "should" be satisfied. The persuasive argument appears as the super-ego, which emerges when the formerly external obstacles of the parents are internalized in the form of moral prohibitions against the original desire for the mother. The super-ego is thus made up of the ideals of the parents translated from the external world into an internal conscience. It is that part of the id which embodies the prohibitionary moral laws that operate in repression and sublimation. Though I have mentioned these laws only as the internalization of parental ideas, they also represent other authority ideals present in the external world impinging upon the unreconstructed id.

Freud's picture of the personality has the largest part of the self located in the id, which is comprised of unconscious wish-impulses. This is the spontaneous self, the basic, true being. Its wishes are neither normal nor abnormal; they simply *are*. Left to demand and expect without guidance, the id would be rebuffed by an external world which does not exist to gratify its wishes. To survive, the id develops a means of perceiving its limitations—the ego—and a set of prohibitions having the force of law which the ego employs—the super-ego. A huge part of the self is therefore naturally and appropriately unconscious. If the ego were always conscious of just how far the id could go in the real world, and if the super-ego were always consciously and realistically reflective of the world, the self would be in harmony. No unreasonable demands would be made of the id; no unsuccessful repressions or sublimations would result.

Such, of course, is not the case. The ego too often lacks the range of consciousness necessary for the successful unification of the poles of the self, very much in the same way that the poles of the society and the individual seem incapable of fusing perfectly. The ego has its own area of unconsciousness, and it is from this unconsciousness that most personal trouble arises. The mechanics of repression require that a wish of the id which cannot be satisfied by the external world be rechannelled in a direction which can lead to satisfaction. The son takes a wife instead of a mother. But let us say that the external world in the form of the mother treats the son ambiguously, on the one hand behaving toward him like a lover and, on the other hand, refusing to satisfy the desires she helps arouse. She herself, of course, is unaware of the nature or the effects of her behavior. Let us also say that the father provides inadequate strength for the successful formation of his son's super-ego. The original wish-impulse of the Oedipus complex is neither completely sublimated nor completely denied. It remains unresolved and unsatisfied. Because the id has not been provided an adequate substitute, the wish presses upon the ego for gratification in its original form. Reacting self-protectively with its eye on the reality principle, the ego represses the wish. Such an illegal wish threatens the ego. It does not want to know that the wish exists. A clash results between the wish, now lying in the ego's unconscious, and the ego's consciousness. Such a clash produces neurotic symptoms. The grown son, his original wish unresolved, seeks to gratify it in other forms—for example, Don Juanism. Or the pressure of the unconscious wish upon the ego might produce that form of neurotic anxiety characterized by groundless fear. In the case of Don Juanism, obsessive promiscuity might be explained as an attempt to gratify an original ungratified wish by engaging in activities similar to that wish beyond the range of "normal" desires. The symptom thus becomes a substitute for what was originally denied.

> In the case of a neurosis these [obsessive acts] are clearly compromise actions: from one point of view they are evidences of remorse, efforts at expiation, and so on, while on the other hand they are at the same time substitutive acts to compensate the instinct for what has been prohibited. It is a law of neurotic illness that these obsessive acts fall more and more under the sway of the instinct and approach nearer and nearer to the activity which was originally prohibited.[17]

The above case demonstrates the crucial role of consciousness in mental health. The original wish was unconscious, but it grew naturally out of the id and should have been satisfactorily dealt with by the ego in its relations with the external world and the id. When a desire is not so dealt with, it exerts pressure upon the ego in its original form. The ego takes, so to speak, emergency measures to keep the supposedly destructive wish under control. The applied control is repression, and this is where the ego-unconscious comes in. A neurotic symptom is the result of the ego's keeping an unresolved wish unconscious, though it must be emphasized that not all repressions lead to neurotic symptoms. A neurotic symptom comes into being in the tension between pressure exerted by the wish and the resistance to that pressure by the ego. Symptoms are thus signs of a malfunctioning ego rather than a malfunctioning id. Anxiety in any form, for example, is unique to the ego. It does not make itself felt to the unconscious. A symptom is a symptom because its cause is unconscious, "unknown to the sufferer."[18] Thus, the wish and the reason for repressing it may remain unknown, which indicates that the ego also operates unconsciously. The ego represses something it is not conscious of for reasons unknown to it. We have something "in the ego itself," says Freud, "which is also unconscious, which behaves exactly like the repressed—that is, which produces powerful effects without itself being conscious and which requires special work before it can be made conscious."[19] Thus, Freud postulates two kinds of unconsciousness: the primordial unconsciousness of the id, which always remains unconscious in its natural state, and the unconsciousness of the ego, which usually takes the form of a cause of a neurotic symptom. That is, the ego is conscious only of its neurotic symptoms, not their cause. In the nature of things it is impossible, unnecessary, and undesirable to make conscious all of the id's unconscious. But it is possible, desirable, and necessary—if the neurotic symptoms are to be dispersed—to make conscious what is unconscious in the ego. The ego functions consciously according to its nature, the id unconsciously. To deal with neurosis the psychotherapist wants *to make conscious* what the errant wish is and why it is being repressed. Until that happens the individual's freedom of choice is curtailed by neurotic symptoms that are compulsive, his authentic self is hidden, and his individual satisfaction is diminished.

Psychotherapeutic success does not mean that the wish will disappear or that it will be gratified in its original form. It does mean that the ego will be able to dispense with the neurotic symptom, for symptoms occur only when the wish and the reason for repressing it remain unconscious. Make these conscious, says Freud, and the symptom disappears. But what does bringing these things into consciousness mean? It is not simply a matter of giving the patient some knowledge of the cause of his symptom. "There is knowing and knowing," writes Freud, and "they are not always the same thing." Intellectual knowledge "does not have the effect of dispersing the symptoms." The "necessary condition" for such dispersal "is that the knowledge must be founded upon an inner change in the patient which can only come about by a mental operation directed to that end."[20] This statement is compatible with one of the assumptions of the "open decision": consciousness is not defined simply as an intellectual reflection upon an idea. Indeed, as our novelists suggest, if life and consciousness are identified only with the intellect—Herzog does this—trouble results. Consciousness is an individual experience, a *feeling* of a situation in such a way that it "makes a difference" internally to the subject. As Whitehead says that his actual entity is subjective feeling, so Freud suggests that at the core of the human experience is also subjective feeling uncontaminated by compulsions or the limitations of unconscious bias and prejudices.

The most important single tool that Freud uses for "knowing" the cause of the neurotic symptom is "free association," by now a word current in every kitchen and parlor of the western world. The technique is to allow a man to say what comes to his mind about any given element in a dream, even to let a proper name or number occur to him.[21] This method is based on the conviction that the most pressing wishes, those most likely to cause trouble, will guide the individual's mental operations when the usual controls are removed. If, for example, frigidity arises from the clash between the id's legitimate sexual appetite and an internalized social code that says such an appetite is wrong and therefore represses it, free association may break through the strong control of the super-ego and reveal to the subject both the sexual wish and its naturalness. It thus throws off the excessive prejudices and restraints that might be imposed upon us by our traditional assumptions. In doing so, free association is intended to liberate something of the primordial self, that part of the whole which has been undesirably repressed. Too many or too cruel controls lead to illegitimate repression, and produce those neuroses that result from the clash between the individualistic id and the internalized laws of parent and society, an echo of the dilemma posed by Niebuhr and McIver. When the internalized laws gain ascendancy, the individual is thwarted.

In this way, Freud's clinical theories reflect the philosophy of the "open decision." Neurosis is in effect a diminishment of individual freedom, a closing of the self's authentic possibilities. The culprit in this closure is not the id in its normal state of unconsciousness, but the ego which represses certain wishes under the authority of a single point of view, refusing consciousness to any other view that threatens it. Thus, free association is analogous to the method of physics as described by Bohm, of the social sciences as described by Weber, and of the phenomenological reduction as described by Husserl. It suggests a way of dealing with Heidegger's inauthenticity, Sartre's bad faith, and Mannheim's false consciousness. By acknowledging the influences at work upon the self, the ego-consciousness frees itself from the dominance of any single force, and brings more possibilities of self-development into being. Unconscious dependency on any force—whether it be the wish-impulses of the id, the stern laws of the super-ego, or the prohibitions of society—assumes the guise of an absolute and leads to false consciousness or bad faith, the assumption that things can be only one way. Such dependency requires cultivation of one facet to the repression of another. Let the individual make the repressed desires conscious through free association, let him realize the nature of the forces that lead to repression, suggests Freud, and he may free himself from the absolute determinism of his neurosis and open up the possibilities of his total self.

It must be emphasized that his total self is not exhausted in consciousness, any more than the elementary particle is exhausted in our models of it. The self is a totality made up of an id and two of its modified areas—the ego and the super-ego. This being is no less "itself" when it is unconscious than when it is conscious. Like Whitehead's actual entity, Freud's self can be divided into parts for analysis, but its selfness is defined by the atomic unity of its parts in all their paradox and ambiguity. A vast part of us, therefore, must remain beyond the reach of our consciousness in either its reflective or its emotional form. What consciousness can—and must—do is to take up an attitude which acknowledges the presence of the unknown, which acknowledges the limitations of its own purview, which acknowledges that what it perceives does not constitute totality.

I have said that the process of free association has a liberating effect upon the individual which puts him in the way of operating freely and spontaneously. Freud, however, rejects the notion of psychic freedom—what Whitehead might call "causal independence"—and postulates a strict psychic determinism: Freud writes ". . . there is within you a deeply rooted belief in psychic freedom and choice, that this belief is quite unscientific, and that it must give ground before the claims of a determinism which governs even mental life."[22] The word "even" here implies that determinism reigns supreme in all reality, a concept prominent in some twentieth-century thought (as it was in some eighteenth- and nineteenth-century thought), but to which I have given no attention. I must stop a few moments on this issue: the relationship between Freud's claims of determinism and the claim of freedom in the "open decision."

What is determinism and what is "psychic freedom and choice?" Classically, determinism assumes a transcendent first cause which sets in motion a system whose components more or less passively do the bidding of antecedent forces. What is Freud's first cause, the original instance of psychic activity which determines all subsequent instances? He rejects the idea of God, but he does not clearly deal with the metaphysical problem inherent in his scheme without God. He says that the cause of behavior is in "important inner attitudes of mind, which are unknown to us at the moment they operate."[23] But this begs the question. What determines those "inner attitudes," and what determines the determinant of those attitudes? If we say, with Freud, that behavior derives from a particular response to an early traumatic experience, we still have not solved the problem. Why do different people have different responses to similar situations? Why is one experience damaging to one individual and not to another? The imputation of a deterministic relationship between an early experience and a later behavior-pattern does not successfully refute the concept of freedom to choose. The presence of this freedom does not mean that it is possible to justify logically the choice made to respond in a particular way. Indeed, this is what freedom is, and it is why freedom is so frustrating. As Sartre says, there is no ultimately justifiable reason for choosing one response or another. Our freedom lies in just this fact—that no system of logic or politics forms a necessity that closes our possibilities.

Another problem comes with the question, What do the "inner attitudes" determine? If we answer "mental life" or "ego," we must assume that they are different in kind from their determinant. If "mental life" is determined, it cannot be the same as its determiner. Yet Freud has said that the unconscious is the basic psychic reality or mental process, that the id contains both the ego and super-ego as modifications of itself. That is, the self is divisible, as I have said above, but not divided. Working from these definitions, to say that the unconscious or the id determines an individual's "mental life" is logically to say that the unconscious or id determines itself. The activity of the unconscious is the activity of the self, just as much as is the activity of the consciousness—at least as Freud sees it. The word *determines,* then, cannot mean that the unconscious or the id either is the agent or is itself a transcendent entity that is not a part of our self but a cause of the way our self behaves. We *are* our unconscious just as much as we are our consciousness. This is the reasoning of Whitehead, who deals with the problem of determinism and infinite regress by maintaining that the ultimate units of reality are self-caused, drawing their material and their goals from the world around them.

Whitehead's metaphysics also comprehends Freud's psychic being. For its data, the self-creative being depends upon the environment, which is both itself and the external world. The way the actual entity responds to these data is not determined by any transcendent power or other agent. It is, in fact, metaphysically indeterminate but statistically predictable. The Freudian psychic being may also be seen as an atomic, self-creative whole. His freedom lies in the fact that his form originates nowhere but in himself. The degree to which he achieves his potential depends both on his own creativity and the order of his environment, whose limitations are indirectly determinants, but not absolute determinants, of what the individual may become.

The machinery of Freud's psychoanalysis and his personality theory—whatever his attitude toward determinism—operates to preserve the authentic self. The self is authentic in proportion to the amount of freedom it enjoys from unacknowledged antecedent forces. Freud recognizes the ambiguity in this authenticity. Eros—love for oneself and one's fellow man—draws men into communities; it is the name of a force that is essentially spontaneous, free, "authentic." But the consequence of this spontaneity is its opposite—Death. In *Civilization and Its Discontents,* Freud opposes these two forces against each other, Eros leading to community and community to the death of the individual as an individual. There is an implied frustration here similar to that which appears in Sartre's concept of the human being as a "useless passion," a sense of unresolvable contradiction. For some this brings nothing but pessimism. For others, the ambiguity either is unimportant or central to the self's spontaneity and authenticity.

Eric Fromm, one of the most prominent of the "neo-Freudians," recognizes the threat of "civilization" to the individual. As Fromm sees it, that threat is most dangerous when men surrender voluntarily, through fear and a failure of self-confidence, to what Jaspers calls the "apparatus." In such a surrender, man flies from his natural freedom, revealed by the modern world, to find security in a new bondage. In doing so, he loses "the integrity of his individual self." Fromm's concern is the way by which man can realize his individual self through the expression of his intellectual, emotional and sensuous potentialities, by which he can "overcome the terror of aloneness without sacrificing the integrity of his self." The "way" is through "spontaneous activity." The two components of spontaneity are those also recommended by Jaspers—love and work:

> Not love as the dissolution of the self in another person, not love as the possession of another person, but love as spontaneous affirmation of others, as the union of the individual with others on the basis of the preservation of the individual self . . . not work as a compulsive activity in order to escape aloneness, not work as a relationship to nature which is partly one of dominating her, partly one of worship of and enslavement by the very products of man's hands, but work as creation in which man becomes one with nature in the act of creation."[24]

Fromm tends to idealize what Freud saw with rather more skepticism, and in that idealization he sounds like Jaspers and Mannheim. That is, he generalizes the preferred situation and the way to achieve it by admonishment, by "musts" and "oughts," omitting details and inherent obstacles to the ideal. What practicality he does employ, after his almost passionate discussion of individual freedom and spontaneity, makes him more a social thinker, finally, than a psychoanalytic theorist of personality structure. Fromm sees that the only means by which "genuine activity [can] be restored to the individual" is through the "planned economy" in which "the purposes of society and of [the individual] become identical, not ideologically but in reality. . . ." This would not, of course, be an authoritarian society. Indeed, says Fromm, "We must replace manipulation of men by active and intelligent co-operation, and expand the principle of government of the people, by the people, for the people, from the formal political to the economic sphere."[25] Thus Fromm, in words almost exactly the same as those written by Mannheim, would have the ideal Whiteheadian society, in which the social order is dominated by the principle of individual intensity, in which its durability and its ability to grow like an organism lies in order rather than anarchy or authoritarianism. At the same time, Fromm makes clear that the ends are purely individual and so can be referred to no other authority than the individual himself. His cooperation must be voluntary, and his satisfaction must arise from the free operation of his spontaneity.

Karen Horney also emphasizes the need for a free authentic self if a state of mental health is to be preserved and if we are to achieve the highest possible individual satisfaction. Neuroses, she says, adopted to compensate for wishes thwarted by a hard and difficult existence, inhibit the expression of our true spontaneous self. Therapy attempts "to help the patient [not] to gain mastery over his instincts but to lesson his anxiety to such an extent that he can dispense with his 'neurotic trends.' Beyond this aim there looms an entirely new therapeutic role, which is to restore the individual to himself, to help him regain his spontaneity and find his center of gravity in himself."[26] Similarly, Erik Erikson declares that the ultimate aim of the individual should be to acquire "ego integrity," the acceptance of one's self. Only through ego integrity can individual fulfillment, the establishment of order and meaning in life, be achieved. Ego integrity is a sense of the self's validity, of the richness of one's own "life style," together with a respect for other life styles. It is the awareness of the self's integrity as part of the world it perceives and a loving commitment to that world. It is a spontaneity that expresses freedom from compulsions of any sort.[27] This spontaneity, and its accompanying ability to love, is one of the main elements of authenticity and individual satisfaction. The contemporary American novelist takes it as a fundamental value. It is the absence of such spontaneity in adults that so repels J. D. Salinger's Holden Caulfield in *Catcher in the Rye,* and the search for it that turns him so frequently to children. Lacking spontaneity, bereft of the power to feel, character after character is depicted as suffering the agonies of heightened isolation and dryness of soul that diminishes his humanity. The point is not simply that these values are cherished by our novelists, but that our novelists are preoccupied with them, see the important personal issues of our day in terms of them. Perhaps one of the most broadly and deeply documented aspects of our age is this deficiency in modern man of spontaneity.

C. G. Jung is enough different from his teacher Freud and Freud's many disciples to warrant treatment on his own merits. He makes explicit some of the implications of Freud's psychology, while at the same time he introduces a historical and philosophical frame of reference into the psychological approach to individual fulfillment. He starts from the ground of Freud's postulate of the unconscious, emphasizing the need to regard the "self" as something more than what we consciously know of it. The self is our whole mental being, made up of both conscious and, perhaps more important because they have so long been ignored, unconscious contents. That part of the self which we know in the form of consciousness is *ego.* The goal of life is to disabuse the ego of the illusion that it represents the whole self, to give it a sense of being part of a larger whole, "the object of an unknown and superordinate subject." The achievement of such a sense is self-realization, which results in the emergence of a familiar attribute—the self's individual and collective uniqueness, "the completest expression of that fateful combination we call individuality, the full flowering not only of the single individual, but of the group, in which each adds his portion to the whole."[28] The self's center is a fulcrum, slightly below the level of ego-consciousness, upon which the conscious and the unconscious balance. Shift this center or fulcrum either way and the result is a loss of equilibrium.

Jung realizes that this "self," like Einstein's world "watch," is a postulate, a model of something we know only through its effects. But such an awareness does not diminish the validity of the model. The atom of the modern physicist is only a model, too, Jung is quick to point out, but for all that it is a powerful tool with which to investigate the nature of the things that elude perception. One can draw another analogy from atomic physics. We do not know what the electron is like or what it is doing between its changes in energy states. We do not know what the unconscious is like, or what it is doing between its manifestations in thoughts, actions, dreams, fantasies. In both models, indeterminacy and indefinability are radical factors of reality. With the unconscious unknowable, the whole self can never be perceived in itself. It can only be sensed or subjectively experienced. Nevertheless, through the postulated model we can establish certain hypotheses.

The unconscious part of the self is "the *unknown psychic* . . . everything of which I know [*sic*], but which I am not at the moment thinking; everything of which I was once conscious but have now forgotten; everything perceived by my senses, but not noted by my conscious mind; everything which, involuntarily and without paying attention to it, I feel, think, remember, want, and do; all the future things that are taking shape in me and will sometime come to consciousness . . . [and, finally,] the psychoid functions [unconscious physical processes] that are not capable of consciousness and of whose existence we have only indirect knowledge." This large area of our mental self Jung further divides into the collective and the personal unconscious. As the adjective indicates, the personal unconscious is the repository of those contents which derive from the individual's own personal experience and the contents of the collective unconscious which assume the form of personal experiences. The collective unconscious is the psyche that all humans are born with. The central importance of the unconscious as a whole lies in its nature as precedent to consciousness. As the more primitive, the unconscious in part determines the form of consciousness, acting as a kind of "ground plan lying dormant in the individual from the beginning." Since the future develops out of the past, the unconscious "is the *sine qua non* for shaping the future."[29]

The collective unconscious plays a far more important role in the shaping of the future, according to Jung, than does the personal unconscious. The collective unconscious is the primordial part of the human being, what he comes into the world with. It is an array of possibilities which in their original form are unfulfilled—as Jung says, "*a priori* categories of possible functioning."[30] The potential psychological functions are collective in nature; they are shared by all men and link every human individual to his species. The presence of these functions makes it statistically probable that each individual will behave, not only like other members of the collective around him, but like former members of the collective.[31] The contents of the collective unconscious, in other words, are those functions which make a human being act like a human being, functions by which the human being is defined. All that is "determined" of the future shape of the individual is the probability that he will act like a human being rather than some other species. The psychological functions of the collective unconscious are thus analogous to the biological functions of all organisms. In life, biological functions fall into patterns that take the form of types or images and have the effect of instincts: "The instinct of the leaf-cutting ant fulfills the image of ant, tree, leaf, cutting, transport, and the little ant-garden fungi."[32]

In the human, the psychological functions of the collective unconscious similarly fall into images which Jung calls "archetypes." These are potential modes of behavior which may be more or less mechanically determining in their effect. The more fully they "intervene in the shaping of conscious contents by regulating, modifying, and motivating them, [the more] they act like instincts."[33] That is, the less power consciousness has over these archetypes, the more demanding and autonomous they will be as mechanical determinants of behavior. Thus, the more primitive the human being, the more his behavior will be determined by the unconscious archetypes and the more limited will be his possibilities.

The archetype is that content of the collective unconscious which is given; it is, as Jung says, "pure unvitiated nature."[34] In its natural state it is not an articulated image waiting to be perceived by the spectator consciousness. It is by definition unconscious and consequently it is "irrepresentable" to the consciousness in itself. It is made knowable through the mediation of images and ideas, the material of conscious experience. For example, one of the archetypal psychological functions of the human being is the tendency to hide from his consciousness that side of himself which for some reason is repugnant to that consciousness. As the actual operating tendency the archetype remains unconscious. When represented to the consciousness, this function takes the form of what Jung calls the "shadow." This is a personification of "everything that the subject refuses to acknowledge about himself," all of his "inferior traits of character."[35] The dress which the shadow dons to be representable comes from conscious experience, for the archetypes in themselves remain strange and unknowable to the conscious mind. Jung writes, for example, that often Americans give their shadow the form of a Negro or an Indian, while Europeans, lacking such convenient ethnic "inferiors," choose other white people to embody their inferior side. It must be remembered that "every archetype, when represented to the mind, is already conscious and therefore differs to an indeterminable extent from that which caused the representation"—that is, the archetype in its natural state.[36]

The archetype may be represented in dreams or fantasies. It may also appear in projections. If, for example, the individual ego refuses to acknowledge the presence in himself of some quality which he deems to be inferior, he may repress it, prevent it from becoming conscious. Such a person, says Jung, "imagines he actually *is* only what he cares to know about himself."[37] He is in what Sartre would call "bad faith." Thus repressed, the unconscious archetype will exert a counterforce to bring the balance between the consciousness and the unconscious back into equilibrium. One form of this counterforce may be projection, in which the individual refuses to acknowledge his own shadow and insists that his inferior qualities actually reside in some one else. The American may find his own unconscious inferiority in the Negro, the Indian, the Communist; the Arab in the Israeli; the Chinese in the Russian. When projection reaches the intensity of neurosis, Jung would say that an "autonomous complex" goes to work, determining the behavior of the consciousness without its knowledge. Projection is a sign that some aspect of the collective unconscious is being denied expression by the consciousness and is being forced to find expression in some unconscious form.

Other archetypal images are the feminine side of the male (the anima), the male side of the female (the animus), the Mother, the Father, the Hero, the Magician, and variations upon these. They represent the instinct patterns of the human being which form polar opposites similar to those described by Whitehead. They act as mediators between the completely physical world of the unconscious "psychoid functions" and the completely mental world of the consciousness, embodying these two aspects of the self in a unit. They are "intuitions" of physical phenomena. That is, the physical process of the human being may be represented to the consciousness as the psychological "imagos" of Mother, Father, Hero, and other archetypes that figure into the unique patterns of human behavior. These patterns are similar to the images of the cutting-ant, except that its pattern, so far as we know, remains unconscious, and hence deeply instinctual. The cutting-ant's behavior, therefore, is completely determined by its "archetypes." The human being, on the other hand, is a human being because his consciousness gives him a relatively greater freedom from the mechanical determinism of instinct. "Man's capacity for consciousness," writes Jung, echoing Scheler, "alone makes him man."[38] It stands to reason, therefore, that the less conscious a man is "the more numerous the psychic contents (imagos) which meet him as quasi-external apparitions, either in the form of spirits, or as magical potencies projected upon living people (magicians, witches, and the like)."[39] As the "open decision" requires, a wider consciousness is for Jung an escape from the determinism of the past in the form of the archetypes.

That part of the self which Jung calls the ego is generally identified as consciousness. "The ego is the only content of the self that we do know."[40] Ego-consciousness is a "reflected state," which is the only thing we have "immediate experience of," and it is by definition "conscious and known."[41] While this consciousness holds out the promise of individuality and freedom from the instinct, it also brings the possibility of trouble. So long as a living organism has only one psychic system which is identified with the unconscious processes of the physical body, no conflict is possible. That organism does the bidding of the unconscious instinct with no questions asked and no desire to do otherwise. Consciousness introduces a second psychic system which in its very nature leans toward a denial of the unconscious. It is the peculiarity of the human being that these two systems tend to compete with each other for whatever psychic energy the self may contain. Consciousness, says Jung, acts as the unifier and the controller of all psychic forces. It organizes them and directs them to some end. In this role it must choose those forces which seem most likely to advance the end and exclude those which seem inadequate. It is its nature to make the choices on the basis of the known rather than the unknown. Thus, consciousness has the capacity to deny expression to the archetypal forces. If this does happen, if the consciousness concentrates only upon the data that it can know, the organism will develop an imbalance on the side of the consciousness and call into action the counterforces of the unconscious, demanding equal expression.

In this case the cause of the imbalance is an unhealthy sovereignty of the ego-consciousness, a shift of the self's center toward consciousness. When this occurs, too high a premium is laid upon conscious data. If unconscious data come from the archetypes of the collective unconscious, conscious data come from the "collective conscious," the reservoir of those "universal ideas" and "generally accepted truths" by which men consciously guide their private and public behavior. The collective conscious views the unconscious as irrational and dangerous and so excludes its data from conscious acceptance as guides. The principal image ego-consciousness takes from the collective conscious is what Jung calls the "persona"—"a complicated system of relations between individual consciousness and society, fittingly enough a kind of mask, designed on the one hand to make a definite impression upon others, and, on the other, to conceal the true nature of the individual." This produces a one-sidedness whose main danger is that the ego will identify with the images of the collective conscious, mistaking its persona for the whole self. "These identifications with a social role," says Jung, "are a very fruitful source of neuroses."[42] In Sartre's terms they are examples of "bad faith."

All neurotic imbalance, whether toward the conscious or the unconscious areas of the self, leads to a domination of the consciousness by the unconscious and acts as the prime obstacle to successful self-fulfillment. The basic problem in neurosis, as Jung sees it, is that the consciousness has not adequately penetrated into the unconscious. When the two sides of the self fail to integrate.

the unconscious reacts in the same way the stomach reacts to physiological imbalance. It gets sick and causes trouble. ". . . when an individual or social group deviates too far from their [*sic*] instinctual foundations, they then experience the full impact of unconscious forces."[43]

Jung provides an example of the way in which the ego's identification with the persona may lead to domination by the unconscious. A man who thinks that his persona "is" his whole self may become a good businessman who keeps everything in order and maintains control of himself and his employees. He is regarded as strong and manly. But in leaning so heavily upon his conscious manliness, he represses his feminine side, the anima. It does not seem compatible with the "masculine" factors of control and strength to admit to "feminine" factors of emotion and weakness. The ego refuses even to "sense" the anima and tries to keep it unconscious. But as with the shadow, the anima will get out and one of its channels of expression is projection. In this hypothetical situation, the man projects his anima, which takes the form of the helpless female in direct contrast to the strong male, upon an appropriate woman—a helpless female. Her helplessness comes to be the force that enslaves her husband, binding him to her by her inability to take care of herself. It is unlikely that such a problem would result in the man choosing a wife who was literally domineering and overbearing, because this would not correspond to the extremely feminine anima provoked by the one-sided imbalance toward the completely masterful persona. The anima, in other words, remains unconscious and dominates the man through his wife.

Such one-sidedness blocks the development of the self toward "individuation," which Jung defines as "becoming a single, homogeneous being, and, in so far as 'individuality' embraces our innermost, last, and incomparable uniqueness, it also implies becoming one's own self. We could therefore translate individuation as 'coming to selfhood' or 'self-realization.' "[44] "Individuation" is Jung's manner of expressing the achievement of a high intensity of individual satisfaction. It is the normal, healthy goal of human experience and development. When this cycle is blocked by neurosis, psychotherapy functions to remove the block, thus serving the emphasis of the psychological approach upon the individual rather than upon his society. The proper direction of the cycle is restored when the balance of the conscious and the unconscious is restored, and that can take place only when the problem-making unconscious elements are brought to consciousness. Psychotherapy thus assumes that the unconscious is not some dark, forbidding demon which in itself is a threat to the ego, but a "natural entity" which is neither good nor bad except as thinking makes it so. In performing this reconciliation between the conscious and the unconscious, Jung stresses the need for "experience" rather than interpretation. The aim is for the consciousness to live and feel the unconscious in such a way that the two forces become familiar enough to work out a settlement of their opposing demands.

The main tool for achieving this aim is what Jung calls "amplification," which is analogous to but not identical with Freud's "free association." Like Freud's method, amplification seeks to free the consciousness from the control of the presuppositions that reside in the collective consciousness. Therefore, to perform amplification, one must voluntarily adopt an attitude that suspends the "critical attention," which is regulated by the collective conscious. This suspension will allow the unconscious contents to enter into conscious experience. The specific way in which amplification is performed is up to the individual. Jung asked his patients to elaborate, through free fantasizing, a particular dream image or association. This may be done, he says, "in any number of ways, dramatic, dialectic, acoustic . . . [or through] dancing, painting, drawing, or modelling."[45] The images that emerge in these activities, if the critical attention has been successfully suspended, are "guided by unconscious regulators" rather than by conscious ones, and so represent the unconscious rather than the conscious. The more effectively the trouble-making unconscious elements are brought into conscious experience, the less autonomous they are in their influence, for they cease to require an unconscious channel of expression such as neurotic identification or projection. They are taken as a natural part of the whole self rather than as threatening aliens.

If amplification is successful a definite change should result in the personality. This does not mean that the "original hereditary disposition" will be altered. There is no magical transformation of one's identity. Whatever change there is, is in attitude. The archetypes of the collective unconscious are there to stay; they cannot be altered. But our conscious attitude toward them can. If our attitude does not change in the normal course of events, we can try psychotherapy. But it will be successful only if the individual really does admit into his experience the forces of his unconscious.

The joining of the poles of consciousness and unconsciousness is what Jung calls the "transcendent function." This is the state of being that rises above the autonomous one-sidedness of unconscious complexes or the excessive control of the ego-consciousness, and by its own efforts, by the very rising above the two opposites, liberates the individual into the freedom of being his whole self. This does not mean a bland armistice between these sides of the self in which they both surrender their claims upon each other. Individuation, the achievement of the transcendent function, "means open conflict and open collaboration at once. That, evidently," says Jung, echoing Reinhold Niebuhr, "is the way human life should be."[46] It is precisely this ambiguity which lies at the heart of the "open decision." The crucial word in Jung's statement is *open*, for openness is the basic condition of self-realization, where openness means to be free of those unconscious complexes that have the effect of mechanical instinct. Openness is the unique and individualizing feature of the human being. Once one does realize his individuality by reconciling his whole self to a kind of friendly enmity, he ceases to be a victim of collective consciousness, frightened of the natural part of himself and the external world as well. He enters into what by now is a familiar state, a "binding, and indissoluble communion with the world at large."[47] Individuality, then, is not a withdrawal of the self from its milieu, but a discovery of the self's own uniqueness so that it may strengthen itself in what Jaspers would call its "ties" with the world.

Nor is individuation some plateau of static changelessness on which the self rests in a kind of angelic apotheosis. Like Whitehead's actual entity, the self is in constant process. Neither one's natural development nor psychotherapy provides some final answer to the problems of the self and its existence. They only offer the possibility of dealing with those problems effectively. "There is no change," writes Jung, "that is unconditionally valid over a long period of time. Life has always to be tackled anew."[48] At this point, Jung's psychology becomes philosophical, and identifies him even more closely with the attitude of the "open decision." ". . . we stand with our soul suspended between formidable influences from within and from without, and somehow we must be fair to both. This we can do only after the measure of our individual capacities. Hence we must bethink ourselves not so much of what we 'ought' to do as of what we *can* and *must* do." One should behave toward the unconscious as he does toward the external forces of nature and society. Up to a point, our consciousness bows to their demands without being overwhelmed as an identifiable, self-realized entity; but some demands must not be given "unqualified consent." Once the consciousness forfeits its power to judge and choose, it becomes the pawn of the unconscious. Only through the effective judiciary of the conscious ego can men preserve their human dignity and avoid becoming "the unresisting shuttlecocks of unconscious forces."[49]

Both the sociological and the psychological approaches to individual fulfillment emphasize consciousness because it frees one from assumptions which, remaining unexamined, have the force of binding instincts and thereby limit the human being to only a few of his potential circuits of experience.

This desire to be liberated from traditional assumptions, this need for broader and more numerous alternatives accounts for the tendency in many of our novelists to formulate their ideas in unfamiliar contexts. Saul Bellow sends Eugene Henderson away from America to a simultaneously primitive and civilized Africa. John Barth turns to late seventeenth-century England and America in *The Sot-Weed Factor* and to an indistinct future in *Giles Goat-Boy*. Kurt Vonnegut sets *The Sirens of Titan* and many of his other novels not only in a future age but on other planets. And the whole genre of science fiction does the same thing. Nor are the novelists I have mentioned writing utopian or anti-utopian novels. They are slipping the restrictions of the present, going away from the status quo—like Thoreau does at Walden—in order to take a clearer fix on the here and now. Other novelists send their characters into the primitive consciousness as a means of exploring otherwise closed circuits of experience. Berger's Jack Crabb becomes, temporarily, a Cheyenne Indian in *Little Big Man*. Probably one of the best "long" short stories written by a contemporary novelist, "Among the Dangs" by George P. Elliott, is about a black student anthropologist who becomes a member of a South American Indian tribe. And Peter Matthiesen, in *At Play in the Fields of the Lord*, has one character who has gone to live with another tribe of South American Indians exclaim over "the extraordinary experience which had befallen him—the *perceiving*, through the Indians, of a wilderness which heretofore had seemed to him a malevolent nether world, poisonous and stagnated, miasmal." These novels do not celebrate the inhabitants of their relatively unfamiliar worlds as some breed of noble savages or future supermen in order to reject the present. Jack Crabb's Cheyenne Indians, for example, have their own limitations. The aim seems to be to break free, at least momentarily, of the familiar earth and examine new categories, especially the category of the primitive, as if, like the id and the collective unconscious, it held potentially valuable secrets for the civilized man. More explicitly, writers like Colin Wilson, in *The Outsider*, admonish contemporary man to embrace not only the civilized persona, but the "wolf man" in himself, the savage whose power, when incorporated, will endow men with powers nearing the godlike. For some novelists, like those I deal with in Chapter 6, the value of spontaneity becomes the rationale for a cult.

Modern man, says Jung, seeks the "way he can live his own individual life, however meagre and uninteresting it may be. It is because every form of imitation seems to him deadening and sterile that he rebels against the force of tradition that would hold him to well-trodden ways." "He wants to live with every side of himself —to know what he is."[50] The properly planned state is one proposed avenue to the achievement of such a condition. Psychotherapy is another. Whichever way one chooses, it is clear that the historical development of twentieth-century thought—in this chapter represented by sociological and psychological thinkers—reflects and contributes to the situation which modern man regards as preferred, the state of the "open decision." As Allen Wheelis writes, ". . . there has occurred in society as a whole during the past two generations a development analogous to that which occurs in an individual during psychoanalysis, an expansion of awareness at the expense of the unconscious."[51] The result of such expansion is a heightened spontaneity, an increased freedom, and a more human individual. It is precisely these values, and a concern for their absence in individual lives, that attract the contemporary American novelist. The novelist takes such assumptions and broadens them into a consideration of morality and ethics.

Neither psychology nor sociology supplies any specific moral rules of action, only an attitude. The attitude is that of the "open decision," in which organic change and a certain ambiguity are part of the definition of the human being. A conception of man as a being fixed and static denies what he is in the human world and equates him with the abstract Ideas of Plato, the formal *primum mobile* of Aristotle, whose immutability suggests just that which is not life. To be human is to be an individual, living in the world, limited but free, responsible, self-creative, developing. It is to recognize the potentialities of freedom and consciousness and the limits of environment, chance, death. It is to be characterized by what Gabriel Marcel calls "ingatheredness," the inability to stand outside one's situation at a point of absolute rest. Though we must use abstractions to represent "truth" to ourselves, says Marcel, who writes in terms we have heard before, there is no "global abstraction, any final high terrace to which we can climb by means of abstract thought, there to rest forever; for our condition in this world does remain, in the last analysis, that of a wanderer, an itinerant being, who cannot come to absolute rest except by a fiction, a fiction which it is the duty of philosophic reflection to oppose with all its strength."[52] Such opposition, similar to that of the rebellion spoken of above by Jung, does not lead Marcel—or many of his contemporaries—to the pessimistic conclusion that all is lost. As I suggested earlier, it affirms the nature of man as we know it, not as we can conceive it. It affirms that quality of man that makes him conscious of a freedom in which he must live, as Camus says, "without appeal," without appeal to God, to ultimate Ideas, to a "global abstraction." It is this opposition which provides the moral posture that man must take in order that he may create his humanity from moment to moment through his freedom.

One of the central metaphors of the morality of the "open decision" is *play*. Its function in a world of human freedom and consciousness is discussed by Sartre in connection with his notion of man as a useless passion. The for-itself, says Sartre, aims to become the in-itself without surrendering any of its own character. This is impossible, for when the for-itself completes the work it is condemned to do, it perishes, never knowing as itself the goal that shaped its life. What recourse is there from this impasse if we are not to despair of ever gaining the thing we want most: repose? There is no recourse in Sartre's ontology, as he says, but there is in his existential psychoanalysis. Existential psychoanalysis probes for "the original way in which each man has chosen his being," the manner in which he projects himself toward his end, the "feeling" that gives unity, as Whitehead might say, to the human actual entity. This probe inevitably reveals that no choice is ever justifiable in terms of some absolute criterion. Knowing this should, says Sartre, "make us repudiate the *spirit of seriousness*."[53]

To be "serious" is an act of bad faith, for seriousness assumes that there is some attainable absolute, one right way things ought to be. The man who thinks he can "be" a waiter is in bad faith because he is serious about the possibility that his being can ever exhaust itself existentially in the abstraction of the waiter's role. Learning that the original choice of being can never be justified, learning that no individual can ever "be" his choice in the sense of achieving completeness and equilibrium and content, shows us that we can only "play" at certain roles. The concept of play emphasizes consciousness and freedom as the condition of man's choice of what he will play. Play, in a sense, is what the philosophy of the "open decision" means by "being." It is an experience of choice unjustified by any other ultimate standard than that of the unity of the individual existent, an experience in which man creates his values by his choice, an experience which is characterized by the simultaneous presence of plan and openness to whatever possibilities are available to the chooser.

The concept of play is more thoroughly explored by Johan Huizinga. Like Sartre, Huizinga writes, "To our way of thinking, play is the direct opposite of seriousness." Play is the act of mind breaking down "the absolute determinism of the cosmos."[54] There are areas in which the elements of play do not apply, as in the commands of the natural process—the beating of our heart, the flow of our blood stream, the involuntary responses of the body. These actions all living creatures share with each other. Play is distinctly human, for it is conscious and voluntary, requiring free acts of the will. It liberates the individual from nature's imperatives. It is disinterested, directed to the moment, yet it is not random, blindly impulsive, or forgetful of the past or the future. It demands an order made possible through the consent of the individual, not one that is imposed by an antecedent lawgiver.

Sometimes play is elevated to the level of sacred ritual. When it is, it does not seek any end beyond itself, but establishes an existing desired situation. "The participants in the rite," says Huizinga, "are convinced that the action actualizes and effects a definite beatification, brings about an order of things higher than that in which they customarily live." Though such an order may not exist in a measurably scientific way in the world of nature, the ritual itself is not merely a dream, but a real experience that "makes a difference" to the private subject, very much like Freud's reenactments of early traumas and Jung's fantasies. In its most salutary forms, the ritual produces effects that linger after the play itself stops, influencing the nonplay world for the better, creating "order and prosperity for the whole community." This does not mean that the players mistake their play for the seriousness of some ultimate reality existing apart from the world of their experience. Indeed, unlike the single-mindedness and determinism of the spirit of seriousness, play is ambivalent, permeating ritual with a sense of humor and detachment that prevents the player from being utterly submerged in what Heidegger calls the "everydayness" of experience, or in bad faith or false consciousness. Play retains its vantage point even while participating in life. In play one maintains intellectual freedom while simultaneously committing himself wholly and consciously to his created existence. This is the creative unification of the indivisible "belief and unbelief, the indissoluble connection between sacred earnest and 'make-believe' or 'fun.' "[55]

Civilization, says Huizinga, is founded on play, for it presupposes the idea that the self "is enclosed within certain bounds freely accepted." Civilization can exist only so long as its citizens voluntarily obey the rules. The spirit of seriousness tends to reject the factor of voluntarism in favor of the assumption that cultural rules are absolute admonishments from a preexistent being. The player *is* a player by virtue of his ability, through free consciousness, to appreciate his own creativity and responsibility in the act of choosing those bounds and thereby investing them with value. He might have chosen other bounds, and that possibility is a relativity which he accepts. "In our hearts," says Huizinga in the characteristically modern vein, "we know that none of our pronouncements is absolutely conclusive. At that point where our judgment begins to waver, the feeling that the world is serious after all wavers with it. Instead of the old saw: 'All is vanity,' the more positive conclusion forces itself upon us that 'all is play.'"[56]

If the player comes closest to the full affirmation of the human state and achieves the highest possible intensity of individual satisfaction, the opposite may be said to be what Eric Hoffer calls the "true believer," the fanatic for whom all things are serious and whose behavior is always in the service of an absolute truth to which only he has the key. The fanatic cannot understand the playful man who can experience belief and disbelief at the same moment, who can participate in a symbolic action whose rules are his own without the need that they be absolute. For the fanatic, says Hoffer, "no doctrine however profound and sublime will be effective unless it is presented as the embodiment of the one and only truth."

> To be in possession of an absolute truth is to have a net of familiarity spread over the whole of eternity. There are no surprises and no unknowns. All questions have already been answered, all decisions made, all eventualities foreseen. The true believer is without wonder and hesitation.

He is also without the openness of possibilities, and he falls under the categories of bad faith and inauthenticity. He assumes that his values come from outside the world and that they represent an explanation that corresponds totally with all that is "real." The fanatic has failed to come to terms with himself or with reality and so craves, like Heidegger's inauthentic Dasein, to submerge himself in a larger entity so that he may escape all responsibility for himself and his world: "Fanatics," says Hoffer, "fear liberty more than they fear persecution."[57] Absoluteness is the fanatic's element; order and openness are the player's.

Play is not a means of retreating from the world. Quite the opposite: It is a means of putting our consciousness in the way of grasping that world more completely. Were the twentieth century convinced that the universe is a crystalline sphere, closed to further possibilities, completed by an artificer who foresees its end in time, then the principle of the "true believer" might have some validity. His demand for absolute completeness would correspond to reality as it was thought to be constituted. But since the twentieth century tends to see the universe as a constantly developing process, the player's acceptance of the relativity of any one set of assumptions or beliefs corresponds more closely with the modern concept of reality. Play, with its voluntarily accepted rules, provides the social order Whitehead speaks of as being necessary for the healthy nurturing of the actual entity. Play also preserves the centrality of the individual entity and the openness that must characterize that entity if it is to approach identification with its own reality in the world and achieve a high intensity of individual satisfaction by means of its individuality.

At this point an ambiguity shows itself. Huizinga says that play "lies outside morals." There are serious things in the world for him; man does have an absolute moral duty. If there is a question as to whether a particular action is "a serious duty or licit as play," says Huizinga, we find the answer in our "moral conscience," which he seems to think of as being in touch with a universal standard that precedes an individual experience. "As soon as truth and justice, compassion and forgiveness have part in our resolve to act, our anxious question loses all meaning. One drop of pity is enough to lift our doing beyond intellectual distinctions."[58] Huizinga's "moral conscience" is a kind of intuition of absolute values. That conscience has similarities with Heidegger's "It," which instructs the Dasein from obscure layers of being, uttering the words of the gods. The difference is in the source of the ultimate principle. Huizinga seems to see that source somewhere outside the individual field, transcendent and apart, appearing to all men who will allow it to appear. Heidegger locates it in the field of the individual Dasein, rising up from within, not appearing from without. In this way, play becomes the expression of our absolute self, absolute in the sense of its being the ultimate reality, not in the sense of its being utterly and completely reposeful. The difference between the classical and the modern appears in the difference between the completed absolute substance and the incompleted absolute of process. It is significant to the distinction Huizinga makes between play and "moral conscience" that, in his biography of Erasmus—the great Renaissance humanist for whom the classical ideal meant so much—he writes: "The whole Renaissance cherished that wish of reposeful, blithe, and yet serious intercourse of good and wise friends in the cool shade of a house under trees, where serenity and harmony would dwell."[59] That sense of harmony reflects the assumption that fundamental reality is "reposeful" and "blithe," and according to Sartre, the twentieth century still yearns after that ideal but sighs disappointedly over its conviction that reality cannot yield it up.

The philosophy of the "open decision" breaks with Huizinga's notion of an intuition of absolute values. If we carry the assumptions of incompleteness and play through to their conclusions, we must admit that, given the premises, we neither possess nor need a moral conscience which intuits universal moral imperatives, appearing to us from a transcendental source which is eternally "right" and "good." This does not mean that we have—or need—no moral conscience. The moral conscience we do have does not produce abstract absolutes. But this is only right, since it holds that the highest good, the source of values, lies in the individual. The result is that morality is a matter of the individual, where right and wrong are judged not according to a fixed standard of preexistent values, but according to the individual and his situation, the game he consents to play at a particular time. As Dewey says, each individual situation has "its own irreplaceable good and principle." A cosmos in which morality is a fixed system, derived from a transcendent absolute, is a prison in which the individual is bound rigidly to antecedent determinants, existing as a kind of tool or artifact rather than as a self-creative creature. The modern world requires the freedom, as Dewey writes, of "a belief in a plurality of changing, moving, individualized goods and ends . . . a belief that principles, criteria, laws are intellectual instruments for analyzing individual or unique situations."[60] The philosophy of the "open decision" takes issue with Huizinga, not in the value of pity (which Camus, as we will see, justifies metaphysically in terms of the "open decision"), but in the interpretation he puts upon its source.

The morality of the "open decision" is based on the absolute of the individual process. The test of the values we choose to order our play is the degree to which they assist in the achievement of the individual end of a high intensity of satisfaction. This does not claim that data arise spontaneously in the individual, but that values arise in the individual as he selects the data for the construction of his life. The way the subject seizes the world about him is more human and satisfactory as it is more individual. That individuality may be thwarted by factors which limit the data available or which weaken the data as firm building blocks. Prejudice or self-delusion or tyranny may prevent the subject from availing himself of many possibilities. Chaos, anarchy, and disorder may limit the number of possibilities. The individual experience is made more unique and intense in proportion to the amount of psychological, political, and economic freedom on the one hand, and social and physical order on the other. These two factors are the poles in every individual's world and they must exist in precarious balance if the highest good is to be realized. Let the scale tip in either direction and the subjective satisfaction is jeopardized. When writers find that these poles are irreconcilable, as do some American novelists of the Second World War, tragedy results and the individual is sacrificed to one of the poles. Morality starts, then, with the individual. Sartre says that the validity of this proposition lies in Descartes's famous statement: I think; therefore, I exist. "There," writes Sartre, "we have the absolute truth of consciousness becoming aware of itself." There is no other absolute truth that we can verify. All other observations are only probable. But "In order to describe the probable, you must have a firm hold on the true." In order to approach the world in which we are a being, we must clearly understand ourselves as a subject. In this admonition the unity of human thought is demonstrated. Socrates' favorite dictum was "know thyself." Both Western and Eastern thought are full of men who have insisted that the world is only probable. The heritage of Aristotle and Ptolemy is the idea that man corresponds to the physical world and that to know the macrocosm one must study the microcosm that reflects it. One of the famous English philosophical poems of the sixteenth century is John Davies' *Nosce Teipsum—Know Thyself*. And Pope's line has become a cliché: "The proper study of mankind is man." But as a statement of the twentieth-century attitude, Sartre's notion is distinguishable from those previous propositions. He does not mean that there is a physical parallel between man and his world, but that man is in his world as a participant and that the only certainty that he possesses is his own existence in that world: ". . . before there can be any truth whatsoever, there must be an absolute truth; and this one is simple and easily arrived at; it's on everyone's doorstep; it's a matter of grasping it directly"—that is, I think; therefore I am.[61]

The way in which these assumptions about play and self-knowledge can serve as a ground for moral action is best formulated by Albert Camus. He searches for a justification of living without appealing to a higher authority, to a "serious global abstraction." He looks for a "rule of action" in this world rather than in some antecedent absolute world. His beginning point is the same as that of Sartre and Descartes and it assumes the same thing: that justifications and rules must be based on known certainties. "What I know, what is certain, what I cannot deny, what I cannot reject—this is what counts." His certainty is the consciousness of being alive. Paradoxically, that consciousness is made up of doubts, the awareness of basic ignorance: "I don't know whether this world has a meaning that transcends it. But I know that I do not know that meaning and that it is impossible for me just now to know it." This becomes the basis for the definition of the human and for his morality. "What can a meaning outside of my condition mean to me? I can understand only in human terms." Part of the "meaning" the individual is certain of is his desire for absolute meaning, total explanation, ultimate repose. The obverse is also part of his meaning: that he cannot know any absolute. The consciousness of this paradox is, of course, the doctrine of the "absurd": "my appetite for the absolute and for unity and the impossibility of reducing this world to a rational and reasonable principle."[62]

The absurd man is analogous to *homo ludens*. Both search for unity and order knowing they are inaccessible as absolutes, inaccessible except by the willed and conscious choices of the individual. For the conscious mind—for the human being—there is no escape from the absurd. Indeed, the absurd is the emergence of Heidegger's being-in-the-world and Sartre's for-itself. It is an experience in which the subject is aware of himself. It is a demand for order and therefore a rebellion against the universal silence that greets men's query for absolute meaning. This demand, this consciousness, this sense of the absurd, so much like play, puts the individual in opposition to his world, placing him in the position of simultaneously refusing and accepting his condition. The justification for living and the basis for a rule of action appear in this assumption. The absurd condition is the only truth that the individual can *know;* it is his only certainty. Consequently, it has, for Camus (as well as for the philosophy of the "open decision"), value. "What I believe to be true," he writes, "I must therefore preserve."[63] Since the truth of the absurd exists only in consciousness and since consciousness appears only with life, life becomes for Camus "the only necessary good."[64]

I stop briefly to deduce from Camus's thought its connection with the rationale of the "open decision." The logic of that intellectual construct is this: If the good, as Aristotle says, is that toward which all things aim, then indeed life is the highest good, for that is what all things aim toward. We may go further and say that the more intense the life, the higher the good. If human life is fundamentally consciousness, then the highest good is the highest intensity of consciousness. And if, further, human life appears only in the individual subject, then the highest good is the highest intensity of individual consciousness.

For Camus, the value of life is the basis for the human rule of action. If life is awareness, a rebellion against the universal silence, then the aware individual must perceive that his is not an isolated rebellion, but one participated in by all human beings in one degree or another. By being what he is—a creature in the pursuit of the unity in the face of chaos—he enters the human community. If he chooses to preserve, as the physicist does with the principle of indeterminacy, the awareness of the absurd that is the most human characteristic of life, he affirms his own condition. By doing so, he also affirms his solidarity with others like him who share the aspiration for freedom and unity. From the basic premise of the "necessary good" of life, Camus thus moves to the proposition that to accept this value is to confirm the value of humanity. The true rebel says, "I rebel—therefore we exist," in a paraphrase of the Cartesian statement. The rebel's slogan is "We are," which puts "in the first rank of its frame of reference an obvious complicity among men, a common texture, a solidarity of chains, a communication between being and human being which makes men both similar and united." For Hegel, says Camus, self-consciousness distinguishes man from animals. Through that self-consciousness man denies the world apart from him, though at the same time he wants to possess it. But in possessing that world, man destroys it, hence his act is negation. Against Hegel, Camus argues that the destruction of objects is essentially unconscious and animalistic. True self-consciousness desires the confirmation of itself through the recognition of others, not the possession and destruction of the world: "Only in association do we receive human value, as distinct from animal value," writes Camus, recalling Jaspers. Thus, the true rebel, whose awareness lies in his solidarity with other human beings, makes that solidarity his rule of action: "The freedom he claims, he claims for all; the freedom he refuses he forbids everyone to enjoy."[65] The life he affirms for himself, he affirms for everyone.

The origin of these values is not in intuition but in the way we understand reality. Reality lies in the individual existent. He can be the only origin of values, for they cannot, in accordance with Whitehead's ontological principle, exist in abstraction.

The rebel is an earnest player, a creator of rules and values through his sense of the absurd. When he abandons the play of the absurd, he becomes inauthentic and should be called a "revolutionary." The revolutionary—a true believer—claims to possess a key to total explanations and absolute values. He maintains that he can see beyond the present to the end of history, toward which human life is moving. In the service of this end, he would sacrifice others. The revolutionary declares that he has an unlimited view of existence, and that this view endows him with an absolute freedom to realize that view, even if it means that others must die for it. The revolutionary puts what the rebel would call abstract principle before concrete individuality. He rejects the other side of the doctrine of the absurd—that transcendent meaning is not part of the human condition. The rebel claims that if there is an end to history that men "ought" to serve, only God can know it, and God does not communicate with men. For the revolutionary to suggest that he knows what God knows is to be in bad faith and to make immoral demands upon others. This does not mean that the rebel assumes that one who dies for a cause he regards as valuable is in bad faith. He might, indeed, be precisely the rebel. But when one would execute those whose values are different, he claims a freedom that cannot be justified by the only certainty we have—that of the absurd. The revolutionary refuses to accept the limits inherent in his condition, and mistakes human freedom for absolute freedom and power. He assumes, through that supposed power, the right to kill, the right to impose the strong's values upon the weak. But that assumption simply locks him into a set of absolutes and binds him to the standards of the true believer. He thereby constructs a nonliving society and diminishes the individuality of his own and others' satisfaction and consciousness.

The rebel accepts the limits of his condition, understanding that freedom is not to be confused with power over others. He acknowledges that he cannot see the end of history and so must undertake any project, make any choice, not with certainty, but in ignorance. The rebel puts himself in risk. He accepts these limits as the sphere of his value and finds in them the choice of "moderation" over "excess." Excess is the assumption of the absolutes of freedom, power, and certainty about the future. It results in tyranny and the debasement of the individual. Moderation is more human, if we define human as the conscious knowledge of oneself in the world and the limitations which that presence presupposes. The real world of the human being is neither a world of god-like, immutable abstractions nor chaotic animality. Camus suggests, as I have tried to document in these introductory chapters, that it is instead made up of modified forms of both these contradictory elements. Moderation chooses both of these elements and exhibits them simultaneously in the organism of the living being. The rebel says that "The real is not entirely rational, nor is the rational entirely real." When the rebel demands unity, he does not surrender the irrational for the rational. He wants both, for both compose the fullness of existence, lying at the heart of the absurd. These two poles exercise restraints on each other in the experience of the human being. "The irrational imposes limits on the rational, which, in its turn, gives it its moderation." The irrational makes total rational explanation impossible, but the rational saves us from complete irrationality. By this reasoning, says Camus, it is clear that "essence" is not the only form that "existence" can take, and that "existence" is not merely "being." The human experience combines the abstract and the concrete, the plan and the act, the rational and the irrational. The absolutist would insist that the "real" is only in the abstract, the plan, the rational—or their opposites. He would have total explanation. In that demand, says Camus, he would be a nihilist, refusing "to live life as it is offered."[66]

The rebel, working on the principle of moderation, sees that limits are fused with possibilities, freedom with laws. Only the absolute is entirely rational and free of chance and indeterminacy. Our real being in this life is an organism composed of united opposites. Rebellion claims no absolute and so opts for life, not death; nature, not certainty about the future; balance and moderation, not excess and absolutism. The rebel, operating on the premises of the "open decision," chooses this earth and this life and all that the human condition entails: ". . . he who dedicates himself to the duration of his life, to the house he builds, to the dignity of mankind, dedicates himself to the earth and reaps from it the harvest that sows its seed and sustains the world again and again."[67] Thus, beginning with the assumption that reality lies in the individual, and that the highest individuality lies in human consciousness, Camus concludes that individual worth results in the worth of human solidarity, and that moral man is not the hedonist who pursues the selfish course of complete gratification of the senses, but the rebel who seeks unity in the context of his human world. The highest intensity of individual satisfaction lies in the rebel's affirmation of his human condition and his complicity with his fellow man. The poignancy that characterizes so many contemporary novels is in the defeat of love and human solidarity and the correlative destruction of individual satisfaction. The victory of the contemporary American novel is the success of love, the triumph of solidarity, the achievement by the individual of an intense consciousness of himself in his condition as given.

TWO

INTRODUCTION

I HAVE BEEN TRYING to define what I mean by the phrase "open decision." It expresses one of the most important conceptions of what the twentieth century takes to be the highest good. The "good" is almost always identified with the "real," and the "real" is that to which men give assent when it satisfies their need to explain the nature of things. That need seems to be satisfied when the explanation put forth deals with what men assume to be the most real, the ultimate, that beyond which they cannot go.[1] Our own age is in the last stages of a revolution in the conception of the real. We have experienced a shift from the absolute to the relative, from the universal to the individual. The "open decision" postulates this new reality, implying at the same time the values that accompany it. The most real thing in the philosophy of the "open decision" is the human individual. The more human, the more individual one is; and the more individual, the more "real." The good appears in a high intensity of individual satisfaction. Satisfaction potentially reaches its highest intensity in human consciousness. Human consciousness in its most authentic aspect recognizes its own nature, accepts the fact that an important part of its being is to choose and that it does so in freedom as itself. It acknowledges the responsibility for the consequences of its choices, knowing that the consequences cannot be infallibly predicted and that no choice can ever certainly be "right." It concludes that it alone is the ground of its value and that the choices it makes in terms of its values are not ultimately, absolutely, or rationally justifiable. It knows that it plans and abstracts, but that its plans and abstractions do not totally correspond to or account for its existence. Individual satisfaction is served when this consciousness is "truly" conscious: when it understands the inadequacy of traditional categories of perception; when it opens itself to the possibilities of new circuits of spontaneous, authentic existence; when it realizes that it and the world it occupies are both one and separate and that the world always eludes total explanation; and when it honors itself by honoring the dignity and the validity of the human community through love. The "open decision" is the choice of human existence in all its impurity; it is the choice of life unsupported by a transcendent perfection; and it is the affirmation of human solidarity.

In one form or another, this conception of the real and the good is the subject of the novels I now turn to discuss. Their dominating concern is with the achievement of the highest good—individual satisfaction. This concern usually appears in two basic forms. The preferred situation may be impeded by the obstacle of social or institutional tyranny, emptying the individual of his spontaneity, forcing him into predetermined grooves, depriving him of alternatives. Or it may be thwarted by the characters' deficiency of consciousness, producing an inability to embrace the conditions of life—uncertainty, ambiguity, death, other people, their own choices. Some novels focus on the obstacles of social tyranny, others on rebellion against that tyranny, still others on the deficiency—and sometimes the discovery—of consciousness. Whatever the emphasis, the tacit or expressed good is clear: the achievement of self-fulfillment through the affirmation of the human condition, the establishment of social freedom, and the cultivation of "true consciousness."

I have divided the novels I discuss in this Part into three categories, each representing a particular emphasis upon the issues raised in Part I. The socio-political war novel, both early and late, is concerned with the way in which the military serves to thwart the realization of individual satisfaction. The business novel takes up almost identical issues but works them out in a different setting and with more various results. The "hip" novel focuses upon the need to break clean from all social conventions, sometimes urging an indiscriminate rebellion and laying the foundations for a cult of spontaneity.

4

THE WAR NOVEL: A BLOOD-SPATTERED UTOPIA

As Chester E. Eisinger says, "Everyone—everyone and his brother, one is tempted to say—wrote a war novel."[1] The truth of this has led me to abandon any attempt to provide a comprehensive survey of this voluminous genre. I will concentrate on two groups of novels about the Second World War whose main preoccupation is with the way in which the individual does and does not attain a high intensity of individual satisfaction. The first group of novels, whose roots are in the political radicalism of the 1930s, expresses this preoccupation in socio-political terms. Most of the works contained in this group appeared between the years 1948 and 1952. They include Norman Mailer's *The Naked and the Dead,* Stefan Heym's *The Crusaders,* Irwin Shaw's *The Young Lions,* John Cobb's *The Gesture,* Dan Levin's *Mask of Glory,* Ned Calmer's *The Strange Land,* James Jones's *From Here to Eternity,* Herman Wouk's *The Caine Mutiny,* and Fred Booth's *Victory Also Ends.*[2] These titles do not exhaust the novels that might be included here, but they represent what I judge to be the best of the genre.

These socio-political war novels, with one or two exceptions, see the military organization as the prime inhibitor of individual fulfillment. The instrument of this organization is the totalitarian officer or enlisted man, and its analogue is the literal totalitarian in Germany and Japan which the apparatus was created to fight. It is a specific example of the apparatus Jaspers feared, and bears

For Notes to Chapter 4, see pages 401–403.

similarities to Heidegger's "they." The novelists specifically identify it as fascist in that it enforces obedience and submission through fear and violence, minimizing individual contrasts and possibilities in order to strengthen its own structure. The main tool of the fascist is the machine, which consigns the individual to a role of secondary importance, ties him to a rigid mechanical pattern, and empties him of the power to resist. The two main victims of the fascist apparatus and the apparatus's tools are an idealized American society which is seen as the provider of both order and freedom, and the individual soldier who is put into the impossible position of having either to surrender his humanity to the system or lose his physical life in resisting it.

The emphasis in these novels is not philosophical but social and political. They derive the pattern of their concern from the Depression years. The misery of that period of national pain is now part of the American legend, and like most legends, this one has its stereotypes. The basic conflict is the struggle between the classes. The hero in this struggle is the proletarian worker. The villain is the businessman, the chairman of the corporation, the owner of the factory. The prophet or historian of the struggle is the liberal intellectual. The businessman, who in the 'twenties had been credited with the country's prosperity, in the 'thirties was blamed for its poverty. The stereotype of the "boss," the "economic royalist," the "economic imperialist" was pot-bellied and soft-handed, with diamond rings adorning his fat fingers. He cared for nothing but profit and power, using both harshly and brutally for the exploitation of the worker. On his side were all the forces of the law, which he wielded with a silent contempt for democracy.

The proletarian worker formed the masses that the economic royalist held in cruel fealty. If the businessman lived in a mansion on the hill, the worker huddled, cold and hungry, in a shack at the bottom. Inarticulate but innately intelligent, possessed of a heroic determination to get what was rightly his, the worker became the opposite stereotype from the businessman. His courage was quiet but positive. He was resourceful and ingenious, possessing practical abilities given heightened value by a sensitive imagination. He was poor, unprotected, and oppressed, but he tried to live within the law. He was above all a moral man, whose natural rectitude contrasted sharply with the corruption of those whom the law of the apparatus favored. His society inevitably drove him to irrevocable acts of lawbreaking. The principal weapon of the proletarian hero was his collective will, which challenged the machines of the businessman. But typically the hero acts, not as a digit in a mob, but as an individual with personal convictions who never surrenders his identity to the collective. As opposed to the businessman, he was a true American democrat, seeking no more than his due, appealing to majority rule, and respecting himself and others as individuals.

If the worker was inarticulate, the intellectual was not. He volubly described the disparity between the very wealthy and the very poor. He wrote articles and books urging the workers to organize against the concentrated power of the industrial elite. The evil was capitalism; therapy was collective action. The intellectual gave shape and meaning to the class struggle and, unlike the worker, was committed to doctrines. His economic philosophy was Communism. Columnists, news correspondents, scientists, novelists—that large community of educated thinkers who sit, essentially, on the sidelines of direct action—saw in the Communist doctrine a panacea for the patent weaknesses of Capitalism. In an economy where all goods were held in common, democracy could flourish and men could be judged on their own merits, not according to what they managed unscrupulously to wrest from their helpless fellows. Liberal magazines espousing this program reflect in their titles the temper of the times: *Nation, The New Republic, Masses, The New Masses, Partisan Review, Liberator, New Leader.* These and dozens of other journals carried writers who raised the banner of social awareness, protesting against the *status quo,* demanding reforms of the prevailing ideology.

The struggle between the proletariat and the capitalists was given sharper point by the gradual unfolding of what seemed a similar struggle in Europe and Asia. The Japanese war machine was smashing into defenseless Manchuria. Mussolini leaped upon an unprepared Ethiopia, sending the steel of tanks and cannons against the flesh of men and horses. And Germany, sometimes noisily, sometimes quietly, was gobbling up central Europe: first Austria, then Czechoslovakia, and finally Poland. These were all totalitarian powers, allowing no opposition among their own people, using fear and force to gain their ends, binding their members to a social order that saw an enemy in individualism. Their emergence gave American writers of social protest a symbol for their own enemies in America, and it was not long before there were dark references to the fascist tendencies of the American businessman.

The most powerful symbol for the liberal intellectual of the 1930s was the Spanish Civil War. Begun in 1936, that local conflict soon drew the attention of most of the world. For the intellectual it became a *cause célèbre,* in which the forces of justice were fighting for their lives against the forces of oppression. This small war turned out to be a preview of the larger holocaust that was to follow. The totalitarian countries—Italy and Germany—contributed money, men, and arms to their protégé, Generalissimo Franco. On the other side, the Loyalists were championed by the international Communist Party, which was considerably less able financially to run a war than its fascist foes. Typically, the principal democratic capitalist countries of the West made no appreciable contributions one way or the other. But sympathizers of the Loyalist cause came from all over the world to fight against the archenemies. Those intellectuals who did not go, as the American war novel gives ample evidence, were saddled with a guilt they expiated only with difficulty.

In the socio-political war novel, the *dramatis personae* of the class struggle are translated into military terms. The military organization becomes the totalitarian society; the authoritarian officer or enlisted man becomes the oppressor; the soldier who resists out of individual integrity becomes the hero. As more than one novelist suggests, the significant experience was not the conflict between the American army and the enemy, but that between the apparatus and the individual.

These novelists equate the power-hungry officer with the grasping American businessman and the military organization with the corporate business hierarchy, thereby suggesting that the oppressive quality of the military society is not confined to a unique and temporary situation such as war, but extends to the whole fabric of American life. Ned Calmer,[3] a World War II war correspondent, in *The Strange Land* has a panel of generals determine the fate of an entire division of troops. Lounging about a firelit room in a comfortable French chateau, while their soldiers slog through rain and mud toward the front, the generals plan, mainly out of the desire for good press releases, what is clearly a hopeless attack. Major Lowell Harrod, an intelligence officer, muses to himself as he surveys the group: "How much it is all like the standard board of directors meeting . . . how much the whole war is run like a vast corporate enterprise by groups of men like these sitting in comfortably warm rooms after hearty meals, by pot-bellied executives pushing buttons in office buildings hundreds of miles behind the lines. . . ." Irwin Shaw's Michael Whitacre, in *The Young Lions,* enters a London bar and stares at the generals collected there, taking their ease far from the front: "He did not like their faces. They looked too much like the American businessman, smalltown merchants, factory owners, growing a little fat and over-comfortable, with an eye out for a new sales campaign."

Stefan Heym,[4] in *The Crusaders,* uses the businessman more directly. His Major Willoughby, though a lawyer, is the prototype of the mogul who grasps after money and power under the sanction of a business ethic that removes itself from normal moral considerations. As the junior member of an American law firm, Willoughby spends most of his time during the battle for Europe trying to establish a cartel between a steel company client of his firm and the Delacroix steel company in France. As the American army sweeps toward Berlin, it "liberates" the starved and tattered victims of the concentration camps. But when Willoughby learns that some of the inmates have been mining ore for the Delacroix furnaces, he keeps them on the job, rags and all. One oppressor is substituted for another. Business comes before humanity.

Norman Mailer and James Jones depict a much more disturbing character, a deliberate, self-conscious authoritarian. Each selects a fascistic general who formulates into sinister philosophical principles the instinctive actions of Willoughby and the generals in *The Strange Land.* Their aim is simple: to establish authority in the hands of the few and obliterate the dignity and independence of the individual. It was precisely this kind of organization which opponents of Mannheim's planned society feared. In this case, the planners are generals acting like businessmen. Mailer says of his General Cummings that when he smiled his expression "was very close to the complacent and hard appearance of any number of American senators and businessmen." Jones's General Slater insists that the authority he advocates has up to now "been handled by the great corporations like Ford and General Motors and U.S. Steel and Standard Oil. . . . The men who control the corporations and our senior officers are really very much alike."

Coldly and rationally these two generals propose that an efficient army may be formed only when power is accumulated under the control of a very few men. The way to this end is fear. General Cummings maintains that the best armies are those with a "superior material force and a poor standard of living." Since America has a high standard of living, its soldiers "have an exaggerated idea of the rights due themselves as individuals and no idea at all of the rights due to others. It's the reverse of the peasant, and I'll tell you right now it's the peasant who makes the soldier." Consequently, the individual must be forced to submit to a "fear ladder." "The Army functions best," says Cummings, "when you're frightened of the man above you, and contemptuous of your subordinates." The hate produced by such an arrangement can be directed outward against the enemy. The fear ladder concentrates power in the hands of the few, which fits the "realities" of modern life: "The machine techniques of this century demand consolidation, and with that you've got to have fear, because the majority of men must be subservient to the machine, and it's not a business they instinctively enjoy." By nature, that is, men lean toward their own individual spontaneity, a tendency which authority must check. Therefore, the general—or any officer—who possesses power cannot think of his men as individuals. "In the Army the idea of individual personality is just a hindrance. . . . I work with grosser techniques, common denominator techniques."

Such a doctrine is fascist in every way, and General Cummings minces no words in making the connection: "The concept of fascism, far sounder than communism if you consider it, for it's grounded firmly in men's actual natures, merely started in the wrong country, in a country which did not have enough intrinsic potential power to develop completely. In Germany with that basic frustration of limited physical means there were bound to be excesses. But the dream, the concept was sound enough." And then, as though to give validity to the fears of the liberals of the 'thirties, Cummings declares confidently that "America is going to absorb that dream, it's in the business of doing it now." The "morality of the future" is a "power morality." Power flows from the top down; "when there are little surges of resistance at the middle levels," efficient authority will simply exert more power downward.

General Slater expresses a similar doctrine, seeing the army as a metaphor of society. They are both like a machine whose parts have no value except as they make it possible for the machine to function. Consequently, the individual must subordinate himself to the machine: "the majority of men must be subservient to the machine, which is society." To enforce this principle, "we must have complete control." But how is this control to be achieved? It used to be that soldiers obeyed authority, not because they were afraid, but because they thought it virtuous to obey. They subscribed to such moral values as Honor, Patriotism, Service. With the ascendancy of the machine in modern life, these abstractions have been emptied of their capacity to command allegiance. "You cannot," Slater echoes Cummings, "make a man voluntarily chain himself to a machine because its 'Honorable.'" You can do so only by making "him afraid of *not* chaining himself to his machine." You threaten him with death.

Slater and Cummings exist outside the apparatus, running it, so to speak, for their own pleasure. Specifically, their responsibility is to govern, and to do that they must consolidate power in their own hands and demand unquestioned control of that power. The highest good is the good of the whole. To achieve that, the individual personality must be destroyed: says Slater, "anyone who governs must be cruel."

Through Cummings and Slater, Mailer and Jones speak for a good many American war novelists. The real danger to American democracy is not the armies of Germany and Japan, but the fascists within our own system, bent on establishing what Whitehead might call a nonliving society. This thesis is not merely tacked on in the socio-political war novel; it is part of its structure. This is especially clear in *The Naked and the Dead* and *From Here to Eternity*. For General Cummings the war is a huge chess game and his men are the pieces. As the player, manipulating his men from outside the fear ladder, he cannot permit even the slightest resistance to his authority from the lower levels. Yet it comes and it comes from two sources.

One of the sources is General Cummings' army, advancing up

the small peninsula of the Pacific island of Anopopei. It slows, stops, and slips into lethargy, resisting all the General's attempts to get it moving again. The other source is his young aide, Lieutenant Hearn. The military stalemate creates a strain between Cummings and Hearn. Capriciously exerting his power, the General sets out to humiliate his aide. He forces Hearn to execute pretty duties and embarrasses him in front of the enlisted men. To these petty annoyances Hearn reacts pettily. When Cummings is absent from his tent, Hearn stamps a cigarette out on the spotless floor, desecrating the cleanliness that Cummings has been unreasonably forcing him to maintain. This gesture of defiance is altogether futile, but Cummings sees it as a symbol of his troops' resistance. Hearn's act and the men's refusal to move ahead against the Japs threaten the stability of the fear ladder and Cummings' own omnipotence, both representing the kind of independence that subordinates must not be allowed if the power morality is to remain intact. Cummings sets out to crush the resistance by applying power from above.

He begins with the easiest problem—Lieutenant Hearn. Summoning Hearn to his tent, Cummings acts upon his theories. He throws a cigarette upon the floor and orders Hearn to pick it up. Hearn balks feebly, but lacking the courage of his indignation, he stoops ignominiously and recovers the burnt butt. Cummings easily stifles one source of resistance.

The troops are a different matter. Cummings decides to destroy their apathy by forcing them into an attack which will secure the island. But if he is to prove the validity of his power philosophy, he must be the one-man engineer of the assault, the chess player *par excellence*. His strategy requires a reconnoitering of the Japanese rear. In a last splurge of power over Hearn, Cummings assigns him to the leadership of the reconnaissance patrol. This mission commences an action which mirrors the conflict between Cummings, Hearn, and the troops, and further examines the fascist mentality. The platoon chosen for the patrol has up to now been headed by Sergeant Croft, an enlisted counterpart of General Cummings, who feeds his appetite for power by making his men afraid of him. Croft sees Hearn, as an officer and the official commander of the group, to be a threat to his position. During the mission Croft becomes obsessed with the wish to climb Mt. Anaka, the peak that dominates the island and that symbolizes absolute power. The wish is analogous to Cummings' desire completely to dominate his army.

As with Cummings, Croft finds obstacles in his men, who do not want to make the arduous climb, and in Hearn, who recognizes it as irrelevant to their mission. Like Cummings, Croft has an easy time with Hearn, deceiving him and maneuvering him into a Japanese ambush in which he is killed. But there are still the soldiers to deal with. Realizing that because the Japanese have discovered their presence their mission cannot now be productive, they wish to return to the base. But Croft forces them up the mountain. Just as he is about to reach the summit he kicks a hornets' nest and out of the paper cone fly hundreds of insects and attack the exhausted men. Capitalizing on this chance to cut short their march, they throw away their rifles and flee down the mountain, ignoring Croft's enraged commands to return. Croft is prevented from seizing absolute power by chance and his own men.

What happens to Croft foreshadows Cummings' fortunes. Another phase of his strategy to regain complete control over his men takes him away from the island to enlist naval support for his attack. While he is absent, it develops that the Japanese have pulled back. The troops, under the command of a mediocre subordinate, follow the line of least resistance and move forward in spite of themselves. Although the men secure the island, they do so without the pressure of Cummings. The power morality is rendered ineffective in part by an implausible sequence of chance events which, as some critics have already remarked, is artistically unacceptable, since it empties Mailer's carefully built power morality of its sinister potential. But the important point for us is that Mailer makes the men the victors over the danger of fascism. Like the members of some aimless but persistent union they triumph over the power mongers. Even though they have no systematic purpose, as a group they possess a will over which no general or dictator—or businessman—has total control. In the end, General Cummings irritably acknowledges this: "The men resisted him, resisted change, with maddening inertia. No matter how you pushed them, they always gave ground sullenly, regrouped once the pressure was off. You could work on them, you could trick them, but there were times now when he doubted basically whether he could change them, really mold them."

Mailer has no hero who achieves a high intensity of individual satisfaction. He shows confidence not so much in the promise of individuality as in the impossibility of establishing a planned society enforced by consolidated power. James Jones has a hero and creates a world in which fascism is a grave danger to that hero's self-fulfillment. The danger is dramatized in the conflict between Private Robert E. Lee Prewitt and the apparatus of the American army. Prewitt has transferred into a line company at Schofield Barracks, whose commander is Captain "Dynamite" Holmes. Holmes is also the regimental boxing coach and a diligent pursuer of the station's boxing trophy. Prewitt, a good middleweight, has quit boxing after inadvertently blinding a friend in a sparring accident. Holmes cannot bear to see so promising a point-getter escape, so he begins, in the tradition of General Cummings, applying pressure to Prewitt in the form of "the treatment." The athletes of the company, the instruments of Holmes's oppression, launch a campaign to badger Prewitt into fighting, but he resists and sticks to his decision.

Prewitt's intransigence is to Holmes what Lieutenant Hearn's rebellion and the troops' lethargy were to General Cummings. At this point, Holmes becomes indoctrinated by General Slater, who explains his power theories to the junior officer at a party. In the course of their talk the matter of Prewitt comes up. Slater admonishes Holmes that he must not back down from an enlisted man: "You can break any man," says Slater. "You are an officer." Yes, claims Colonel Jake Delbert, Holmes's immediate superior, they broke Dillinger right there in the Schofield stockade. Holmes insists that Dillinger was only killed, not broken. Into this argument steps Slater and articulates the sentiments that give Jones's novel its main form: "They never broke Dillinger. You might as well be honest, Jake, and give him his due. . . . But the important thing is they did kill him, like they always kill them. The only thing wrong with Dillinger was that he was an individualist, and you can't understand that, Jake. But that's why they had to kill him." The apparatus cannot tolerate the value of individual satisfaction. Prewitt must be throttled because he *is* individualism. Holmes is commanded to "give this man Prewitt the goddam book."

Jones illustrates the way in which the balance between individual freedom and social order has shifted to the social order, requiring so many concessions from the individual that he must die either in resisting or in surrendering. This rather simple conflict is enriched by a human ambiguity in *From Here to Eternity,* for Prewitt, far from hating the army, loves it; he is a thirty-year-man. But how does an individual, in the full sense of the word, reconcile his integrity with an authority which insists that he abandon it? How does he come to live in "harmony" with the "powers of the world," as Jaspers urged him to do? This is the paradox that gives Jones's book the overtones of tragedy. Given the original conditions—Prewitt's individuality and the army's fascism—only one outcome is possible.

Prewitt, true to his individual style, refuses to budge from his decision not to fight. The army, true to its social style, railroads him into the stockade. Here are what Jones would call the army's true individuals. But for the army they are simply dangerous misfits who must be herded together and kept from damaging the apparatus. The stockade interlude performs the same function as the reconnaissance episode in *The Naked and the Dead;* it mirrors the main action. Major Thompson, the commander of the stockade, and his assistant, Sergeant Fatso Judson, are representatives of pure and unsullied tyranny, the brutal strongarms of legal power, Slater's consolidated control set forth in high relief. In the stockade Prewitt meets Sam Slater's opposite, Jack Malloy, who preaches the doctrine of extreme individuality carried out in the passive resistance and civil disobedience of Mahatma Ghandi.

When Prewitt observes the impersonal cruelty of Fatso Judson, he decides to kill him. After he is released from the stockade, he meets the guard in an alley in Honolulu, knifes him, but is himself wounded by Judson. Thinking his own wound will reveal his guilt, he goes AWOL. After the Japanese attack Pearl Harbor, he attempts to join his company bivouacked on the beach, but is gunned down by an MP patrol when he fails to halt at their command. Prewitt refuses to let himself be absorbed by the apparatus and is destroyed by it.

The judgment against the authoritarian and the society he seeks to establish is expressed by the socio-political war novelist mainly through showing them as oppressors of the individual. He has, however, other ways of reinforcing this judgment. Some novelists suggest that the megalomania of the fascist is a symptom of a deeper sickness. Jung has suggested that outwardly manly behavior, when carried to extremes, is compensation for an inner womanliness, and it has often been noted that the desire to dominate is a compensation for an inner failure. Erich Fromm writes that when he speaks of a neurotic with these symptoms he uses the word "sado-masochistic," and Cummings and Slater come close to fitting into this category. When Fromm speaks of the "normal person" with these symptoms he uses the word I have employed: "*authoritarian character.*" This character must convince himself that he is strong in order to hide his shortcomings. "If I have power over another person to kill him," writes Fromm, "I am 'stronger' than he is. But in a psychological sense, *the lust for power is not rooted in strength but in weakness.* It is the expression of the inability of the individual self to stand alone and live. It is the desperate attempt to gain secondary strength where genuine strength is lacking."[5]

This weakness takes another form in the war novel, a sexual one. No authoritarian character is allowed to have a satisfactory heterosexual relationship. Either they attempt to dominate the woman for little more than masturbatory purposes or there are faint hints of homosexuality. Both Slater and Cummings have something feminine about them. After his discussion with Slater, Holmes felt "suddenly for no reason like he had been seduced, the way a woman must feel," and Slater summarizes his position "with a curiously feminine satisfaction." In a similar situation, after Cummings has described his theory to Hearn, the latter is agitated by a personal turn in the conversation. Hearn feels that Cummings' eyes are "beseeching" and "that if he remained motionless long enough the General would slowly extend his arm, touch his knee perhaps." Getting up, Hearn steps aimlessly toward the other end of the tent, only to find himself staring at the General's cot and thinks, "No, get away from there, before Cummings grabbed that interpretation." Cummings, with obvious self-pity, calls his wife a "bitch." Holmes is habitually promiscuous.

The war novelist had a good precedent for hinting at the homosexuality of his fascist characters. In the 1930's suspicions of Hitler's sexual abnormality were widespread. And the bourgeois businessman of the Depression years was often depicted in the radical social novels of the period as having homosexual tendencies. Walter B. Rideout remarks: "Particularly the incidence of homosexuality among the *bourgeoisie* by contrast with that among the proletariat is placed astoundingly high, so high, in fact, that it quite reverses the findings of Professor Kinsey's celebrated study of sexual behavior in the American male. One suspects that for the proletarian novelist homosexuality came to stand arbitrarily as a convenient, all-inclusive symptom of capitalist decay."[6] If we substitute the word "fascist" or "authoritarian" for "capitalist" in Rideout's last sentence, we may see the effect of the hint made by Jones and Mailer. One way to discredit the authoritarian doctrine is to invest its administrators with hints of sexual aberration as a signal of moral decadence. Mailer himself states that he had conceived Cummings' homosexuality as "the core of much of his motivation," because he had believed there to be "an intrinsic relation between homosexuality and 'evil.'"[7] Interestingly enough—and we see it in the novels of James Baldwin and Gore Vidal—the homosexual has come more and more to be used as a symbol of the misunderstood and mistreated, whom a brutal society tries to bend from his spontaneous self to a rigid conformity. Mailer, too, later concluded that his early attitude had been biased and inaccurate.

The homosexual aspect of the authoritarian character is usually accompanied by a high degree of rationality which isolates him from humanity. General Cummings, for example, looks up at Mt. Anaka and thinks, "Both of them, from necessity, were bleak and alone, commanding the heights." These characters start from the premise that the highest value lies not in individual satisfaction but in the smooth working of the apparatus. Reasoning from this position, they remain uninvolved with individual human beings at the subject level. All their relationships are external. They are incapable of taking up ties and so remain humanly impotent, a feature which emphatically differentiates them from the individualistic hero.

Less intelligent authoritarians than Slater and Cummings are simply bigots. General Mallon, in *The Strange Land,* calls the newspaper correspondent Marks, a "Jewboy," and, because Marks questions the validity of the attack that Mallon wants to launch, accuses him of "making trouble." Sergeant Dondolo, in *The Crusaders,* when pressed by a young Jew to say whether he is fighting the war for his children, replies, "Sure I'm fighting for my kids. I'm going to get back to 'em, too! It's because of people like you I had to leave 'em. . . . Bunch of Jews get themselves into trouble, and the whole American Army swims across the ocean. This fellow Hitler, he knew what he was doing, and Mussolini, he, too. Everything is wrong. We should be fighting with them, against the Communists." Irwin Shaw has his lisping Sergeant Rickett say, "Ah ain't got no use for Niggerth, Jewth, Mexicans or Chinamen. . . ." One of the soldiers in Rickett's platoon tells Shaw's Jewish protagonist, Noah Ackerman, "You people got us into the war. Now why can't you behave yourselves like human beings?" In John Cobb's[8] *The Gesture,* the daring pilot Willie Turk, a Southerner, refuses to accept a Negro officer as a roommate. Turk's buddies throw the Negro's clothes out in the street and Turk smashes him in the jaw at the officers' club.

Whether the authoritarian appears as a philosopher of fascism or simply an emotional bigot reflecting the narrowness of his social order, he bears more similarities to the Nazi than to the democratic American. Much of the time the fascist deludes himself with the notion that the oppression he practices is really simply a benevolent despotism that actually works in favor of the individual, if only the individual had the sense to see it. Captain Holmes sees the consolidation of power as a potential agent of great good for raising "humanity to new heights despite humanity's own mulishness and inertia." General Farrish, in *The Crusaders,* thinks in the same way: "We must have a purge. We must weed out the undesirables—the crooks, the politicians, the guys who talk back and always have dozens of considerations. There is too much democracy in the Army, and that doesn't work. . . . A war has got to be run on the basis of dictatorship."

The validity of these positions depends upon the way in which they are presented. Clearly, Jones and Heym mean to discredit the views of Holmes and Farrish. But if Farrish's statement is put more favorably, the authoritarian position can be justified according to what Joseph Waldmeir calls "expedient fascism,"[9] the adoption of authoritarianism during a crisis in order to preserve a higher good. The dilemma is that it is quite true that an army cannot function efficiently if everyone in it is equal and independent. Waldmeir cites James Gould Cozzens' *Guard of Honor* and Herman Wouk's *The Caine Mutiny* as the main spokesmen for expedient fascism. Cozzens' Colonel Ross, in civilian life a judge, realizes that the "gigantic machine" of the army might injure the individual here and there. But the gravity of the war threat requires a "postponement" of individual freedom.

Wouk is less convincing in his defense of this thesis. For well over half the novel, the reader is confronted with the most overpowering evidence that the *Caine's* commander, Captain Queeg, is unreasonable, overbearing, incompetent, and probably mentally ill —in short, a typical authoritarian. He is not only a fool but a coward. He wastes time on trivialities when there is a war to fight. At the height of a typhoon he insists insanely upon following a course that seems to lead to destruction. When the admirable Lieutenant Maryk mutinies, every reader has been conditioned to experience only relief. But after Maryk is exonerated in a court martial that ruins the careers of both himself and Queeg, Wouk turns all his sympathy upon the heretofore despicable captain. Barney Greenwald, Maryk's cynically idealistic defense lawyer, tells the crew of the *Caine* that Queeg was on guard against fascism when the rest of them were having a good time in civilian life, oblivious to the mounting dangers. The logic of Wouk's narrative is not very clear, but his conclusion is. Queeg may not have been the best sailor that America had and he may have commanded the *Caine* with an almost sick unreasonableness, but in those circumstances he was all America had and should be deferred to for that reason. The middle class hero of the book, Willie Keith, formulates the theory in comfortably pedestrian words: "The idea is, once you get an incompetent ass of a skipper . . . there's nothing to do but serve him as though he were the wisest and best, cover his mistakes, keep the ship going, and bear up. . . ." Wouk sells a valid position short by defending it with gimmickry and unacceptable logic.

Most of the war novelists accept the fundamental principle of expedient fascism, though they do not like it. Their real objections are directed toward those who would make fascism the permanent form of the American system. And for these objectors the real danger comes not from the overt enemy which can be fought out in the open battlefield, but from the viper within our own society, gradually eating away the freedom which nourishes it. The danger of the American fascist is that he is given free license to practice, indeed, almost encouraged. Both Willoughby and Dondolo, in *The Crusaders,* commit legally punishable crimes, yet both escape punishment. As the protégé of General Farrish, who advances him to a colonelcy, Willoughby is above the law. After being apprehended for some black marketeering, Willoughby is merely sent back to the States, successful in all his endeavors, including his attempt to work out the cartel with the Delacroix company. Dondolo, who maliciously terrorizes a combat veteran suffering from war neurosis, is also caught in some black market dealings, but he too is sent to the rear lines, a fate he welcomes. Our real enemies are not the Germans or the Japanese, these novels suggest, but those who exploit slave labor, maneuver for the centralization of power both industrial and military, brutalize individuals, and advocate dictatorship within and without the army. These are the supporters of a society so rigidly ordered that most individual possibilities are closed.

The most verbal opponent of authoritarianism in the war novel is the politically liberal intellectual. He appears in many different faces, but from the diversity a composite emerges. Like his predecessor of the Depression years, the intellectual of the war novelists tends to look for solutions in abstract doctrines. Generally he does more talking and observing than acting, articulating the meaning of the war in the terminology of the class struggle of the 'thirties.

Ned Calmer's Major Harrod is typical of the intellectual as an observer. He is not a combat soldier, but is at times in combat. He is not a member of the general staff, but he attends staff meetings as General Mallon's aide. He is thus committed fatally to neither side, though his sympathies always lie with the combat soldier. He sees and responds to the faces of individual men, the dull fear in their eyes, the misery of their movements. He is disgusted with his superior officer, General Mallon, for exploiting the soldier, but neither his rank nor his temperament equip him to confront that ambitious man with his sins.

Some of these intellectuals are brave men. Major Harrod has a quiet strength which gives confidence to the men around him, making them "feel better just being up here with us." His courage under fire impresses the toughest and most experienced combat men. These attributes qualify Harrod to speak and judge as he does. He formulates the values implicit in the action of the novel, explains the essence of combat and the ineffable relationship between the members of the combat group, defines fascism and sees the war as a struggle against it. And he judges against the selfish generals and opportunistic parasites like John C. Wexel, the temporary war correspondent who will commercialize and distort the small corner of the war he is permitted to see.

Private Elbrus, in Levin's *Mask of Glory,*[10] has the same courage and capacity for love that Calmer gives to Major Harrod. Although he is uneducated, a second generation "hunkie," he must be ranked as an intellectual. He is accused of thinking too much and in a way this is true. His ties with the proletarian movement of the 'thirties are explicit. He cites religion as "dope for the poor people," preventing them "from getting in unions and fighting for their rights." He feels guilt that he did not accompany a friend of his when the latter went to fight in the Spanish Civil War. "I always asked myself, if it's for the workers, shouldn't you go? . . . That's why, I guess, I picked on the Marines. Every time I go in I try to think, this is for the workers." He is called a Communist by his company commander and the pretentiously cynical news correspondent Morton links Elbrus with the "social thinkers" he knew in his newspaper guild. Most of Elbrus's intellectual energy is expended in trying to bring order out of his troubled thoughts over the meaning of the war. His moment of truth comes as he kneels beside a dying Marine. He feels compelled to tell the youth only what is true and the truth is that love makes us what we are, love is what we are fighting for: "It isn't for nothing, boy, I tell you I know. . . . You are loved by men, whoever you are, and by the common people in the world. It is for them, in some way, and some day we will all know. I am guilty because you are gone for good, and I am here, but you did something swell I tell you. Now be peaceful, and it doesn't matter what happens or if you stink or what happens to your body because it is all for the working people." Elbrus desperately clings to the liberal statement of purposefulness and the ideals of his background, but a few moments later he is blown to bits by a Japanese mortar shell.

The type of intellectual represented by Harrod and Elbrus appears only in a minority of the war novels. Almost always he is linked sympathetically with the liberal causes of the 1930's—Communism, the Spanish Civil War, the proletarian movement. But the sympathy usually is only with the position and not with the intellectual himself. The typical war novelist shows a basic distrust of this character. The reason for this distrust is simple: the intellectual talks but does not do. Lincoln Steffens reports a speech given by Lenin in the days when he was still competing with Kerenski. "He may think socialism," says Lenin, "he may mean socialism. But comrades . . . I tell you Kerenski is an intellectual; he *cannot* act; he can talk; he cannot *act*." General Cummings says the same thing about the doctrinaire liberal: "The root of all the liberals' ineffectiveness comes right spang out of the desperate suspension in which they have to hold their minds."

The intellectual entertains all ideas, rationally examines all positions. He remains detached so as to keep himself free of bias. Only in the atmosphere of such freedom can he prevent himself from falling prey to an obsessive idea which reason cannot penetrate. Up to this point, these traits fit very well with the ideal of the "open decision." Two important factors, however, are missing—feeling and commitment. The intellectual is the observer. He involves himself with abstractions, not with life. Play is beyond him because he lacks that necessary combination of earnestness and daring which allows him to take up ties with the world even while maintaining his freedom. With very few exceptions, the war novelists place the intellectual on the side of the oppressed against authority. But for the most part he is either ineffective in the good fight or downright harmful.

One of the best specimens of the liberal intellectual in these novels is Mailer's Lieutenant Hearn. General Cummings chose Hearn for his aide because the young officer is one of the few men in the command who can understand and appreciate Cummings' theories. Cummings likes him because he is a natural antagonist, and Cummings enjoys a battle, however uneven the odds. Hearn defends most of the liberal theories in his arguments with Cummings. But he does so without any really settled convictions of his own, out of an irritable reflex against Cummings' smug confidence in his own power. Against the concept of the "fear ladder" Hearn argues the importance of the individual. Against the idea that war is merely aimed toward the establishment of the power morality, Hearn argues that war is to establish democracy in the face of fascism. Upon each point, Cummings soundly trounces his fuzzy-thinking opponent. Yet Hearn disturbs him: "There was something unapproachable and unattainable about Hearn which had always piqued him, always irritated him subtly. The empty pit where there should be a man."

This is a heavy indictment against a thinker who defends the rights of the individual. Yet, this is exactly Hearn's problem. His ideas remain ideas. They do not affect him internally. Theoretically, he has a passion for the proletariat, but in effect he remains detached: "Several people had at one time or another made it a point to tell Hearn that he liked men only in the abstract and never in the particular, a cliché of course, an oversimplification, but not without casual truth." Hearn's background is very much that of the young rebel of the 'thirties. He grew up in the midwest. His father was a large, crude, and successful man who did not understand his shy, burly son. Aimlessly, Hearn rebels against the authority and materialism of his businessman father—he goes to Harvard when he learns that his father wants him to attend Yale. He succeeds in nothing, except in assuming a cynical and self-conscious skepticism: "A dilettante skipping around sewers," he thinks. "Everything is crapped up, everything is phony, everything curdles when you touch it." Yet, he feels a romantic yearning for something he cannot define. His indecisiveness stems from his ambivalent sense that there is something beyond the surface of experience that may be sought and discovered, and the opposite contemptuousness that "everything is crapped up." On the ship going overseas he thinks, "There is the phrase 'I'm seeking for something' but it gives the process an importance it doesn't really possess. . . . You never do find out what makes you tick, and after a while it's unimportant." Beneath his self-protective veneer of childish skepticism is an equally childish idealism, and because he can commit himself to neither the acceptance of the phoniness nor the hopefulness that the "process" is important, he is no match for the authoritarians against whom he is pitted, who are blind to every other possibility than their own convictions. Hearn lacks the transcending capacity for play which joins belief and unbelief.

Hearn's character determines his fate. Weakened by his own indecisiveness but driven by a petulant sense of grievance, he first stamps out his cigarette on the General's floor and then backs down from Cummings and picks up the cigarette which the General, in turn, has purposely dropped. Cummings transfers him, then assigns him to Sergeant Croft's platoon for the reconnaissance mission behind the Japanese lines. As they make their trek toward the pass at the base of Mt. Anaka, Croft, with the subtlety of instinct, attempts to undermine Hearn's authority. Hearn, living up to his liberal theories, tries to befriend the men, but meets only surly resistance. The patrol is ambushed, a man is wounded. Hearn must decide whether to go on or to return. Reason tells him the effectiveness of the mission is nil because their presence is known by the enemy. Croft, however, is bent upon wresting power from Hearn and climbing Mt. Anaka. Hearn decides to return, but then makes his fatal, and typical, error. He reverses his decision and allows Croft to persuade him to send out a scout. If the pass is clear they will continue the patrol.

After the scout has been dispatched, Hearn agonizes over his decisions and indecisions. He recognizes with disgust that he enjoys commanding these men, especially having made even Croft back down. He wants the satisfaction of returning to Cummings with a successfully completed mission. Both of these points alert him to the fact that he is acting according to Cummings' power morality. To continue would be to manipulate these men simply to gratify a selfish desire for power. At this point he brings his liberal views back into play, and their wrong-headedness is apparent. Fascism, he muses, must not win out. He would return the men to the base after this mission and resign his commission: "That was the thing he could do, that would be honest, true to himself." You had to "keep resisting" the fascists. "You had to do things like giving up a commission." But Hearn sees even his own idealism cynically: "Hearn and Quixote," he thinks. "Bourgeois liberals." Hearn simply cannot make the meaningful gesture—or he makes it too late. His indecisiveness prevents him from playing an effective role against Cummings and Croft. The scout returns, having found Japs still guarding the pass, and tells Croft. Croft, with the singleminded determination of a man who knows intuitively what he wants, lies to Hearn that the pass is clear. Leading his men into the ambush, Hearn is killed by a Japanese machine-gun bullet.

In other novels, the intellectual's failure causes damage to men other than the intellectual himself. The doctrine of Jack Malloy, in *From Here to Eternity,* is based on passive resistance, the conviction—which sounds very much like General Cummings' resigned conclusion—that "you cant [*sic*] force the individual who makes up your non-existent masses into anything unless he wants it. . . ." Like Elbrus, Malloy finds love to be the important ingredient in all worthwhile relationships. His god is not Vengeance or even Forgiveness, but Acceptance.

Malloy preaches his ideas to the men in the stockade as a means of resisting brutal authoritarianism which would press the individual into the mass. But at the crucial time Malloy loses confidence in his own ideas as well as himself. When Prewitt vows to kill Fatso Judson, Malloy declares that such an act will be futile; another Judson will spring up in the former's place and Prewitt will be back where he started. Prewitt, however, persists, claiming that the gesture will make him "feel better." The intellectual's approach is through the general principle. Prewitt's approach is through the specific event and the individual. In the face of such determination, Malloy suddenly confesses that he has been a failure: "I've tried to teach people things I saw but they always take them wrong and use them wrong. Its because theres something lacking in me. I preach passive resistance and a new kind of God with a new kind of love that understands, but I dont practice it. At least not enough. Sometimes, I don't think I've ever loved anything in my life. . . ." "The things I've loved have always been too phantasmal, too immaterial, too idealistic. I suffer from the same disease I try to diagnose, the same disease thats destroying the world."

Such a weakness—similar to Hearn's—is not merely a handicap but a danger. Malloy blames himself for the death of young Blues Berry and the dishonorable discharge of Angelo Maggio, both of whom were disciples of his passive resistance theory. "If it hadn't been for me and my talk, neither Angelo nor Berry would have done what they did. Or got what they got. And if I stay here . . . the same thing is going to happen to other guys."

When such behavior is treated less sympathetically, the intellectual becomes the opponent of right conduct rather than its spokesman and formulator. Malloy's heart is in the right place; he simply cannot act upon his ideas. He must hold people at a distance, and that gives him grief. Wouk and Cozzens do not give their intellectuals credit even for good intentions. Both Lieutenant Keefer, in *The Caine Mutiny,* and Lieutenant Edsell, in *Guard of Honor,* are selfish and obstreperous, parroting liberal ideas but using them for ulterior motives. The poignant disabilities of the intellectual in *The*

Naked and the Dead and *From Here to Eternity* become not only dangerous but contemptible weaknesses in *The Caine Mutiny.* Lieutenant Keefer, certain of his own worth, obnoxiously arrogant, is restive under the authority of both captains of the *Caine.* He is, as Willie Keith says, "too clever to be wise." And so he regards the Navy with contempt, thinks of all but a few "excellent" officers at the top as morons, and feels his coevals are beneath him, making him more like an authoritarian than the liberal he professes to be. He parades his learning, which consists of reading in contemporary literature and a smattering of psychology, and advertises his scorn with vitriolic epigrams. Because of Keefer, Captain Queeg and Lieutenant Maryk are virtually destroyed as Naval officers.

As Barney Greenwald bitterly says, Keefer was the cause of it all, but managed to remain detached, to escape untouched. "You bowled a perfect score," says Barney to Keefer. "You went after Queeg and got him. You kept your own skirts all white and starchy. Steve Maryk is finished for good, but you'll be the next captain of the *Caine.*" Although he was the one who planted the seeds of doubt about Queeg's sanity, the doubt which led directly to the mutiny, Keefer backs down in the crisis. He does not stand by Maryk when the latter wishes to carry proof of Queeg's incompetence to the fleet commander; he deftly avoids taking any direct part in the mutiny itself; and he refuses at the court martial to acknowledge his earlier opinion that Queeg was dangerously sick. As though these examples were not enough to establish Keefer's cowardice, Wouk gives him a final moment of ignominy. When the *Caine* is hit in one of the last battles of the Pacific War, Keefer, now the captain, frantically abandons ship, while Willie Keith gallantly brings the cripple into port. Through Keefer, Wouk discredits the liberal intellectual's attack upon fascism.

Most of these intellectuals are not cowards in the way that Keefer is. They merely shrink from human involvement, from the job that must be performed, from taking up ties with the world. In some cases the intellectual is educated during the novel to an awareness of his responsibility. Both Michael Whitacre, in *The Young Lions,* and Lieutenant Yates, in *The Crusaders,* undergo such a development. Whitacre is in the New York theater. He reads Shakespeare and Strindberg and thinks about the Nature of Things and the Meaning of the War. Like Hearn he has a strong sense of self-disgust: "Too fat, too much liquor, too many attachments, a wife who was practically a stranger . . . while he frittered away the years of his youth, drifting with the easy tide of the theatre, making a little money, being content, never making the bold move. . . ."

When the war begins, Michael thinks he has found a way to expiate his sins. Refusing the help of his influential New York friend Cahoon in getting him an easy job in Special Services, he joins the infantry, idealistically assuming that there he would at last walk among the noble army of the proletariat. He finds instead a group of men who are prejudiced, crude, cruel, and without the least sense of why they are fighting. At last he is driven to seek Cahoon's help and in doing so expresses a key idea: "Intellectuals, Cahoon was probably thinking, they're all alike, no matter what they say. When it finally gets down to it, they pull back. When the sound of the guns finally draw close, they suddenly find they have more important business elsewhere."

His inability to endure the infantry heightens Michael's sense of guilt. It brings back his remorse for having failed to go to Spain: "Ever since 1936, ever since Spain, I have felt that one day I would be asked to pay. . . . I remain a private for my guilt." From the infantry training camp he is sent to Special Services in London, where his guilt pushes him to beg a job with Colonel Pavone as jeep driver in Europe. But even that does not quiet his conscience. He wants a transfer to a combat outfit. Pavone is disgusted with him: "Christ, I hate intellectual soldiers! You think all the Army has to do these days is make sure you can make the proper sacrifice to satisfy your jerky little consciences!"

For all his good intentions Michael is constitutionally unable to act effectively. Sitting in a jeep in a French village with Corporal Keane, he is astonished to see a German armored car careen into the main street and race toward them. He fumbles awkwardly with the safety on his carbine, but is unable to release it. Behind him a shot sounds; the armored car wobbles, then crashes. Keane, a loud-mouth who had boasted how he would handle the Germans if he ever saw them, has coolly saved the day. A French crowd gathers and demands the death of the one German who remains alive. Michael hesitates. Swiftly and jubilantly, Keane shoots the man in cold blood. Even while he hates Keane, Michael thinks, "Keane had earned his souvenir. When Michael had faltered and fumbled,

Keane had behaved like a soldier. . . . Inadequate. Michael Whitacre, the inadequate man, the doubtful civilian, the non-killing soldier."

Lieutenant Yates also hesitates in crucial moments. In civilian life an instructor of German in a small Eastern college, Yates prided himself on his "enlightened skepticism." But in the army he finds his detachment a liability rather than an asset. Because he fails to act quickly, Sergeant Dondolo browbeats a battle veteran with combat neurosis into insanity, and Major Willoughby manages to prevent the chairman of the board of Delacroix Steel, who had collaborated with the Germans, from being brought to justice. Two comments by Yates put the danger of the intellectual's weakness into perspective. He compares the inmates of the Nazi concentration camps with the inhabitants of America: ". . . they were Europe, they had made their Europe, or had allowed their Europe to be made into what it was. And there they were, wreckage, freezing, stinking, starving, and waiting for American charity." The inmates had failed to deal with totalitarianism when they should have. They waited and were nearly destroyed. Ironically, Yates is not fully aware that his statement reflects upon his own indecisiveness. The remedy is to act, which is to assume responsibility for one's self. Yates formulates this idea when he speaks to a group of German prisoners who have insisted they were simply following orders when they killed helpless people. He admonishes them that they must, finally, take the responsibility for their own personal actions, that they can hide no longer behind their superiors. Soon all the suffering in the world could be blamed upon one man, and all those who participated in that suffering would get off free. No, says Yates, every man will be held accountable for what he himself does, with or without orders.

Yates and Whitacre do finally learn to assume responsibility in the act, to feel, to be internally changed by experience, to touch life and existence rather than merely ideas. They learn to become subjects. Whitacre turns into an effective combat soldier and Yates, for once, acts quickly enough to expose Willoughby in his black market dealings. They become heroes, but not before their intellectuality has caused damage. And so the majority report on the intellectual is negative. Whether his motives are suspected or sympathized with, his detachment keeps him from the real grime of battle. The intellectual in these socio-political war novels tends to be a negative dramatization of the need for assuming ties, taking up internal relationships with his world if the apparatus is to be prevented from inhibiting the achievement of individual satisfaction. The intellectual only formulates positive values; he does not live them. To live them is the role of the hero.

The hero is everything the intellectual is not. In him the values of the "open decision" are fully realized. He is no preacher of formulated ideas, but his integrity is unassailable. He moves in the real concrete world, not the world of abstractions. He has strong though usually unarticulated convictions, and he acts upon these convictions whatever suffering they may cost him. He is willing to gamble in his choice of possibilities. Prewitt refuses to withdraw his refusal to fight and is saddled with the worst details in the company. Noah Ackerman fights consecutively the ten biggest men in his platoon when they badger him for being a Jew; his nose is broken several times and his ribs are smashed. Steve Maryk mutinies in spite of the fact that it probably means a court martial.

The hero acts. Captain Troy, the efficient commander of an armored company in *The Crusaders,* relentlessly hunts down the Nazi Captain Pettinger and destroys him. Prewitt kills Fatso Judson. Noah leads a patrol out from under a German ambush and is cited for bravery. These are not compulsive actions, the result of mechanical instinct. They arise from the unique individual, who exists through them the novel experience of the living subject. They are gestures of the sort John Cobb has his narrator speak of: ". . . gesture is spontaneity and what is spontaneous is what we feel rather than reason through. It may be quite futile, but it comes out of the inner man and his personal faith, and in this way it alone is not subject to failure." In Cobb's sense, gesture is the unique style of an individual's existence. The hero's gestures are free acts, unconditioned by tradition or prejudice or expedience, undetermined by biological instinct or social pressure. They are moves in that earnest game which derives its significance from the commitment of the individual.

The hero dares to expose himself to life. The form of this exposure is love, which recalls the theories of Jaspers and Fromm, both of whom see in the ability to love an intensity of subjective experience that both protects the self from the machine of the apparatus and confirms that self's solidarity with the rest of the human community. Jack Malloy tells Prewitt: "I'd give whatever place in heaven I've got coming to have been able to love something as much as you love the Army. . . . When a man has found something he really loves, he must always hang onto it, no matter what happens, whether it loves him or not. And . . . if it finally kills him, he should be grateful to it, for having just had the chance. Because thats the whole secret." Significantly, it is usually the intellectual who formulates the "secret," but it is the hero who lives it. The secret that Malloy speaks of is that individual spontaneity which frees the authentic self from the constraints of false consciousness, bad faith, authoritarianism. It is the capacity to be changed internally by the stream of life, and it cuts through the insulation of the *status quo* and the abstract to the very heart of the individual self. The intellectual rues his attachment to phantasms, can like people only in the abstract. The authoritarian seeks to dominate others because he cannot stand alone. The hero, because he can stand alone, is able to love without destroying. Prewitt loves the whore Lorene with an intensity that disconcerts her. Noah's love for his wife Hope drives him to break the laws of the army to see her. Glenn Manson, in *Mask of Glory,* falls deeply in love with Isabella and with her comes "to have peace that grew like a seed in a tortured fruitless desert." Indeed, love, it is suggested in almost all of these novels, is the prerequisite to growth, a risk of the self before unpredictable consequences, the achievement of awareness that is the quintessence of human life. And love in the "open decision," is the force that links the individual to other human beings, creates internal change, and leads to a high intensity of individual satisfaction.

In the hero, open and authentic, lies the highest good. But the conditions of his environment often lead to his destruction. Prewitt's integrity sets in motion an inexorable series of events that concludes in his death. Noah's courage does not prevent him from being picked off by a degenerate remnant of the defeated German army. The naive enthusiasm of Glenn Manson explodes under a Japanese mortar shell on a numbered hill in the Pacific. And to satisfy the vanity of a single National Guard general, a whole company of admirable men is sent to be slaughtered in *The Strange Land*. A frustrated sense of ambiguity seems to prevail here. The very qualities which make the individual most valuable seem to be the ones which his society—the apparatus—is least receptive to, at least the authoritarian society. There is an irreconcilable conflict between the individual and the Fascist order. What pessimism there is in these socio-political war novels appears in the conviction that the authoritarian threatens to win the war, even though our armies will be victorious over the enemy. The outcry is against that system which exploits the individual who gives himself to death, as well as to life, with such tragic eagerness.

Probably the most bitter expression of this thesis comes in *Mask of Glory*, whose irony begins with its title. Sergeant Lewicki survives the Pacific war and returns to look up the parents of Glenn Manson. Talking to Glenn's brother, Lewicki says bitterly that all the straight young men, who "needed so much to be heroes," believed the propaganda of the "big shots" who sat safely at home urging patriots to their deaths. The youngsters fought and died and asked nothing for their heroism. "Treated like dogs, killed like flies . . . it's a mortal sin if a country sends its best young kids out, scared as hell and not knowing from nothing but volunteering, taking it on faith because they love their country so much—and it sends them out to be killed like flies dumped in a ditch, and then it just goes ahead and lets everything start all over again, the same way it was."

The bitterness here is not so much existential or cosmic as it is specific—social—directed against a country that "lets everything start all over again, the same way it was." The young heroes who go off to war have a capacity for a high intensity of individual experience. It isn't that nature itself is so disordered that they are denied their self-fulfillment, it is the particular conditions of war and the army organization. There is a sense of having been betrayed by a present world which destroys rather than cultivates individual uniqueness. Give the hero a land where he could be himself, free of the suffocating apparatus, and he can achieve his fulfillment.

And for all the pessimism in these stories, many of the war novelists do just that. The leftist spokesmen of social protest during the Depression envisioned a socialistic utopia, in which the proletarian might live out his life in dignity, love, and equality, in which part of his satisfaction comes in the personal contributions he might make to the order of his life and to other subjects. Such was the society envisioned, too, by Mannheim, Jaspers, and Whitehead. And such is the society envisioned by the socio-political war novelist. Ironically the utopia is combat; its citizen is the hero. In spite of its brutality combat gives the hero a freedom unknown to the rear echelon soldier. Under fire there is no inequality, no oppression, no jealousies. Captain Mike Andrews, in *Victory Also Ends,* after having been in Florence on a brief leave, wishes desperately to be back in action with his men. "No matter what they say about the war . . . up front it's honest and it's freer of phonies, fraud and selfishness than any other place on earth. False fronts won't stand up here, and it's almost worth the killing to find things that way."

The combat soldier hero is different from other men. It is not merely that he has faced personal danger, but that he has faced it with other men, in a way that changes him, contributes to his growth—and perishing. This feature of the war was seized upon early by almost all the war novelists, whether they took on political and social themes or not. Frederic Wakeman's narrator in *Shore Leave,* reflects upon the group of Navy fliers he has accompanied to San Francisco: "A fighting man is a very special fellow—and because he exists for destruction and lives with death, he can only be completely understood by his fellow-specialists who have met his own test of battle. Fighting, like flying, is a brotherhood. Although I had seen a little action, more as a spectator, I was not of the brotherhood of these combat fliers."[11]

Fighting itself is not glorified when the novelists are defining this "brotherhood of combat."[12] They concentrate upon what happens emotionally to the men fighting. Combat becomes a rare experience, whose participants find in it a means of scraping away all the preconceptions about existence and getting down to their own authentic selves. It is the throwing off of their identification with the persona: the front tolerates no "fronts." There is an aura of spirituality here that is sometimes so intense that the fighting soldier is virtually beatified. Major Harrod thinks of the heartaches suffered by a company commander. But in return for those heartaches "a company commander gets the reward of war that only

GI's understand, though none of them could describe it. This thing is something beyond what we mean by the words loyalty, comradeship, exaltation, pity, love, self-sacrifice. It is beyond words at all. It can be known only to those who experience it, the small percentage of actual combat troops in the huge armies of the modern world. . . . It's something that is given freely by one man to the other and all to the unit. . . . Sergeant Vorak always has it. This is what has put those lines so strangely like sainthood in Vorak's face. This is what is hidden behind the noisy bitching of a man like Selig. In the selflessness of an old hand like Boyce. . . . I doubt if General Mallon ever caught a glimpse of it."

The combat soldier participates in and helps create the ideally ordered society through his voluntary contributions to the group. The threat of physical death does not, in this case, inhibit self-realization; the apparatus does that. Combat and combat soldiers are regarded as models of the real America and the real American in these novels. This vision sees an America that is an amalgam of free and equal individuals who, while retaining the integrity of their own souls, work for the common good. The army with its inequities and restraints is a microcosm of an America riddled with prejudice and oppression, closing men's possibilities. Combat seen as a brotherhood is a microcosm of what America might be. The celebration of the hero in combat is nothing less than an expression of the deepest patriotism in novels that on the surface seem to be devoted to criticism. Stefan Heym puts his patriotism in wholly explicit terms. The German had been defeated at the Bulge.

> He was defeated by men. They were average men, without rank and name. But they had that remarkable American quality: They were able to put down their foot and say, *Wait a minute, Bud. Don't push us around. Let's see what this is all about.* Perhaps they didn't say it in these words. But they felt it, and they acted on it, and they stood fast, and many of them gave their lives. And this collective attitude came in spite of the difference in personal background—in spite of the fact that some didn't know what it was all about, and what the Bulge Battle meant; that some of them did; that most were afraid, and few weren't; that all of them were miserable and cold and tired and worn with nerves frazzled. In the hour of crisis, they proved themselves citizens of the Republic.

The hero is a "citizen of the Republic" in a way that neither the authoritarian nor the intellectual can ever be. The combat man stands firm, acts upon his convictions without wasting time talking about the moral values involved. Thus, after the cynicism and the bitterness, after the attacks upon the businessman and capitalism, these war novelists turn out to be patriots, confident of the People, proud of the "forgotten man," and given to idealizing a way of life uniquely American—a way of life based upon the concept of the individual as an end in himself. The fullest formulation of this combat utopia is made by Irwin Shaw. As Michael Whitacre makes his way toward the front with the battle-scarred Noah in the lead, he thinks,

> Somewhere just ahead of him . . . under the constant trembling of the artillery among the hills, he was going to find that America he had never known on its own continent, a tortured and dying America, but an America of friends and neighbors, an America in which a man could finally put away his over-civilized doubts, his book-soured cynicism, his realistic despair. . . . Noah . . . had already found that country, and it was plain in the quiet, assured way he spoke to sergeants and to Generals alike. The exiles, living in mud and fear of death, had, in one way at least, found a better home than those from which they had been driven, a blood-spattered Utopia, now on the fringe of German soil, where no man was rich and none poor, a shell-burst democracy where all living was a community enterprise, where all food was distributed according to need and not according to pocket, where light, heat, lodging, transportation, medical attention, and funeral benefits were at the cost of the government and available with absolute impartiality to white and black, Jew and Gentile, worker and owner, where the means of production, in this case M1's, 30 caliber machine guns, 90's, 105's, 204's, mortars, bazookas, were in the hands of the masses; that ultimate Christian socialism in which all worked for the common good and the only leisure class were the dead.

This combat Utopia, in spite of its dangers, opens more possibilities for subjective satisfaction than the rigid hierarchical society of the rear lines. Most of the metaphysical principles of the "open decision" are put into play in this utopia. Here the individual is freed from compulsive behavior, liberated from the strict determinism of the past, and allowed to feel, to love, to honor the value of others regardless of class or race. The preferred America is the land of combat, a tragic alternative to the regimented society of fascism. The front, as Glenn Manson came to feel, was a place "where Americans were made."

In the second group of war novels I include Mitchell Goodman's *The End of It*, Joseph Heller's *Catch-22*, James Jones's *The Thin Red Line*, Stephen Linakis's *The Spring the War Ended*, George Mandel's *The Wax Boom*, and James E. Ross's *The Dead Are Mine*.[13] These novels relate ideologically to the first group in their assumption that the army apparatus destroys the individual, but they are more notable for their differences. Except for Mitchell Goodman's novel, they drop the preoccupation with business and politics. The earlier pattern of the socio-political novels, with their authoritarian, intellectual, and hero, dissolves into a simpler pattern of hero against the apparatus. Combat ceases to be an ennobling brotherhood and becomes the tool by which the apparatus exploits the helpless individual. The change in attitude toward combat is accompanied by a disappearance of the intense patriotism that characterized so many early war novels. These later novelists concentrate more upon what the individual does in his own behalf rather than upon the way in which America can be made democratic. Seldom does the hero of the socio-political novel defy the apparatus outright and refuse to fight. He is too patriotic. The hero of these later novels is characterized by his defiance. He seeks to survive without surrendering his self and he finds that he can do that only by saying "no" to the apparatus, and that takes the form of refusing to fight any longer.

The differences and the similarities between these two groups of novels are most clearly seen in *The End of It*. On the surface this novel appears to be socio-political in the same sense as the first group was. Even more explicitly than Jones and Calmer, Goodman[14] makes the army out to be a corporation, the generals to be businessmen, and the men workers. His professed theme is the dehumanization of men by the machine. All the trappings of the socio-political war novel are here: the army is "one of the biggest corporations the world had ever seen." The soldiers, like laborers, mark time at their boring jobs; the generals, captains of industry, are "impatient to practice their trade. . . . Business is business." Working with the big guns of the artillery is "like working in a factory." The explosion of a gun barrel which kills several men is merely "an industrial accident." The war "begins as a mission: to save the world. It ends as another victory for the machine." The hero of the novel, ironically named Lieutenant Gilbert Freeman, hates his assignment to the artillery. He wants to be up in the front lines—and in this he links himself with his precursors: "up there, the mystery: men walking through fire, at one, the at-one-ment of living and dying together. Each separate man, not chained to the machine: one man and one man and one man, together. . . ."

The problem with these symbols in this particular book is that they do not really express what is on Goodman's mind. They are imposed by the author; they do not rise naturally out of the action. The action shows no conflict between the protagonist and the machines except the conflict that Goodman tells us is there. The narrative of *The End of It* is a very simple one. It traces, through scenes conveyed by a kind of static impressionism, scenes presented by symbols rather than coherent action, the slow advance of the American army and Lieutenant Freeman through Italy. The end of the narrative is not the result of conflict between man and machine.

Lieutenant Freeman has gone beyond the front lines as a forward artillery observer to direct the big guns upon a German regiment. His informants are some Italian partisans. From his perch in the hills above the valley where the regiment is bivouacked, he radios back the coordinates and orders the guns to commence firing. At the moment he does so he realizes that only the officers of the unit are German; the soldiers are Italian Fascists. They have been betrayed, Freeman realizes with horror, by their own countrymen. The regiment is slaughtered, to the satisfaction of the partisans. But Freeman is numbed by what he sees and he withdraws into a kind of symbolical death. At a hospital he is sent even deeper into psychological shock by the callous and morbid nurses who question him about the details of the slaughter. Finally he is sent to a small Italian village as an occupation officer. Here he is awakened from his dark night of the soul by the Italians, simple and joyful, who have endured the war. They welcome him with childlike hospitality, smiling at him, seizing his hands, touching him. Suddenly, in the midst of these spontaneous human beings, "There was strength in his hands; the blood beat fast in his body; he was warm. Warm and cold, as if he were a corpse being warmed into life by the sun." By the last line of the book, Lieutenant Freeman has discovered that "Many were dead, but he was not dead."

The real crisis in Lieutenant Freeman's life has nothing to do with the elaborate symbolical warnings against the business corporation and machine. He is shocked by something very simple: seeing humans die and realizing that some of them were the victims of their own countrymen. The implications of Goodman's novel illustrate the difference a decade has made in the way the war was depicted. Freeman, though he pays lip service to the brotherhood of infantry combat, finds no ties in war, only dehumanizing terror. The important point is that he is resurrected. He circumvents the apparatus in his madness and survives, not as a creature of the machine, but as a human being among other human beings.

Defiance is not always rewarded with success in these novels. Those by Mandel, Ross, and Linakis[15] hark back to earlier novels of the war which show tremendous resentment of an incompetent officer class. In *The Wax Boom*, "A" Troop's Captain Stollman is awarded a Silver Star for the action of his unit in France; he supposedly masterminded the operation, but because of his ineptness, two good combat men are unnecessarily killed. Disgusted to see such a man rewarded, the book's protagonist, Sal Riglioni, turns in his sergeant's stripes and refuses to fight any more. The men, sullen and filthy, follow his lead. They have been driven to the edge of insanity by their unconscionably long exposure to combat and have taken to melting down the wax religious figures they find in the French houses and churches. Making candles out of the wax, they hole up in an abandoned house and sit around staring at their flames, like madmen. When various rearline officers appear to urge them to take up their arms again, the men threaten to shoot them. Hypnotized by their candles, the men in "A" Troop lose their alertness and are destroyed by the advancing Germans. They have virtually committed suicide.

The apparatus is named as the cause of their death—not simply the army organization, but the whole society that creates it. One of the survivors, Gingold, rails against a psychiatrist who is trying to learn why the men had quit. They had been "turned into wax by hypocrites," says Gingold, by a society full of "happy affirmers . . . whose basic characteristic is an inability ever to detect in your own bloodstream the cold neon tube of falseness." Sal realizes from the beginning that the greatest danger is not getting killed by the Germans but getting caught in the "chain-of-command," in the "institution," which appeals to his "blind, murderous lust to survive." It is clearly not the "lust to survive" that drives Sal to refuse to fight, but a rejection of his role as a tool of the apparatus. His friend Lieutenant Enshaw adduces "expedient fascism." Sal is not bucking simply men, says Enshaw, but an institution: "Stollman, Simmons, they can't fight it any more than you can. Because to fight it you have to disown it, and none of us are about to join the Nazis." This is precisely the point upon which the socio-political novelist stuck. He tended to accept Enshaw's reasoning and found an escape through seeing combat as utopia. But for Sal, joining the Nazis is not the only alternative. When he defies the system he feels no guilt.

The hero of *The Dead Are Mine,* Terry Lewis, is like Sal Riglioni: courageous, skillful as a combat man, devoted to his comrades, and bitterly resentful of the superior officers who expose him and his buddies to destruction while they prosper. Terry is ordered by his platoon commander to take his squad on an unnecessary mission. The officer fails to inform the artillery of Terry's location and in the barrage all but Terry are wiped out. Like Riglioni, and for the same reasons, Terry "quits." But in a paradox which Ross does not, I think, intend, the apparatus, in the form of Terry's battalion commander, recognizes Terry's contributions as a combat man and saves him from a court martial. He is assigned to Graves Registration and given the job of collecting and cataloguing American dead.

He continues his rebellion when he unearths a supply of Italian wine. One of his main resentments is the preferential treatment given officers in such things as a relatively plentiful liquor ration. So instead of turning the wine over to his superiors, he distributes it to the enlisted men. His strong sense of morality is concentrated in his dedication to the American dogface, the individual fighting soldier. When he surprises a rear echelon American trying to steal a ring off the finger of one of the corpses, he beats the man unmercifully. When a German spits on an American corpse, he shoots down not only the offender, but three other prisoners too. Terry Lewis is an angry man, hating the easy self-serving hypocrisy of the officers and men who refuse to respect the individual. Finally, he accepts reassignment to combat where, after all, he feels more comfortable, and on his first mission he is killed.

Ross does not quite manage to make Terry's death anything but fortuitous, as though he had to kill him off simply because he could find no other way to end the novel. It does not result from any series of occurrences that illustrate the main conflict. Nor does his rebelliousness produce any clear results; it is not because of his defiance that he dies. This loose end is the major weakness of the novel.

Nick Leonidas, of *The Spring the War Ended,* is more systematically and effectively angry than either Sal Riglioni or Terry Lewis. His defiance takes the form of criminality which Linakis attempts to imbue with the colors of a higher morality than the laws of the U.S. Army. During a battle in the Hurtgen Forest, Nick goes AWOL. As Linakis presents it, this is neither dishonorable nor uncommon. Nick is justified because as a combat man he has been outrageously exploited. Only a few men, maintains Nick, did the actual fighting while the noncombat men got the rewards. "Some had the mistaken notion that millions were fighting, or that Eisenhower was fighting. The only thing Eisenhower fought was his desk. There were millions all right, all behind us, supporting our rear, strutting like soldiers, but they were not soldiers at all." The combat man takes all the shock of the actual fighting but never gets the attention received by the rear echelon soldier. "During the war, a dogface never saw a U.S.O. show like Benny or Bergman. That was only for troops that did not do the fighting. . . . Morale was very high at SHAEF. They were hiding in a chateau nearly four hundred kilometers behind us when we had our asses torn at the Hurtgen."

It is not simply that the combat man is not given his due, but that once in combat he is kept there. Nick is on the lines for a solid six months. He feels no allegiance to a society which rewards the drones and penalizes the producers. His anger finally breaks out during the Hurtgen campaign, when everything goes wrong. The men are caught in a murderous artillery barrage. "That," says Nick, "was when you saw your infantry taking off, going AWOL by squads, yelling their heads off, 'Fuck the war! Fuck the lousy war!' and nobody tried to stop them." It is this categorical rejection of the whole project of the apparatus that characterizes this second group of war novels. Why should these men not go AWOL, Linakis is asking. What obligation do they have to a system which sought always to destroy them? Linakis has Nick say in a documentary tone that our combat soldiers quit in disgusted droves so that "damned near a fifth to a quarter of the actual front line was over the hump." These are the bearers of life—rebellion—against death.

When Nick goes AWOL, he becomes an outlaw, but Linakis invests him with the legendary quality of the famous outlaws of the past—Robin Hood, Jesse James, Joaquin Murietta—driven to lawbreaking by an insufferable oppressor. He takes up with other AWOL's in Brussels, impersonating officers, stealing from supply depots, working on the black market, deliberately getting into scuffles with the MP's. But the army is always on the lookout for him and eventually his hatred of it delivers him into its hands. But before he is caught, the point has been made; it is more moral to rebel than to surrender.

None of these men succeeds in his rebellion and there seems to be more personal bitterness in the making of these stories than thoughtful assessment of the situation. A slightly more positive, as well as more intelligent note is struck by James Jones in *The Thin Red Line.* In this story of the army on Guadalcanal, the familiar themes occur. Lieutenant Stein, commanded by his superior to deploy his men in a murderously dangerous area, realizes that today he will obey the order (though eventually he defies it) and tomorrow it will be someone else obeying it. He sees all the inhabitants of the world running to their deaths at the command of some authority, all doing the same thing and all "devoutly and proudly believing themselves to be free individuals. . . . It was the concept—concept? the fact; the reality—of the modern State in action." Storm, the mess sergeant who accidentally gets into one of the battles, finds in it no "pageant," "spectacle," "challenge," or "adventure" for the frontline soldier. Everybody but the officers who run the battles "was a tool—a tool with its serial number of manufacture stamped right on it. And Storm didn't like being no tool."

Neither Stein nor Storm finds in combat a noble but blood-spattered utopia. They do not rebel in the same angry way that Nick Leonidas does, but they do conclude, along with Lieutenant Freeman, that to survive is better than to die and that survival does not necessarily mean surrendering to the apparatus. Some who scramble for life are cowards. Others, like Stein and Storm, have proved their courage and found that it is not worth it. Relieved of his command when he fails to obey an order, Stein wonders later if he acted in order to save himself rather than his men. At the bottom of his concern is what his father will think, who loved to tell stories about his own heroism in World War I. Then he realizes that he does not care at all what his father thinks, concluding with some astonishment that "Men changed their wars in the years that followed after they fought them, made them more glorious, made the alternatives simpler." Patriotism and morality are qualities imposed upon combat after the battle is over. To die for one's country is an act made into a noble abstraction by those who do not die. Many people would live through the war, Stein sees now, and he "intended to be one of those if he could."

Stein does not retreat or expect others to fight the war for him. The validity of the war is not an issue for him. He simply finds in combat no compensation for its horror, as many of the earlier heroes did. If he can survive, he is going to; for the dead there is no meaning in brotherhood. Storm comes to see things as Stein does. Having acquitted himself well in combat, Storm now has the choice of returning to the front lines or to his kitchen. He feels no tie with the men he fought with and no urge to rejoin them. He decides to stay with the kitchen. He does not, as he has said, like to be a tool; nor does he like the idea of dying in a conflict that would be followed by an eventual union of the combatants: ". . . many more people were going to live through this war than got killed in it; . . . as soon as it was over all the nations involved would start helping each other and be friends again, except for the dead. And Storm—[Stein] like him—did not feel at all guilty" for withdrawing from combat.

For Jones (almost exactly ten years after his first socio-political novel), as for most of the novelists in this group, there is no compensation for being caught fighting in the apparatus's battle. Those who get a warm feeling of comradeship out of combat are those who are least exposed to it. They are also the most cowardly. Corporal Fife, as Lieutenant Stein's clerk, does practically no fighting, and when he is exposed to fire he cringes ineffectually. He is promoted to squad leader when several of the original leaders are killed and immediately he feels a sentimental "protective love" for his men and is certain they reciprocate. But Fife is not the selfless warrior that Major Harrod describes in *The Strange Land*. He is a vain little martinet, held in contempt by his men, and more worried about his status with the other squad leaders than about the members of his unit. Combat makes men more animal-like. They help each other not out of any sense of brotherhood but because they know their own lives may some day depend upon what they do for someone else. They gather together in little cliques of two or three men, hating the other cliques, and shifting from one to another with the suddenness of petulant children. The men of Charlie Company have little *esprit de corps*. They get drunk after a battle and, on their hands and knees, bay like wolves at the moon, get into fights with each other, and stagger to the tent of their new company commander to tell him how much they hate him. There is no saintliness here, no brotherhood, no cooperative utopia—only debasement and degradation.

With Joseph Heller's *Catch-22*, the theme that lies only partly formed in these novels is fully developed and given a positive conclusion—the theme of survival through defiance. Heller claims that his novel does not attack the war or question its legitimacy; it deals with "contemporary, regimented society." His satire is directed against the institutions that make up this society, business, psychiatry, medicine, law, the military, assuming, as he says, that certain people and social groups act the same in war as they do in peace. These institutions form that familiar entity, the apparatus, which operates according to the principle of "Catch-22." Better than almost any other single war novel, *Catch-22* illustrates the main issues of the "open decision," laying out clearly the factors which inhibit its highest good and suggesting ways in which those factors can be overcome.

"Catch-22" is the law which the apparatus uses to bind the individual to only those possibilities which strengthen the society rather than the individual. The book's protagonist, Yossarian, is a bombardier serving in Italy, who spends most of his time devising ways to get out of combat. He asks Doc Daneeka if a man can be grounded if he is insane. Such a man can be grounded, says Doc, but he must first submit a request to be grounded; this is the catch —Catch-22. If a man does submit such a request, that is clear evidence he is not insane. Only the insane voluntarily continue to fly. This is an almost perfect catch because the law is in the definition of insanity. To see it, one must be able to step outside of the system. When Yossarian tries to understand the nature of Catch-22 he is reminded that he also does not understand Orr's claim that Appleby has flies in his eyes. Appleby cannot see them himself because they are in *his* eyes; the system is closed. Appleby's flies and, by analogy, Catch-22 are a parody of the epistemology of relativity. Measuring instruments in one system "change" when that system speeds up or slows down relative to another system, but the change can never be detected by the system's instruments, for they will measure only themselves. The change, furthermore, is intelligible only with the postulation of another system.

Appleby's flies are a metaphor of Catch-22, and Catch-22 is the great social tautology that imprisons every individual who takes it as a natural absolute and does not see that it is a kind of language-game. As with measuring rods and clocks, Catch-22 shrinks or expands, speeds up or slows down, to cover the situation, obscuring its own relativity. An old Italian woman tells Yossarian that the Army has run all of her prostitute daughters out of Rome, leaving her penniless. The authority for the action is Catch-22, which says, according to the old woman, that "they have a right to do anything we can't stop them from doing." Yossarian is outraged. Did they show her a paper explaining Catch-22? "They don't have to show us Catch-22," she answers. "The law says they don't have to." What law? asks Yossarian. "Catch-22." Catch-22 is the way in which Heller expresses his understanding of the old view of reality and shows how that old view comes to invest the social apparatus with absolute power over those who are taken in. It comically exemplifies how solipsism can be taken as an objective absolute. Those who do not see its relativity become bound to it as prisoners, performing its commands in a way that reduces the avenues which, as more spontaneous beings, they might pursue.

Catch-22 promulgates values that serve itself rather than the individual. Yossarian senses that something is not quite right but does not see clearly what it is. He knows that there is a contradiction between the values of Catch-22 and his own values. Catch-22 says that the highest value is the preservation of the system, expressed in words like Patriotism and Service, which recalls the theories of Jones's Sam Slater. Yossarian says that the highest value is his own survival, stating with comic explicitness what most of these other later war novels state with a sense of seriousness. "Ex-Pfc." Wintergreen, an immensely influential clerk who profits on the black market, supports the *status quo* preserved by Catch-22. He maintains that it is Yossarian's job to make his bombing runs even though it endangers his life. "Why can't you be a fatalist about it the way I am?" says Wintergreen. "If I'm destined to unload these lighters at a profit . . . then that's what I'm going to do. And if you're destined to be killed over Bologna, then you're going to be killed, so you might just as well go out and die like a man." The tone in which Wintergreen speaks is ambiguous. He both knows that he is exploiting a situation profitable to himself at the expense of another man and deludes himself that what is good for him has the force of objective morality. He is acting in "bad faith." Another form of bad faith is that practiced by Clevinger, the patriot who regards risking his life for his country as an objectively valid moral position. He is in bad faith because he sees no alternatives, because he lives the role given him by the apparatus. He accepts without examining them the values that favor the system.

When Clevinger asks Yossarian whether winning the war or staying alive is more important, he isolates one of the main problems that confronted both groups of war novelists. The earlier group concluded, in general, that, tragic though it was, winning the war took precedence over saving individual lives. Yossarian shows the way the second group has widened the problem by answering Clevinger's question with another: "Important to whom?" "It doesn't make a damned bit of difference *who* wins the war to someone who's dead." As Yossarian sees it, whoever wants to kill him is the enemy. When his commanding officer, Colonel Cathcart, sends him into skies filled with flak, the Colonel is as much an enemy as the Germans. In Yossarian's eyes, the apparatus obscures its status as enemy by justifying its use of individuals on the grounds of its own values. It is like writing a book of laws to legalize one's behavior, then citing that book as proof of the behavior's legality. The only way that the circular justifications of Catch-22 can be dealt with is by breaking out of the circle. Yossarian moves toward that break with his question, Important to whom? He completes it by deciding to desert.

Throughout most of the book Yossarian behaves according to Whitehead's proposition that without the living subject there is nothing, nothing, nothing. Heller's presentation of the conflict between this subject and the society that attempts to kill it claims, in principle, that right is on the side of the subject. But in specific instances the conflict is not simple. In principle, to defy the apparatus appeals to our sense of individual values. But to make that defiance more than cowardice and selfishness is a difficult task, and Heller does not quite succeed in being convincing. If Yossarian quits, what are the possible consequences? He may gain his freedom, and that is good. But he may also contribute to a Nazi victory, which would cancel out his own gains. Even worse, he leaves his buddies to do the fighting for him. He says that it is no fight of his and deserts. The contention that nothing can be important to a dead man, however true, cannot justify a man's running off from the field of battle to let others die in his place. The "open decision" is not an invitation to evading one's responsibility to other humans.

Heller realizes this, and tries to justify Yossarian's decision to desert. His attempt, unfortunately, saps Yossarian of all his zany vitality and destroys the comic tone of the book. In a conversation with Major Danby, Yossarian adduces arguments in support of the morality of his deserting. He says that he has done his part; now it is time for someone else to do his. "I earned the medal I got, no matter what their reasons for giving it to me. I've flown seventy goddam combat missions. Don't talk to me about fighting to save my country. Now I'm going to fight a little to save myself. The country's not in danger any more, but I am." If he were to die now, says Yossarian, it would not be for America, but for the hated officers of the hated apparatus. The assumption is that dying for one's country is, under certain circumstances, worthwhile, but nothing in the rest of the novel supports this as a basic principle. The war is insane and brutal, says most of the novel, and the people who perpetuate it are equally insane and brutal. It kills and maims the helpless on both sides, and makes millionaires and bemedaled heroes out of the callous and the stupid.

In spite of the discrepancy between Yossarian's argument with Major Danby and the rest of the novel, what Heller wants to do links him with the other war novelists in this group. He wants to provide a way in which Yossarian can survive both the spiritual death of submitting to the system and the physical death of combat. Heller hints at one way to do this which would make Yossarian's desertion unnecessary and maintain the comic atmosphere of the novel at the same time. When all of his attempts to get grounded have failed, Yossarian simply refuses to fly. Like Sal Riglioni and Nick Leonidas, he says "no" to the apparatus while remaining within it. His rebellion affects the other men in his squadron profoundly. Colonel Korn tells Yossarian that the men had been "content to fly as many missions as we asked as long as they thought they had no alternative. Now you've given them hope, and they're unhappy." Alternatives, as so frequently suggested in Part I, establish freedom. And Yossarian might have led the men in a break from the system. A mass sit-down strike by all the airmen on the base would have been in keeping with other outrageous improbabilities which so delight the reader in the rest of the book. And what simpler solution to the insanity of following a safe general's order to expose themselves to death by killing others than for all the soldiers in actual combat—on both sides—to refuse to fight? It is sad to think that such behavior can only be regarded as a comic improbability. But Heller does not pose this solution.

Because Yossarian is causing so much trouble refusing to fly, Korn and Cathcart tell him he can go home without a court martial if he does not reveal their part. At first Yossarian agrees, but when he realizes he has sold his soul to the apparatus, he withdraws from the conspiracy. To go home under those conditions, he says, would be to "lose" himself. At this point, Heller provides a gloss on the theme of the novel. In the course of the narrative, occasional references are made to Snowden, a young gunner whose insides are shot out as his plane flies over Italy and who dies in Yossarian's arms. The experience profoundly affects Yossarian. As the narrative advances, the reader is given longer and longer glimpses of the incident. But not until Yossarian decides to try another way of getting out of combat than to agree with Korn and Cathcart do we get Snowden's full story. As the boy whimpers, "I'm cold," Yossarian, horrified, sees his entrails slither to the floor. There is a message in those entrails that teaches Yossarian, finally, what he must do. The message reads: "Man was matter, that was Snowden's secret. Drop him out of a window and he'll fall. Set fire to him and he'll burn. Bury him and he'll rot like other kinds of garbage. The spirit gone, man is garbage." Man is spirit, as Scheler suggests. Stifle that spirit and you kill the man. Combat kills and discloses man's frailty. But there is also death in the apparatus. Were Yossarian to accept a deal with Korn and Cathcart he would be co-operating with the apparatus in the stifling of his own spirit. He would, as I have said, "lose" himself, become submerged in the "they." He must, therefore, defy Korn and Cathcart, seize upon an "alternative." As he sees it, the only viable alternative is desertion. Its validity and its high probability of success is demonstrated when the Chaplain brings news that Orr, who had been thought lost at sea after a bombing raid, has turned up safely in Sweden. Yossarian suddenly understands what Orr has been trying to show him throughout the novel—the possibility of breaking out, of seizing a new vantage point. Orr provides Yossarian with an alternative, an "or." For months Orr had one mishap after another, almost every one involving his ditching his airplane at sea. Now Yossarian realizes that Orr was simply practicing. The practice paid off; Orr is free.

But for Yossarian to desert to Sweden, says Danby, would be running away from his responsibilities. On the contrary, says Yossarian, echoing the values of the "open decision," he would be running to, not from, responsibilities. Away from the rigid pattern of the apparatus's data, he will be thrown upon his spontaneous self. Those who submit to the apparatus are the ones shirking their responsibility. Again, Danby warns that Yossarian's conscience will bother him. Yossarian answers with the typical individualistic thesis: "I wouldn't want to live without strong misgivings." Those who do live without misgivings, he implies, live in false consciousness, deluding themselves that the apparatus makes all well. They are, as Mandel's Gingold says, "happy affirmers" who are blind to their own falseness. At last Danby gives up trying to dissuade Yossarian: "You'll have to keep on your toes every minute of the day. They'll bend heaven and earth to catch you." "I'll jump," says Yossarian.

Yossarian discovers that Catch-22 is not necessarily the way things have to be, that one can break out of the system because its rules are not absolute. The chaplain provides another means by which this can be accomplished than by escape. The novel opens with the line, "It was love at first sight," which refers to Yossarian's instant liking for the chaplain. Their affection for each other links them in such a way as to establish them as two aspects of the same thing—defiance of the army organization. The chaplain is a young Anabaptist who comes into the outfit a timid, doubting man, afraid of the superior officers and not quite sure God exists. His great strength is his humanity. As Yossarian's determination to escape grows, the chaplain gains confidence in his struggle with the apparatus's officers to reduce the number of required missions. When he hears of Yossarian's plan to go AWOL, the chaplain cheers him on. As for himself, "I'll stay here and persevere. Yes. I'll persevere. I'll nag and badger Colonel Cathcart and Colonel Korn every time I see them. I'm not afraid. . . . If Orr can row to Sweden, then I can triumph over Colonel Cathcart and Colonel Korn, if I only persevere."

It is proper that the chaplain be the one to elect this course, for he is not a combat man and so his physical life is not threatened by staying. His form of defiance is resoluteness in the face of the apparatus, the determination of the authentic self to preserve its uniqueness. The chaplain qualifies the method of what seems like anarchy pursued by Orr and Yossarian. He will remain within the system, endangered only psychologically. Through the chaplain Heller suggests that going away is only a start; permanent withdrawal is not the ultimate solution to the threat of the apparatus. The chaplain is Yossarian's tie with the society that now threatens his physical life. He stays and perseveres, but says that he and Yossarian will "meet again when the fighting stops." Yossarian's escape will allow him to save himself from his immediate threat, to take up, as well, a "saner relationship" to the system's institutions. The chaplain's perseverance allows him to retain his spontaneous self in the midst of a society that would rigidly channel it. Heller promises that flight and perseverance will lead to a proper relationship between the individual and his society, a relationship which, as Jaspers advocates, will allow the self to live in harmony with the apparatus without being overwhelmed by it. In order to triumph, however, both the chaplain and Yossarian will have to "jump."

The principle of Catch-22 is a metaphor of the "world" of Husserl which must be bracketed, the "inauthenticity" of Heidegger, the "bad faith" of Sartre, the "false consciousness" of Mannheim, the refusal of the scientist to acknowledge all evidence. By deserting, Yossarian will scrape away all of those restrictions, prejudices, and preconceptions that confine him in a shell of reduced possibilities. Thus, Yossarian, like most of the other protagonists discussed in this chapter, seeks to preserve his authentic self against a suffocating system. The earlier war novelist resigns himself to the assumption that the apparatus will eventually claim the individual's physical life, but not his humanity. They tend to concentrate, therefore, upon the virtues of the hero, who experiences the stream of life, takes up internal ties with others, and lives in his own novel way most intensively in combat. The later war novelists write at the end of a decade of unprecedented prosperity and complacency, in which those who had suffered insecurity during the Depression years, welcomed with something near obsession an economic security due in some part to the growth of industry during the war. Accompanying that security was the growth of what President Eisenhower called in his farewell address in 1960 the "military-industrial complex," precisely the beginnings of an apparatus against which Karl Jaspers and the earlier war novelists warned. The later war novelists help to usher in the rebellion of the 'sixties against that complex and all it stands for. They emphasize the need to survive, and their method is through defiance. Heller carries that defiance against the military hierarchy—the symbol in all these novels for a rigid society—to its most positive end. He focuses upon the need to break with the present, as Sartre might say, and then suggests how that break might be accomplished. All the war novelists, both early and late, are concerned with the integrity of the individual and the morality of the society in which he lives. They tacitly assume the values of the "open decision": that the individual must be free to grow toward his own novel end and that the society he lives in be based on the principle of contrast, not upon rigidity or conflict. The business novelist also focuses on these issues, and it is to the business novel that I now turn.

5

THE BUSINESS NOVEL: THE TYCOON AND THE TORTURED THINKER

WORLD WAR II was an immense experience for the young writers who lived through its dark years, and it occupied a large amount of their attention into the early 1950s. Then in 1952 General Dwight Eisenhower was elected President and he carried with him to the White House the determination to establish a "businessman's cabinet." Here was an ironic fulfillment, it seemed, of one of the prophecies of the early socio-political war novelist. The army general, frequently linked by the war novelists with the businessman, seemed literally to be setting up an alliance between two huge and powerful institutions for governing the country. Would not this result in a social apparatus so rigid as to limit unduly the freedom and awareness necessary to the realization of the highest good? Would not such an apparatus reduce the vividness of one's sense of individuality, binding men mentally as well as physically to values and forms of behavior preestablished by a society inimical to spontaneity?

The sociological literature of the post-World War II era seems to answer these questions in the affirmative. David Riesman's *The Lonely Crowd* and William H. Whyte's *The Organization Man,* prototypes of this literature, turn from the theory-building of the first several decades of the century to more specific studies of classes of people working at their jobs and going home to their radios and television sets. Both of these books are heavily indebted to writers like Cooley, Weber, Mannheim, Fromm, and

For Notes to Chapter 5, see pages 403–404.

Scheler for their basic sociological theory, but their conclusions do not so much express plans and suggestions about how to provide an auspicious environment for men's self-fulfillment as they present evidence that the human being in the post-war world has lost his struggle to remain unique, has surrendered to the apparatus. Riesman's *The Lonely Crowd* declares that ours is a society of "other-directed" people, with their sensitive antennae out to pick up their directions for behavior from a mass-society made up of other persons with identical antennae employed in identical actions. Society in general reflects business in particular. Whyte's organization man does not seek an intensity of novel experience or expose himself to the risks of the "open decision." He retreats to the bosom of the large corporation and there exchanges his painful authenticity for the comfortable security of the collective mold of commercial certainty and unimaginativeness.

The individualistic hero of the war novel, if we are to believe the social commentators of the 1950s, succumbed to the gray "theyness" of business. He becomes, in Whyte's words, "the well-rounded man: obtrusive in no particular, excessive in no zeal." He has ambition, but not very much; he desires to advance, but not to assume the inevitable burdens of responsibility that go with advancement. He has adopted the "social ethic"—what Whyte calls "that contemporary body of thought which makes morally legitimate the pressures of society against the individual."[1] One of the principal executors of this ethic is the large corporation, that safe and unadventurous home allegedly sought for by so many of the "silent" college generation. There the organization men harvest the fruits of the social ethic they have internalized. "The Corporation," writes Vance Packard, "tames people, clips their wings. Those who stay . . . feel a shrinkage of impulse, inventiveness, desire."[2] According to the sociological writers, the war novelists seem to have been accurate in their warnings. Americans flocked to volunteer their souls to the business of America, the establishment of a complacency that dulls the sense of one's own individuality and thus works in opposition to the highest good. The angry determination to defend the last inviolable stronghold of the self against the apparatus, it was said, disappeared. By 1960, Eugene V. Rostow could write that "one is struck by the atmosphere of relative peace. There seems to be no general conviction abroad that reform is needed. The vehement feelings of the early thirties, expressing a sense of betrayal and frustration at a depression blamed on twelve years of business leadership, are almost entirely absent."[3]

Whyte declares that the values of the social ethic were picked up by many American novelists and celebrated as the foundation of the preferred situation. For example, Sloan Wilson's *The Man in the Gray Flannel Suit*,[4] says Whyte, is an almost perfect case study of the organization man. And indeed the novel does seem to be just that. Tom Rath, Wilson's protagonist, goes to work for the United Broadcasting Company, writing speeches for Mr. Hopkins, the company president. Mr. Hopkins is a prototype of the big businessman who is the apotheosis of the "protestant" as opposed to the "social" ethic. He has virtually illimitable energy and is possessed by a demon which drives him to work fifteen hours a day. Men like him have built the great companies which employ men like Tom Rath. In the eyes of the organization man, the Hopkinses are rather strange exotic birds, operating in unfamiliar spheres, occupying a frighteningly demanding world with which the subordinate executive has not—and does not want to have—anything to do. The Hopkinses in the business world constitute a distant "they" which orders the life of and provides the wherewithal for the organization man, who is glad to take it without upsetting the system or asking too many questions. Where, in a previous ethic, Hopkins might be drawn as a man to be imitated, Wilson presents him as a man who has devoted his energy to the wrong things. In his fierce drive for personal satisfaction, he has lost his wife and children and alienated his friends. There is a certain awe that he inspires, but not emulation.

For Tom this total involvement in one's work is not the way to achieve satisfaction. He turns down a promotion because it would require that he spend too much time working. Yet, he wants to stay with United Broadcasting in a job with a salary that will provide him the material comforts he sees his contemporaries enjoying. According to the social ethic he has the very best reasons for his position. He wants to be free from the entanglements of the organization in order to spend more time with his family. Whyte calls this "self-ennobling hedonism." In Wilson's world, this is a virtue and it must be rewarded. At first Mr. Hopkins is outraged by Tom's expectations of reward from the company without being willing to devote himself to it entirely. But soon he gives Tom what he asks for, agreeing that "there are plenty of jobs around that do not require [Tom] to do an unusual amount of work."

Wilson implies that Tom's candor with Hopkins is admirable. It characterizes Tom's whole attitude toward life, suggesting an openness and a concern for others that constitute important elements in the morality of the "open decision." The implication is that with the individual at the center of an essentially chaotic—even deceptive—universe, deception and selfishness on the part of conscious creatures thwart value and satisfaction. Tom's honesty also governs his personal life. In Italy during the war he had a love affair with an Italian girl, while his wife Betsy waited faithfully for him at home. Tom kept this from Betsy, and his deception rightly caused him pain. In the course of the novel, however, he learns from an old army buddy that the girl bore him a son. Conscience-stricken, he can relieve himself only by confessing the affair to Betsy and declaring that he wants to contribute to the child's support. Betsy reacts at first as Hopkins did, in outrage. But also like Hopkins, after thinking it over, she concludes that Tom's honesty must be rewarded and lovingly approves of his setting up a trust fund for the boy.

On the face of it, Tom's behavior seems to be an attempt to maintain his individuality against the threat of the corporation. But in the end, one must agree with Whyte's conclusion that the novel is an affirmation of the values of the organization man. Tom Rath does not preserve his integrity under the pressure of the apparatus. He appears thoroughly undeserving and weak. His candor—taking the form of confessing his self-indulgences—seems more like a surrender of responsibility than its acceptance. His satisfactions are without individuality and intensity, emerging from the lives of countless other men just like him, whom business suckles and society rewards for conforming. He has so completely absorbed the values of the social apparatus that he regards them as unassailable virtues. Tom exemplifies a dulling of consciousness that signals his complete submersion in the apparatus. When we see that the symbol of Tom's brave new life—in which he courageously acknowledges an illegitimate child and becomes a well paid corporate drone—is his decision to trade his old car for a new one, we must conclude with Whyte that *The Man in the Gray Flannel Suit,* whatever it purports to be, is a celebration of the other-directed corporation man in whom the intensity of individual satisfaction has hit a low pitch. Wilson seems unable to embrace the essence of the "open decision," which requires risk and danger, and which cannot promise a neatly packaged conclusion to the difficult questions of human existence.

Most business novelists reject the social ethic of the organization man. And some find in business no drag upon self-realization, but many encouragements to fulfillment. Indeed, for Ayn Rand in *Atlas Shrugged* there can be no satisfaction, properly defined, outside of the true business world, that world which is based upon unconditional free enterprise, and a full-blown *laissez-faire* individualism. And Miss Rand has a carefully constructed philosophy to support her position, which is a curious blend of the values of the "open decision" and their outright denial. The highest good for her is the life of the individual, and the virtuous man will not surrender that life without a fight. As with Jaspers and Heidegger, Miss Rand suggests that human death is not simply physical; it may occur with the submergence of the self in the apparatus, the values of the "they." The man who wants to live must guard against humanitarianism, often passed off as a virtue but, in Miss Rand's view, a vicious softness which requires one to sacrifice his life for another. The greatest wealth that one can own is the outright title to his own life, unentailed by other claims or debts. The moral purpose of one's life, says Miss Rand, is "the achievement of happiness," but that happiness is not assured simply by possession of title. It comes from growth: "Every living thing must grow . . . or perish." Life is growth—not biological growth, but intellectual. The form of that growth is familiar. It is conceiving an aim and then shaping matter to the purpose of that aim. Thus created objects like motors have life "because they are the physical shape of the action of a living power—of the mind that had been able to grasp the whole of this complexity, to set its purpose, to give it form." The function of life is action, and action is the harnessing of thought to the production of goods. There is more, however, to happiness than mere action in Miss Rand's world. Part of the moral purpose of life—that is, happiness—is payment for services rendered. *Giving* is a pernicious word in her vocabulary. The more one produces the more wealth one ought to have; the contrary also holds true.

Those who live by these values experience the highest satisfaction. They declare their freedom from responsibility for other people. They reject irrationality and feeling and celebrate reason. They organize transportation networks, build bridges and tunnels, invent motors that get their power from the static electricity in the air, and develop synthetic metals stronger and lighter than steel. They compete for markets, meet deadlines with efficiency, and expect nothing from anyone but what they earn.

The society organized on these values is not simply auspicious for individual satisfaction, as Miss Rand sees it; it is virtuous in what approaches a religious sense. Those who reject such a society are represented as wicked and evil, malevolently bent upon destroying life itself simply because they are too weak to live it and would spite everyone who is strong. In *Atlas Shrugged* such men appear within the very business world which is presented as carrying our salvation. Their presence is corrosive, and one of the duties of the good is to rid the world of this corrosiveness. These men, together with those in government gradually strangle the country's practitioners of free enterprise, professing patriotism and concern for the social good. Frustrated and enraged that, in their weakness, they cannot compete with the truly good and the truly strong, they pass laws controlling what and how much is produced in the country, how much is sold, and to whom it is sold. These evil men preach a vicious social ethic: obedience rather than argument, belief rather than understanding, adjustment rather than rebellion, compromise rather than struggle. They speak hypocritically of brotherhood and the common good, and of the conviction that all must share each other's burdens. They are the "enemy," and they scorn reason as illusion, have a "leering hatred of the human mind." The "moderation" and the ambiguities of the "open decision" are here represented by Miss Rand as sinister threats to her conception of reality. Men who live by these antivalues (as Tom Rath does) ride ungratefully upon the backs of the capable, demanding what they neither earn nor deserve, and declaring that the deserving rich need them more than they need the rich.

Miss Rand has created a world composed of all that she most vehemently resents. This she represents as a true assessment of the present structure of reality, and she proceeds to attack that structure with strong vindictiveness. The weaklings must be taught a lesson; they must be punished for their ungratefulness. In *Atlas Shrugged,* the main punisher is John Galt. After getting out of college, Galt decides to drop out of the society that thwarts his satisfaction with such deliberate malice. He secretly persuades the best men in the country—the top industrialists—to go on "strike" with him. They retire to a hidden section of land in Colorado and build the ideal business community. Galt calls the area Atlantis. Its insignia is a dollar sign. The mythical Atlantis, as one character tells us, was where "hero-spirits lived in a happiness unknown to the rest of the earth." Galt's Atlantis and the men who populate it do not differ appreciably from their mythical counterparts. In the meantime, the baleful conspiracy of weakling businessmen and grasping government officials has reduced American business to chaos with its leveling ways. Goods are diminishing, transportation is breaking down, the people are becoming restless. This is proof that John Galt and the titans like him are "uncommon men" upon whom the "common men" depend. Without the uncommon men the country disintegrates. The confusion and deprivation and panic are well-deserved punishment for those who fail to acknowledge the irrefutable facts of the relationship between men. As Galt and the last of his Atlantis enlistees fly toward their heavenly valley, the once flourishing countryside below them rapidly darkens and the millions of ungrateful inferiors receive their due.

Atlas Shrugged is more myth than novel. Miss Rand's heroes and heroines are god-like creatures who, in their leviathan strength, resist the wickedness of the pernicious weaklings around them and achieve their ends at will, though not without devoted and gigantic effort. Their tool is reason, their aim is individual satisfaction. While the enemy collapses of his own evil, the godlike producers retire to reap the harvest of the world. For Miss Rand there are no contradictions inherent in the human condition between man's image of himself and the ability to actualize that image. The notions of moderation and absurdity she flatly rejects. The for-itself *can* become an in-itself. One *can* achieve full identity. The real and the ideal *can* merge under the direction of the human mind. And, to complete the repudiation of the "open decision," a sense of human solidarity is represented as an obstacle to the achievement of the highest good, for it smacks of humanitarianism. Yet, only Miss Rand's heroes and heroines, who would find the love ethic of Erich

Fromm an intolerable concession to weakness, can experience real love. Its best expression is sexual intercourse, which she invests with the romantic masochism of a Swinburne. The first sexual experience of Dagny Taggart and Hank Reardon seems more painful than pleasurable: "It was like an act of hatred, like the cutting blow of a lash encircling her body: she felt his arms around her, she felt her legs pulled forward against him and her chest bent back under the pressure of his, his mouth on hers." Miss Rand's treatment of sex, which is a function of the values which her giants apply to their business dealings, suggests that the novel is a massive expression of wish-fulfillment. Dagny Taggart, her one heroine, is the only woman invited by John Galt to Atlantis. There she will live in a paradise in which she is the only queen, passionately and devotedly loved by the three strongest men in America, two of whom surrender their claims upon her to the king of all the gods, John Galt.

It can be said that the values which move Miss Rand to create such characters relate more closely to nineteenth-century economic individualism than to the concerns of the "open decision," that Dagny Taggart and John Galt would be more comfortable in the company of a John D. Rockefeller or an Andrew Carnegie than such "absurd" heroes as Camus's Meursault in *The Stranger* or Sartre's Roquentin. The truth of such a statement, however, simply demonstrates what I have avoided dealing with because it lies beyond the scope of this book—that is, the kinship between nineteenth-century romanticism (along with its corollaries of laissez-faire economics and the biology of evolution, with their emphasis upon growth and change) and the more thoroughly formulated metaphysical foundations of the "open decision." Miss Rand may sound like an economic romantic, but her values reflect those of the "open decision." True reality lies in individual experience, whose worth is measured in terms of growth and risk. It could even be said that Miss Rand celebrates individual spontaneity in that she deplores all structures that would blunt the self's sharp striving for the realization of its novel end. Where the difference comes between the assumptions in *Atlas Shrugged* and those of the "open decision" is in her imputation to certain stereotypes a jealous cowardice that envies strength in others and seeks to destroy that strength. The human solidarity so valuable to thinkers like Whitehead, Dewey, Jaspers,

Fromm, Camus, and many others Miss Rand represents as dangerous to her romanticized giants.

There are other business novelists, also, who look back more to an idealized earlier age of individual freedom than to what Jung would call the dark uncertainty of the modern abyss. They, like their other twentieth-century counterparts, take as their assumed fundamental value the free exertion of the spontaneous self that leads to a high intensity of individual satisfaction. But, like Miss Rand, they see an idealized system of free enterprise—business—as the only environment in which such satisfaction may be achieved.

What the socio-political war novelists found to be the greatest danger to the authentic self, these novelists find to be the only system in which that self can be preserved and nurtured. Like the war novelists, those who celebrate their preferred system assert that its integrity is under attack by forces intent upon diminishing individual freedom and intensity of satisfaction. This conflict is the plot device common to many business novels. In some novels, the agent of totalitarianism is outside the business system. Garth Hale,[5] in *Legacy for Our Sons,* traces the gradual strangulation by the government of America's free enterprise system. In the bright days before the Depression, when virtue reigned and work was rewarded, "The individual," writes Hale, "was largely on his own. He chose his work and kept what he made by his work. Or he was free to be shiftless, but for his shiftlessness he eventually paid the price. The only limitation on how far he might go, up or down, was the limitation of his own ability or choice." But too soon this desirable society is undermined by government welfare and spending programs. Men who used to expect to earn their wages are corrupted by the "gimme complex." Laziness replaces industry, profligacy thrift.

Nor is this tragic transformation innocent. It is the work of satanic forces that hate virtue. By the end of World War II, as Hale sees it, it seems clear that an insidious and malicious conspiracy, an "alien group," is laying a "deep design whose ultimate result was to subvert the traditional American way." The unions are part of this deep design. Union men strike, not with the heroic conviction depicted in the protest novels of the 'thirties, but with blurry-eyed, stubble-chinned glee, as if they are revenging themselves upon a system they know to be superior to the one they advocate. In their spitefulness, these union men are the proletarian counterparts of the weaklings in government and business that Miss Rand draws. Moreover, government supports the unions. Harrison Day, Hale's protagonist, fires a railroad employee for being drunk on the job. But soon an NLRB official insists that the man be taken back on. Because of the omnipotence of government, Harrison is helpless. He has to give in, while, shuffling behind him, the slothful unionists grin slyly and triumphantly. And finally, Harrison is forced out of the job he loves because he would struggle against the great apparatus which is hostile to honest work and the concept of earning one's money. His freedom and, thereby, his satisfaction are thwarted.

Frequently, in these novels that celebrate precisely what the socio-political war novel attacked, a vigorous and honest young man rises up to champion the preferred system and to preserve it from the threat against it, much as John Galt does in *Atlas Shrugged.* There is, however, an important basic difference. The actions of this hero are motivated by a strong sense of social service so alien to Miss Rand. Cameron Hawley, for example, not only describes what a good system is, but why it is good. In his system, as in Rand's, it is the strong men who flourish. They are artists of investment and management, princes of commerce, dominating huge empires and possessing tremendous power. These men feel responsible for preserving their society, not only because it is right in the scheme of things but because it serves the good of all. In *Executive Suite,* good business is represented by Avery Bullard, head of the huge Tredway Furniture Corporation. Bullard is a big man, spiritually and physically. Strong, domineering, forceful, he single-handedly creates Tredway. His philosophy is that of America's great moguls: "A good company is a one-man show," a little empire ruled by a stern but benevolent monarch. The aristocracy to which Bullard belongs is not cultured or effete. It is impatient with ideas and anxious to get on with the action. Bullard, like Miss Rand's giants, is a "builder." But his aim is not simply profit. It is to live with integrity, devoted to his work. As one of the characters says, Bullard is "one of the most uncompromisingly honest men that I've ever known in my whole life." For him the company is not a toy, to be manipulated according to his whim and appetite. It is a "living, breathing organism" made up of many parts, all of which must be served. It must embrace not only the hard-headed businessman but also artistic sensitivity and creative imagination.

In this society, of course, not everyone is to the manner born and this fact links the novel more strongly with the nineteenth century than with the twentieth. Some people simply are born with a lower capacity for individual satisfaction. But Hawley's scheme does not deprive these naturally inferior creatures of their means to feeble fulfillment. Indeed, it supports them in a way they hardly deserve, given their low intrinsic worth. The Tredway factory in Millburgh, Pennsylvania, provides work for one of every three families living there. Some of the workers are fourth- and fifth-generation employees, and, unlike Miss Rand's inferiors, few of them do not feel a kind of grateful awe for the great creature perched in the executive suite of the Tredway tower symbolically overlooking the city, who moves in seemingly infallible ways and produces for them their livelihood. For Hawley, some "actual entities" are less "causally independent," as Whitehead would say, than others.

When Bullard dies, leaving no successor, the preferred scheme is threatened. Loren Shaw, the firm's cold and intellectual chief accountant and newest member of the board of directors, begins an insidious campaign to install himself as president. Shaw represents, in Hawley's eyes, all that is bad about business—an emphasis upon figures and profits. He sees the company functioning solely as a money-making operation for the stockholders. This means that it is to be conducted on paper rather than in the plant. It means paying the lowest wages, buying the cheapest materials, and turning out an inferior product. Don Walling, however, the combination artist-businessman hired by Bullard to design furniture and run the plant, carries Bullard's values into the crucial board meeting during which the new president is to be chosen. A company, says young Walling, is more than money. It is like a man, and a man's dignity and pride tell him the work of his hands must be good. It is true that the board has an obligation to the stockholders; but it also has an obligation to the mystical body of the company, to the workers and the product they manufacture. This is not only good morality, it is good business. Quality furniture will make them all both proud and commercially successful, and this, one senses, is the sign of virtue. Walling claims that Tredway can command a much larger part of the market if they follow his advice. His rhetoric persuades the vacillating members of the board to elect him president and he dedicates himself to implementing, with the necessary modifications and updating, the principles of Avery Bullard.

In Hawley's view good business does not thwart individual satisfaction, nor does it, as Packard claims in his remarks on large corporations, shrink inventiveness and desire. Indeed, it encourages these virtues and must be protected against those who would subvert it. Its custodians follow no social ethic, but adopt an aristocratic toleration and *noblesse oblige*. Thus, the values of the "open decision" are served. The individual is granted freedom in a "live" and auspicious society to work out his own satisfaction. Yet, in the end, it seems that possibilities are open only to some. The system Hawley lauds provides data for only certain kinds of satisfaction. Who cannot meet the demands of that system—like the weaklings on the board of directors or the workers who do not aspire to the heights of the executive suite—are either destroyed or relegated to diminished fulfillment. The weakling only gets what he deserves and the worker could not handle any more than he gets. In Hawley's hierarchy, some can achieve a greater individuality than others. Were it not so, the system would crumble. The social arrangement the war novelist found repressive, Hawley finds to be the only free condition. His heroes protect that arrangement and in doing so are presented as deserving the gratitude of all who truly understand.

Hawley and Miss Rand see good business as a kind of religion. Their emphasis is upon the preservation of the tenets of business as the *sine qua non* of self-fulfillment. They seem to assume that left to its own devices the human spirit will spontaneously seek out individual satisfaction in the organization of the production and marketing of commodities, and that freed of such satanic threats as accountant Shaw and government interference, they can achieve their authentic existence. More complete practitioners of the "open decision" would accuse these novelists of bad faith, of limiting possibilities to artificially imposed bonds, of assuming this is the only way things can be. Howard Swiggett and Amelia Elizabeth Walden[6] shift the emphasis to a concern for preserving individual integrity when it is threatened by corruption within the system. A powerful business executive, working through the rigid power structure of the corporation, requires his admirable subordinate to behave counter to his convictions, expecting him to sacrifice honesty in personal relationships to serve the reputation and the profit-making capacity of the company. In each case the tacit assumption is that the system itself would be weakened were the business executive to succeed in his demands. But the focus is upon the preservation of personal honesty. That is where the highest good lies for Swiggett and Mrs. Walden. This view of the preferred situation argues against the validity of the social ethic on the one hand and demonstrates that individual integrity strengthens the business system on the other. The point is not that business stifles the authentic self, but that there are corrupt forces within it that must be dealt with, implying that one's own individual satisfaction is tied in with, as Whitehead says, the contributions one can make to the freedom of others in the society. This point is made explicitly by Bill Tarrant, a young man on his way to the top in a Boston investment house in W. H. Prosser's[7] *Nine to Five*. Bill is momentarily discouraged by the immoral behavior of two of his colleagues who scheme to win promotions by destroying others. The business itself is worthwhile, as Bill sees it, benefiting people materially, but it is sick: ". . . it seemed that somewhere in the core of it there must be a substantial corruption like a cancer—not the corruption of business dishonesty, but a kind of personal decay. . . ." Bill's first reaction is to run in order to preserve his integrity. But he decides to stay, "to do what he could right here, here where he could function." The business world is both salvageable, and worth saving.

For Swiggett and Mrs. Walden business is not only hospitable to honest men; it requires such men in order to exist. Their heroes possess all of the virtues of the "open decision"—they are candid, open, capable of love and human ties, and able to see beyond specious business expediency to the larger issues of community and solidarity. For maintaining their individual authenticity, these characters are rewarded by the business world. Here personal and business considerations are intertwined, emphasizing the importance of a central personal integrity which, as the "open decision" states, unifies a chaotic universe into a moral reality. Both Mrs. Walden and Swiggett open up new dimensions of the business world for fictional treatment. The private lives of the characters are guided by principles similar to those of their business lives. This is something Hawley did not see. And in *Atlas Shrugged* the personal lives of Miss Rand's characters seemed to be simply business transactions.

Swiggett and Mrs. Walden construct their plots to demonstrate this interconnectedness. In Swiggett's *The Power and the Prize,* Cleves Barwick, a comparatively young man in his middle forties and vice-president of Allied Metals Corporation, is sent to London to negotiate some business with a British firm. There he wins friends by refusing to be the stereotyped American who aggressively and indelicately insists upon the superiority of American business skill. Instead, he displays a genuine and respectful interest in the British and a candid admiration of their customs and values. He is more than a single-minded business ambassador; he is a human being conversing with other human beings. While in London, he falls in love with Rachel Linka, a refugee from Austria whose husband was killed by the Nazis. She works for a charity institution which some Americans suspect of having Communist connections. When the negotiations take Cleves back to New York, he asks Rachel to follow him so they can be married.

Back home he is confronted with the powerful George Salt, president of Allied Metals and, up to now, Cleves' main patron. When Cleves tells him about Rachel, Salt explodes, complaining that the woman is not only a foreigner but a Jew. If a high executive of Allied Metals were to marry a woman of such a shadowy past, it would make a bad impression on important people. Because Salt is unable to conceive of a true love match, bound as he is to a hypocritical business ethic, he suggests that Cleves has gotten Rachel pregnant and must marry her. If that is the case, Rachel is not really worth the risk. The company, says Salt, would be glad to pay her off to protect itself. Enraged at Salt's lack of insight and delicacy, Cleves walks out of the office. In the ensuing struggle, Cleves' weapons are the private virtues: honesty, integrity, fidelity to his personal obligations and feelings. Salt's weapons are bigotry and the power that comes with his position at the top of the corporate fear ladder. The issue is referred to the corporation's board of directors, chaired by the scrupulously honest Henry Dennison. It becomes clear to Dennison that Cleves is more valuable to the company than Salt, and he has got that way by being warm and human. The contract being negotiated with the British is crucial to Allied, and the British will deal only with Cleves. In his own investigation of Rachel, Dennison finds her free of Communist association, but he asks Cleves to guarantee the board that she is not a Communist. Resentful of such suspiciousness, Cleves risks his career—and at the same time demonstrates his personal worthiness—by refusing to acknowledge the need for such a guarantee. Cleves' loyalty convinces Dennison. He recommends to the board that Salt be removed and Cleves be installed as the new president of Allied. Not only are good business and personal integrity identical, but business, for all its dangers, is auspicious to the achievement of individual satisfaction.

In Swiggett's world, feeling and uniqueness are prerequisites for business success and the improvement of the business community. The integrity of the subjective experience must be given priority. Swiggett's *The Durable Fire* reaffirms that priority. Stephen Lowry is a younger copy of Cleves Barwick. He and his wife, Rosalie Lainvee, an Estonian refugee from the Communists, love flowers, trees, and the outdoors. To avoid being submerged in the apparatus of business, they work in their leisure time upon a book —"The Principal Errors of Judges and Potentates." Steve takes an executive position with Continental Industries Corporation. He does not seek merely business success, but the exhilaration of enjoying his work, of spontaneous pleasure. He disturbs the company's rigid president by wondering if the job will be "fun."

Steve steadily resists becoming an organization man. Those who do not resist—those who identify themselves strictly with the aims of the company—end up as embezzlers or drunkards or worse. They allow the organization to determine their choices, rejecting their inherent freedom. And when they are willing to commit any act for the company, they surrender their own sovereignty. Nor do they profit the company by their behavior. Dishonesty and personal corruption only damage it. The new president of Continental is such a person. When it is discovered that the company's bid on a project in South America is $500,000 in error, the president asks Steve to work some sharp practice in order to protect the firm's advantage. Steve refuses. At this point, the president becomes upset by an incident in Steve's personal life. During an innocent nude swim in the surf with some friends, Rosalie saves one of the other men in the group from drowning. The tabloids pick up the story and give it sexual overtones. The president is furious. Willing to stoop to any dishonesty in business, he maintains a hypocritical sanctimony in his personal life. He demands Steve's dismissal. But as in *The Power and the Prize,* the board of directors supports individual integrity. In a hearing on the South American project's irregularities, Steve testifies about the president's behavior, but he remains steadfastly honest and detached, disavowing any sympathy with the president's proposals but refusing to accuse him of improper conduct. The board, however, recognizes the situation. It replaces the president and retains Steve. Neither Steve nor Cleves Barwick is without ambition and energy, unlike Wilson's Tom Rath. They are willing to upset the corporate hierarchy. But that willingness does not empty them of the capacity for close human ties.

A similar situation occurs in Mrs. Walden's *The Bradford Story.* Bradford Tool is the business of an old New England family, whose officers are taken only from the family circle. The head of the family, stuffy and unimaginative Spencer, is the president of the firm, but his patrician self-confidence is not matched by ability. The man who actually runs the business as plant general manager is Mark Galloway, who has made his way out of the slums, got an education, and married Spencer's sister Nina. Soon, the familiar crisis arises, and Spencer and Mark take different sides. Spencer wants to appoint an inexperienced distant relative to the open chief engineer's post, while Mark backs a brilliant young engineer already in the company, Steve Emrich. Nina, as tradition-bound as her brother, throws the weight of her company shares behind Spencer, declaring that Mark would never have got where he is had he not married her. The bitterness of their disagreement causes Mark to separate temporarily from Nina and he takes refuge in the arms of an old flame, Claire Elliott. Spencer becomes worried that Mark will divorce Nina and produce gossip adversely affecting the reputation of the company. He proposes that Mark remain married to Nina technically, but carry on a discreet liaison with Claire. Spencer is willing to degrade human relationships in the interest of business, but Mark cannot conduct his personal life by giving precedence to the concerns of the company. He resigns Bradford Tool, leaves both Nina and Claire, and takes another job. It becomes clear, however, that business does not thrive on hypocrisy. Spencer cannot run the company without Mark. The business needs the strong hand of the independent and honest man. One of the strong old Bradford aunts, who has supported Mark throughout, forces Spencer to resign. Mark is lured back as company president and he and Nina—unconvincingly—rediscover their love for each other.

The structure of these plots is built upon the whole intellectual construct of the "open decision." The business worlds of George Salt and Spencer Bradford are rigid—"dead"—providing minimum alternatives and thwarting the free play of individual energies. Salt and Spencer Bradford are imprisoned in the specious "theyness" of the apparatus, fearing the censure of some vague absolute that allegedly frowns upon the display of the authentic self and the preservation of integrity and independence. Both are measured according to their allegiance to trivial superficialities: the reputation of a business entity that has no actual existence and the assumption that conformity to an assumed social ethic is good business. Cleves Barwick, Steve Lowry, and Mark Galloway defy the apparatus, refuse to fall into "theyness," and seek to keep open their own possibilities for growth. Their task, however, is made easy for them by Swiggett and Mrs. Walden, whose business world is—unlike the "immoral society" of Niebuhr, the "civilization" of Freud, the "apparatus" of Jaspers, which by definition impose limits upon the free individual—inherently auspicious to the honest man. Their heroes not only find peace, as Jaspers suggests, with the apparatus without being absorbed by it; they are rewarded by that apparatus for refusing to be so absorbed. Thus there is in Swiggett and Mrs. Walden a tendency I have already remarked upon—a tendency to disregard the difficult ambiguities of the human condition implicit in the "open decision" and to find, with traditional optimism, a kind of state of rest in which the virtuous win an eternal happiness, and the sinful are punished by being deposed from their positions of power.

A little more explicitly, however, than the other novels I have discussed so far in this chapter, *The Bradford Story* shows an attempt to deal with the ambiguities of the "open decision" in the setting of business. The Bradford family and the business they run are analogous to the old world of objective certainty and self-confidence that are said to close individual possibilities because they assume that only one choice is open, the "right" one as decreed by tradition. Mark Galloway is free from that limiting certitude in a way the Bradfords, bound by family tradition, are not. But, like the modern man whose consciousness has led him to the absurd, Mark pays a price—his freedom is "dreadful." With the deterioration of the comfortable and unquestioned order of his work and his home, Mark is plunged into anxiety, a condition totally unfamiliar to and impossible for the rigid Spencer. Mark experiences a fear "more swift and devastating than any he had known before." The source of his panic is the disappearance of the old familiar landmarks of meaning and truth and identity. "What is truth?" he wonders. "The terror screamed at him. Who are you? There is no truth about you or marriage or love or anything else." In the absence of what he once took to be the absolute warrants of his own purpose, he can find in his anxiety only two certainties: despair and death. The note of Heidegger, Camus, and Sartre is strong here. But as with Camus, Mrs. Walden does not conclude on a note of despair. Mark has been forced into freedom, out of the shelter of "everydayness" or "bad faith." If objective absolutes dissolve, where can he go? In the openness of his freedom he can turn only to himself, and when he does, he discovers something closed to the Bradfords: that existence and identity are not conferred by organizations or tradition. They originate in the self. "Each must reach through to the truth about himself and his universe, and an essential part of that search was loneliness." Mrs. Walden rejects the social ethic and embraces the "open decision," maintaining that business is more hospitable to a high intensity of individual satisfaction when the social ethic does not prevail. Furthermore, it is Mark Galloway, the "modern" man, who triumphs over tradition, and in the depth of his "angst" achieves fulfillment.

Novelists like Miss Rand and Mrs. Walden, Hawley and Swiggett find in business the possibilities of independence and integrity. But these writers present a minority view. The majority of business novels see business, even when one is successful, as a system inherently antithetical to individual freedom and openness. This attitude recalls the attitude of some of the war novelists, who drew the connection between business and the military. In some novels, it is business itself which thwarts the individual, and because of that the protagonist finds that he must abandon it if he is to retain any chance of choosing his own alternatives. Business, in these novels, as opposed to those of Swiggett and Mrs. Walden, is represented as unsalvageable. It must be escaped. The protagonist is confronted with a moral choice, at whose center is the question of his freedom, his very existence as a human being. In the bright light of the crisis, the hero recognizes the tyranny of the business structure and the essentially immoral men who control it. There is, he decides, no living within this structure, and so he abandons it. Pete Cody, for example, in Joe Morgan's[8] *Expense Account,* is a traveling public relations man for Cartwright Tool. His position in this business firm forces him to live a life of constant tension, in which he is provided with no substantial alternatives and in which he fears to choose from those alternatives with which he is provided. He eats in expensive restaurants and lives in high-priced hotels during the week, but when he returns to his family on the weekends he is plagued by economic troubles because his salary is insufficient. Nor is his work compensation for the anxiety produced by his fiscal position. He is saddled with responsibility but given no power. And he finds it necessary to control the expression of his own ideas because they often conflict with those of the more conservative and affluent members of the firm. It is in this atmosphere of *dis*satisfaction that Pete is confronted with his moral choice. At the height of his own financial crisis, he is offered a bribe to help overthrow the company's existing board of directors. Acquiescence would provide him quick cash and, in the likely event the coup succeeded, assure him a comfortable future. In accepting the bribe he would place the values of the social ethic—economic security and material comfort—over the values of the "open decision"—personal integrity and freedom. It is the choice between the collective and the individual, and certainly Morgan is conscious of the sociology of the 1950s when he confronts his character with his dilemma.

Pete, of course, makes the choice for the individual. He refuses to take the bribe, refuses to sell himself for the security said to be of paramount importance to the "silent" generation. With Pete's honest assistance, the board of Cartwright Tool puts down the insurrection. He has demonstrated both integrity and ability and the board moves to offer him a vice-presidency. But that is no more attractive than the bribe. His dissatisfaction with business is more than economic. Not only would the gap between income and expenditures be even greater than before, he would be required to give more and more time to the company. He would cease to be his own man. Morgan finds no resolution to these limitations within the business system, as Sloan Wilson does. Nor does Pete's behavior save both himself and the business, as in *The Power and the Prize* and *The Durable Fire.* If Pete is to achieve any kind of satisfaction, he must get out of business. And he does, deciding at 34 to go to law school and eventually into partnership with an old friend.

Paul Marrow, in Frederick Laing's[9] *The Giant's House,* and Alex Harris, in Stanley Kaufmann's[10] *A Change of Climate,* come to the same decision. Marrow, though he shows remarkable business ability, concludes that the personal freedom that would allow him to make unique choices for his own novel satisfaction has been preempted by the old man he works for, John Horgan. He grows restive in the rigid community run by the crusty old Horgan, who demands unquestioning obedience from his employees. At the crucial point, Marrow rebels; he says "no" to the force that would diminish his individuality and "yes" to what he knows is right in himself, even though it eludes rational description. His rebellion deprives him of the security he had once considered paramount—Horgan fires him. But with that dismissal comes liberation, "a sense of freedom, a kind of elation that more than made up for the sudden financial insecurity." Suddenly what was missing in his life is no longer missing. With his freedom comes a heightened awareness and with that awareness comes the ability to risk himself by taking up ties with others. While he had been in business, he had backed away from his sweetheart, Prudy, unwilling to expose himself. He was too careful a part of the organization to gamble on the intensity of love. Freed from that situation, he finds himself open to a more intense satisfaction: "He knew that what had been lacking in his life was lacking no more. He knew now [with his love for Prudy] that if there was at least one living being whom you loved unselfishly, life was richer, needs fewer and pleasures were more real. Especially if the love were mutual and mutually unselfish." He decides to leave business and return to what he deems to be the freer world of journalism.

Alex Harris is disturbed by the common twentieth-century problem: the loss of the old system of absolute values. Without such a system, he laments, the intensity of one's existence is diminished. He hopes to recapture some kind of value standard by leaving his college teaching post and going into business with Charles France. France, however, as a businessman, asks Alex to help him avoid a congressional investigation into his shady business dealings during World War II. Alex reluctantly agrees, because he likes France and has fallen in love with France's daughter Linda, who is to be kept innocent of her father's past indiscretions. But in doing so he reactivates his old despair. He has violated a moral law. He has acted dishonestly. That people he likes and admires could plan something illegal and that he would accede simply confirms that all values have disintegrated, that we have lost our ground for moral behavior and hence any meaning in our existence.

Kaufmann self-consciously confronts Alex with the modern dilemma. Equally self-consciously he provides the modern solution to the despair over the loss of the old values—the absolute worth of the individual and the corollary worth of all human beings. Alex's instructor in the new morality is old Rube Isaacs, the self-taught father of one of France's ex-wives. The truth and validity of Rube's position is implied by the fact that he has discovered it individually. He has remained free of the distorting prejudices of traditional education. He has, in a sense, bracketed the conventional presuppositions and set them aside, leaving the core of truth. That criterion of moral behavior which Alex regrets violating, says Rube, is simply an abstraction, concocted by the intellectuals of many ages, many religions, many nations. We used to regard this abstraction as the word of God, but history shows that this abstraction changes and shifts its meaning. It is this recognition of the relativity of moral codes that causes our despair. But, says Rube, we do have an absolute criterion for moral behavior. Codes may come and go, but people remain. Therefore, "We've got to take our bearing from our relations with each other." Rube is not advocating anxious other-directedness. He is advocating that Alex recognize the worth of the human individual as the basis for moral action. When he does, he will see that he acted morally in helping France, for the ground of his behavior was "caring for other people."

Alex is impressed. He comes to recognize the assumption of the "open decision": that it is not necessary to believe, as Alex says, in abstract "final causes or ultimate purpose" in order to behave morally and meaningfully. Concern for the integrity of others is cause enough. Such concern commits a man to his own life, which can be lived only here in this world. It abolishes the impulse to look for immortality in the old moral codes, to waste oneself even while trying to save oneself. Alex decides to align himself with men, to find "a continuity in the race. Instead of hoping for a ghost to survive him when his body wears out, he can survive and progress in others: sons; kin; friends; strangers." This is almost a direct paraphrase of Whitehead's assertion that consciousness reveals to the self that one's own value "will be preserved, and that there are elements of value in the lives of others." It is in this world that one comes to the highest intensity of individual satisfaction, the sense of oneself as a unique being related to other unique beings. "And the marvelous thing," thinks Alex about surviving in others, "is that although there is no compulsion to do this, divine or otherwise, yet we want to do it." This "want" is a most personal thing, individualizing our experience. It is through such an experience that we receive "the assurance that we exist, really exist. And that is all we need to know." In Whitehead's terms, Alex has decided that the awareness of existence is one of our basic "subjective aims" and that the achievement of that aim is "something individual to the entity in question." It is the emergence of this awareness that distinguishes between low and high intensity of individual satisfaction. Alex has disclosed to himself his own unifying and meaning-giving "world-center." In finding himself he has also found his relationship with the truly human community.

It is not the business world, however, that provides the most hospitable theater for exploiting the principles of behavior that Alex has discovered. As in *Expense Account* and *The Giant's House,* business is presented as an impossibly limiting society for the "actual entity" who has gained a high degree of self-awareness and is searching for a high intensity of individual satisfaction. Alex has discovered that no absolute standard of value is available to him and that in spite of this fact he can live "without appeal" to higher abstractions. But now he must leave the business world, marry Linda, and reappraise his whole moral position.

In what I consider to be the most interesting business novels, business is not so easily escapable, and complete satisfaction is not quite so accessible. Business, in these novels, is dealt with as an analogue to the human condition. Its limitations are not merely social or economic but metaphysical, similar to those treated in

Part I. That is, civilization requires men to sublimate or repress some of their most fundamental and spontaneous desires; it requires concessions of individuality that inevitably diminish the intensity of satisfaction the human mind can conceive of in terms of absolute power and absolute gratification of one's desires. At the same time, the human being, left alone to face a powerful and indifferent nature without the accumulated strength of his organized fellows, though he may not be required to repress his appetites, yet he will find his puny strength too scant to gratify those appetites. Civilization, for all it takes away, gives us considerable return. Indeed, in the "open decision," the idea is that the social apparatus is the only theater we have in which to seek out our individual satisfaction. Part of the ambiguity of our condition lies in this warring relationship. Life in business, like life in the world, is by definition a moderation of one's will, a qualification of one's freedom. The pathos implicit in these novels is that men can conceive as gods but not achieve as gods. The real and the ideal are mutually exclusive, and this invokes a resigned sadness with the fact that men fall short. In business one inevitably sacrifices something to the apparatus. This does not mean that the characters in these novels are organization men, bland drones who define their apathy as virtue. They are men caught in the contradictions and paradoxes of human existence. Theodore Morrison, in *The Whole Creation,* captures the tone of these novels when he has one of his characters say: "We can ask to be grounded in the depth of things; we can hardly ask to escape waste and mischance, and I do not think any profound moral literature has ever encouraged us to make such a request." To be "grounded in the depth of things" and to be unable "to escape waste and mischance" are part of our condition, touching us with pathos and the regret of things dreamt of but unachieved. Nor can this pathos be explained away by science. "Even where [science's] discoveries are most certain, its explanations most satisfactory, it doesn't touch bottom, it doesn't exhaust the mystery."

Many of these novels are success stories, like *Executive Suite, The Power and the Prize, The Bradford Story.* The difference is that every success is seen to have its element of loss. Martin Brill, in George de Mare's[11] *The Empire,* is ambivalent about his success with A.T. & T. He is an admirable man—thoughtful, sometimes troubled, but always strong and efficient in the arts of persuasion and decision-making. He enters the company full of skepticism about business in general. He is determined to maintain his own independence, to avoid becoming the organization man who eagerly sells his integrity to the corporation. Free from the fear of upsetting his superiors, and unafraid of violating company taboos, he explores new responses to the System's problems, displaying courage, inventiveness, and willingness to make and take the responsibility for independent decisions. In a union dispute, the company orders its negotiators to humiliate the union leader. Martin realizes that the company can win its major points without such tactics. Moreover, deliberate embarrassment now will create future enmity, making the union harder to deal with and creating a disadvantage for the company. Martin issues a press release that allows the union leader to save face without jeopardizing the company. Because of his skill and his independence, Martin is given a promotion that assures his reaching the top—the very top.

But the value of that promotion is equivocal. Martin realizes that he has become what "he had fought against and hated": the corporation man, "tough, smooth, knowledgeable." "He had started out to be something else, something entirely different: the whole man. And he had ended in the old formula. He had fulfilled the pattern." Now he could not go back. He feels that, having won the game, he must remain bound by its rules: "The Empire had bought and paid for him, and he would have to keep going up. . . ." Ironically, it was because he originally possessed the vivid sense of his own freedom and individuality that he has become imprisoned. Now he has fallen into the groove of the successful businessman: "handsome man in his forties, the hair gray at the temples, wearing the dark, expensive suit. There is the gray Homburg; there is the brief case."

Martin Brill is too successful and too willing to assume responsibility to be classed as an organization man as Whyte defines the phrase. But that de Mare is thinking of the danger of the great corporation is explicit, and probably his focus upon this issue owes as much to the sociological writers of his time as to the pervasive presence of the principles of the "open decision." The ambivalence he expresses, however he comes by it, is inescapable in the world he creates. He admires the successful man, but in that success there is the pathos of another kind of failure. John P. Marquand takes up the same theme. More explicitly than de Mare, he suggests that business and society are ruled by the same limitations. Charles Gray, the hero of *Point of No Return,* is up for the vice presidency of the Stuyvesant Bank in New York City. Charley wants the promotion because it means success, and yet he is troubled because such success does not seem to promise full satisfaction. As an officer in the bank he will have passed the point of no return; he will have committed himself unconditionally to its rules. What he will leave behind is the small town of Clyde, Massachusetts, nostalgic memories of which flood his daydreams at this crucial point in his life. But the romantically free Clyde of his memories is only a vision. It rapidly becomes clear that the real Clyde was a cruelly rigid society of rituals and hierarchies, in which the street of one's birth could determine irrevocably where one stood in the system. By leaving, Charley breaks the bonds, becomes the hometown boy who makes good in the big city. In a brief sojourn in Clyde, Charley realizes he could never go back.

Charley sees that his situation in New York is analogous to that of the real Clyde. The bank is organized into a rigid system of protocol in which voice inflections, gestures, and the use of first or last names have subtle but important significance. This is Charley's only alternative now that he has abandoned the dream of Clyde. Yet, he returns to it and the decision of his fate with trepidation. He has worried that he will get the promotion, and he has worried that he will not. When, upon his return, he is convinced by the tone of the president's voice that he has been passed over, he feels a tremendous relief that he has escaped the system. But he is wrong. He has not been passed over. The vice-presidency is his. When he discovers this, he feels numb and tired, partly from the strain of having been kept ignorant and partly from the fear of what this means to his freedom. He is proud to be advanced but troubled that he has been advanced. His clearest regret, however, is that he knows now that he has voluntarily accepted the system. And this, suggests Marquand, is one of the inescapable ambivalences of men's satisfaction. And the point is not that Charley might have squared his dreams with his existence had he done something differently, but that every realization of an aim is by definition defective. A confirmation of this appears in the character of Malcolm Bryant, an academic sociologist who has studied Clyde's social structure. Unlike Charley, Malcolm travels freely, follows his own bent. But Malcolm is also dissatisfied, his freedom is deficient. He boasts that he is interested in people only "academically," but he feels the pain of having no close ties. And his freedom is too often more rootlessness of which he grows tired. In the end, it is Charley's sense of responsibility to himself, his work, and his family that wins our approval. And what Charley finally saves is the consciousness of what he is and what he has done.

In Marquand's *Sincerely, Willis Wade,* Willis does not have quite the power to transcend his situation through consciousness. Unlike Charley, Willis never questions the business ethics that guide his life. Unattractively aggressive, Willis *is* sincere, as the title states. The money and power he seeks appear to him to be the highest goods, and far from apologizing to anyone for pursuing and attaining them, he assumes that everyone else is motivated by the same principles. But not everyone is. The Harcourt family, whose business is the Harcourt Belt Factory in Clyde, is in the genteel tradition of New England business, much like Mrs. Walden's Bradford family—stable, thoughtful, self-confident. In its quiet, aristocratic arrogance, the family implies that it rightly occupies its position of privilege, which position obliges them to their inferiors, Clyde's working families. It is the Harcourt family that gives Willis his start in business by putting him through school and employing him in his early career. When Willis becomes president of several merging companies, including Harcourt Belt, he decides to close the Clyde plant down. It is losing money, and from Willis's standpoint closure is both moral and good business. But for the Harcourts, shutting down the plant means that many of Clyde's faithful will lose jobs they have held for years. Willis does not understand. Their sense of obligation is alien to him, and he is hurt and bewildered when the Harcourts express bitterness at his decision. Marquand does not condemn Willis for what he does, even though the humanitarian principles of the Harcourts seem more attractive. Nor does he attack business as the source of the evil. He invites the reader to sympathize with a character who is repudiated for what his morality tells him is right. What is saddest about Willis is that his sincerity is blind, that he lacks the consciousness of a Charley Gray or a Martin Brill to be able to see what he has done to himself.

Seymour Epstein,[12] in *The Successor,* creates a character who combines the traits of Willis Wade and Charley Gray. Ray Tolchin has both fierce ambition and considerable consciousness of his situation. As a youngster he goes into the business of David Altman, a manufacturer of cheap novelties. Altman's son, Jerry, is totally indifferent to the business, and Ray comes to occupy the position David had hoped Jerry would assume. Ray is driven not only by the desire for success, but by a need to be able to confer gifts. He seeks the power of a larger business and the higher profits it will bring. With those profits he can indulge his generosity, bestow upon almost anyone almost anything. The demands and responsibilities such a power will put upon him, the devotion a larger company will require he assumes eagerly, willing to "accept any consequence. He would have to. He was committed." He persuades the reluctant David to buy up an old, established company and branch out into other lines. Then just as Ray finds himself becoming an executive in a growing company, David discovers that he has cancer. The question becomes whether it is morally right to seek profit and do business while David is ill. Some say that it is not, that all of Ray's concern should be for David. But Ray insists that business is impersonal and has no connection with David's illness. David, too, on his sickbed, realizes that he had never allowed even his concern for his son to interfere with what he took to be good business. He urges Ray on.

Ray does succeed. He brings David's old company into the big time and becomes a man with a briefcase who attends to his business in all parts of the country. When David dies while Ray is away in Los Angeles, closing a crucial deal, the real motive behind Ray's drive is revealed. Flying back to New York, Ray laments that now "there was no one to whom he could bring the banners and trophies." With David's death, the vital spirit has fled Ray's frantic struggle for success. But, as Ray says, he is "committed." Like Charley Gray, he has reached the point of no return. He proceeds mechanically to build the business into a large corporation. But his satisfaction is muted. His wife resigns herself to a pale life in suburbia married to a man who is too busy for his family or any other human ties.

Like Marquand, Epstein does not criticize the institution of business as an evil or suffocating system in itself that can and must be done away with so that men can be free and happy. It is simply another theater of human activity in which life exacts its inevitable payments. The actual entity, says Whitehead, perishes at the moment it achieves its novel end; the for-itself, says Sartre, cannot ever become the in-itself without ceasing to be a for-itself. Ray Tolchin cannot be the kind of powerful businessman he seeks to be without sacrificing something of his humanity. This is the principle of uncertainty at work in human existence. In the sub-atomic world, when we focus upon the electron's speed, we surrender our ability to locate it as a particle; when we focus upon its location, we surrender the precision with which we can measure its speed. When we try to represent its subjective existence to our intellect we get only ambiguity. Analogously, when Martin Brill or Charley Gray or Ray Tolchin seek a contented equilibrium in which satisfaction is complete, they find only ambiguity, disappointing because it constitutes a gap between the aim they conceive of and its realization. This, however, is the definition of the human state, and that state is no more to be repudiated because it does not grant us a godlike completeness of satisfaction than is the electron to be denied because it does not disclose itself in terms of clearcut Newtonian physics. There is, indeed, a good in the human state that is at the heart of the "open decision," the consciousness of oneself as an individual. It is in that consciousness—which is essentially *of* the ambiguity in the heart of our existence—that our human satisfaction lies. That is the core of our existence. Thus, the Martin Brills, the Charley Grays, the Ray Tolchins in these business novels live what is most human, the disappointment that arises only when we are conscious of ourselves as experiencing beings. That consciousness relieves us from the bad faith of the organization man who retreats into the protective "theyness" of the apparatus. It delivers to our lives that high intensity of individuality that is our highest good. And it may occur in business as well as in any other human activity.

Yet, it is obvious that what is affirmative in the novels of de Mare, Marquand, Epstein, and writers like them is implicit rather than expressed. The pathos of loss rather than the discovery of something positive is what they emphasize. The tone of that pathos is also captured by Robert Molloy[13] in *The Other Side of the Hill.* Gerry Crofts, past 50, the affable, efficient, well-liked general manager of Acme Handbags, tries to change his life at this late date. But the neurotic young woman for whom he was going to leave his waspish wife commits suicide, and the whining owner of Acme Handbags persuades him not to quit, but to remain on the job long enough to see the company through a difficult time. He is left with a sense of mild desolation, diminished only by his sardonic sense of humor. As Gerry walks from the owner's office, having agreed to stay, he glances into the vacant cubicle of the recently dead company vice-president: "It was lonely and empty and so was I." What is good and positive in *The Other Side of the Hill* is Gerry Crofts himself. He does not cry out that he has been unjustly victimized. The life he has lived is he; it has been, perhaps, characterized by "waste and mischance," but no one can evade that.

The explicitly positive affirmation of lives like that led by Gerry Crofts in business appears in such novelists as Ralph Maloney[14] and John Brooks. Charlie Riley, in Maloney's *Daily Bread,* like Gerry Crofts, comes to the point where he believes he wants to change his life, to abandon the public relations business he has created with his partner Sandy Brooks, and to leave his wife and start anew with another woman. But to do so would be to ask for a new life because he does not like his old one. The granting of such a request is beyond any agency we know. Then he is drawn back into the world he has created for himself. Brooks begins an underhanded campaign to change the nature of their business operations and Charlie undertakes to preserve the firm in its present form. In the course of his defense he learns something about his romantic desire to transform his life. He had refused to accept the limits imposed by the human condition, assuming that the presence of dreams guarantees the possibility of actualizing them perfectly. But, he comes to see, "It is impossible to do the very best [with life] because you have only one chance; no dry runs." Nor is there any going back on what one has become. This might be "unfair," thinks Charlie, to tantalize one with visions of perfection which in their very nature are not open to realization, "but that's how it is: unfair." One answer to such a discovery is to turn cynic; another, to despair—both are repudiations of life. Charlie's answer, however, is that of the "open decision": "So fight anyway." Charlie becomes the rebel. Not a melodramatic fighter for great causes, but a conscious man who refuses to delude himself. One does not create values by rejecting past acts. Indeed, one affirms those acts as the identity of that one unique, conscious, individual self. Thus, Charlie, newly awakened, goes back to his wife and the business he has saved, "Not because I liked it so much as because that's who I am. The man I am is the man I have become. Not by accident, not overnight, but in the accumulation of years spent working to become that kind of man."

John Brooks, in *The Big Wheel* and *The Man Who Broke Things* gives this theme its most explicit expression. The business apparatus he presents as neither a sanctified system with a monopoly on individual freedom, as Miss Rand and Hawley see it; nor a totalitarian order which viciously thwarts men's fulfillment, as the war novelists and some of the business novelists see it. Like the world, it is incontrovertibly *there*, simultaneously putting limits to our power and providing us with possibilities. It is simply one more realm within which the human being may feel his individuality, and that, in the view of the "open decision," is what satisfaction is. It is to be neither rejected, out of cynicism or despair, nor surrendered to out of fear or apathy. One need not become an organization man to live with it, either. As Jaspers advises men to come to terms with the social apparatus without surrendering their individuality, so Brooks suggests that the business world is to be lived in the full consciousness of its nature and both the limits of one's power and the freedom of one's choice within it.

Some men blindly worship business; others hold it up to contempt. Ed Masterson, editor of the feature-story magazine *Present Day*, in *The Big Wheel*, regards business as a religion in which he has absolute faith. As a religion, it rightly demands the conscience of all its votaries. He believes that *Present Day* has the right to expect its employees to agree in their hearts with the magazine's conservative editorial policy. If his employees withhold their agreement they cannot morally justify taking their salary. Herb Katzman, a bright young cynic on the staff, holds the opposite position. Contemptuous of the whole business world, he regards *Present Day* as a kind of prison to which he sacrifices part of his integrity in return for a salary that gives him other kinds of freedom. He owes, in his view, no allegiance of conscience to the firm and finds nothing immoral in writing articles in which he does not believe. Indeed, there is a kind of virtue in it, for he is winning a victory, he thinks, over a system he detests.

Brooks presents both of these positions as inadequate for dealing with the human condition as represented by *Present Day*. When Ed Masterson learns about Katzman's attitude, he fires him. But that creates a small office rebellion. Work is disrupted, the meeting of deadlines is threatened. The board of directors, oblivious to the devotion and energy Masterson has given to the firm in building it into a successful business, forces him to resign. At the same time it gives Katzman the option of staying on. The board's action simply confirms Katzman's convictions about business: that it is an impersonal mechanism bent only on piling up profits. For him the good in life is the dynamic tension between individuals facing each other in conflict. Contemptuously he quits. He has missed seeing the real character of the business apparatus, however. Masterson meekly resigns, too used to obeying papal edicts even to conceive of rebellion. Masterson also has failed to plumb the nature of the firm. He has surrendered himself to the business like a monk, whose temple is the building that houses the magazine where worship is conducted daily. Such a rigid faith, like the old world view, is always vulnerable to attack. And certainly Brooks uses Masterson as an analogy of the set of values said to have been destroyed by the "acids of modernity." With his dismissal, Masterson finds his "belief broken" and he comes to live "in despair."

Dick Peters, Masterson's young cousin, neither despairs nor retreats into cynicism. To be effective in one's existence, thinks Peters, one must be a kind of player; he must possess that freedom that allows him, as Huizinga suggests, to doubt and believe at the same time. Indeed, "sound belief," he says, can only be built upon "doubt and resignation." Doubt and resignation appear only with consciousness, and consciousness provides the means for transcendence, which is simultaneously repudiation and affirmation. There is no avoiding the fact that the huge *Present Day* company is "partly evil . . . part giant and part monster." And it is clear that to give in to this monster "is nothing less than to die." But if one is to remain a man, one must acknowledge its nature and learn to live with it without being stifled by it. Men, says Peters, may not be masters of the monsters they create, but "the monsters [are not] masters of the men, either." As Peters walks away from the

Present Day building, he sees "neither Masterson's cathedral nor Katzman's dungeon, but only a building standing among others; neither blessed nor accursed, but only there." Men achieve their freedom and the sense of individuality that goes with that freedom by taking up an attitude, by saying "no" to the monster even while they recognize that their negative does not make the monster go away. Were it to do so, men would lose their possibilities for satisfaction. Business, like life, paradoxically limits and frees, and it is in that paradox that men come to the satisfaction of consciousness. Practically, Peters' attitude allows him to make a compromise with the new editor of *Present Day.* In return for not expecting ever to reach the top of the executive hierarchy, Peters wins the concession that he will not be asked to compromise his conscience by having to write articles that run counter to his convictions. He learns to live with the apparatus without submitting to it.

Dick Peters' counterpart in *The Man Who Broke Things* is Bob Billings. He begins as a cynic about business, a romantic who asserts a self-righteous sensitivity that seems less defensible than the practices it condemns. He refuses to go into business, especially the firm in which his father is on the board of directors, the Great Eastern Company, a staid and conservative firm. But when he discovers that his father acted unethically in business during the late 'twenties, he seeks a kind of revenge by going to work for one of his father's enemies, Henry Haislip. He determines to maintain the purity of his values, but he is confronted with a situation for which his values have no answer. Haislip, like Willis Wade an insensitive and ambitious man and an apostle of that business ethic which justifies every decision on the basis of its effect upon the commercial enterprise, undertakes to gain control of Great Eastern Company. His aim is to change it into a more modern and effective business instrument. But to do so he must destroy some of the men on the firm's board of directors. Bob is perplexed. Deliberately hurting people is not right, he reflects. On the other hand, the chairman of the board, the object of Haislip's campaign, is indeed a senile old man and he has made the company as sterile and as static as himself. At first outraged by Haislip's methods, Bob is educated to reality. He comes to see that he has sought to avoid "the doubts and complexities and impostures of modern life," illustrated here in the fight between Haislip and the Great Eastern directors, by taking refuge in "a sort of archaic simplified world of fixed and known weights and measures." Again Brooks self-consciously invokes the twentieth-century dilemma. To insist upon "fixed and known weights and measures" when they are no longer relevant is to reject the things we are certain of and to dismiss our own possibilities for fulfillment. Without condoning Haislip's behavior, Bob concludes that life in business "when you get involved in it, was after all just life." With that notion, Bob moves away from cynicism and opens himself to freedom without business.

The main preoccupation of these novelists, whether celebrators of business like Ayn Rand, detractors of business like Stanley Kauffmann, or supporters of the social ethic like Sloan Wilson, is the good of the individual—as opposed, say, to the good of the social order or the glory of God. That preoccupation shows how general and how basic is the pattern of thought represented in the "open decision." None of the writers I have discussed in this chapter has been hailed by critics or readers as the best of our period. For that reason, perhaps, the issues of the age are simplified and isolated with more obviousness in this group of novels. Whatever the position of the novelist, he pictures the individual beset on all sides by forces (business, social, or governmental) that would deprive him of his freedom. So deprived, according to the metaphysics of the "open decision," he becomes less alive and less human. The forces of the government, as Ayn Rand and Garth Hale see them, intrude upon the individual in such a way as to make an object out of him, as to force him into patterns of choice and behavior that debases the value of his subjective intensity. Business is the world in which the individual is allowed to keep his subjective indeterminacy and his unique possibilities. For other novelists, like Ralph Maloney and Robert Molloy, business is the limiting feature, the "non-living" society. And from it the individual cannot escape.

John Brooks offers the fullest conclusion about the novelists in this chapter. He has his characters take up a position toward business that neither condones nor attacks it. It cannot be dealt with, anymore than life can, by moralizing for or against it on the basis of values once assumed to be absolute but now no longer relevant, any more than the physicist can deal with the atom solely on the basis of Newtonian physics. Brooks makes explicit what most of the novelists discussed in this chapter tacitly assume. The human condition, as suggested by the "open decision," is inherently limiting, and business is a way of representing that condition. One may surrender in despair or retreat in cynicism because of those limitations. Or one may submerge himself in the apparatus—the social ethic—and avoid the responsibility of being himself. When one does none of these, his final recourse is to choose to live within those limits. That choice entails a certain sadness, the pathos of dreams dissipated by awareness. But that choice is also the choice of our humanity, our consciousness of being an individual that embraces simultaneously success and failure. Such a state will not satisfy those who refuse to credit any experience as satisfactory that does not involve making the ideal real. But for men like Dick Peters, Bob Billings, and their analogues in the rest of these novels, such resistance constitutes a closing off of possibilities and a deficiency of consciousness. Satisfaction lies in the consciousness of the paradoxes of our lives, and it is in those paradoxes that we gain a high intensity of individuality. Business, like life, either forces men to protect that inviolable core of the self or it drives men to surrender it and to take the social ethic as the highest value. All of these novelists are aware of the issues. Most of them choose, implicitly or explicitly, the values of the "open decision," the sense of freedom within limits by which our experience is defined.

6

THE "HIP" NOVEL—THE FIGURE OF CAIN

MAX DEMIAN, in Herman Hesse's novel *Demian*, interprets the Cain story by making Cain the injured party and the repository of virtue. He has been given his mark, says Max, because he has chosen to violate the shibboleths of a stultified group of social conformists. He is called criminal because he would jar this group loose from its bourgeois platitudes.

The group of novelists to be discussed in this chapter includes Alexander Trocchi,[1] J. P. Donleavy, Elliott Baker, Alfred Grossman, Jack Kerouac, John Clellon Holmes, Chandler Brossard, and William Burroughs.[2] The similarity that joins them is not the setting of their novels, as with the war and business novelists; it is the fact that they see the issues of their world in terms of the Cain celebrated by Max Demian. They are preoccupied with the repressiveness of an industrialized, middle-class, technological society, and with the value of spontaneity by which the individual—Cain—fights that repressiveness. Their conviction is that, as one of John Clellon Holmes's characters says, only the rebel and outlaw can "feel freshly" anymore. In some of these novels, the mark of Cain is the needle scar of the heroin user, that most sinister of all outlaws for the American middle class. In other novels, especially those of William Burroughs, the needle marks are "stigmata," tokens of the junky's victimization. Cain throws off the wraps of conventional wisdom, embarks upon what Norman Mailer calls the journey into "the rebellious imperatives of the self." He does so both by rejecting the social standards according to which he is judged an outcast,

For Notes to Chapter 6, see page 404.

and by "going away"—figuratively through heroin and marijuana, and literally by removing himself physically from society. His aim is to discover himself, to find the seat of his spontaneity, to locate what Husserl calls the "eidos." Cain "brackets" the world and sets it aside, leaving only his irreducible and authentic self, which is metaphysically the ultimate reality and morally the highest good in the "open decision."

The prototype of these novels is Trocchi's *Cain's Book.* It is narrated by Joe Necchi, who seeks to find himself by breaking down the barriers of convention, tradition, and social expectation that separates his outer and inner selves, and by opening up the ambiguous possibilities of his life. These possibilities, says Joe—echoing the epistemological principle of the "open decision" in general and Brooks's Bob Billings in particular (cf. p. 197)—wait "beyond what is fixed and known," in an unpredictable land outside that conforming America whose machinery has "impressed its forms deep into the fibres of the human brain so as to make efficiency and the willingness to cooperate the only flags of value, where all extravagance, even of love, [is] condemned. . . ." This America is essentially urban America, and in it Necchi finds conditions that threaten his existence as an intensely authentic human being who is free to exercise his spontaneous self in choosing from many possibilities. Joe has a "horror of groups," because they claim "the right to subsume all my acts under certain normative designations in terms of which they would reward or punish me." In the city he is bound to preestablished responses and feelings. In the city "Things moved or they were subversive." The city fixes and knows. It would objectify the living individual and close possibilities. It purports to be the ground of its citizens' existence. But Joe Necchi cites the manifesto of both Cain and the "open decision": "*I* am the ground of all existence." Therefore, he must turn away from the group, like Thoreau—and Theocritus and countless other pastoralists before him. *Cain's Book* is his account of what he has done, his "inventory" of what remains "after his eviction." It is "Cain's book," because he breaks the law of society by defying it. Like Demian, Joe Necchi sees Cain, not Abel, as the aggrieved party. Abel is a "butcher" and Joe says he always "felt it strange that the butcher Abel should be preferred to the agriculturist Cain." Abel is a capitalist, soon the owner of "vast herds and air-conditioned slaughterhouses." But Cain's crops are blighted, and Cain himself becomes destitute and thin. Seeing him so,

> Abel approached his brother, saying: Why don't you give up and come to work for me? I could use a good man in the slaughterhouse.
> And Cain slew him.

Certainly justifiable homicide. More than that, the act of a genuine man.

Necchi slays no one. He simply rejects the standards of his contemporary urbanized Abels. First he uses heroin and marijuana. Heroin, he says, brings him to the present moment, to his own experience. The ritual of the "fix" demonstrates "respect for the whole chemistry of alienation." Marijuana also takes "one more intensely into whatever experience." It intensifies the "pleasures of poetry, art, and music" for those whom the pressures of the group have made insensitive. Echoing Sartre and Huizinga, Necchi declares that marijuana produces the "ability to adopt play postures," to become involved and remain detached simultaneously. Necchi does not use marijuana and heroin merely for kicks. Heroin especially can be a way of life that both defies and accepts. The junkies with whom Joe turns on talk too frequently about "kicking" the habit. For Joe, this simply plays into the hands of the enemy, whose standards are invoked by the talk of kicking. When one declares he will rid himself of his habit, he is truly hooked. "Get high and relax," Joe advises his friends. The junky is in a situation similar to that of the rebel. They are both caught in a condition which they can control only by their attitude. They cannot escape that condition. They can only accept it. Joe tells his companions "that there was no way out." But as with the formulators of the "open decision," who look for a way of living without appeal and who find their satisfaction within the bounds of the human condition, this need not cause frustration and despair. Its acceptance could itself be a beginning, so long as one retains his integrity by rebelling, too. Joe thus exhorts his friends "to accept, to endure, to record. As a last act of blasphemy I exhorted them to be ready to pee on the flames."

Joe also goes away from society physically. He takes a job on a scow that operates on the waterways around New York City. The means of separation, though, reflect an important facet of the Cain figure, and recalls Whitehead's conception about societies. From the scow, Joe can see Manhattan "like a little mirage in which one isn't involved." He can feel himself free of that city; had he not gone on the scow his alternatives would have been only "prison, madhouse, morgue." Yet, that scow is tied by hawsers to society's dock. His separation has not been total. There is danger in extreme isolation just as in the heart of the city. "I often wondered," writes Joe in his journal, "how far out a man could go [away from society] without being obliterated." When his scow is being towed in a storm, Joe has the tormented "sense of being adrift," tied as he is to the tugboat by only one line. If that were to go, he would float out into the Atlantic, be "obliterated." He is frantic to make sure the line holds and unspeakably relieved when he is saved. One cannot expect to go too far away from society and remain intact. In the same way that space and motion are meaningless without the presence of bodies in some relation with each other, the concept of an individual (an "actual entity") apart from a society of other individuals providing data for self-creation is senseless. Yet, the individual must fight any tendency in the prevailing social order that would lead to a nonliving society, which in turn would diminish the potential for satisfaction. Thus, the suffocating embrace of the city must be broken and Joe takes heroin and uses the scow as his wedges in the operation. His aim is to mobilize "raw memory," to participate in "the existential," to remove all "barriers to the gradual refinement of the central nervous system," to escape the "unquestioning acceptance of conventional abstractions."

Another attack upon those abstractions, which are the binding rules of nonliving societies and the thwarters of individual fulfillment, comes from William S. Burroughs, who is more intense, more frightening, more surrealistic than Trocchi is. One of Alfred Grossman's characters exclaims, "Does not the American scene as daily imprinted on your retina and eardrum make you want to leap up and down with both feet and scream pornographic imprecations into the cold desert night?" Burroughs' books come close to being "pornographic imprecations," hurled against the same America as that described by Trocchi, and his attack is deep and complex. He writes of strange worlds, of people whose actions and feelings are disturbingly unfamiliar, sometimes frightening and sometimes disgusting. His nightmare descriptions are drug-induced—hallucinatory. They are "notes on sickness and delirium," made, as he says in his Introduction to *Naked Lunch,* under the influence of dope and hallucinogens. Burroughs deliberately ignores the apologies and the compromises of the middle class, which by definition is in bad faith. The title of *Naked Lunch* means that he presents the uncompromising truth, "a frozen moment when everyone sees what is on the end of every fork," when limiting assumptions are bracketed and set aside.

The "truth" that he presents is not a photograph of the society from which Joe Necchi escapes into drugs. It is an allegorical truth about the trapped junky, the prisoner of a system which obscenely feeds off of him. The junky is a victim, says Burroughs, and his life exemplifies the life of every individual caught in such a system, for "there are many forms of addiction and I think they all obey basic laws." The world of the addict, which Burroughs depicts, stands for the larger world. Both infect their citizens with a "Human Virus," a psychological sickness that destroys the human being, his spontaneous love, and his authentic impulses. The symptoms of this virus are "poverty, hatred, war, police-criminals, bureaucracy, insanity." The world in which these symptoms appear is one of hideous deformity and terrible perversions, where crabmen devour the translucent flesh of moldy old men, and giant black centipedes, metamorphosed from men, scuttle about in a landscape of Kafkaesque horror. If these are literally the content of a junky's hallucinations under drugs, they are also a way of representing the character of the nonhallucinatory world, for in that world men are, Burroughs suggests, no less helpless prisoners. They are like the constituents of a stone society compelled to follow rigidly laid down courses.

The allegorical connection between the drug world and that of a repressive society is subtle and sophisticated. The junky—analogous to a social conformist—is the prisoner of his habit. In *Nova Express,* the habit is represented as a "criminal" that takes up residence in a "host"—that is, a junky. The junky regulates this criminal through drugs—specifically morphine. Allegorically, morphine acts as a policeman that operates constantly to regulate the criminal. Burroughs calls this agency the "morphine police." They do not, of course, work to rid the host of his "criminal" habit. They are parasitic, purporting to deal with the criminal, but needing his presence for their own existence. They tend to perpetuate the habit. The junky collaborates in order to "protect the disease." But, as Burroughs says, he is "not in a position to act in any other way." This situation is largely the doing of the "Nova Mob," the symbol of a tyrannical society that flourishes on the destruction of its citizens' independence and integrity. The Mob cultivates the existence of conflicting and incompatible forms of life on the planets, causing them eventually to explode and destroy themselves—Burroughs uses the word *nova,* apparently, to mean explosion. Morphine, in other words, drugs in general, and social tyranny—all are incompatible with man's individuality. They produce conflicts which eventually destroy him. The Nova Mob exerts its control through the Nova criminal and the morphine police. It is itself a "syndicate" that is also a "government," and controls the "scanning pattern we accept as 'reality' " through "word and image." Besides the general relationship between this structure and that of American society, there is a specific relation between the morphine police and the urban narcotics squads. Far from curing addiction, argues Burroughs (and many others), narcotics squads simply help perpetuate it. Without it, they would not be needed. Similarly, conventional law enforcement does not want to root out crime for then it would lose its reason for being. Police are parasitic. And the syndicate that controls them, as Burroughs sees it, controls all through the conventional abstractions, through the words of tradition and the images of prejudice, through bad faith, false consciousness.

Burroughs does not claim that contemporary American society —as represented by the Nova Mob and its control of the junky-victim—has a monopoly on thought control and repression of individual spontaneity. In *The Soft Machine,* the narrator takes an imaginary journey into the past and visits a Mayan village. In this primitive atmosphere, so frequently associated with the freedom of the noble savage, Burroughs sees only another example of tyranny. The villagers are controlled in "thought feeling and sensory impressions" by the priests, who are "nothing but word and image." Moving to the other end of the chronological scale, in *Naked Lunch,* Burroughs calls a fantasy town of the future "Pigeon Hole." Its citizens violate human individuality by pigeon-holing people, finding their common denominator. The townspeople of Pigeon Hole regard urbanites with hostility and consider black men as animals. The town is sick with fear and prejudice; it is corrupt, rotten, depraved—a parody of the myth of the decent small country town. No better than the Mayan village or Pigeon Hole, which reflect a form of fascism, is the imaginary "Freeland." It represents the society of the political liberal, but its name is ironic. Freeland is "a welfare state," and as such it is every bit as suffocating as Puerto Joselito and Pigeon Hole (whose similarities are declared by the letters of their names). "If a citizen wanted anything from a load of bone meal to a sexual partner some department was ready to offer effective aid. The threat implicit in this enveloping benevolence stifled the concept of rebellion. . . ."

Drug addiction is both a literal example of human imprisonment and thought control and a figurative representation of similar forces at work in human society at large. It is both a means of control and the result of control. It operates to debase and deceive. Drug addiction, like the Nova Mob, makes promises that only corrupt and destroy. The "syndicates" promise a "Garden of Delights Immortality Cosmic Consciousness The Best Ever in Drug Kicks. And *love love love.*" But the ecstasy they bring is sterile and destructive, and Burroughs takes pains to make this explicit. He tries to show in *Nova Express* as, according to him, he tried to show in *Naked Lunch* and *The Soft Machine*, that the "love" promised is "*love* in slop buckets," and that "Their Garden of Delights is a terminal sewer." This judgment is demonstrated in the pervasive and detailed homosexual perversions which Burroughs recites in all of his books. He has said that the "pornographic" portions of *Naked Lunch* are meant to be "a tract against Capital Punishment." In these passages young boys are hanged, and at the moment of their death, gleeful pederasts symbolically deal the penile death blow, the potentially productive semen of both victim and victimizer falling, at the moment of hideous orgasm, onto barren ground. The apparent pleasure that Americans seem to take in issuing the death sentence and carrying it out is characterized by Burroughs as disgusting sexual perversion. This is part of the Garden of Delights that ends in a "terminal sewer."

There are other aspects to the "syndicate's" promises that also relate to the perverted sado-masochism of death, execution, and illimitable but sterile erotic gratification. They encourage a preoccupation with anal pleasure which leads to the degradation of human sexuality. Ejaculations spurt into the air, onto the floor, against bare stomachs, and into anuses—never into wombs. As Burroughs says, these acts are "terminal," in most senses of that word. The homosexual pleasures are usually related with death (inescapably explicit in the hanging episodes), excrement, sewage. After a homosexual climax in *The Soft Machine,* young Billy lies floating in warm fetid water, "breathing sewage smells of the canal." Puerto Joselito is a nightmare of death, erotic self-indulgence, and the destruction of all that is virile, productive, and natural. The sexual perversions in which the natives engage are, as Burroughs writes in another context, "dreamy and brutal, depraved and innocent." These acts are like the hideous "Black Meat," which is "overpoweringly delicious and nauseating, so that the eaters eat and vomit and eat again until they fall exhausted." The consequences of the Mayan's appetite for sex is associated with an "addiction" to the sexual pleasure promised by drugs. Puerto Joselito's old men are "boneless," "muttering addicts of the orgasm drug," and are eventually eaten by crabmen. Their bonelessness suggests the emasculating effects of drug pleasures and, symbolically, of social tyranny. The young boys, like drug addicts, cooperate in their emasculation by saying "yes" to uncontrolled, unlimited erotic gratification. Such appetites also lead to the destruction of one's biological nature. Carl is transformed into a woman when the Commandments of Puerto Joselito rub him with jelly, shriveling his genitals, and bringing him "orgasm after orgasm." He is converted, like the drug addict, into a quivering red blob, racked with "boneless spasms."

The sterility of drug addiction is represented by the sterility of homosexual ecstasy. Both, in turn, result from the control of the "host" by the criminal representative of a repressive force, a force which stifles independence and selfness. The sterility of that control is suggested by Burroughs in *Naked Lunch.* ". . . control can never be a means to any practical end. . . . It can never be a means to anything but more control. . . . Like Junk. . . ." The society that practices such control would make criminals out of individuals and seek the death penalty of those guilty of "the crime of separate life." In America, says Burroughs' thinly disguised narrator William Lee, we "have a special horror of giving up control, of letting things happen in their own way without interference." It is that horror that on the one hand leads to junk and on the other causes us to interpret as a criminal whoever rejects control.

Burroughs would break free to liberate human spontaneity, which stimulates growth and constitutes identity. And he would do so in ways similar to those of Trocchi. The literal antidote to literal morphine addiction is, writes Burroughs, apomorphine. This is a regulator, but unlike parasitic morphine, it is not habit-forming. Burroughs thus does not think of freedom as unregulated life, nor spontaneity as license. Apomorphine gets rid of the drug habit by establishing a new regulation of the metabolism, which is organic and independent. But once it establishes the new order, it leaves. It does not have to be continued. Allegorically, apomorphine is the Nova Police, who search out the criminals of habit in order to relieve the host of habit's "criminal" control. Having done so, the Nova Police disappear, having put the host back in possession of his authentic self, free to grow and develop. If the Nova Mob controls the "scanning pattern we accept as 'reality,'" the Nova Police seek to "occupy the Reality Studio and retake their universe of Fear Death and Monopoly." In turn, bureaus must be replaced by "co-operatives." Bureaus are "cancers," and like the "virus" of dope kill the host. The bureau cannot live without the state just as the morphine police cannot live without the criminal of habit. The co-operative cannot live with the state. It is a "building up of independent units to meet the needs of the people who participate in the functioning of the unit." Only those free of the destructive force of the totalitarian state—be it fascist or welfare—can operate as individuals and directly contribute to the *functioning* of their own society.

Several of Burroughs' characters call for these reforms. Brion Gysin Hassan i Sabbah adjures, "prisoners, come out," create a new order. Uranian Willy, in *Nova Express,* defects from the Nova Mob and urges, "Souls rotten from the orgasm drug, flesh shuddering from the ovens, prisoners of the earth come out." He recommends a revolution against the thought control of the "virus" of words and images, the "conventional abstractions" of the Nova Mob, which lock the mind into "habits" and suppress freedom. If the Nova Mob controls through language, which symbolizes and is symbolized by dope, then, says Willy, we must "Cut word lines—Shift linguals."

For example, take a recording tape upon which has been recorded some ten minutes of conventional speech. The words of that speech fall into certain patterns. This is analogous to the tape of the mind, upon which have been fixed, according to rigid conventional patterns, certain assumptions that guide our reactions, our feelings, our perceptions. Run the tape back and record new words on it at random. When the newly recorded tape is played back, the old patterns are abolished. The assumptions of the past, seemingly absolute, have been transformed. "You have," says Burroughs' narrator in *Naked Lunch,* "turned time back ten minutes and wiped electromagnetic word patterns off the tape and substituted other patterns." In this way, "The old mind tapes can be wiped clean." These new patterns are similar to the new order created by apomorphine, and to the co-operatives that replace the bureaus. It is an order, as in Whitehead's living societies, in which spontaneity can flourish, but which is regarded as criminal by the repressive state of addiction and bureaucracy.

Northrop Frye defines satire as a genre which depicts reality as a demonic underworld, pervaded by executions and emasculations, in which man is a helpless victim of diabolical forces. Burroughs' work fits this description. The figure of Cain, of course, is not a helpless victim, but an infuriated rebel taking action—however futilely—against what he considers to be injustice. The Cain in Burroughs' novels is Burroughs himself. There is a rage in the way he presents his world that cannot easily be pacified, and that rage expressed in satire is a violent blow directed at the conditions he depicts. He taunts the perpetrators of those conditions with an exaggerated "truth" that has a close enough correspondence to the actual world for it to strike home with effect. The same fury appears, though with less intensity and less success, in some of the work of Alfred Grossman, J. P. Donleavy, and Elliott Baker. In their novels, the Cain figure is in the characters they create rather than in themselves as author. Their protagonists are restive under the constraints of a repressive society. Their rebellion—their search for integrity and freedom—takes the form of cheating, lying, hurting—even murdering—with very little sense of guilt. They nurse a grievance which justifies them in whatever strikes they make against the enemy. By the standards of that enemy they are thoughtless, selfish, immoral, self-indulgent. Though their creators, perhaps, do not unconditionally approve of them; yet they are presented as advanced guerilla units engaged in warfare against the totalitarian and emasculating social monolith.

Sebastian Dangerfield, in Donleavy's *The Ginger Man,* is an American student in Dublin, the husband of a proper Britisher, and the father of a child. He attends the very traditional law school at Trinity College. But he feels hemmed in and his behavior wins him no supporters from the establishment. His teachers disregard him. His father, who disapproves of him, refuses to bequeath him his inheritance until he reaches 47. And his wife, Marion, admonishes him for insulting her friends, for sabotaging any chance they might help him with their influence, and for ruining her "socially"—"Daddy," she cries reprovingly, "was so right." This is a world in which wealthy "public schoolboys" will talk to Sebastian and his friends but consider them "a little coarse." It is a world of grasping landlords and stuffy government ministers who belong to an elite by birth.

Sebastian reacts to this world with an air of injured innocence. How "can I get away from evil in this world?" he asks. "How to put down the sinners and raise the doers of good." He declares, "I want to show them the way and I expect only taunts and jeers." Not only is he misunderstood; he is sacrificially victimized: "I may be just a bit younger than Christ when they tacked him up but they've had me outstretched a few times already." And with characteristic self-pity, his last words in the novel are:

> *God's mercy*
> *On the wild*
> *Ginger Man,*

that is, himself. He has been driven, he implies, to wild acts by a hypocritical society that squelches all moves toward spontaneity and freedom. His innocence and the wickedness of society justify almost any kind of behavior. He is a confirmed philanderer and an irresponsible prodigal with money—judgments, it should be said, typical of the society he strains against. He damages both of the houses he and his wife rent in Dublin. He neglects his studies and abuses Marion. When she leaves him, he finds her out, moves back in with her, and sponges off her until she runs from him again. In London, he helps start a destructive brawl in a pub. And later, at a

New Year's Eve party, he insults the gathered guests, proclaiming loudly that "Christmas is a fraud. This room is filled with knaves and thieves. Jesus was a Celt and Judas was British. . . . Now I have it from good sources that some of you own pig sties and I must confess that the rearing of pigs to me is extremely distasteful. . . ."

Donleavy's portrait is not without its satiric side. In claiming monopolies on truth and virtue, as well as a resemblance to Christ, Sebastian perhaps inadvertently displays his posturing, unjustified sense of innocent grievance. His selfishness hurts not only his wife, who is strong enough to maintain her independence, but weaker, unsuspecting persons. After he seduces the timid and love-hungry Miss Frost, his boarder, he snores away guiltlessly by her side while she agonizes, as a Catholic, over her mortal sin. Yet, the final implication is that Sebastian is justified in defiantly violating a stuffy society's most cherished values: familial devotion, marital fidelity, ambition, respect for property and money. As Cain he is a hero. Coming out of the hospital after the fight at the London pub, he and two of his friends form a "tragic trinity." The night of the New Year's Eve party, when he indiscriminately insults many people he has never seen before, is described as "honesty night." And the time of the party—the closing of the old year and the birth of the new one—suggests that Sebastian has achieved a kind of purge. His violence and venom are not the signs of a childish tantrum. They contribute, as Donleavy would have it, to the creation of new life.

Grossman, too, says that violence is fertile, that it produces life in the midst of social death. Charles Kraft, the protagonist of *Many Slippery Errors*, does acknowledge the desirability of "law and order." But, he cautions, "Perhaps we have too much law and order in this country [America], in any country highly industrialized and rationalized. . . ." When such a condition prevails and the lives of young people have fallen into boredom and their work has become "routinized, circumscribed, deprived of interest," then "a little excitement, tension and overt violence in their youths will give them at least a memory of color down the tunnel of the long gray years." Kraft, a respectable 29-year-old demographer for the U.N., seeks for color and renewal in his own life, partly through violence and partly through flight. He takes up with a gang of young hoodlums in Brooklyn, whose weird initiations violate all the conventional sex taboos, and falls in love with one of the slum girls—Pia. At the same time, he enters into an agreement with old Dicherty, the night watchman where the gang holds its meetings, to blow up one of the city's power plants. In the end, his romance with Pia is frustrated when she marries one of the gang members, and his move toward destruction he himself backs out of because it seems poorly planned and badly conceived. But these results do not show that the violence of the streets is an undesirable response to the character of a social law and order "over the formulation and imposition of which the individual has so little control." The time is simply not right. He still anticipates "another, better, Pia, a true unknown, a true new country, but one I will be permitted this time to explore. More practically, there will come, I am sure, another, better Dicherty, a Dicherty who not only knows that something must be done—everybody knows that something must be done—but who knows how to do it, who has a plan. Perhaps, just perhaps, it may be that I will find a plan myself."

The violation of sanctified social mores takes another form with Charles besides violence. He breaks the laws of marriage and the taboo of incest. His wife, Sally, follows all the latest fashions, true to the track society has put her on. She works, concerns herself with chic psychological explanations of human motives, and she expresses feelings of insecurity though she is the thoroughly emancipated woman. Charles feels more comfortable with Sally's sister, Kate. Kate, like Charles has with Sally, has become involved with a male representative of the phony society—a pompous lawyer named Robert Richard Russell, who wants to marry her. Kate, on the other hand, openly tries to persuade Charles to make love to her. Refusing at first, Charles finally realizes that the road to at least partial freedom is in divorcing Sally and marrying Kate, and he shocks Sally by letting her find him and her sister in bed together.

Grossman formulates a rationale for defiance and outright violence that recalls Niebuhr's *Moral Man and Immoral Society:* ". . . we must live in a tension between the commands of society and the demands of the individual, not acceding wholly to one or to the other," says Charles Kraft. We must not, he goes on, allow "law and order" to mean acceptance of "the monolithic and unquestioned dicta of society without opposition." Ethical behavior is not conformity to a system over which the individual has no control. It is fidelity to the order which the individual creates himself, which has validity because it arises from the authentic self rather than the imposed conditions of his society. This is one of the basic principles of the "open decision," and the hero of Grossman's first novel, *Acrobat Admits,* articulates that principle. Going under the alias of "Hugo," he enters into an affair with a girl, Stephanie, under the laws of truthfulness with and fidelity to each other that they themselves have created and that do not require social sanction to be valid. Most people, says Hugo, blindly and slavishly submit to an order given them. But he and Stephanie "haven't inherited any order we can use. So for us to create an order was to do in little the most important thing our mutual species ever did. We re-enacted Genesis, and the departure from the jungle." In a world in which man has no access to transcendent meaning, the best he can do is create his own. But Hugo mistakenly thinks that words can produce the "meaning" of their relationship. Stephanie heatedly declares that this is not so, that Hugo must "involve" himself—must live and act the values he only speaks of. Hugo sees that she is right, and that the anger she displays in reaction to his demands of fidelity from her is justified. He does not arrive, however, at an involvement with Stephanie that will allow them to start anew. Instead, he learns another kind of action. When Stephanie maintains that her relationship with a German businessman, Eric, is none of Hugo's affair and threatens to begin sleeping with him, Hugo counters with a rage of his own. He drives his sense of having failed Stephanie out of his mind by deciding to kill Eric.

As in *The Ginger Man,* so in *Acrobat Admits* the author's judgment of his Cain-like protagonist is equivocal. Murder is hardly to be regarded as the virtuous solution to any human problem. The sanctions against murder have been rigidly institutionalized in almost all human cultures. Nor has Grossman presented Hugo as the most honest creature in the world. Hugo has sought to counter the dullness and pallor of his life by making "something different happen." He deceives both Stephanie and another girl, Cairo Joy, using phony names, telling them lies, and keeping their existence from each other. He is, in other words, something of a Sebastian Dangerfield. With a sense of complete justification he goes out to murder Eric. And he seems to be embarking upon the proper course. His decision is spontaneous and it calls for an irrational act. But the point is that it is action and not words, not his old pursuit for "meaning." The proposition that individual creativity leads to a high intensity of satisfaction is valid in terms of the "open decision." And, as Charles Kraft says in *Many Slippery Errors,* sometimes that creativity must take the form of violence. Hugo is also convinced of this. ". . . there was no need to do anything but burst out in violence that needed no meaning. Good. Good. Good." Hugo has found the ultimate spontaneous act, the ultimate violation of society's laws. The significance of this act does not have a meaning that can be articulated in language. The significance is in the act itself, which, like the ultimate action of the quantum, is enigmatic to an observer who would objectify it. The logical meaninglessness of Hugo's action is emphasized by the ironical fact that he does not kill Eric, the superficial source of his chagrin over Stephanie. Inadvertently, he kills someone else. It is, as I say, difficult to justify the irresponsible aimlessness of his behavior. But in spite of the equivocal nature of the judgment, it is positive. One of the characteristics of the figure of Cain is that his actions do break laws and cannot for that very reason be justified by the standards broken. He violates society's laws. But more than that: he refuses to feel guilty for that violation. Hugo is like Sartre's Orestes in *The Flies,* who murders his parents but rejects the punishing sense of guilt Zeus would put upon him. In remaining thus free, Orestes claims to free his countrymen from the absolute control of Zeus, the super-ego. Similarly, Hugo is untroubled by the murder he commits. He escapes, at first a little shaken, but "By the time I got to the station I was all right." Hugo, like Orestes, exemplifies the rebel against tradition, the traveler into forbidden country, the seeker after new experiences, and the opener, as Trocchi might say, of new circuits of the individual nervous system.

Samson Shillitoe, in Baker's *A Fine Madness,* also seeks freedom, but unlike either Sebastian Dangerfield or Hugo, he seeks it for a clear purpose. His "fine madness" is his passion to complete a second volume of poems. Besides several of his own writing blocks, Samson is impeded by a bourgeois social order that insists each citizen conform to its own rigid laws and no others. He is harassed by the city of New York, the police, a ladies' art society, psychiatrists, and divorce lawyers. The novel is about his attempt both to maintain his integrity in the land of the Philistines, and to find a place serene enough for him to finish his poem. Samson, like the three previous protagonists I have discussed, has no sense of guilt. He is amoral, selfish, and full of appetite. His only guide is his poetry. Divorced, he lives with a coarse but lovable waitress named Rhoda, who is his common-law wife. She understands his need to write but not his poetry. He is faithful to her emotionally, perhaps, but he, like Dangerfield, seeks women almost automatically. When he is crossed, Samson is a wild animal. He has no more respect for property than did Dangerfield. His behavior is so counter to convention—so full of life and intensity and individuality—that society cannot safely tolerate his "madness." A neurological psychiatrist claims that Samson is a danger to himself and his community and that the only way to handle him is by frontal lobotomy. Samson's very passion finally brings him under the psychiatrist's knife. He returns to the doctor's hospital to recover his precious manuscript. When he cannot find it, he becomes a wild man, furious and raving. That great natural power is suddenly imprisoned. Samson is shot full of drugs and the psychiatrist removes his frontal lobe.

But as with *The Ginger Man, Acrobat Admits,* and *Many Slippery Errors, A Fine Madness* ends with hope for renewal. Implausibly, the lobotomy affects Samson only slightly. He can still function and he is determined to complete his poem. Taking Rhoda—an indication of his generosity and fidelity—Samson escapes New York, the police who are after him, and his ex-wife's lawyer. He retreats to the small town of Cob City, Indiana. There he can live safely and write his poem. That he has successfully asserted his unconventionality against a restrictive society is signaled first by the fact that his "fine madness" is proof against the lobotomy, the symbol of all the stultifying tortures of the modern world, and second by the fact that Rhoda, as they approach Cob City, tells him she is pregnant. The possibility of new life suddenly illuminates the theme of his poem: birth. He is ecstatic. "Then the fourth part of the poem broke free, its wild wind carrying him higher and higher. And the words, like hard-brined fists of fire, beat back at the sun." His superficial rebellion is over. His poem becomes the expression of a higher consciousness that frees Samson to be his own spontaneous self. Now he will "beat back at the sun," challenge through his own consciousness even the power of nature, and in doing so assert the intrinsic value of his own novel satisfaction.

The figure of Cain that appears in the contemporary American novel has another side to him. He is not always bitter, aggrieved, violent. The characters in Jack Kerouac's *On the Road* do reject American middle-class society, complaining that it has throttled the spontaneous life of the inner self in its obsession with deodorants and shiny new cars. They do smoke marijuana, steal, drink, engage in free love, violate many cherished bourgeois standards. They race about madly in old cars, constantly broke and constantly on the move, searching indiscriminately for "kicks," and impatient with delay. Dean Moriarty says, "Man, let's eat, *Now!*" Finding the hindrances of convention intolerable, Kerouac's people in his various other novels go underground, become "subterraneans" or "Dharma bums," abandon the values of work, success, cleanliness. But they are not marked by the bitter aggressiveness of a Sebastian Dangerfield or the apocalyptic helplessness of a William Burroughs homosexual. They possess a kind of joyous naïveté, searching for pleasure out of an exuberant enthusiasm for life rather than a mindless hedonism, for in that pleasure they find the highest intensity of satisfaction and the clearest and firmest expression of themselves.

But contemporary American society is not, as these novelists see it, hospitable to that enthusiasm, and Cain is characterized by a nostalgic sense of its loss. In John Clellon Holmes's *Get Home Free,* Paul Hobbes laments "that we'll never make it in this century, because we've lost touch with something—something wild and natural, call it bliss or reality, a capacity for spontaneous love, whatever—but it's the only thing that can renew the consciousness when it's exhausted by anxiety. . . ." Modern America, with its technology and engineering, its profit-seeking and thing-getting, has stifled the authentic human being in its citizens. In his first trip to Cob City, Samson Shillitoe resentfully muses over what has been done to the countryside by the new turnpikes, symbols of the subtly totalitarian society of the big cities. They represent the priority given to speed over "character" and the interest of the countryside: "No wildflowers, no loafing cows, no limestone quarrys, no apple trees, cherry trees, pear trees, neither rye nor clover to decorate the way of the itinerant bus. . . . The anesthetists and the slide rule boys had been here and that was that."

Ironically, the lost wildness and naturalness, the lost spontaneity, is to be recovered in America, though not, of course, middle-class America. "I suppose what I'm really doing," says Paul Hobbes, "is searching for the natives, for the lost America." The true natives are not those who have submitted to the apparatus, who have consigned themselves as prisoners to the common circuits of the collective nervous system. They are the "rebels, the oddballs, and outcasts." They are the Cains—the only ones who, as I remarked earlier, "can still feel freshly any more." Who discovers these natives discovers life, growth, self. For Kerouac, that discovery may be made through the very geography of America. Sal Paradise, the narrator of *On the Road,* traipses back and forth across the continent three times in the novel, singing songs of praise to the beauties of the land, digging America as Walt Whitman and Carl Sandburg dug America. He sees across the mountains and the prairies to the sea, "over the rolling wheatfields all golden beneath the distant snows of Estes. . . . Now I could see Denver looming ahead of me like the Promised Land, way out there beneath the stars, across the prairie of Iowa and the plains of Nebraska, and I could see the greater vision of San Francisco beyond, like jewels in the night." There is a gospel to be taught about this land and Sal envisions himself teaching it, arriving in Denver, appearing before "all the gang, and in their eyes I would be strange and ragged and like the Prophet who has walked across the land to bring the dark Word, and the only Word I had was 'Wow!' "

The significance of America is not to be formulated in easy phrases and intellectual constructs. The rebels and oddballs who are its "true" natives—"the old bums and beat cowboys" Sal meets on Denver's Larimer Street—are often wordless and laconic, implying that words fix and know, as Joe Necchi might say, and in doing so distort the living moment of experience. For Samson Shillitoe, "Lean, burnt [country] men told him by their stance that they'd seen more of life from their siloes than he had in all his wanderings." That stance is another form of Sal Paradise's "Wow!"

This side of Cain speaks in nonverbal eloquence and one of its most effective languages is jazz, a music that comes spontaneously straight from the soul of one kind of native American. That music expresses all of the ambiguity in this attitude toward America, an ambiguity made up of love and hate, bitterness and joy, respect and contempt. Holmes has a young black piano player say that jazz

> has always been a celebration of—Of what? The hard winter light on American rooftops? . . . The dark bars? The tenement ghettos? The sun-merciless highways? The radio that buzzes through the interminable afternoons in every furnished room across the continent? . . .
>
> Yes. But of the enigmatic beer can, too, that lies in the densest thicket, in the remotest glade, beyond the farthest country road, where someone has gone off (as Americans have always gone off) into the leafy wildness that still waits just out of any town. . . . And of America that has always been bigger than any man, *forcing* him to think, to imagine, to create, just to keep from drowning in sheer, insentient nature, and that has made Americans slaves to rhetoric, abstraction, idealism, in an effort to match the manless Rockies always looking in the corner of their America that cannot admit that out of imperfection all perfection comes, but which, despite everything (the ugliness, the hate, the greed and the hypocrisy), has always been an infinite possibility to match man's infinite desire. Yes. Jazz was as much a celebration of this American reality (everything, *everything!*) as a protest against it. Yes.

The positive part of this vision—the land, the "lean, burnt men," the infinite appetite to grow and be—is an invocation of the American frontier, the self-reliance of the country town. It is a conservative vision, strangely enough, whose view is backward rather than forward, whose impulse is to escape from the present into the past rather than the future. It is a romantic vision, an assumption that the invoked past was a time of serenity and achievement. In *Get Home Free,* May Delano experiences a surge of longing for "a distracted companion to live silently beside through days and days and days of nothing at all. I longed for it the way we (who never knew it) sometimes long for that tranquil summerworld before 1914. . . ." This nostalgia is not very rebellious or very violent. It is Cain's softer side, and it demonstrates the universality of the pastoral ideal, the continued conflict between the city and the country, the conviction that when men live in the country they are living nearer to nature and that this nearness makes better and more authentic human beings of them.

This side of Cain results in a style common to so many of these novelists, the reminiscent style. Time after time they turn to their own past for material. Kerouac's first novel, *The Town and the City,* deals with the narrator's childhood and adolescence in Lowell, Massachusetts, full of family portraits and mild conflicts with friends. *Maggie Cassidy* is about the innocence and completeness of adolescent first love and the pathos that results when the youngsters mature and become more cynical. The characters in *On the Road* spend a great deal of time sitting knee-to-knee on mussed beds, facing each other over a bottle of wine or a joint of marijuana, recalling their past.

At its weakest, the novel of reminiscence, with its gentle Cains refusing to come into the present, is a series of incidents strung together by a narrator under the assumption that any detail about the past, when it is charged with the bitter-sweet character of sunny memories, is inherently valuable and interesting. Typical is Herbert Gold's *Therefore Be Bold,* an apparently autobiographical account of Gold's teens just before World War II. It contains a few set scenes, narrated by Dan Berman and full of youngsters who want to become writers and seek to model themselves after Thomas Wolfe or James Branch Cabell. Dan edits the school newspaper. He and his friends go out into the woods by Cleveland and get drunk. Dan falls in love with Eva Masters, but when he allows himself to be run off by her father, the affair cools. Eva begins going with one of Dan's friends, and Dan takes up with a new girl friend. This is aimless and self-indulgently sentimental. The same characteristic shows up in Gold's writing style, which is self-consciously literary, falsely energetic, and full of straining for the unusual phrase:

> Chuck sucked flaps of food from his teeth and clicked his palate in important labor, shaking his head to dislodge the day's scruff of ideas. Circularly I exercised my pseudo-argyled ankle in a distracted gesture I had not made up—it had just honestly happened

to me. I let them talk, Chuck jutting toward us, Eva tranquil in her plans by my side. We swayed thus through the rumor and hullabaloo of the city, the hauling cries of work and the ruling purr of machinery, these echoes of that time's pure music of pleasure and pain.

At its best, the reminiscent novel tells, impartially, a well-honed, unsentimental story about childhood and adolescence, a story as old as story-telling but illuminating when told honestly. For example, Chandler Brossard's *The Bold Saboteurs* functions like *The Town and the City* and *Therefore Be Bold*, though it is not characterized by the latter's professional nostalgia and sentimentality. It does resemble both of these novels in its setting: the 1930s. George Brown, the narrator of the story, lives in the slums of Washington, D.C. His father is a drunkard who occasionally returns home to beat up on his family. Finally, George's brother Roland kicks the old man out, gets a job, and runs the family with a 15-year-old's authority. He raises George as a substitute father, guiding him and punishing him. George himself is a picaro, what R. W. B. Lewis might call a "picaresque saint." As narrator, he displays a detachment from and an involvement with life. Seeing his father walk down the street with two other men, staggering drunk, George is "torn with the terrible conflict of wanting to save and yet wanting to stand apart, unnoticed and untouched." This simultaneous detachment and involvement, characteristic of Huizinga's play, makes George a kind of youthful, male, and American Moll Flanders, who travels up and down through several social planes. At each plane he stops to comment, with an ironic detachment and uncompromising honesty that prevents the sometimes shocking incidents from becoming pretentious melodrama.

For Brossard, reminiscence serves to characterize the figure of a Cain more familiar than that of Gold or Kerouac. As a youngster, George enters the underworld of his city, taking to the streets, making crime a way of life. It was, as George sees it, a means of revolting against a society made up of "pathetic, misguided soul-savers," who fail to realize "that charity is the mother of self-destruction and that Christianity breeds contempt, to say nothing of dirt and disease." Like Burroughs, Brossard suggests that the welfare state does not contribute to the welfare of the individual. And individuality, says George, carries with it a high premium for the young members of the gang he runs with. They do not, he says, have it themselves, but at least they have not yet joined "society's war on the individual." Instead, they wage war on society. And for George, that war is an esthetic experience. Crime is an art in which the artist is involved immediately and directly with his product, in which he experiences with high intensity and thereby achieves an individual satisfaction not available to him in society. The only difference, says George, between the "premeditated criminal act" performed alone and other kinds of creative experiences "is that you live this form; it is not something that exists apart from you in musical notes or words on paper. There is not the safety of distance. Form and content are inextricably one, and it is as if you yourself, for example, and not the fourteen lines are the sonnet. The demands of this particular art form are stricter than most and the margin for error almost nonexistent. You can write a clumsy short story and get away with it but you cannot bungle a crime with very much impunity."

In crime, concludes George, that tension between distance and closeness that caused him pain when he observed his drunken father is dissolved. The individual self emerges as the pure rebel, challenging restraint with a clear and logical plan of action. But as in *Cain's Book*, the separation between the individual and his society cannot become too great without some kind of mechanism starting up to close the gap. When one goes too far away, he becomes annihilated. Similarly, when one becomes too engrossed in the past, he loses his only reality—the present. In an impressive concluding sequence, George takes a surrealistic, dreamlike journey. In the real world he has left home. In the dream world he comes to an empty house where his brother Roland tells him that everyone thought he was dead. That is, he has gone too far away—so far, indeed, that he will be unable to recover his identity. A sudden reappearance, says Roland, will not convince people that George is not dead. Exasperating, restrictive—even tragic—as the social apparatus might be, it is only in its context that the human being can experience his identifiable self. And he does so by differentiating himself from his surroundings. This is the meaning implicit in George's references to individual premeditated crime. But the act is performed within society. In the end, George finds himself down at the waterfront, "running from pier to pier, looking for the boat which I hoped would take me back."

Brossard suggests that there is a balance in the relationship between the individual—the actual entity—and the society which he helps to form. When repression becomes too dehumanizing, the rebel Cain seeks to burst out, destroy the system, hold the principles that identify the system in contempt. At the same time, when rebellion becomes excessive, when the self loses its social orientation, it turns once more to the frame of society.

In Part I of this book, I emphasized the acute awareness, especially in the science and the philosophy of the first three decades of the century, of the apparent impossibility of producing an absolute correspondence between logical constructs—like verbal statements and scientific models—and the existing subject, the "buzzing blooming confusion" of living immediacy. For those who see the most important issues of their time in terms of the figure of Cain, who deliberately break the laws of their society in order to disclose new circuits of experience more nearly their own, this is still one of the prime concerns. They are confronted with the paradox of trying to express the inexpressible. This is especially difficult for those who come down so hard on the assertion that ultimate reality—the spontaneous individual experience—is inexpressible, the conviction that in terms of traditional logic the present moment is meaningless. Joe Necchi, in *Cain's Book,* makes a familiar point: ". . . below the level of language the facts slide away like a lava." And, he says, for the "possibility" and the openness of immediate, subjective, human existence "there is no language." Necchi picks up the point that Whitehead makes—that every subject is mutually exclusive, that no subject can ever communicate itself as itself to another. Says Joe, "One could be in another's world . . . only indirectly; one had recourse to a kind of expression appropriate to that ambiguity, was masked always, even at the moment of discarding the mask, because for another the act of exposure stood equally in need of interpretation. . . ." No intermediate instrument can transfer one world to another.

On the basis of this premise, Cain should eschew language of any sort and withdraw into the isolation of his own psyche. That, however, as I have already noted about these novelists, yields only obliteration. The "hip" Cain, the musician, turns to jazz as the means for expressing the inexpressible. The rationale for this position is formulated by the literary hipster, especially the writers associated with the Beat Generation. The definitive feature of jazz as the hipster sees it is improvisation, which best expresses the joy of the spontaneous act, for it is not confined to a rigidly predetermined pattern, though its spontaneity is given meaning and shape through certain principles of musical form. It resembles the intense individuality and satisfaction that Brossard describes in the "premeditated" crime. For the hipster the jazz improviser is a high priest. Each note he plays, supposedly, is thought to emerge spontaneously from the center of his authentic self, where "true" religious experience originates. Jazz is thus a feeling of an "emotion," to paraphrase Whitehead, that constitutes the identity of the self. The jazz experience at its best is for the hipster religious ecstasy, sacred and holy. Sal Paradise and Dean Moriarty, in *On the Road*, go to Birdland to hear George Shearing. Both enter into the frenzy of the moment like votaries before a deity:

> . . . a smile broke over [Shearing's] ecstatic face; he began to rock in the piano seat, back and forth, slowly at first, then the beat went up, and he began rocking fast, his left foot jumped with every beat, his neck began to rock crookedly, he brought his face down to the keys, he pushed his hair back, his combed hair dissolved, he began to sweat. The music picked up. The bass player hunched over and socked it in, faster and faster, it seemed faster and faster, that's all. Shearing began to play his chords; they rolled out of the piano in great rich showers, you'd think the man wouldn't have time to line them up. They rolled and rolled like the sea. Folks yelled for him to "Go!" Dean was sweating; the sweat poured down his collar. "There he is! That's him! Old God! Old God Shearing! Yes! Yes! Yes!" and Shearing was conscious of the madman behind him, he could hear every one of Dean's gasps and imprecations, he could sense though he couldn't see. "That's right!" Dean said. "Yes!" Shearing smiled; he rocked. Shearing rose from the piano, dripping with sweat; those

were his great 1949 days before he became cool and commercial. When he was gone Dean pointed to the empty piano seat. "God's empty chair," he said. On the piano a horn sat; its gold shadow made a strange reflection along the desert caravan painted on the wall behind the drums. God was gone; it was the silence of his departure.

Jazz is simultaneously a representation of an experience—that of the musician to the listener—and an experience in itself. For many of these novelists, it is the same with language. Writers like Trocchi, Kerouac, Burroughs, and Gold compose a kind of literary jazz. Sometimes, they mean for their words to cease being denotative and to become simply expressive, like colors and chords and melodies. Words like *hip, cool, swinging* suggest emotional states, but they are meaningful only to the initiated; they lack the logical precision demanded by the "square." This is the language of a cult, setting its users apart—as they want to be—from their enemy. This particular language is designed to do what jazz does, to create an emotional experience rather than formulate abstractions. "Hip," says Norman Mailer in his essay "The White Negro," "is a pictorial language, but pictorial like nonobjective art, imbued with the dialectic of small but intense change, a language for the microcosm, in this case, man, for it takes the immediate experiences of any passing man and magnifies the dynamic of his movements. . . ."[3] Jack Kerouac has described this language at some length in an essay appropriately entitled "The Essentials of Spontaneous Prose." He advises the Beat Hipster to go counter to the traditions of the *status quo,* traditions which linguistic conventions help perpetuate. He recommends a language of disengagement, one which will emphasize the individual self, the *me* that is free of the enemy's coercions. In this view, whatever comes spontaneously from the inside must come from that uncontaminated self and must therefore be "good." Cain's language breaks laws.

Kerouac's basic prose principle is to write the first thing that comes into one's head. Write "without consciousness," he says, sounding like a Freudian analyst instructing a patient in free association. Write without plan, in a kind of semi-trance. Admit to the page "in own uninhibited interesting necessary and so 'modern' language what conscious art would censor." Follow the "laws of orgasm, Reich's 'beclouding of consciousness.'" Do not revise, either, for that empties language of its spontaneity. Write as a jazz musician plays:

> Begin not from preconceived idea of what to say about image at *moment* of writing, and write outwards swimming in sea of language to peripheral release and exhaustion—Do not afterthink except for poetic or P.S. reasons. Never afterthink to "improve" or defray impressions . . . tap from yourself the song of yourself, *blow!—now! —your* way is your way—"good"—or "bad"—always honest ("ludicrous"), spontaneous, "confessional," interesting, because not "crafted." Craft [he writes in a thundering cliché] *is* craft.[4]

Much of Kerouac's prose looks as if he has taken his principles completely seriously. Sometimes it has a certain impact—like the passage I quoted earlier from *On the Road,* in which he employs the old technique of trying to capture the rhythms of the situation (Shearing playing at Birdland) in the rhythm of the words he uses to describe it. There are also satisfying passages in such widely separated novels as his first one, *The Town and the City,* and one of his last ones, *Desolation Angels.* But too frequently, following his own rules only leads him into trouble and demonstrates the weaknesses of his theory. For example, in *The Subterraneans,* his syntax is rambling and ungrammatical. He violates parallelism and cares little to make his pronoun references clear. It would not do to suggest that one finds echoes of James Joyce and William Faulkner in his associational style, for it lacks the surprise, the vitality, and the originality that are the earlier writers' hallmarks. The following passage, from the first page of *The Subterraneans,* establishes immediately what the reader is in for:

> I was coming down the street with Larry O'Hara old drinking buddy of mine from all the times in San Francisco in my long and nervous and mad careers I've gotten drunk and in fact cadged drinks off friends with such "genial" regularity nobody really cared to notice or announce that I am developing or was developing, in my youth, such bad freeloading habits though of course they did not notice but liked me and as Sam said "everybody comes to you for your gasoline boy, that's some filling station you got there" or say words to that effect—old Larry O'Hara always nice to me, a crazy Irish young

businessman of San Francisco with Balzacian [*sic*] backroom in his bookstore where they'd smoke tea and talk of the old days of the great Basie band or the days of the great Chu Berry. . . .

The "essentials of spontaneous prose" are more acceptable in the breach than the observance. Yet in them lies an example of the way in which Cain uses language to rebel. There *is* a language for Cain, and even Trocchi suggests that there is, briefly citing his own principles of spontaneous expression. Expression is independent only when it abandons cultural linguistic taboos, such as Kerouac advises. Thus, Necchi eschews euphemism, propriety, conventional courtesy. He employs, as he says, "a certain crudity of expression, judging it to be essential to meaning, in a slick age vital to the efficacy of language."

The argument made here for language, even though it cannot communicate the perfectly authentic individual experience, is the same one made by those who argue for the validity of the scientific model. Both simulate a reality that can never be completely known, and in doing so they illuminate areas of experience and of being that would otherwise remain dark. Joe Necchi, Cain's principal theorist in these matters, remarks that "it is not the power to abstract that is invalid, but the unquestioning acceptance of conventional abstractions which stand in the way of raw memory, of the existential . . . all such barriers to the gradual refinement of the central nervous system." This is one of the reasons that Kerouac calls for a "spontaneous prose," one which refuses deliberately to select details from the past, but lets them well up as "raw memory." By such means the writer releases what is most authentic and most individual in himself, a jazz musician of prose.

By the same token, whole novels are valid to the Cain figure. But the novels of which he approves lean toward formlessness, at least in terms of the critical logic of traditional form. The word *formlessness* must be qualified, and when it is, it shows the trickiness of attempting to use language in any way to express complete spontaneity. Even the most apparently formless novels of William Burroughs reflect a principle of selection, a principle designed to simulate freedom and spontaneity. Again, Joe Necchi articulates the basic assumption. Sounding very much like the French anti-novelists—Alain Robbe-Grillet in particular—Necchi rejects the traditional notion of structure and plot, with its emphasis upon a hierarchy of important acts and details. Such a structure presupposes a certainty and an order that distorts existence, for it embodies the "fixed and the known." Writes Necchi:

> I am unfortunately not concerned with the events which led up to this or that. If I were my task would be simpler. Details would take their meaning from their relation to the end and could be expanded or contracted, chosen or rejected, in terms of how they contributed to it. In all this, there is no it, and there is no startling fact or sensational event to which the mass of detail in which I find myself from day to day wallowing can be related. Thus I must go on from day to day accumulating, blindly following this or that train of thought, each in itself possessed of no more implication than a flower or a spring breeze or a molehill or a falling star or a cackle of geese. No beginning, no middle, no end. This is the impasse which a serious man must enter and from which only the simpleminded can retreat.

Cain's Book is an attempt to demonstrate that impasse, to present the reader with a symbolic experience of an existence that has no neat bounds, no ending that results inevitably from events that lead up to it. Joe Necchi tells us about his past, about his present. He records excerpts from his diary and from his manuscript of "Cain's Book." But he concludes nothing from his "inventory." It is simply a way of imitating existence, which has no objective meaning that can be indicated by a "significant" ending. As his own manuscript comes to a stop, Joe says that after he informs his publishers that it is ready, he will take a fix, "knowing again that nothing is ending, and certainly not this." Only the abstract and non-"existent" can be fitted neatly into objectively meaningful bounds. Existence cannot be. *Cain's Book* tries to show this in the language of the abstract and the certain, tries to express the inexpressible. The artist, like all of his twentieth-century contemporaries, must be careful not to confuse the linguistic formulation with subjective experience.

Art, for Cain, serves life. And art, says Necchi, is the spirit of play. Without that spirit "there is only murder." Play refuses to take abstractions seriously, refuses to regard them as completely correspondent to subjective existence. When abstractions are given priority over the reality of the individual, the result is horrors such as Auschwitz and Buchenwald. Those horrors still contaminate our world: "Man is forgetting how to play." The solution? "Art as the way, symbol, indirect, transcendence." Art can simulate existence without pretending to "be" it. It is the only way of transporting from one to another the most important truth of our lives: our spontaneous subjectivity, our difference from the stream of experience, our rebelliousness. "Existential" truth can, Cain might say, be expressed in no other way than the indirect, representative symbol. Trocchi's position—and he speaks for most of the Cain novelists—compares with Plato's. In the parable of the cave, the "reality" that lies outside the cave in the form of the sun cannot be directly communicated to those chained to the stake inside with only their fire behind them and their abstracted shadows in front of them. One who has looked upon that reality can express it only indirectly: in metaphor, symbol, poetry. The parable itself is an example of that proposition.

It is the same way with the novelists I have dealt with in this chapter. The figure of Cain they jointly construct symbolizes that spontaneous reality of our individual subjective existence that refuses to be bound by abstract laws and conventions. He breaks forth in both language and action. He must, however, like the jazz improvisor, remain within the meaning-giving order of society or lose the data out of which he must shape his novel satisfaction. The tension between the individual and his society is part of that paradox and ambivalence so central to the "open decision" as defined in Part I. The experience of that tension *is* the highest individual consciousness. To surrender wholly to the apparatus is to give in to bad faith and resolve the tension. But that is to destroy the presence of life.

The novelists I have discussed in this Part see the issues of their day in terms of society's danger to life, that is, to the experience of the individual as something free, as something full of the possibilities of growth and choice and spontaneity. Whether it is the army organization, the business organization, or the middle-class social organization, the apparatus must be exposed as the danger it is. Their emphasis, therefore, is upon external conflict rather than psychological conflicts within the self. Even so, they are always careful to reaffirm the metaphysical necessity of the organization to the individual, and in doing so, reaffirm the "open decision's" metaphysical foundation of value and the preferred state. That is, the highest good lies in the human individual and the liberation of his potential consciousness. What best serves that good—a free society or modified flight from an oppressive one—is the preferred situation. In this way do these novelists work out their concerns according to the logic of the "open decision."

THREE

INTRODUCTION

THE NOVELS DISCUSSED in this Part do not constitute a genre in the same sense as those dealt with in Part II. They are united only by an awareness of the issues, values, and implications of the "open decision." Except for three or four of the war novels already discussed, these pieces exemplify the best prose fiction in America since World War II. They are good not simply because of the vividness of their style, the soundness of their structure, or the effectiveness of their characterization; but because they express so incisively the quality of the modern experience. I do not claim to have included all of the best novels by all of the best novelists writing in America for the last quarter of a century. Some may score me for both my omissions and inclusions. I hope, however, that my selection is representative of both the quality and the scope of serious American fiction since the War, and that what I say about the novels I do discuss will be useful for approaching those I do not discuss.

One last note to this apologetic opening. Because of the number of works taken up here, I omit many considerations of plot, character, and theme which in these rich novels demand attention. This is not the place to give them that attention. Instead, I approach each book and author from the central reference point of the "open decision," demonstrating that their controlling principle arises from and contributes to this construct of thought. Because that is the case, I turn now to a review of some of the basic premises and values of the "open decision." Its main assumption is that reality lies in the individual thing—the "process" of the actual entity. The highest good is the enactment of that reality, which is the achievement of the highest possible intensity of individuality. That good is most accessible through human consciousness, for the basis of human consciousness is the sense of oneself as a unity that is different from the world of which it is conscious. Consciousness used in this sense does not mean simply a state of intellectual lucidity in which one forms abstract explanations. It means the recognition that the self is not identical with or exhausted by self-consciousness, that there is a great reality to be felt though not explained. This is what Saul Bellow's protagonist, Moses Herzog, calls "true consciousness . . . simple, free, intense realization." True consciousness brings with it a sense of wholeness, though not completeness, for it acknowledges and affirms the ambiguities and paradoxes of which, by definition, the individual is constituted.

Consciousness is one of the defining features of man's nature. To deny it or to attempt to escape from it into bad faith or false consciousness is to diminish the possibility of satisfaction. Whitehead has said that subjects are "causally independent." Consciousness increases that independence and burdens us with freedom. Subjects cannot exist any life but their own; therefore, they cannot "be" as themselves in the past of another subject. Consequently, no subject can have a mechanically deterministic influence upon any other subject and in turn cannot be mechanically determined. In their "causal independence," subjects are responsible for the way in which they go about choosing from the world around them. This responsibility is intensified when men become conscious of it. They must accept the responsibility for what their choice leads to, regardless of their intentions, for no one can make that choice for them. This is not a statement of morality: that a man "should" be responsible because some higher good declares that it is right to be so. It is a statement of what, in the "open decision," is regarded as the true condition. The painfulness of this condition is that our choices may not produce the results desired or intended. We cannot predict consequences; we can only suffer them. No one but a god can rise above history, look to its end, and judge infallibly the correct choice in the present. The subject is immersed in life; he has no access to complete knowledge of an objective goal which would assure him in the choices he makes and the acts he performs in the present. He must, therefore, gamble, risk himself in a commitment which contains few certainties and no promises. The assumption that one has been given the absolute criterion of choice by God or a special insight into history signals a deficiency of consciousness and a corresponding reduction in the intensity of satisfaction. The consciousness, and the freedom it entails, is a terrible burden, but it is the foundation of our existence and our highest good.

To be deprived of consciousness is to be thwarted in the achievement of a high intensity of individual satisfaction. It is therefore necessary to maintain an openness, to avoid absolute and total explanations which fix the self in grooves and prevent him from moving through new categories and feelings. True consciousness is to be free of any tradition or prejudice which claims the final truth and binds itself to predetermined possibilities, to transcend the demands of a single society, to engage life in all its ranges. This consciousness, as I have remarked in Part I, is a kind of play, characterized by an earnest wittiness which nourishes itself on ambiguity. It believes only one thing absolutely: that the subject is the chooser and unifier of its experience and that the ambiguity it knows is one of the defining characteristics of the human being. It affirms its conditions by opening itself to all known possibilities, and by seeking other possibilities unknown. The playful man devotes himself earnestly and sincerely, but not "seriously," to the actions of his life. "Serious" commitment assumes that one particular act can be justified according to an objectively verifiable value and therefore shuts the self off from other possibilities. This repudiates the human state, which is defined as that condition which is always open to the future. The difference between seriousness and earnest playfulness may be explained by noting the function of abstraction in the characteristic human experience. Abstractions are categories of thought drawn from the "buzzing, blooming confusion" of existence to render that existence rationally knowable and meaningful. They may be laid upon the future as a means of controlling it by prediction and a way of guiding our choices in the present. But the abstraction is only a way by which consciousness experiences itself or its world and must not be taken for the most real or as a total explanation of the most real. To do so is to limit consciousness. "Seriousness" is giving abstractions objective validity, saying that God has given them to us. This does not mean that one avoids abstractions. Without them we would be less than human. We would have no art or civilization. They are our means of satisfying our appetite for unity and clarity. It does mean that we must not blind ourselves to the whole of our existence by being willing to settle only for a total explanation of it as embodied in our abstractions. The player remains conscious of both the utility of abstractions and their inadequacy, of our need for them and their relativity.

The contrast between the abstraction and the experience of existence itself suggests an important feature of freedom and of the whole human condition: that our freedom is not absolute. Absolute freedom is the power to actualize every abstract plan that one can conceive. This is to be a god. To be human is to have one's freedom limited by death, chance, ignorance of the future, other people—in short, by life. By definition, human life is consciousness of being a self in the stream of experience, of the horizon that limits that self, and of the rebellion against that horizon. It is the paradox of wanting to be something we cannot be in the nature of things. It is part of our nature, too, to seek absolute rest and contentment—"being," the identification of the abstract blueprint and the throb of life. It is equally a part of our nature not to be able to make such an identification and to know that we cannot. Our highest good is in the embracing of that paradox, for only in the subjective experience of the individual human being does that paradox exist. To keep separate the conceptual and the emotional, as Whitehead says, is to produce a "life-tedium." The highest good is served when we recognize and choose this life and all its entailments.

The paradox and contradictoriness of human life are not some exasperating imperfections which, if we strive long enough, we can rid ourselves of. They are definitive features of human life. To accept life is to affirm this condition. Unlike previous attitudes toward this duality—in which one term was taken to be "better" than another (God better than man, form better than matter, Idea better than individual copy)—the attitudes of the novelists discussed in this chapter, as well as those I have already discussed, imply that the good is in both of the terms as they are joined in the individual. These attitudes are tinged with a sad regret for the passing of an innocence that relied upon a knowable transcendent deity which resolved bothersome dualism. But the human being that emerges in these novels is proper to our time and illuminative of our peculiar experience. Alone in the face of an absolutely enigmatic world, without appeal to a higher, wiser, more benevolent power, bereft of any assurances or certainties beyond himself, the human being forges his own identity. The characters in these novels seek for the freedom to do this.

It is important to emphasize that these novels do not issue in the happiness of romance. The ideal of harmony, contentment, certainty, and safety is important. That it fares badly in a world inhospitable to it is the source of much of the suffering these novels depict. What emerges is a new "ideal," one that employs both poles of the "real" and the "ideal" within the organism of a living existent, conscious of his freedom and of his limitations. Aristotle speaks of the "privation" of matter—its inability, by definition, ever fully to realize its form. Sartre's "lack" is analogous to privation, defining the inability of the for-itself ever to become identical with the in-itself. But "lack" and "privation" mean simply that the human being is not a god. To be human is the highest good, for in the human state the sense of individuality reaches its highest intensity. Therefore, the "failure" of lack and privation is, as John Barth says in *Giles Goat-Boy,* paradoxically success. It is this paradox that preoccupies, in one form or another, the following novelists. And probably their most pervasive theme is the question of whether or not a character is willing to be what the "open decision" finds him to be.

7

NOVELS OF AMBIGUITY AND AFFIRMATION: THE DRAMA OF CONSCIOUSNESS

Consciousness may be the foundation of human reality, in the view of the "open decision," and as such the source of our highest good. But it is also the source of pain and fear, the creator of dreams which cannot be realized, the sense of separateness and aloneness. The drama of consciousness is the common denominator of the following ten novels, which in most other respects are quite different from each other. Some of the characters in these novels seek to evade the pain of awareness, afraid of their freedom and unsure of themselves without absolutes. Some regard awareness as liberation and seek to smash all institutions that would limit that awareness. But all are confronted with their nature and are forced to come to some conclusion about themselves in the midst of a world that never answers the questions they put to it. "The manhood of man," writes Allen Wheelis, "depends upon his alienation and his awareness of mortality. Without them he would be less than human for they are the perils, not of nature, but of the human condition."[1]

In many American novels written since World War II, the drama arises from the refusal of the central character to enter manhood and affirm the human condition. Probably the best known illustration of this refusal is J.D. Salinger's Holden Caulfield in *The Catcher in the Rye.*[2] This novel reflects that inability to accept the limits of our

For Notes to Chapter 7, see pages 404–405.

condition that is one of the main dilemmas of our age. In that dilemma we lament that we are not self-sufficient, not full, not complete, but alone and afraid by ourselves before life. Holden feels separated from his world. In the opening pages he stands alone upon a hill while the rest of Pencey Prep's students watch a football game in the stadium below. Earlier, he has been ostracized by the fencing team for leaving the foils on a New York subway, making it impossible for them to play their match. He has, furthermore, just been expelled from school and is preparing to return to New York without telling his parents. The effect of this separateness is to make him feel as if he were "disappearing." The sensation attacks him in the first few pages and establishes one of the novel's main motifs. The occasion of his feeling is almost as important as the feeling itself. It occurs when he is crossing a road the afternoon of his departure from Pencey. He describes that afternoon as one of the "crazy" kinds, "terrifically cold, and no sun out or anything, and you felt like you were disappearing every time you crossed a road." This sensation recurs more intensely later in New York, when he crosses the street at the end of a block and feels that he will not make it to the other side, that he will "just go down, down, down, and nobody'd ever see me again." He prays to his dead brother Allie not to let him "disappear."

Crossing roads becomes for Holden a symbol of dissolution. It comes partly from the fact that Holden, at sixteen, is on the verge of entering the new territory of adulthood. The change means that he will "be" something else when he moves from his familiar identity as an adolescent to the unknown of the adult. Change means obliteration of the self in Holden's view, and his fear of change leads him to represent it as something dangerous and undesirable. What Holden wants to preserve is the authenticity and spontaneity that is the hallmark of the "open decision," and he sees these qualities only in children and childlike grown-ups. He likes Mrs. Morrow, who leaves her bags in the middle of the railroad car aisle; the nuns at Grand Central Station, who talk of *Romeo and Juliet* with unabashed pleasure and enthusiasm; Jane Gallagher, who at checkers keeps her kings in the back row and at the movies touches Holden on the back of the neck; the little girl at the ice rink, who says "thank you" when he tightens her skates; and especially his little sister Phoebe, who has a curious blend of maturity and childlike naïveté in her eagerness to experience the world. Holden sees himself as the protector of these values, a "catcher in the rye." He fancies himself as the only grown-up standing in a field of rye grass at the edge of "some crazy cliff." In the field children play, and his job is to keep them from running over the edge of the cliff. The edge of the cliff, analogous to the curbs of the street and the roads that Holden must cross, suggests the end of childhood genuineness. Falling over the cliff is falling into the "death" of adulthood.

Adults—or children who have absorbed adult ways—corrupt the authentic spontaneity of childhood by introducing practice, contrivance, hypocrisy. Sally Hayes wants to go skating because of the effect she can create by wearing a short skating skirt to show off her figure. The roller skaters who perform in the theater pretend to skate easily without practice, but Holden is put off by the thought of their spending hours going through their routine. Ernie, the piano player, turns out superficially intricate music only to dazzle and impress. The Lunts are so practiced that Holden cannot suspend his disbelief in watching them. For Holden, there is a poison in the adult habit of rehearsal and self-consciousness and in referring to it, Salinger has given an old word a new force. The adult world is "phony." Phoniness is bad faith. Its almost desperate self-consciousness is not the liberating awareness of the "open decision." It is the false consciousness that Mannheim speaks of. It operates to stifle that which is authentic in the self by enforcing conformity to imposed, preexistent, and collective grooves of behavior, thwarting individuality rather than increasing it. For Holden this is death.

Holden tries to escape this world. He urges Sally Hayes to go off with him to Vermont where they would live in "cabin camps," evade the world and establish their own idyll. He fantasizes a withdrawal to a cabin in Colorado where he will live alone like a hermit. When visitors come he will pretend to be deaf in order not to converse with them. And as his own odyssey nears an end, he plans to run off to the west. What he would forestall by doing this is the change to adulthood. The value by which he operates is changelessness. The "best" thing about the Metropolitan Museum of Natural History is that "everything always stayed right where it was. Nobody'd move. You could go there a hundred thousand times, and that Eskimo would still be just finished catching those two fish, the birds would still be on their way south, the deer would still be drinking out of that water hole, with their pretty antlers and their pretty, skinny legs, and that squaw with the naked bosom would still be wearing the same blanket." The trouble with life is illustrated in the contrast between the museum display and those who come to view it. Though the display never changes, supposedly, the viewer does.

For Holden change means the destruction of all that is good and desirable. But change and the death it inevitably leads to are the defining features of human life. To reject them is to reject the unnegotiable conditions inherent in one's situation, to reject life itself. Mr. Antolini, one of Holden's old teachers, warns Holden that he is riding for a "terrible fall" in which he will just keep "falling and falling," the sensation Holden later feels while crossing the streets in New York. This fall, says Mr. Antolini, comes to those "who, at some time or other in their lives, were looking for something their own environment couldn't supply them with." Mr. Antolini's assessment of Holden's attitude is valid. Holden is a romantic who identifies adulthood with phoniness, phoniness with change, and change with death and dissolution. This does not mean that many of the observations Holden makes as he moves through society like a picaro do not strike home. People are insensitive, cruel, hypocritical. But as Mr. Antolini says, Holden is not "the first person who was ever confused and frightened and even sickened by human behavior." Every experience is characterized by "lack." Thinking that Mr. Antolini, at least, will harbor him, Holden awakens to find his old teacher stroking his head. And the validity of the advice that Mr. Antolini gives Holden is vitiated by the fact that he is drunk when he gives it. Holden cannot bear imperfection, the discrepancy between the ideal and the real. He runs from it: he runs from Pencey Prep, from his parents, from "phonies," from Mr. Antolini. In the end he plans to run from New York.

Life, however, does not allow itself to be run from. The pressure of his weekend of wandering the city and the lack of sleep and food cause Holden to collapse physically, and his condition is exacerbated by his mental condition. He is sent to a sanitarium out west to recover. This does not indicate that Holden never achieves any kind of repprochement with his experience. Though he never comes to the kind of mature affirmation found, as we shall see, by characters like Bellow's Herzog or Barth's Ebenezer Cook,

..e does discover that he has unbreakable ties with the world. After an argument with his sister Phoebe in which he refuses to let her come with him in his flight from New York, he buys her rides on the carrousel in the amusement park. As she goes toward the ride for the third time rain begins to fall. She turns, goes back to Holden, reaches in the pocket of his coat for his red hunting cap, and puts it on his head. This gesture of love and care has tremendous impact on Holden: "it damn near killed me." And later, writing from the sanitarium, he implies the value of all the people he has talked about—even the phonies—by saying he is going to "miss" them. Yet, in both of these instances, designed by Salinger, it seems, to emphasize Holden's essential ability to accept what he has been rejecting, there remains a deficiency of consciousness. As Holden sits by the carrousel he feels so "damn happy" he almost cries, for he is watching Phoebe going "around and around," describing a circle whose perfection cannot be broken. And his "missing" the people he has met is not a genuine embrace of life but a condescending forgiveness for its not corresponding to his ideal. There is in Holden's final words an illimitable confidence both in his power to forgive and the necessity of forgiving. Holden sees only one half of the "open decision": the ideal of spontaneity and authenticity. Genuine affirmation takes in the other pole, too, the limits placed by life upon the ideal. Because Holden cannot accept these limits—because Salinger cannot—he falls short of achieving that high intensity of individual satisfaction, that chastened maturity and clear vision that are at the heart of the human experience.

In *Rabbit, Run,* John Updike presents a grown man with the same problems as those of the adolescent Holden Caulfield, but he does so with less approval of his protagonist and more compassion for the blind than does Salinger. Harry "Rabbit" Angstrom cannot face up to the conditions of being human, the conditions of time, change, responsibility, nothingness, and the demands placed upon him by other people. The title indicates Harry's means of dealing with his situation: as Holden tries to do, Harry runs—at the beginning of the novel and at the end, literally. He runs from crying babies, a slovenly pregnant wife, having to sell used cars, the pressures of parents. Unable to control the world, he wants it to go away. He runs in fantasy to his days as a high school basketball hero, a time when he felt all-powerful. He runs in his automobile away from the town he lives in. He runs from his wife, Janice, to a sometime prostitute, Ruth. His anguish is that these redoubts provide no real protection from what he most fears. Harry's fear takes the same form of Holden's. Dreaming of his triumphs in high school, the pleasure vibrates and turns to flight: ". . . he feels he's on a cliff, there is an abyss he will fall into when the ball leaves his hands."

The abyss is nothingness, and for Rabbit nothingness is literally adulthood. When the Episcopal priest, Eccles, out to save Rabbit from destroying himself, suggests that Rabbit is not mature, Rabbit says that maturity is "the same thing as being dead." For Harry, maturity means accepting responsibility for one's actions even when they bring consequences different from those originally intended. Maturity means his returning to his wife and the world of cluttered apartments and dirty diapers, of selling cars and answering the expectations of parents. Maturity means smothering what he regards as his true self by surrendering absolute freedom. The world outside himself has no values useful for him. It only threatens him. "All I know is what's inside *me,*" he says. "That's all I have." This is not Updike's way of setting up Rabbit in the "open decision." People like Camus and Sartre, Whitehead and Dewey, do say very much the same thing: we can know only what our consciousness tells us and the good is that which we confer upon an act by choosing to perform it rather than another one. "Goodness lies inside," says Rabbit. But where in the "open decision" this is a metaphysical basis for taking up ties with the world, in Rabbit this insight is perverted into a protective shell, which he uses to justify self-indulgence and illusion in a parody of the "open decision." He does not carry the insight further to the conclusion that if he knows only what he feels, then he must be responsible for those feelings and must see their consequences through to the end; and that if he is responsible for himself he is also responsible for—and to—others.

Rabbit cannot bear the "guilt" inherent in this responsibility. He must put the guilt on others. At the funeral of his tiny daughter, drowned inadvertently by Janice during a lapse into drunkenness, Rabbit finds his usual form of relief from the human condition. As the minister intones, "Casting every care on thee," Rabbit sees that this is precisely what he can do: put himself into the hands of God, repudiate his own human responsibility. With this revelation Harry believes he has found freedom from himself. He is guilty of nothing and to confirm his own innocence, he looks at Janice, "dumb with grief," and says, "Don't look at *me*. . . . I didn't kill her." He is simply stating the truth, he feels: that the baby is dead and he did not kill her. But the gathered mourners do not join him in the acknowledgment of that truth. Instead, they close him out, even Janice. He feels helpless, suffocated by injustice. He does the only thing he knows: "He turns and runs."

Nothingness is what we "are"; it is constituted of "lack." It means that we "are" not some final and complete thing that is fully itself, free of change. It means that by definition we stand out from the world, alone with the question of our own identity. Before the funeral of his daughter, Harry walks to his apartment with Janice. The once familiar and safe world has come to seem unfamiliar under the impact of this tragedy. The strangeness confronts him with the "childish mystery" of the "ultimate" question: "Why am I me?" At this moment another abyss opens up before Harry, and we are reminded of Holden Caulfield trying to cross his streets. His body becomes cold and he feels detached, outside of things. The details of his street lose their familiarity and immediacy. He feels as if he has gone out of his body into nothingness, as if the "he" that was once his identity now had no way of returning to its locus. This is the prototypical twentieth century experience—the fright that comes with the awareness that our identities are not shaped beforehand and inserted into the envelope of the body as an irreducible, constantly intelligible particle; the fright that comes from consciousness itself. Our identity is in the acts we perform and the thoughts we think and we produce those identities through choice. The colossal responsibility for living what is "inside" us, as Rabbit might say, is more than some can bear. Rabbit is one of those moderns who cannot shoulder the burden. Jung writes that the modern man is the one who "has come to the very edge of the world, leaving behind him all that has been discarded and outgrown, and acknowledging that he stands before a void out of which all things may grow."[3] For Rabbit, the nothingness of the void that looms before him is not a realm of growth and possibilities. It is an intolerable demand placed upon his weakness, the snuffing out of his life.

When Rabbit runs, whether it is to his fantasies of his youthful basketball success or simply physically away from the scene of his troubles, he runs from nothingness, the openness of his condition. He also runs from the limitations of a repugnant home, wife, and family. Harry's is one of the modern world's main problems. Remove the certainty of traditional values (Why, asks Harry, were youngsters taught such things as a belief in God if such beliefs were no longer held valid?), place the responsibility for one's being upon the individual, and we run the risk of producing a race of Harry Angstroms. Harry has too much human freedom—too much responsibility for giving his experience its unique spiritual quality—and too little god-like freedom—the power of making reality what he wants it to be. Harry's anguish is that in running from the one in his search for the other he finds no shelter. He runs from his daughter's burial in the cemetery into a long-abandoned grove of trees. Consider this grove to possess the same symbolic meaning as Frost's woods, which are "lovely, dark and deep" and appear to offer respite from the demands of the world. Rabbit expects to find there the sanctuary which Frost's observer is drawn to but finally renounces regretfully. But when Rabbit reaches the woods, he finds that "he is less sheltered than he expected." The woods are a primitive unconscious world in which he is an alien creature. The trees rise above him, obliterating his perspective. He can spy out no clearings, no redoubts of civilization in this primitive landscape. He feels as if a spotlight is focused upon him, that all the dangerous and mysterious forces menace him from the edges of darkness about him. Typically, Harry turns to his childhood as a protective device, recalling that he had often walked, as a child, through these trees. But then he had been protected by some kind of magic. Now his awareness exposes himself and the protection he identifies with his childhood has disappeared. He has taken the woods as a sanctuary of comfortable childhood certainty, a sanctuary he has continued to seek as a means of escaping from the abyss of nothingness, which constitutes the reality of adult consciousness.

But the woods turn out to be unsafe nature, to which Rabbit brings a human consciousness which makes him all the more vulnerable. Indeed, this episode emphasizes that the human condition is by definition vulnerable. It is the display of all the risks we run. In the woods he comes across a place that "was once self-conscious," but now the crumbled walls of the house are only a remnant of "human intrusion into a world of blind life." This applies to Rabbit's own humanity, whose modified consciousness is an intrusion into the world, and now in the woods he once more feels alienated and frightened. The very thing that makes him human—his consciousness—exposes him to the hostility of the woods: "He feels more conspicuous and vulnerable than in the little clearings of sunshine; he obscurely feels lit by a great spark, the spark whereby the blind tumble of matter recognizes itself, a spark struck in the collision of two opposed realms, an encounter a terrible God willed." This is Heidegger's sense of being-in-the-world, of being-there, but the *angst* it arouses in Rabbit produces the desire to flee, not the "care" that leads to "resoluteness."

Consciousness, in its very nature, can find no protection, no sanctuary. Harry feels with each "escape" that he begins a new life, hoping for a transformation akin to magic, one in which he has to make no concessions. But each escape is only into the woods. Coming out of the woods above the cemetery, he decides to run to Ruth. But for her he is simply bad news—"Death." Stymied again, Rabbit feels a kind of ecstatic desperateness, as if his desperation licenses him to throw off all care: "I don't know, he kept telling Ruth; he doesn't know, what to do, where to go, what will happen, the thought that he doesn't know seems to make him infinitely small and impossible to capture. Its smallness fills him like a vastness." For the man who affirms all of the conditions of the human situation, nothingness is the obligation to create his self with the resoluteness of one who does not confuse his illusions with reality. Rabbit continues to turn to his illusions as a means of escape. He sees his nothingness, once so fearsome, as a protection. The smallness that will make him "impossible to capture" is the same feeling as the one he experienced as a basketball player. When, guarded by two men, he passed the ball, he had the sensation that he was no longer there. Now, figuratively disappearing, he will no longer be there. And that is what Rabbit yearns for, because if he is not "there," he will no longer have to choose and act. But Rabbit decides inauthentically. He is in bad faith. He cannot choose not to choose, for that denies the undeniable conditions of his humanity. He cannot abrogate his freedom and discard his responsibility. He carries his attempt to do so to its farthest extreme, by depositing himself into the hands of other forces over which "he" has no control: "His hands lift of their own and he feels the wind on his ears even before, his heels hitting heavily on the pavement at first but with an effortless gathering out of a kind of sweet panic growing lighter and quicker and quieter, he runs. Ah: runs. Runs."

Rabbit, Run indicts neither society nor Harry Angstrom. It simply depicts the pathos of the modern situation, the inability of a man to deal with his experience when he finds himself bereft of the certainties of his past and confronted with that "lack" which is nothingness. Salinger represents this dilemma in terms of the adolescent passing into adulthood. Updike represents it in terms of a young man who never passed out of adolescence. Carson McCullers chooses a similar metaphor: the period of transition from childhood to puberty, adolescence, and the adulthood that lies just beyond. In the spring before her novel *Member of the Wedding* opens, twelve-year-old Frankie Addams has entered just such a period. Like Holden Caulfield and Rabbit Angstrom, she becomes conscious of herself in the world and with that consciousness comes the awareness of lack again. She feels an isolation and separateness from the world that frightens her. Her fear, like that of Holden and Rabbit, is of the new self which gradually comes into being through that consciousness which is the distinction of the course of awareness—the "I"—from things of which it is aware. Being afraid is a response to her change, a resistance to development.

What Frankie "Lacks" is a oneness with the world and with others, a oneness which ironically can come about only when consciousness and the "I" are extinguished. Like Rabbit Angstrom, Frankie is frightened by the awareness of "being-there," of being irrevocably an individual who cannot ever "be" some other individual. This awareness is the sign that she is leaving the childhood world of relative unconsciousness—perhaps the protective "magic" that Harry Angstrom sees surrounding the child's world. At the same time this change frightens her it also makes her sad. ". . . always I am I, and you are you," she tells the Negro maid Berenice. "And I can't ever be anything else but me, and you can't ever be anything else but you." Nor can people ever live each other's experience, compare sensations directly. People are simply separate. Frankie is dissatisfied with this new reality. She wants to "know"

"Everybody in the world," just as she "knows" herself. She wants to gather the world to her so that it will be familiar, inviting, friendly, comforting—so that she will not be alone.

Bernice puts Frankie's thoughts into her own words, explicitly defining the truth of the human condition: "We all of us somehow caught. . . . And maybe we wants to widen and bust free. But no matter what we do we still caught. Me is me and you is you and he is he. We each of us somehow caught all by ourself . . . as all human beings is caught." Frankie holds the two ideas in her mind at the same time—the desire to "bust free" and the impossibility of doing so. She recognizes the metaphysical truth of this absurd situation. But she can say without petulance, "I don't want to be caught." As her consciousness intensifies, Frankie is both liberated and imprisoned, but on the threshold of her new life, she can see only imprisonment. During this crucial summer, she attempts to escape that imprisonment by conceiving a dream that runs counter to reality.

Her plan involves her brother's approaching wedding, in which she sees her salvation from being "caught." At first the prospect of the marriage only intensifies her sense of fear and sadness and longing. Jarvis, her brother, and his fiancée Janice make her feel sad because they make up what Frankie takes to be a united self of which she is not a part. She is "sickened" by her feeling of isolation, but then she contrives the thought that "They are the we of me." Others, she thinks, are joined, can refer to themselves and their other egos as "we," while she is alone, a single "I." Now with the wedding, Jarvis and Janice will absorb her into the community of their lives. By becoming part of a world and a self larger than what her condition grants her, she can escape being caught. In this period of her life, identity is not separateness and independence; it is union with the world outside of her from which, in her consciousness, she feels alienated. But with her dream, "At last she knew just who she was and understood where she was going. She loved her brother and the bride and she was a member of the wedding. The three of them would go into the world and they would always be together. And finally, after the scared spring and the crazy summer, she was no more afraid." There is a tidy fullness and completeness about Frankie's dream: "The telling of the wedding had an end and a beginning, a shape like a song." She convinces herself, resisting her change, that her life can be like a story, fully accounted for, rounded out, enjoyable in its totality all at once, like the state of absolute equilibrium and rest in Sartre's "repose." Frankie's is a metaphysical delusion in which she refuses to acknowledge that the beginnings and the endings of a human life are not accessible to the human being living it. It is constantly open and unpredictable, a lack which in its nature is indeterminate and incomplete—always open. Her view is similar to the one Camus describes in *The Rebel.* Seen from a distance, he writes, the lives of others "seem to possess a coherence and a unity which they cannot have in reality, but which seem evident to the spectator. He sees only the salient points of these lives without taking into account the details of corrosion. Thus we make these lives into works of art. In an elementary fashion we turn them into novels. In this sense, everyone tries to make his life a work of art."[4] The lack that Frankie feels lies in her own openness, in that conscious self that becomes aware of itself as a being that stands out from the world it lives in. In her dreams of the wedding, just as in the spectator's observation of others' lives, she seeks to cancel that lack by creating a storied life with nothing left over and nothing lacking.

But Frankie's period of transition cannot remain static. She must either regress to the unconscious abandon of childhood or move forward to the higher consciousness of her next stage of growth. The world itself forces her forward. Simultaneously certain that Jarvis and Janice plan to take her with them and doubtful that her hopes are anything more than illusions, Frankie sneaks into the waiting honeymoon car with her own suitcase. When her family tries to remove her, she clings frantically to the steering wheel, crying to the newlyweds to take her along. This is the climax of Frankie's childhood, the last desperate attempt to make life something it is not, to escape the inescapable. In the aftermath of her disgrace, she attempts to run away, but is discovered by a policeman and returned to her father. Her response is typical. She has not quite made the leap into her adolescence, and seeing the destruction of her dream, she despairs that she will ever be included in the world. Judged from the standpoint of her demands, her life can be nothing but worthless. The human being, however, develops, grows out of his fears—at least if he is lucky and has enough time. Frankie does grow. When she progresses beyond the childhood dream of completeness and unmixed joy, she is ready to accept what the human condition confronts her with. First she makes a new friend, a girl two years older than she, who introduces her to the tastes of adolescence. Next, her father decides to move in with some relatives and Berenice quits her job with the family. And finally, John Henry, the six-year-old playmate of the "old" Frankie, dies of the childhood disease meningitis, symbolizing the death of Frankie's childhood. With Berenice and John Henry gone from her life, Frankie quietly moves toward the acceptance of her limits. There is a pathos in what is lost in this acceptance, but also a triumph in what is gained.

Member of the Wedding is not an admonitory novel. It is descriptive, showing what occurs to people who happen to be born into life. There is nothing we can "do" to modify that life in its basic characteristics and hence we must content ourselves with separateness and the peculiar freedom that accompanies that separateness. This does not mean that our condition denies us the warmth of human love and understanding. The heart, as Miss McCullers suggests in the title of her first novel, is a "lonely hunter." But as Frankie says, there is a connectedness between people which she cannot explain, which indeed is beyond the human being to explain, and that connectedness is illustrated in the scene following the discussion about the inescapable loneliness of humans. Frankie, nervously confronting a deep and important truth, sits for comfort on Berenice's lap; little John Henry leans against her ample hip. In the dusk of the kitchen they all begin to cry, and all for a different reason. For all their differences, however, they are in one sense united. The scene dramatizes the sad fact of human existence—the impossibility of ever filling up consciousness without turning it into something else, the necessity of remaining separate, and, most important, the beauty of sharing these human deprivations. Their weeping is like their singing: ". . . their three voices were joined, and the parts of the song were woven together." People's lives are like this song and this weeping, each separate strand contributing to a whole and deriving from that whole a satisfaction missing without the others. If the condition of the human being is to "lack," he can share that condition with others through love. Metaphysically, it is the actual entity committing himself to his society as an element of his individual satisfaction. As a child, this is not good enough for Frankie. She demands absolute communion. As an adult, suggests McCullers, she will learn that this is the way we fulfill ourselves.

Other novelists are preoccupied with the attempt, not to overcome the lack of the human actual entity, but to replace the reality of existence with abstractions—especially written stories or historical narratives which give recognizable order to that which is inherently unordered. Such abstractions are analogous to the attempts by physicists to explain the observed phenomena of the atom by Newtonian mechanics. They ignore what Sartre calls "transphenomenality," the impossibility of ever capturing the ultimate reality of the existence they purport to reflect or embody. These abstractions are one more means of escaping the irrational. They establish equilibrium, balance, and harmony—a state of self-sufficiency and completeness. James Purdy's *The Nephew* and Thomas Pynchon's *V.* exemplify this preoccupation. These novels do not recommend that we abandon our abstractions. Explaining our existence and making stories out of our lives is what humans do. What they do recommend is the adoption of a consciousness that recognizes the limits of explanations and the relationship of awareness to existence.

The Nephew is a low-key, tightly organized novel of two old people who try to create a past that never was in order to help themselves in the present. The setting of this unspectacular tale is the ingrown neighborhood of the small mid-western town of Rainbow Center. Some five or six years before the novel opens Alma and Boyd Mason, a brother and a sister who have lived with each other since Boyd's wife died, take in their nephew, fourteen-year-old Cliff. Though Boyd is away a good deal on real estate trips and Alma teaches school in a nearby town, Cliff gives them someone to be responsible for. When he goes off to Korea, the old couple begin to remember a closeness and intimacy which did not exist in the real relationship. Cliff's letters give them no confidence that they are right in their memory, for they are short, uninformative, and noncommittal. When Cliff is reported missing in action, they enlarge the romantic picture they have begun to draw of him and remember more and more a model young man who loved them in appreciation for the affectionate care they gave him. Alma is especially insistent upon creating the fiction that Cliff was someone very special, to whom she meant a great deal and who meant a great deal to her.

When Cliff leaves, Alma becomes preoccupied with both her memory of him and the problems of her neighbors. The two are connected. For dealing with her neighbors she seems peculiarly unprepared. She has spent most of her life tending her invalid mother and teaching school and so has never acquired an understanding of "the main things about life." She is short and peremptory, jealous and resentful toward the other people in her world, regarding them more as troublesome objects to be controlled by her than human subjects to be loved for their own value. She does not try to understand these people. She bosses them. She gives advice no one listens to. Alma assumes that life is to be directed and manipulated by an act of will according to a rigid set of rules that tell her the way things "ought" to be, to some higher abstraction that is inherently good and true. Similarly, she sets out to manipulate the past. As her preoccupation with Cliff's memory grows, she finds herself devoting more and more time to "a dim dream-like reshaping of Cliff's life," a kind of "silent commemoration of his brief career." This "memorial" is to be a record of his boyhood and a portrait of his character. Both the memorial and her attempts to shape the lives of her neighbors reflect her distance from life. She believes that she can skate on abstract surfaces of her own making. She would create a neighborhood that fits her sense of propriety. She would create a Cliff that confirms the thing she most wants verified: that Cliff loved her and Boyd, that he understood how they cared for him. The memorial is thus more than an expression of her feeling for Cliff; it is a proof that her feeling had value because Cliff loved her back.

In reconstructing Cliff's life, Alma tries to do what Frankie Addams tried to do with her brother and his fiancee—enter completely into another person's existence by means of a kind of story. That story is meant to substitute for the actual experience of the years when Cliff lived in her house. But in her search for proof that the past was as she wants it to be, she discovers precisely what Frankie discovered. She laments that she never "knew" Cliff. And the picture that slowly emerges is different from that of her dim dream. She uncovers a Cliff who was lonely and anguished and restless, ill at ease in the home she and Boyd had made for him. And she finds that the "real" Cliff is not accessible to her. Troubled, Alma begins to learn something about herself, if not about the "real" Cliff. She comes to suspect "that in planning the memorial she had set out to do something which was not only the height of folly, but had made everyone else in the neighborhood behave like fools." And so she puts the memorial away, promising herself that she will return to it at a more propitious time.

But Alma has to learn the futility of such a memorial and to see that there are other aspects of the human experience which are more painful, perhaps, but also more satisfying than the creation of substitute abstractions. She cannot put off learning some things about Cliff she would have preferred to remain ignorant of. Life forces that experience upon her. She discovers a friendship between Cliff and a suspected homosexual. The possibility that Cliff had shared this aberration shocks Boyd into a heart attack. The significance of this situation, however, is not Cliff's brush with homosexuality, but Alma's emergence as an open human being. She becomes responsible for nursing Boyd back to health, protecting him from further anxiety. When the telegram comes notifying her that Cliff has been killed in action, she is confronted with what she always sought to avoid. It is as if the discovery about Cliff serves finally to kill off the image of the "missing" Cliff that Alma had sought to erect in the memorial. In that death and in the emergency of Boyd's attack, she gains a new strength and insight. It is not necessary that she abandon her memory of Cliff. But at last she turns to the living, determined to be strong enough for Boyd and to keep Cliff's death from him until he is strong enough to bear it. With a new humility she realizes "that it was Boyd who cared for him [Cliff] perhaps the most, while you see it was I who always talked and talked . . . and was going to write a book."

Alma tries to capture Cliff, fix him in her memorial, partly in order to "know" him and partly in order to secure the investment of her love. She learns that no person may be fixed, completely objectified, by another. As Boyd tells her, echoing Frankie and Berenice, "We none of us, I'm afraid, know anybody or know one another." Again we are presented with that sad separateness that arises from the contemporary conception of reality—that individual entity which, as a subject, is causally independent. But the human condition is not without its means of satisfaction, and those means stem from the very notion of reality that cause us our sorrow—subjective independence. The individual self may intensify its sense of being, not by occupying the existence of another subject—not by "knowing" and thus capturing another person—but by loving, by feeling *for* another in one's own private experience. It is just this intensely personal emotion which Alma learns to set free in herself. She discovers that Cliff's friend, in his love for Cliff, had given him money in order that he might escape Rainbow Center, thus doing for his friend Cliff what he was not able to do for himself. Alma is struck by the unwanted knowledge that Cliff ever wanted to flee Rainbow Center. She sees suddenly what the real Cliff must have been going through. Instead of feeling sorry for herself that Cliff did not love her enough not to want to run off, she loves Cliff more, "Because I see how much more he needed the little love anyone can give." At last her love has become a spontaneous response to another's need, not a deliberate investment that expects a return. Moreover, she learns to love a real Cliff rather than an image reshaped in a fatuous memorial. This love, though painful and seemingly deficient, is "all we dare hope for in this life." Even the pain of Cliff's desire to escape loses some of its sting, for, as one of Alma's neighbors says, "who doesn't want to run away from those they love, and at his age?"

All the human has, suggests Purdy, is the certainty of his own love for another. Alma learns, in addition, that she has jurisdiction only over herself, not the lives of her neighbors or the image of Cliff in the past. Nor is this ground for despair or cynicism. It makes possible the spontaneous positive gestures of love and affection which invest life with its value. Thus, in the end, Alma can admit, "I'm so glad you've been here, Boyd. It would be pretty all-alone by myself." Boyd returns her gesture by trying to assure her that Cliff did know of their love for him and that in knowing, returned it. This, however, Alma no longer needs and she remains silent in the darkness of their living room: she and Boyd, together as human beings, no longer in need of words or misled about the place of stories and abstractions in the human experience.

V. is a much more elaborate examination of the relationship between rationality and irrationality, between abstractions and existence. It reflects the "moderation" that Camus speaks of and that I have named as one of the basic features of the "open decision." Pynchon establishes two main narrative lines in his novel, one dealing with existence, the other with "history"; one with aimless feeling and experience, the other with explanations and significance. Benny Profane's narrative emphasizes existence, meaning here a wide range of immediate experience in the present. Benny, by his own definition a "schlemiehl," wanders through a series of episodes in which he descends into the sewers of New York to shoot alligators, lives on the West Side with a Puerto Rican gang, has an affair with one Rachel Owleglass who accuses him of not being able to love, and eventually is persuaded by Herbert Stencil—the protagonist of the other narrative line—to go to Valletta on Malta where his odyssey stops, apparently in suicide. The reason for the suicide is not made explicit, but it may be inferred. As his name suggests, Profane is an unsanctified man, irreverent though not rebellious, passively allowing himself to be carried by the current of experience rather than attempting to steer his own course toward discovery according to some goal. His life, however, though eventful, has had little significance. It has taught him nothing. Brenda, an American college girl he picks up in Malta, envies him "all these fabulous experiences," but when she wonders whether he has learned anything from them, he answers, "No . . . offhand I'd say I haven't learned a goddamn thing." Later, after these words—which are the last Benny utters in the novel—Valletta's lights suddenly go out, darkening the entire city, suggesting a connection between Benny's condition and the city's. As benighted and as unenlightened as when he entered the story, Profane runs "through the abruptly absolute night . . . toward the edge of Malta, and the Mediterranean beyond." It is not that Benny is so ignorant or apathetic that he cannot or will not learn. He simply despairs of any "true" knowledge and so renounces all knowledge. The gap between subjective experience and rational explanation renders, for him, all explanation fatuous. He refuses to search for forms in the world. The perception of causes and effects, the awareness of intelligibility and significance—these are for him purely illusory. Benny is a good-natured nihilist who lets himself float with the stream of experience. It is not enough. He cannot love, and darkling he runs toward death.

In the other narrative, Herbert Stencil searches for significance, but in that search, he seals himself off from experience. Born in 1901, in the same year Queen Victoria died, he represents a form of twentieth century man, one who, as Stencil says of himself, "sleeps" between the two world wars and then awakens with an appetite for making sense out of the years of his life. The way that he seeks to do this is similar to Alma's memorial to Cliff. Stencil sets out to put together a history of V., an entity both imaginary and real in the same way that the world we know and experience is imaginary and real. V. has as many facets as there are eyes to view her (it, him). V. is Victoria Wren, who, between 1898—when she appears in Alexandria and allows her innocence to be violated —and the Second World War, turns up in Florence as an experienced but still youthful mistress of Evan Godolphin, in Paris as a lesbian fetishist, in Malta as an anti-British revolutionist named Victoria Manganese, and as a mysteriously mechanized "Bad Priest" who is taken apart by a group of gleeful children in a surrealistic orgy of amorality in which the Victorian age (V.) is finally dismantled after a period of deterioration under a new ideology. V. is also Vheissu, a territory in Africa so colorful, as old Hugh Godolphin says, that it can drive men mad with its vividness. It is the V-Note in New York City where the Negro jazz musician McLintic Sphere plays. It is Veronica, the New York sewer rat that wants to become a nun. It is the Vergeltungswaffe, Hilter's last weapons of revengeful war which one Mondaugen helps to invent.

Out of a welter of symbolic names and tantalizingly meaningful events, Stencil (the copier of reality rather than reality in itself) draws a vague pattern. His sources are his father's journal, where he first saw any reference to V., and interviews with those who might give him information. In this pattern, Stencil sees a "grand cabal," and thus gives an intelligible form to the past. But that form is "history," in which facet upon facet appears, detail upon detail, all flashing in and out of the investigator's sight like the constantly changing reflection of light off the prisms of a crystal chandelier. Herbert's father, Sidney Stencil, an agent for the British Government, concludes before his son is born "that no Situation had any objective reality: it only existed in the minds of those who happened to be in on it at any specific moment. Since these several minds tend to form a sum total or complex more mongrel than homogeneous, The Situation must necessarily appear to a single observer much like a diagram in four dimensions to an eye conditioned to seeing its world in only three." This notion of the relativity of knowledge leads us to question young Stencil's search. Herbert searches for The Situation, the "identity" of V., seeking to objectify it in a form recognizable to the intellect. But in its nature the past that V. represents cannot be objectified, except as history. It is like the "structure of the totality of natural law" that Bohm speaks of, which is virtually infinitely-faceted and can never be "known" absolutely. It is like Einstein's analogy of the observer who attempts to understand the inside of a watch through the evidence of its surface characteristics. The picture we imagine of the interior mechanism can never be compared with the "real mechanism." The figure of the letter V. for which Stencil searches embodies the elusiveness of the identification of intellectual explanation and subjective experience. As Benny Profane walks down a street in Norfolk, Virginia, he sees that the streetlights overhead form an "asymmetric V," and in the distance the V's legs converge in the darkness. But it is a convergence which, as he approaches it, recedes. This is precisely the experience of Stencil in his search; it is the experience of any investigator who probes for some absolute truth that appears to make itself accessible in the patterns we perceive. Absolute comprehension and absolute existence are mutually exclusive.

Stencil looks for knowledge. The way he goes about it demonstrates the theoretical exclusiveness of history and existence. He strives to remain free of his subject, avoid becoming involved in it. To do this he puts on the various classical disguises of political espionage, "not out of any professional necessity but only as a trick, simply to involve him less in the chase, to put off some part of the pain of dilemma on various 'impersonations.'" As an impersonator, he remains on the surface, referring to himself always as an object in the third person, never as the subject "I." Unable to exist subjectively in his investigation, he gathers dossiers from others, as a kind of vicarious existence. But the investigating mind inevitably distorts reality in itself in the attempt to objectify it; hence, the dossiers develop "a nacreous mass of inference, poetic license, forcible dislocation of personality into a past he didn't remember and had no right in, save the right of imaginative anxiety or historical care, which is recognized by no one." This is the weakness of all historians: their knowledge is neither an objective knowledge of some ultimate reality nor a subjective knowledge of existence. Stencil can experience the *dramatis personae* of the past whose center is V. only through the information of others. Whatever else he adds is "impersonation and dream." The episodes he shapes out of his evidence—which form his account of the past—are pictures that result from guesses, models of a reality he can never know fully, rather than reproductions of the reality that once throbbed with life. Any model he creates, because he does not have access to the original, will be the result more of invention than of observation. This inventiveness is a literary license which appears as Stencil's "compulsive yarning," his *creation* of the V. "situation." For Stencil the pictures begin to be more important than the past itself. When Kierkegaard claims that one can learn nothing from history about Christ, he is speaking of the same problem confronting Stencil: "For whether now one learns little or much about him [Christ], it will not represent what he was in reality. Hence one learns something else about him than what is strictly true. . . ."[5] History shows only the intellect abstracting, not existence in itself transpiring as the individual subject.

But because history cannot reproduce existence does not mean it is not basic to man's life. The pursuit of historical explanation is one of the poles of the human condition's paradox. When that pursuit is absent, we as human beings die. In V. the metaphor of this notion is Vheissu, once visited by Old Godolphin and described by him as a place where the colors are unbearably gaudy and the coats of iridescent spider monkeys created the impression of living "inside a madman's kaleidoscope." Tourists, says Old Godolphin, "want only the skin of a place, the explorer wants its heart." The heart is subjective existence, something we can never get from the tourism of history. Tourists and historians, touch only the surface and remain inanimate. They follow their Baedeker, conform to certain expectations, and avoid the deception and the ambiguity of the "heart." As an explorer Godolphin had gone to Vheissu, and at its heart had found, as he says, "Nothing." The "nothing" of Godolphin's Vheissu is not precisely the "nothing" of Sartre. It is the sense of life without recognizable pattern. It is existence—iridescent, gaudy, changeful, overpowering. This vivid force is everywhere, emerging to blind the ascetic simplicity of the clear explanation. Old Godolphin tries to escape the clamorous color of Vheissu by taking refuge in the monotonous white waste of Antarctica. But there in the ice he finds the corpse of a Vheissuvian monkey, having come to be there through the earth tunnels dug by the Vhessuvians—like the tunnels of the mind beneath consciousness—and penetrating with its urgency the cool detachment of that distant place. Vheissu and the "buzzing, blooming existence" it represents conflict with the conscious self-reflection of the historian, the man of knowledge. It is, Godolphin concludes, "a dream of annihilation." What is annihilated is the intellectual consciousness, which maintains order and unity, sees pattern and purpose. In terms of that faculty, Vheissu is indeed annihilation. Both appear simultaneously in the human being and both would destroy each other. So long as they do not, human life persists.

Even Stencil senses this. He fears that actually finding V. will mean his annihilation, for that would be the equivalent of substituting history for existence. ". . . where else would there be to go but back into half-consciousness? He tried not to think, therefore, about any end to the search. Approach and avoid." The "sense of animateness" that Stencil feels in his search for V. both betrays existence in itself and makes him feel like a human being. Yet, when history and explanation are unmixed with existence, it constitutes the death of rejecting its opposite. At least Stencil, in the end of the novel, is still open, still pursuing leads. Profane, for whom explanation is futile, runs into Malta's darkness toward the sea.

In the novels I have talked about so far in this chapter, the issue has been the degree to which the characters are willing to live the human condition as it is given. Some are not willing and seek to escape from the pain of existence's uncertainties into the certainties of complete explanation or the dreams of absolute power. The tacit assumption underlying this issue is that human reality is the paradox of rationality and irrationality and that to deny either is to deny human life. The problem dramatized by the novelist is that the human being, by definition, seeks to resolve the paradox and does not admit easily the impossibility of doing it.

For some contemporary novelists the issue takes the form of a rejection of irrationality. That is, they invent characters who renounce that faith which is willing to entertain the irrational, and they suffer because of that renunciation. When the issue is the affirmation of faith over skepticism, the main antagonist is the rational empiricism of modern technology.[6] Against that empiricism these novelists assert the reality and the validity of irrational faith. Their point is that the highest consciousness and hence the most intense human existence includes faith, which, while not rational, is yet among the most certain of our certainties. Their note is positive and affirmative, though it does not exclude the mixture of pain and regret that we have learned to expect from the contemporary novel. Faith is a function of the consciousness which affirms those aspects of ourselves and our world that never come into consciousness, but lie on its outskirts as dark presences that reveal themselves only in ambiguous and inarticulate shadows, something like Jung's archetypes of the collective unconscious. This faith appears as religious faith in its most fundamental form and as simple faith in the potential of the human being to live worthily in the midst of a stultifying and dehumanizing machine world. The metaphysical basis of this position lies in the "open decision," which locates human value in that most real thing—the human individual. That individual is a unique subject, whose novel constitution spills over any rational explanation of it. To insist that what cannot be dealt with through rational empiricism is to debase the value of the transphenomenal individual.

Probably the most unlikely of our contemporary novelists to be identified as "contemporary" and linked with the philosophical background of modern western thought is Flannery O'Connor. A southern Catholic fundamentalist, she has claimed to be innocent of all theory, and has asserted her unconditional belief in the literal truth of the old Christian principles of Redemption, Sin, Grace, and the Resurrection of Jesus. Even so, the values she affirms in her Christianity—a religion which is by no means all hearts and flowers—reflect the emphasis upon irrationality and its location in the individual which characterizes many of our thinkers. This reflection comes out nowhere more clearly than in her first novel, *Wise Blood.* In her preface to the 1962 edition of that novel, Miss O'Connor says of her hero, Hazel Motes, that his integrity lies in his inability to rid himself of his faith in Christ. He is unable to escape his most authentic self, which lies in that living core that eludes rational explanation and the will based upon that explanation.

Haze tries to escape his faith. The atmosphere within which he attempts to do this is permeated with the ironic opposition between darkness and light. Here, the "real" truth lies in darkness while the light reveals only a narrow and superficial truth. Christ is the real truth, but Haze represents Christ to himself as "a wild ragged figure motioning him to turn around and come off into the dark where he was not sure of his footing, where he might be walking on the water and not know it and then suddenly know it and drown." For Haze, the truth of Christ is death—the overwhelming of reason, light, and consciousness by the wild, the irrational, and the dark. The dark is the unpredictable and unknown, that which lies beyond cognizing consciousness and the models of reality such consciousness constructs. Haze seeks to escape the ragged figure beckoning him into the dark by disavowing faith. Ironically, the very desperateness of his disavowal only confirms the inescapability of his faith.

Hazel Motes runs, figuratively, from what he is. He determines to "avoid" Jesus by preaching the "truth" that behind all truths lies only one truth—that there is no truth. What he means is that truth and the irrationality of faith are mutually exclusive. Therefore, he preaches relativism and rationalism, in which empiricism is the supposed basis of the only valid knowledge. In his youth he wants to stay in his home town of Eastrod "with his two eyes open, and his hands always handling the familiar things, his feet on the known track, and his tongue not too loose." As a grown man, he declares that "it was not right to believe anything you couldn't see or hold in your hands or test with your teeth." Sanity is reason and clear-sightedness—rational empiricism. And rational empiricism tells us that Jesus cannot have been the son of God or our redeemer because that would require empirical change in our real individual bodies and no such change can be detected. Sounding occasionally like both a Whiteheadian and a Sartrean, Haze says, "In yourself right now is all the place you've got." The Fall, Redemption, and Judgment, if they are "real," must exist in time and space—inside our body. But, he asks, where *are* they? Kierkegaard comes to mind with these words. Contrary to Hazel Motes, Kierkegaard says that the existence of Christ as God and Redeemer is precisely an existence which cannot be determined empirically, rationally, historically, or clearsightedly. His existence can only be determined by faith, and faith is irrational.[7] In *The Sickness unto Death,* he declares that only the "seriousness" of true Christian concern for "the reality of personal existence" is "edifying." ". . . the high aloofness of indifferent learning is, from the Christian point of view, far from being seriousness, it is, from the Christian point of view, jest and vanity."[8] Haze's contention that truth is empirical and can be discerned only in the clear light of reason is not "edifying." He flees the "reality of personal existence" described by Kierkegaard, trying to objectify the Christ of faith out of existence through the detachment of rationality.

Haze is blind while he professes that his sight is clear. The irony of his position is symbolized by his old Essex, a "rat-colored" broken down relic of a car which is on the verge of collapse, but which Haze declares will run forever. It represents the deterioration of rationalism as "edifying" knowledge. The Essex becomes the center of his life, the "vehicle" of his rebellion against and flight from his belief in Jesus. He sleeps in it, and he preaches from its hood the doctrine of his "Church without Christ." The car, he contends, is the embodiment of clearsightedness, "built by people with their eyes open that knew where they were at." So long as the car holds together, so long does Haze hold together his campaign of resistance. But in a series of incidents, related more by sequence than by literal cause and effect, Haze loses the car and his professed clearsightedness.

The first incident in this series is his murder of Solace Layfield. He runs over the weak, tubercular man because Solace has replaced Haze as the "prophet" of the "Church without Christ." It is not being replaced that incenses Haze, but the fact that Solace professes a lie: that he does not believe in Christ when he really does. This, of course, is what Haze himself is doing, and that fact is emphasized by Solace's troublesome resemblance to Haze. With his murder of Solace, Haze reaches the nadir of his own perverse rebellion. The virtual effect of the murder is the beginning of the final deterioration of the car, and by implication, the foundation of Haze's rational resistance. He has used his rationalism to run down another human being. Immediately, the Essex starts going to pieces. Its radiator and gas tank begin to leak and it drips oil. Haze, however, in the blindness of his "sight," insists that it is "just beginning life." But both he and his car have nearly reached the end of the line. That comes in the final incident. The morning after he kills Solace, he drives out on the highway in a car—and a doctrine—on the verge of disintegration. Once again he has taken flight, for his destination is another town where he can preach his doctrine of the Church without Christ. He is stopped by a policeman, who has no reason for his action except that he simply does not like Haze's face. The officer functions as a kind of irrational fury, ironically appearing to destroy Haze's whole flimsy structure of empiricism and clearsightedness. He orders Haze to drive to an embankment to "see the view," and then pushes the old car over, demolishing it completely. Haze, having always sought a "view," is not confronted with it. But what he sees is not something lucid and empirically explainable—something conscious cognition can totally account for. He sees an enigmatic world which does not disclose itself to the sort of clarity which Haze maintains is the only truth: a "distance that extended from his eyes to the blank gray sky that went on, depth after depth, into space." One does not see into that space with one's open eyes any more than one's physical eyes can see into the darkness toward which Jesus calls Haze.

After the destruction of his car—apparently because of it—Haze blinds himself with quick lime. Ostensibly he intends this to be one last gesture of defiance, one last proof that he does not believe in Jesus. But the symbolic nature of that gesture is that he cannot escape his belief. Whom does he have to convince of his disbelief but Christ, and how can he convince an entity which does not exist? Haze himself formulates this question, deciding that you cannot even believe that the way to salvation is blasphemy, that the way to escape sin is by disbelieving in Christ. That would mean you accepted as real what you blaspheme. Having fled from Christ's darkness to the light of "truth," he turns at last, almost panting and at bay, and plunges into that very darkness. It is a last resort—ironically, a way to "see." "If there's no bottom in your eyes," he says, "they hold more."

There are two pieces of evidence which, in spite of his rationality, confirm Haze's act as an affirmation of his faith. The first is the attempt by the phony blind preacher Asa Hawks to blind himself, "to justify his belief that Christ Jesus had redeemed him." After he has worked himself up into a kind of possessed frenzy, he is suddenly unable to go through with it and only pretends to let the lime run into his eyes. He cannot enter that darkness. The reason for his failure is that he suddenly sees himself clearly, unpossessed by the "devils" that would have permitted him to fulfill his vow, standing alone. He is only himself facing Jesus who, having "expelled" the devils, now beckons to him, precisely as Jesus does to Haze, inviting him into the irrational and the unknown with no assurance of what will be found there. He asks Hawks, as he asks Haze, to make the conscious deliberate leap into the darkness celebrated by Kierkegaard. Indeed, Kierkegaard is again relevant to the point. "The Christian heroism," he writes, "is to venture wholly to be oneself, as an individual man, this definite individual man, alone before the face of God, alone in this tremendous exertion and this tremendous responsibility. . . ."[9] In the unbearable clarity of his unsupported aloneness before Christ, in his own unique form, Hawks is incapable of the "Christian heroism." He runs. Haze turns into that darkness to see, having failed with rationality. Alone, he strains into that blackness to take it all in, a Christian hero while trying not to be.[10]

The second piece of evidence that Haze's act is affirmative is his relationship with Mrs. Flood, his landlady. She is a mindless, shallow woman who really does believe in the principles which Haze only professes to believe in: "I believe," she says, "that what's right today is wrong tomorrow and that the time to enjoy yourself is now so long as you let others do the same. I'm as good . . . not believing in Jesus as many a one that does." She, like Haze, prides herself on her clarity of mind. But she lacks the tortured integrity that drives Haze. She is simply insensitive and obtuse. When Haze tells her that he is going to blind himself, she merely marvels that anyone would want to suffer, especially by blindness. As for herself, "A woman like her, who was so clearsighted, could never stand to be blind." Radically faithless, she does not have the morbid obsession with darkness and Jesus that Haze has. Hers is only a superficial common sense, whose faithlessness seals off from her the burning power that lies in the unpredictability of darkness. One avoids it at all costs: ". . . time goes forward, it don't go backward," she says in a paraphrase of some of Haze's own preachments, "and unless you take what's offered you, you'll find yourself out in the cold pitch black. . . ." For her that "cold pitch black" holds no fatal fascination, as it does for Haze.

Unable to marry this corrupted reflection of his own conscious tenets—though she frequently suggests it—Haze limps out into the gray freezing weather and dies of exposure and the blow of a policeman's club in a drainage ditch, having affirmed his faith in his resistance to it and having journeyed at last into the final absolute darkness. The significance of what Haze has done appears in the fact that Mrs. Flood tries, like Asa Hawks, to imitate Haze's blindness but cannot. When the police bring him back to her, she tries to look into his eyes, not blinded by quick lime and death, "to see how she had been cheated." When she cannot see anything, she simulates blindness by closing her eyes in order to "stare" into his for further insight. But for such knowledge there is no help in others; that personal reality is absolutely singular. She cannot go into that darkness, and she senses this. She feels "blocked at the entrance of something," "as if she had finally got to the beginning of something she couldn't begin." Mrs. Flood's very clearsightedness, a parody of the rational empiricism preached by Haze, disqualifies her from entering that murky, passionate, dangerous territory in which faith prevails, existence is set on fire, and the unique single individual faces his Christ entirely alone in the darkling light of "edifying" knowledge. It is just this territory that Haze enters, like Paul on the road to Damascus, when he blinds himself. Mrs. Flood cannot follow him as she attempts to do in a purely safe and simulated darkness. She sees "him moving farther and farther away, farther and farther into the darkness until he was the pinpoint of light." In that new land, Haze achieves, as Mrs. Flood interprets it for us, a stern tranquility: "She had never observed his face more composed. . . ."

In her commitment to the irrational in man—that faith by which we "know" different "truths" from those asserted by reason and empirical observation—Flannery O'Connor reflects one of the ways that the modern mind meets existence. Even though she explicitly rejects the relativism that attaches to the "open decision," yet she cannot escape the atmosphere of her time. Reduce life to its most fundamental factor, she suggests, and you move into regions of indeterminacy. Carried far enough, that indeterminacy does not yield even to the intellectual construct of statistical probability, but only to the intensity of individual existence for which reason and probability graphs are irrelevant, and faith and irrationality are the definitive features of human life.

Faith is the affirmation of one's own integrity and the worth of life even though one can find no rational or objective standards to validate that affirmation. Faith is the confidence the self feels in occupying his own novel world-center, in being-in-the-world in its own unique way and on its own unique terms, independent of any transcendent validating standard. Lacking confidence in the strength of one's own personal authenticity, one becomes vulnerable to the powers of destruction. This is the issue in William Styron's *Set This House on Fire,* which, like *Wise Blood,* opposes the antagonists' faith and technological materialism. Cass Kinsolving is an artist who has lost his faith: "I didn't have," he says, "any more faith than a tomcat." The faith that Cass has lost is not the religious faith that drove Hazel Motes. It is the faith that disappears with the old world-view. The Italian Fascist, Luigi, calls our attention to this whole frame of reference: ". . . existence itself is an imprisonment," he says; "we are serving our sentences in solitary confinement, unable to speak. All of us. Once we were at least able to talk with our Jailer, but now even He has gone away, leaving us alone with the knowledge of insufferable loss." The loss does indeed seem to be insufferable for Cass. He feels only "*half* a person, trapped by terror, trapped by booze, trapped by self." He is "some hulk which had slipped from its moorings and drifted out onto the sea, surrounded on all sides by reefs and ruin and yawning deeps." He dreams of the imprisonment Luigi describes, and of cataclysm, and of the death of God. Bereft of belief in some high court that confers value and meaning upon himself and all he does, Cass reacts with "despair and self-loathing." He loses his artistic creativity and starts drinking heavily to anesthetize himself against the oppressiveness of his existence.

Thus vulnerable, he falls under the sway of Mason Flagg, a rich young man who uses his fortune to indulge his corrupt appetite for sex, machines, and dominance. Mason is a representation of an American society which has become dehumanized and dehumanizing in its capitulation to technology and materialism. He engages in every superficial fashion, sees sex as pornography, man as "a thinking biological complex." Mason's life is a self-indulgent machine existence. His "frenzied desire for speed" is simply "an empty ritualistic coupling with a machine, self-possessed, craven, autoerotic, devoid of pleasure much less joy." When Cass comes into Mason's orbit in Sambuco, Italy, Mason sets out systematically to degrade him. In return for a plentiful supply of liquor, Mason requires Cass to perform debasing acts in front of his guests, and corrupts his artistic integrity by having him draw pornographic pictures.

Cass, nevertheless, struggles to find "the good in myself," that authentic and inviolable center "which is very close to God." Only then will he be able to escape from his stultifying dependence upon alcohol and Mason Flagg. In order to find that good he must settle the question of faith, without which, as Cass says, a man cannot live. The key to that question appears in the Italian peasant girl Francesca. She teaches Cass about love and shows him that life has "some vestige of meaning." In a series of pastoral idylls, Cass and Francesca retire to the primitive innocence of the countryside while Cass paints the girl in the nude, the purity of which contrasts with the degeneracy of the pornography he does for Mason. Francesca's purity and the love and gentleness with which she administers to her father Michele, dying of tuberculosis, bespeak an integrity and a faith in the intrinsic value of the human subject which Cass must find in himself. The source of that faith in part lies in the character of the Italian peasant and the way he reacts to a painful life. For example, Cass observes an old peasant woman, bent under her load of firewood, lose her balance and drop her bundle. She throws up her arms in "a noiseless gesture, touched not with anger or despair but only inevitability, acceptance of the world in which heavy loads fall and must forever be rehoisted." The peasant does not turn to despair or self-loathing. For all the passiveness in her attitude, she displays a force of life, a power for endurance and determination to endure. Later, dreaming of this incident, Cass concludes that God, through some "capricious error had created suffering mortal flesh which refused to die, even in its own extremity."

Cass has sought to destroy himself, morally and psychologically. Now Francesca and her peasant family offer him redemption, teaching him about their faith that urges them to survive and endure. Because of them he begins to break free from Mason. Cass goes to Mason for medicine to treat the sick Michele. Mason agrees to get some in return for Cass's further degradation. Though Cass accepts the bargain, he has taken a step toward freedom. He has, he says, allowed Mason to own him, "out of spinelessness at first, out of whiskey-greed and desolation of the spirit, but at last out of necessity." It is that necessity by means of which his own integrity begins to emerge. His concessions to Mason are no longer permeated with despair and self-disgust. Their basis is his love for Francesca and Michele and, more generally, for life itself.

Mason, however, and the empty materialism he stands for, opposes this life and seeks to destroy its spirit. Realizing that Francesca is giving Cass strength, Mason rapes her. Later she is found dead, and Cass, believing Mason to be both rapist and murderer, kills him in a desperate rage. But Mason is not guilty of Francesca's murder, and Cass later admits that he really knew it at the time he killed Mason, though he tried to hide that knowledge from himself. Thus there is a brutal querulousness, a self-pity, in the action he took. The revenge was in excess of the crime actually committed. Mason raped Francesca but did not kill her. The world he represents polluted an ideal but did not destroy it. For all of Mason's evil, Cass is not without responsibility, and finally he admits this: "It didn't *start* with Mason," he says. The real killer of Francesca is another aspect of the world with which Cass is now inescapably confronted—a kind of *deus ex machina,* a half-wit of the village who became frightened when the girl struggled against his harmless caresses and in his fear mutilated her. The half-wit's crime was irrational, without Mason's malice. Just so are fate and suffering irrational. Why loads fall and must be reshouldered, why Michele suffered and died from disease, why peasants live in wretchedness, why the lovely Francesca was destroyed—these realities cannot be explained by the logic of our intellect. It is folly for men to become angry when such explanations cannot be discovered, as Cass did when he cried that God is dead, and when he sought to gain retribution for Francesca's death by killing Mason.

Paradoxically, however, that act of violence seems to shake him free from the despair he felt when he discovered his faithfulness and the world's degradation; it releases him, too, from total immersion in his ideal of Francesca. It is a rebellion against the inescapable injustices of pain and the chaos of existence. In that rebellion Cass asserts himself, says with Camus's rebel, "just this far and no farther." The faith that this rebellion unlocks is not "that here [in this world] madness might become reason, and grief joy, and no yes. And even death itself death no longer, but resurrection." That is, it is not a faith that there is a higher authority to appeal to for help in escaping, finally, our present condition. It is a faith shot through with mild regret and a kind of fatigue, recognizing that there is in life only a choice between "being and nothing," existence and death, consciousness and unconsciousness, and that "to choose between them was simply to choose being, not for the sake of being, or even the love of being, much less the desire to be forever—but in the hope of being what I could be for a time. This would be an ecstasy." Only man gives existence meaning, and he does so through his powers of endurance, his capacity to survive the suffering of the flesh. Above all man gives existence meaning by choosing to endure. In seeing this, Cass arrives at a higher consciousness than that of the Italian peasant, whose acceptance of his condition is virtually an automatic reflex. Cass's hope lies in his faith in the possibilities of his own being, not as commandments laid down by a rational and meaning-giving deity, but as openings which he must choose by himself on the basis of no more valid reasons than that it is he choosing.

In *Set This House on Fire* and *Wise Blood* Styron and Miss O'Connor tacitly assume the whole rationale underlying the value so many modern thinkers place upon the irrational. Traditional physics and metaphysics assume a close correspondence between the models of reality constructed by the intellect in an attempt to explain that reality to consciousness and reality in itself. Part of that assumption is that whatever lies outside of such explanatory models cannot be very important, cannot, indeed, be considered part of reality. With modern physics and metaphysics, the emphasis has shifted. Relativity and indeterminacy suggest the impossibility that the conscious intellect can ever totally represent reality in itself. That reality—the individual subject, the feeling, experiencing thing—is metaphysically protected, finally, from any incursions upon its integrity. But more important for O'Connor and Styron, and for most of the other novelists writing today, individual satisfaction is intensified and the higher good served when the human being acknowledges and embraces those elements of its being that escape representation in rational explanation, those elements which lie in the darkness of indeterminacy and which give reality its characteristic quality. Individual satisfaction is further intensified, by this thinking, when the human being abandons his assumption that the real and the valuable lie in the totally explainable and recognizes instead that they are to be found in the indeterminate authenticity of the experiencing subject, whose value is confirmed by the act of faith which is the choice of its own being, and not the being conferred, supposedly, by some transcendent agent. The faith of Hazel Motes and Cass Kinsolving is the affirmation—for no objectively valid reason—of themselves as human beings.

All of the novelists I have been discussing assume the good to lie in the elusive individual. That good, in the view of the "open decision," is heightened as the individual becomes more aware of himself. Some novelists focus on awareness rather than on escape from the human condition or a refusal to accept the irrational foundation of man's existence. Heightened consciousness for them is the *sine qua non* of individuality. The concern for such consciousness appears in its clearest form in the last three novels to be dealt with in this section. Consciousness is tantamount to freedom; both words refer, in the metaphysics of the "open decision," to that state in which the human being is most spontaneous, most genuine, most himself. That state can be vitiated by tyranny—social tyranny, ideological tyranny, psychological tyranny; that is, any form of bad faith or false consciousness. Under such tyranny the self fearfully shrinks to the point of disappearance or it dissipates in "they-ness." The aim of human experience, therefore, is to achieve an independence of these forces. It is done through authentic consciousness.

Ken Kesey's *One Flew Over the Cuckoo's Nest* depicts the shrinkage of the authentic self in a suffocating society and tells the story of the liberation of men who have long withdrawn into themselves through fear. The setting is a mental hospital, a deliberately oversimplified symbol of society, whose "Acute" and "Disturbed" wards are run rigidly by the stern "Big Nurse Ratched." The narrator of the story is Chief Bromden, a Northwest Indian who, when the Government refuses to let him live the natural life of his choice, simulates schizophrenia, pretending neither to hear nor to talk. Bromden defines the symbolic meaning of the mental hospital and Nurse Ratched (and recalls Jaspers' "apparatus") when he describes them as parts of a nation-wide "Combine," organized—like Burroughs' Nova Mob—to put the individual in bonds and to prevent him from realizing his spontaneous authentic self. Most of the time the Combine works by installing "things," as Chief says. That is, the Combine conditions the individual self out of existence by seeing to it that he cooperates in the destruction of his spontaneity. The Combine cannot tolerate uniqueness—cannot tolerate life. The patients in the hospital are victims of the Combine, pusillanimous "rabbits" who do its bidding almost automatically. So completely emptied of the will to be themselves, many of them have assisted the Combine in its systematic destruction by voluntarily committing themselves to the institution. It is these men who must be liberated from their cringing refusal to be aware.

Bromden explains that the Combine's main device for controlling the patients is "fog," generated by huge machines and emitted through chutes in the wall like heat. The fog that Bromden hallucinates is one of Kesey's favorite symbols. In his second novel, *Sometimes a Great Nation,* a Canadian goose gets cut off from the flock and loses its way. Frantically searching for an opening in the mist it flies low along a river, crying plaintively, its voice sounding like a "lost soul," not "so much asking where the lost flock was—he was wanting to know where the river was, and the bank and *everything* hooked up with his life. Where is my world? he was wanting to know, *and where the hell am I if I can't locate it?*" Like that goose, modern man has been disoriented. In *One Flew Over the Cuckoo's Nest,* the patients have been alienated from themselves by a systematically malicious apparatus. The fog figuratively dispensed by its huge machines confuses and weakens them. They lose their sense of self. As their identity blurs they become more and more afraid to draw in their own outlines and turn to the fog to hide in. The fog is Heidegger's "they," which provides men escape from themselves.

Into this world comes Randle Patrick McMurphy, a huge redheaded Irishman, who thinks that a term in a mental hospital will be easier than serving out a sentence on a road gang. McMurphy is the prototypical rebel, with a well-developed sense of his own identity, his boundaries sharply set and vigorously defended. He is the liberator of the ward's inmates. His task becomes to train the patients to assert their inviolate identity, to struggle out of the fog, and to overthrow the tyranny of the emasculating Nurse Ratched. When Bromden sees the fog coming he hopes that McMurphy will know enough to hide in it, to retreat from the sense of self that so sharply emerges when its integrity is threatened. But McMurphy does not have to hide in it. He is completely himself and the strength which he derives from that condition allows him to remain clear-headed and conscious, out "in front" of everyone else, fearless. When he is locked in his first major struggle with Big Nurse over whether the patients will be able to watch the World Series on TV, he manages to persuade the Acute patients to vote with him against Nurse Ratched:

> The first hand that comes up, I can tell [narrates Bromden], is McMurphy's, because of the bandage where that control panel cut into him when he tried to lift it. And then off down the slope I see them, other hands coming up out of the fog. It's like . . . that big red hand of McMurphy's is reaching into the fog and dropping down and dragging the men up by their hands, dragging them blinking into the open . . . dragging them out of the fog till there they stand, all twenty of them, raising not just for watching TV, but against the Big Nurse, against her trying to send McMurphy to Disturbed, against the way she's talked and acted and beat them down for years.

Slowly, McMurphy teaches the men in the wards to be less afraid, first forcing them to assert themselves, then persuading them to do so voluntarily. The result of his first successes is described by Bromden. "There's no more fog any place," he says. The Chief's new acuity tells him that McMurphy's strength comes from the fact that he lives his own being, not a being foisted on him by the Combine. The greatest source of inner strength comes from nature, and this McMurphy teaches the patients on a fishing trip. Nurse Ratched opposes the trip from the start, playing upon the timid men's fear of death by noting the formation of ominous storm clouds over the sea. The trip turns out to be exactly what Nurse Ratched feared it would be: therapeutic. Out on the open sea, challenged by the fish and the elements, the men are provided with the opportunity at last to engage in an honest struggle. Nature does not, like the Combine, seek to imprison; it invites struggle to survive. And struggle is the creative act of rebellion by which men define themselves.

The price of the liberation of these men is high—it is no less than the destruction of McMurphy. And he seems to sense what impends. On the way back to the hospital from the fishing trip, Bromden describes his face as looking "dreadfully tired and strained and *frantic,* like there wasn't enough time left for something he had to do. . . ." As his struggle with Nurse Ratched nears its climax, McMurphy puts his life in greater and greater danger. Big Nurse orders electric shock treatments to break the spirit of the great redheaded man, but McMurphy refuses to surrender. So far she has not been justified in calling forth the Combine's ultimate weapon—lobotomy, the operation which transforms the struggling human being into a vegetable. But finally McMurphy gives her justification. He promotes an illegal party in the ward, complete with liquor and a couple of warm-hearted and humanly virtuous prostitutes, clear contrasts to the frigid mother figure of Nurse Ratched. Wholesome, fun-loving rebellion here reaches its maddest peak, and it possesses salutary possibilities. The stuttering Billy Bibbit, long dominated by an overpossessive mother who coyly treats him like a lover, sleeps with the young prostitute Candy Starr, significantly in the cleansing atmosphere of the laundry room. He seems to have snapped the silver cord at last, for he is calm, happy, and unstuttering when Big Nurse discovers him. This is the work of McMurphy. Through an act of spontaneous love and independent behavior Billy has escaped the Combine. But the strength of the Combine to regain control of its victims is huge. When Nurse Ratched admonishes Billy for not thinking of the shame he would cause his mother and threatens to tell her of his indiscretion, Billy collapses. Unable to face such a possibility, he commits suicide.

Billy's death suggests that something more than the rebelliousness of parties inside the hospital is needed to break free, and that something more is the sacrifice of the great life force of McMurphy. The men, indeed, drive him to his own destruction, almost as if he must, in Whitehead's terms, perish as an actual entity before he can become effective data for the creative process of others. McMurphy must risk his own consciousness for that of others. Nurse

Ratched accuses McMurphy of playing God with the lives of these men. And there is an element of truth in the accusation, but not the truth that Big Nurse sees. McMurphy *is* a kind of god. And in his last act of creativity—that is, the last act of rebellion out of which the other men win their liberation—he annihilates himself. Feeling cornered by Big Nurse's accusation, he at last sees there is no other way to free the men. He rips off the starched front of Nurse Ratched's uniform, the severe rigidity that repressed her ample womanhood, and then seizes her throat as if to choke her. He is pulled off of her, but he has finally exposed the weakness of the Combine in Nurse Ratched. Shocked and unnerved, she will never be the same again. But McMurphy has brought on his own death, condemned himself to a lobotomy. His actions, however, have led to the rehabilitation of the patients in his ward. Several check out, some make plans to leave, and others transfer to different wards.

Chief Bromden is the representative beneficiary of McMurphy's sacrifice. McMurphy is wheeled back into the ward after the lobotomy, and Bromden recognizes that Nurse Ratched intends for his vegetable body to be a monument of the Combine's power. Rebels, she would warn future inmates, never succeed. But Kesey would have it that they do, though perhaps indirectly. Now in command of his own consciousness and stronger as an individual, Bromden refuses to allow Big Nurse her victory. He smothers McMurphy and then escapes from the institution. The way he escapes is also symbolic: he rips out Big Nurse's control panel and throws it through the locked ward door, smashing his way to freedom and destroying the central control that the Combine has exercised over him. The Chief intends to return to his own life of an Indian on the Columbia River. He has gone full circle. Disgusted and alienated by an impersonal Government, he retired from the human race. But through the example of McMurphy, he regains his integrity and returns to life determined to live out the rebelliousness that McMurphy has taught him. A symbol of his new life is in the fact that the Indians "have took to building their old ramshackle wood scaffolding all over that big million-dollar hydroelectric dam, and are spearing salmon in the spillway." These people refuse to surrender "their right to be Indians," which the Government sought to buy from them. Now Chief will pass again through that country "to bring some of it clear in my mind again." He has been brought back to the land of freedom, consciousness, and individuality by McMurphy's rebellion. McMurphy has exchanged his consciousness for that of the others.

In Walker Percy's *The Moviegoer* and Ralph Ellison's *Invisible Man,* the issues of consciousness and freedom are given similar, though less dramatic, form. Percy is explicitly conscious of the existentialism of Kierkegaard, Heidegger, and Sartre. Where for Kesey there is a conspiratorial Combine operating maliciously to thwart the intensity of our individual satisfaction, for Percy there is "everydayness," that familiarity with life, that cleaving to conventions, habits, and expectations that moves one to act and react automatically on cue in grooves so well-known that one is not conscious of himself, his actions, or his place. This condition is what Heidegger calls "fallenness," the inauthentic existence in which the Dasein hides from itself in the impersonal collective through the distractions of the banal, the trivial, the objective. What is fog for Kesey is "everydayness" for Percy and "fallenness" for Heidegger. When everydayness ceases to prevail, suggests Percy, a sense of strangeness exiles the individual. Uncomfortable as that strangeness may be, however, it invests him with a more vivid sense of himself in his world. Just this sense of strangeness falls on Binx Bolling—the "moviegoer"—for he awakens one morning to a world made unfamiliar by the fact that he can now "see" it. His belongings on the table by the bed, which he has hardly looked at in years, now become mysteriously "full of clues." No particular event brings about this change, but it is a re-emergence of an earlier experience when, as a soldier in Korea, Binx lay wounded, with his world "upside-down," watching a dungbeetle crawl across the ground. As he lies watching the beetle, he feels an "immense curiosity," as if he is "on to something." What he is "on to" is what he calls the "search," "what anyone would undertake if he were not sunk in the everydayness of his own life." The search creates the possibility of becoming "someone somewhere," rather than just "anybody anywhere." It marks the self as a being-in-the-world, as a significant identity existing "here" rather than diffusing into gray everydayness. Those caught in everydayness are afflicted, though they may not realize it, with "despair" and "malaise." Lacking vivid consciousness of themselves they are deprived of freedom. The man engaged in the search is in his freest and best and most individual state. The week which the novel covers is the week in which the search is at the center of Binx's attention.

The reason that Binx is a "moviegoer" is that movies are "on to" the search, though they always finally fall back into everydayness. Movies and movie actors establish a reality we do not have in our daily lives. As a movie actor, William Holden carries "an aura of heightened reality" about him. When a young newlywed lights Holden's cigaret on a New Orleans street, he wins "title to his own existence, as plenary an existence now as Holden's. . . ." "Nowadays," says Binx, "when a person lives somewhere, in a neighborhood, the place is not certified for him. More than likely he will live there sadly and the emptiness which is inside him will expand until it evacuates the entire neighborhood. But if he sees a movie which shows his very neighborhood, it becomes possible for him to live, for a time at least, as a person who is Somewhere and not Anywhere." The assumption Binx makes is that heightened reality comes with heightened consciousness. Movies are, up to a point, the instruments of consciousness. They fix our attention upon the familiar, bringing us to it from another angle. They carry us out of the collective and the impersonal into a "plenary" reality in which we are conscious of the world in ways we never knew before. The movies are analogous to the story Frankie Addams tries to make of her life and to the novels described in Camus's *The Rebel.* But where Frankie sought to use story to escape from heightened reality, Binx uses it to seek it. The movies Binx uses are analogous to scientific models, not revealing all reality in itself, but illuminating aspects of reality which we would miss without the model and in doing so expanding our awareness and heightening the intensity of our satisfaction. The search he has undertaken is for a reality in which nothing is left over, in which everything is as it might be, if for no longer than a moment. It is the search for satisfaction, and as Percy sees it, it can be carried on only when the mantle of familiar everydayness has been torn away, throwing us out of the conventional, and forcing us to discover ourselves as castaways on an alien shore. Only then does the vivid sense of individuality emerge and we become ourselves in the world: open, risked, unprotected. The movies demonstrate the role in human life played by intellectualizing and abstracting, those functions of the human being that constitute his rebellion against the chaos and the indiscriminateness of nature.

In his own life, Binx is not a passionate rebel. He simply does not understand—and so cannot embrace—the values by which other people live. He loves the people close to him but does not accept their doctrines—neither those of his Catholic mother, nor those of his humanistic Aunt Emily. Aunt Emily tells him:

> I don't quite know what we're doing on this insignificant cinder spinning away in a dark corner of the universe. That is a secret which the high gods have not confided in me. Yet one thing I believe and I believe it with every fibre of my being. A man must live by his lights and do what little he can and do it as best he can. In this world goodness is destined to be defeated. But a man must go down fighting. That is victory. To do anything less is to be less than a man.

This is precisely the thesis formulated by Joseph Wood Krutch, who spoke for the humanist of the 1920s. "Ours is a lost cause," he writes in *The Modern Temper*, "and there is no place for us in the natural universe, but we are not, for all that, sorry to be human. We should rather die as men than live as animals."[11] But for Binx, such statements have no meaning. They are familiar and recognizable to Aunt Emily; they make her world more comfortable. But to Binx, such an attitude leads to death-like complacency. In this century of "scientific humanism," in which "needs are satisfied" and people are "warm and creative," the individual becomes diffused, "everyone becomes anyone . . . and men are dead, dead, dead." Aunt Emily lives in her own kind of bad faith and false consciousness and therefore cannot understand when Binx confesses that he lives by none of the values with which she so carefully sought to imbue him as a child.

Engaged in his search, as he is, Binx feels free of the rules by which Aunt Emily or his mother lives. Therefore, when his cousin, Kate Cutrer—nervous and neurotic and having just made a suicide attempt—begs him to take her with him on a brief trip to Chicago, he acquiesces. Aunt Emily, Kate's stepmother, is deeply upset, disappointed that Binx could have so insensitively violated her ordered world. People in the South, she says, simply do not travel with each other unmarried. She admonishes Binx for being without values in breaking a law of custom and she dismisses him from her favor until he consents to return from his unfamiliar land. The everyday world is too strong a lure for any man long to hold out against. Binx is no hero. Aunt Emily is too much a part of his familiar life to give up. The possibilities of the search do not promise adequate compensation for depriving himself of the people he loves, whatever their ideology. He decides, at first, to abandon the search completely, for "it is no match for my aunt, her rightness and her despair, her despairing of me and her despairing of herself." Without self-consciously determining upon a program of action, Binx allows himself to drift back into her favor, marrying Kate, deciding to begin medical school if Aunt Emily wishes, and entering what she would call a more responsible life. Ironically, where he had felt like a castaway in his world, he becomes one of its stabilizing factors. He helps Kate to verify her own existence by telling her—at her request—what to do, reassuring her, thinking of her in certain ways to give her confidence. When his stepbrother, the gentle, fiercely Catholic Lonnie, falls gravely ill, Binx interprets his impending death to Lonnie's younger brothers and sisters, letting them experience the tragedy of the boy's situation but refusing to indulge in ritualistic and superficial sentiment.

The world, says Percy, clamors for our attention. The "search," in which intellectualizing and abstracting bulk so large, cannot be absolutely and completely successful. In the nature of things, when we come to the end of the line of our intellect, we find nothing there because the full reality of our existence cannot be represented to the intellect. In the end, therefore, Binx is neither defeated nor victorious. He is not forced back into everydayness, but he cannot continue the search in its old form, either. Though he does feel that his "best times" are in the search, the "plenary" reality that lies at its end does not square with the unavoidable encounters one must undergo with the world and the people in it. Intellectual consciousness does raise one from the anonymity of everydayness, but it cannot lead to a paradise in which the real and the ideal, the matter and the form become identical. Something always remains, in human life, left over, unexplained, "transphenomenal." So Binx turns to a compromise. He comes to see that, like Kierkegaard—whom he refers to only as "the great Danish philosopher"—he cannot ever really exist the search, embody it fully in his own life.

The best he can do is to "plant a foot in the right place as the opportunity presents itself." The search is a job for a loner, and life seldom lets one go alone. Something is lost—a vividness and intensity that only the search can bring one to. At the same time, the ambiguity of the "open decision" appears here, for what is lost receives some compensation in a human world occupied by people who are not alone but who make demands on each other, and in doing so enrich the individual consciousness rather than impoverish it. To see this is to free ourselves from everydayness and to see the inherent limitations of the search.

More clearly than either Kesey or Percy, Ralph Ellison focuses upon the issue of freedom and consciousness not simply as a social problem, but a psychological and philosophical one as well. The fact that *Invisible Man* is about an Afro-American broadens the frame of reference, but does not change Ellison's relationship to the principles and values of the "open decision." Indeed, probably more explicitly than any of the ten novels in this section, *Invisible Man* delineates the inhibitions and the freedoms that are laid upon human consciousness. It shows that for the black man in America, for the white man in America, for the human being in America nothingness and openness and absurdity are not the esoteric playthings of educated thinkers, but significant factors in the everyday lives of individuals. Discovery of them puts one in the way of breaking free of the constraints of his system and its traditional preconceptions, of defining himself with greater awareness. The foundation of this freedom—the preferred situation—is that higher consciousness which embraces simultaneously the abstractions of the intellect and the immediate sensations of the emotion.

The main obstacles to arriving at this state of consciousness are the "gangs" that would put the world in a "strait jacket," echoing the Combine of Nurse Ratched. The first "gang" the unnamed narrator of the novel confronts is made up of the whites in the Southern town where he lives. From them he takes his definition, the measurement of his personal value, allowing himself to be used by them for entertainment in return for vague expectations of reward. Convinced by the white apparatus that whatever he gets in life will come from the whites, and ambitious to succeed, he suppresses his spontaneity and designs his behavior to please them. The Southern Negro college he attends is supported by Northern white men, who are no different in effect from the Southern whites. They assume that the nature of things has endowed them with a god-like superiority from which eminence they administer the lives of the child-like Negro. The narrator eagerly collaborates in perpetuating their picture of the world, working hard to become a black white man, an inferior copy of the original. His aim in college is to prepare himself to be a leader in his own community so that he may lead his people, as one white man puts it, along the "proper paths." The extent of his servility to the white man's values is suggested in the sense of shame he feels for those Negroes who are oblivious to white respectability, who fall short of the white ideals of dress, social behavior, and sexual morality.

This is a "strait jacket" world in which the narrator voluntarily submits to the imposed limitations. He is, however, forcibly evicted from that world, when the president of the Negro college he attends sends him packing to New York. In New York, he falls into another circumscribed world, the "Brotherhood," a Communist-like monolith run by Brother Jack and a grim humorless committee of theorists who feed on abstractions and clichés. The ostensible aim of the Brotherhood is to make the world a better place for people to live. History has decreed that the future must, through inevitable dialectic struggle and resistance, bring into being a utopia, which has been "scientifically" formulated. The Brotherhood sees itself as the instrument of this manifest destiny. Its members swear to sacrifice to it whatever is necessary—be it their lives, their individuality, or the lives and individuality of others. Any who resist the historical development, whose shape the Brotherhood claims to know absolutely, will be rightly ground under; any who go outside of that history will be abandoned. There is no room for any but the collective self. In his new independence from the Southern strait jacket, the narrator finds the Brotherhood to be the perfect antidote to his previous deference to the white society. The Brotherhood not only makes no distinctions either between individuals or races, its purpose is to subvert the society the narrator once supported but has now come to hate. In this organization, the narrator enjoys more freedom than he has ever had before. But like the white-dominated Southern society, the Brotherhood has no use for diversity. It accuses the narrator of "petty individualism" and insists, much like Aunt Emily does of Binx Bolling, that he depart in no sense from established doctrine. This, too, like the Southern white society, allows for none of that consciousness which results in individual satisfaction.

Gradually, the narrator works himself out of this strait jacket, too. He loses faith in the Brotherhood, discovering that it is sacrificing the black people of Harlem for its larger plans. By withdrawing its attention from organizing in the ghetto, it helps create rising dissatisfaction. This situation plays into the hands of the black nationalist, Ras the Exhorter, who steps into the vacuum created by the diminution of the Brotherhood's activities, and acts as a catalyst to riot. The narrator realizes that this is precisely what the Brotherhood wants, for social unrest, especially if it is bloody, challenges the *status quo* as does nothing else. Both Ras and Brother Jack espouse totalitarian doctrines. Both would suppress the kind of individual spontaneity and awareness that thrives in a pluralistic society in which contrast, rather than conflict, is the organizing principle. Both claim for themselves a freedom which they would not grant others, the freedom of insisting that they and only they have stood above history and seen its end. With that assertion they would justify any injustice in the present to bring about the future good.

These, however, are imprisoning delusions that thwart the awareness of the self. During the riot excited by Ras, the narrator, running from three white men, escapes from these prisons into a manhole. He discovers, ironically, that it is necessary to go into a hole—to bracket the world, so to speak, to turn away from the past —in order to achieve greater awareness. What men tout as "reality" is only their own strait jacket, and they would cram into that strait jacket all the world, insisting upon strict conformity, punishing unorthodoxy and diversity. One must go into a hole because these strait jackets do not manifest themselves as such until one breaks out of them. So long as they prevail, the values that make them up appear to be absolutely given, like the physical measurements of a closed system which does not allow self-observation. But what does the greater awareness of the underground world bring? Not more order, or new rules, or different demands. "Step outside the narrow borders of what men call reality and you step into chaos . . . or imagination." Chaos is repugnant to the human mind. In fighting it, the mind invents systems which lay order over chaos. Then in the conviction that its invention accounts for all reality—that, indeed, the invention *is* the reality—it calls sin any attempts to reject that invention. From his hole, the narrator observes that those caught in a system do not see each other as individuals. They see instead what the system habituates them to see. Thus, as he tells us in the first line of the novel, he is an invisible man. Though he is flesh and blood, "people refuse to see me. . . . When they approach me they see only my surroundings, themselves, or figments of their imagination—indeed, everything and anything except me." For Mr. Norton, the Northern white college trustee, the narrator is simply "a walking personification of the Negative, the most imperfect achievement of your dreams . . . a mark on the score-card of your achievement, a thing and not a man; a child, or even less—a black amorphous thing." The narrator is a "zombie," who regards Mr. Norton not as a man and a human being, but as "a God, a force." Both are in bad faith, for they see the other's identity as exhausted by an abstraction, and confuse that abstraction with the living being.

The "me" that people refuse to see in the narrator—and each other—is not the image that the sleepwalkers dream when he passes before them. The living subject is not the "little shines" the Southern whites see, or the Brother the Brotherhood sees, or the black African that Ras sees. These are all strait jackets that distort the reality they would force into their own shape. The living subject is "possibility," that Sartrean Nothingness which cuts, in Sartre's words, a "hole in being," and whose nature is "to be what it is not and not to be what it is." "Until some gang succeeds in putting the world in a strait jacket," says the narrator, "its definition is possibility." Now that he has become conscious of his invisibility, he can no longer justify through meek acquiescence the mistaken notions of others. He must go his own way after years of trying "to go in everyone else's way but my own." "Life is to be lived, not controlled; and humanity is won by continuing to play in the face of certain defeat," the narrator writes, sounding like Aunt Emily but without her complacency; sounding more like Camus's Dr. Rieux in *The Plague* or the Randle McMurphy of *One Flew Over the Cuckoo's Nest*. This sentence also takes us back to the game-playing of Huizinga. The narrator is not attempting to force another system on the world. He is simply discovering the paradox of the human consciousness. That is, in his conclusion he does not expect to change the ontological nature of the world. It will be "just as concrete, ornery, vile and sublimely wonderful as before." The difference lies in his attitude toward it: ". . . now I better understand my relationship to it and it to me." And what he understands is that "the mind that has conceived a plan of living must never lose sight of the chaos against which that pattern was conceived." It is through our plans and our abstractions and our inventions that we give ourselves and our lives the intelligibility of form. But we remain free only so long as we remember that the form is given by ourselves and not by the nature of things. Form is not a strait jacket, but a possibility plucked from chaos.

On these philosophical grounds, the narrator arrives at a conception of America that transcends those he has tried to fit himself to. Thinking only in terms of their own limited constructions, Bledsoe, Brother Jack, Ras, and all the rest refuse "to recognize the beautiful absurdity of their American identity and mine." This beautiful absurdity is America's "fate": "to become one, and yet many"—to develop a unified society whose main feature is diversity. The joke is in the attempt of most Americans to escape this fate: "whites busy escaping blackness and becoming blacker every day, and the blacks striving toward whiteness, becoming quite dull and gray." Only from the hole of invisibility, in which liberated consciousness tells us we "are" not what others demand that we be, does the root of America grow—that absurd diversity in which a person can only be himself. And so, more completely than the protagonist of any of these ten novels, the narrator of *Invisible Man* finds himself in the light of the "open decision."

The way I have divided my discussion of the novels in this chapter obscures the fact that all of them are founded on the complete metaphysical system of the "open decision." That is, Frankie Addams' stories, Alma Mason's "memorial," Binx Bolling's movies, Stencil's "history" are all aspects of intellectual abstractions and models through which the mind pursues the rationality of existence and the significance of life, but which, according to the "open decision," fall short because of the indeterminacy inherent in all intellectual constructs representing reality in itself. And the values that guide Flannery O'Connor are very much the same as those which guide Ken Kesey and Ralph Ellison: there is an integrity in the individual which is good in itself and which must be preserved from bad faith and false consciousness and the suffocating embrace of systems demanding conformity of its citizens. These values rest on the assumption that reality in our time exists in a state of relative awareness made up of consciousness and unconsciousness, reason and unreason, mind and matter. The highest good comes in the affirmation of that reality. My division here shows that these ten novelists, as most of the novelists of our time, though working within the framework of the same metaphysics, emphasize different issues. Where McCullers sees the problem of human life to rest in the separateness of individuals and the need for corrective love and the mature strength to accept this aspect of our condition, Styron sees it as a danger of losing faith in the obscure and hidden foundations of our being and the consequent need to find the courage to restore that faith. These novels differ only in the focus they represent, not in their philosophical assumptions.

NOVELS OF AMBIGUITY AND AFFIRMATION: THE MORAL OUTLOOK

THE TEN NOVELS I have just discussed illustrate the ubiquity of the principles and the issues of the "open decision." The concern of most American authors since the Second World War is with the breakdown of the old absolutes and the consequent sense of disjointedness and disconnectedness of our existence. More than that, however, they are concerned with ways to live life affirmatively without appeal. Their affirmation lies in the concept of the individual defined in the "open decision." His value is his humanness, and his humanness is inherently paradoxical. He is both free and limited, conscious and unconscious, rebellious and accepting. The higher consciousness is the intense awareness of these paradoxes, an awareness which does not dissolve them but which receives them as contrasts within the unity of the organism. The five novelists I now turn to—John Barth, Kurt Vonnegut, Jr., Bernard Malamud, Saul Bellow, and Norman Mailer—all question, but ultimately affirm, the values of the "open decision." Their novels dramatize the pain and the conflict that consciousness brings. They do not end happily, but usually on a note of "lack." Yet, it is that lack that makes us human beings, that urges us to marshal the forces of life and rebellion in struggle against our limits.

Some critics have admonished the contemporary American novelist for refusing to place his characters in a recognizable social context, like Dos Passos did, or Fitzgerald, or Hemingway, or Faulkner. Our novelists have, these critics suggest, limited their range of

For Notes to Chapter 8, see pages 405–406.

reference to their characters' psyches and have thus surrendered the opportunity to examine the great issues of our day. I hope it is clear that this criticism is quite invalid when applied to the novelists discussed in Part II. It is somewhat more applicable, on its face, to the writers discussed in this Part. But if left unqualified, it totally distorts the character of the fiction I refer to in this chapter.

The overwhelming moral and metaphysical preoccupation of the western mind in the twentieth century is the integrity of the individual, because that is where reality and value are deemed to lie. From that preoccupation flow most of the issues dealt with in the contemporary American novel. If individual integrity is of prime interest, then we wish to know what the character of that individuality and integrity is. It follows, too, that one of the basic queries of western man will be, not only "What am I?" but "Who am I?" If we are concerned with individual integrity then we will be acutely sensitive to anything that threatens it. What we consider to be threats depends upon what we consider to be good and real—that is, the individual. If he is defined as an "open decision," a paradoxical consciousness responsible for his own self-creation from a wide range of alternatives around him, then the threats upon him will be those things that thwart the implementation of the "open decision." It is true that a good many of the problems arising from these threats as dealt with by our novelists involve a focus on introspection—false consciousness, for example, requires that one achieve a greater psychological openness in order to execute the "open decision." And that openness is a private thing.

But though our novelists' preoccupation with individual integrity leads, through the "open decision," to some introspectiveness in their fiction, it also presupposes a social context, as I have indicated in Part I. Whitehead emphasizes that the satisfaction of the actual entity assumes an acceptable relationship with the society from which that entity receives its data and to which it contributes its own energies and data. Charles H. Cooley writes that the relationship between the individual and his society is a continuum and not a mutually exclusive discreteness. Camus emphasizes the slogans of the true rebel—"I rebel, therefore we exist"; and "only in association do we receive human value." The same attitudes characterize our novelists. Always implied in the introspection of a Frank Alpine (Malamud's *The Assistant*) and a Moses Herzog is what Cooley calls a "saner relation" with society. The assumption is that before the self can acquire a productive relationship with other people he must solve the problems of his private condition. Sartre says that before this can be done, one must "go away" from society—as Ellison's narrator in *Invisible Man* goes away—so that he may return more self-confident and self-aware. Thus, while none of these novelists is a social novelist, all presuppose that human life is simultaneously private and public, and that effectiveness in one sphere is predicated upon effectiveness in the other. The emphasis, however, is upon the pattern of difficulties that arise from the metaphysics of the "open decision"—upon the difficulty with which men abandon their old explanations and their old selves for the new. In a sense, this is what the "open decision" requires—the bracketing of the traditional world and the familiar self and their abandonment; and the embarkation upon journeys into new and supposedly more basic territories of experience and the self. Only when the individual can do that can we hope for a society more auspicious to the needs of the self. Only when the individual can do that can he effectively influence his world. Not all of the novelists treated in this chapter deal with the entire pattern in their novels, from individual discovery to social effectiveness. But all of them imply that pattern even though their novels may focus on only one aspect of it.

At bottom, then, these novelists are moralists, just as, as I indicated in Part I, the "open decision" is moral. Their basic question, expressed or implied, is "What is virtuous action?" And for the most part their answer includes a social service that respects the value of the individual subject, a value as old as the Greeks but in our time justified and rationalized by a new metaphysics—the metaphysics of the "open decision." "Morality of outlook," says Whitehead, "is inseparably conjoined with generality of outlook." A high intensity of individual satisfaction presupposes a high degree of self-awareness. And in the "open decision" a high degree of self-awareness includes in its definition a concern for others and the social pattern they form. Moral action is, therefore, not selfish hedonism. It is a love and a compassion for others which is made possible through the affirmation of the limits, the freedom, and the responsibilities of the human condition. It is a rebellious "moderation" which embraces the valued ties of human solidarity.

More clearly than any other American writer, John Barth,[1] like Sartre, writes novels that examine the logical structure of the philosophical ideas that make up the "open decision." He begins with a tacit assumption: It is in the nature of the human being to justify his life logically on premises of value. The values upon which he grounds his life and actions are his reasons for being—for choosing one thing rather than another, life rather than death, death rather than life. The recognition of values is a function of consciousness and the higher the consciousness the more important is the question of values. One of the more satisfactory episodes in *Giles Goat-Boy* depicts the hero, George Giles, awakening from the relative unconsciousness of animality. He has been raised up to adolescence as a goat, a time during which values as an aspect of choosing between alternatives are not an issue. He acts instinctively and emotionally to the alternatives presented to him. With the emergence of consciousness comes a recognition that there is a condition called "man" which he can be and which is accompanied by the ability—the imperative—of making choices based on value.

If the human being does require logical reasons for choosing one thing rather than another, the nature of those reasons becomes an important issue. When is reason or value a satisfactory ground for action? At what point—and *how*—does a man assume social responsibility? To say that a reason for choice has force when it is logical leads us to ask about the premises which make the reason logical. The question turns out to be, for Barth, whether reasons and values are satisfactory only when they are absolute—only when they are universal, objective, equally applicable to all men in all times in all places. Todd Andrews, the narrator of Barth's first novel, *The Floating Opera*, answers this question negatively, but not before he makes several false starts and undergoes the prototypical experience of the prototypical twentieth-century man, moving from a child-like faith and optimism, through despair and cynicism over the breakdown of old absolutes, to a recognition of openness and relativity.

Todd is a great one for adducing logical reasons to guide his life. The "life" he tries to guide is, figuratively, a heart disease—endocarditis—which he contracts as a young man just out of World War I. His condition, in other words, is mortal; he is bounded by death. This becomes the "great fact" with which he has to live, after a childhood in which he thought he could do anything. To control this "fact" he turns to certain "stances," which are logical in that he "wills" them into existence as responses to his condition. First he becomes a sybarite, arguing that if he has only a short while to live, he will live to the hilt. When this results in a close brush with death, he turns to sainthood—removes himself from the world, becomes a mysterious figure. When his father commits suicide during the collapse of the stock market in 1929, Todd turns to cynicism, suspecting all motives and rejecting all values. At the time, each of these stances seems to be the ultimate solution to the fact of his endocarditis. They are analogous to the absolute values and reasons of the old order, categories which completely embody his identity into which he retreats from his full existence. But the sheer bodily facts of life cannot long be avoided—especially the fact of death. They cannot be forever controlled by the will and the intellect through abstractions. When Todd's mistress inadvertently refers to his clubbed fingers, he is brought up short. They are signs of his heart disease—his mortality—and he suddenly realizes that he has sought to hide from that mortality in his stances. He sees that the stances have been "masks," pretenses whose abstractness Todd has confused with whole existence. He discovers, too, that far from having been in control, he has himself been under the control of his "heart."

This recognition is an awakening from a state of relative unconsciousness into a state of heightened awareness. But with it comes bitterness and despair, for he sees all that he has lost. The central loss is a sense of identity, the sense of control by which he justifies himself and lends significance to his existence. In the aftermath of these discoveries, his heart seems to fill his body, taking over from the masks. He is confronted with "*nothing*." This is Sartre's Nothingness, that awareness that nihilates existence. Todd has been in bad faith, taking his masks for full existence. Now he sees that such an identification cannot be made. He laments the powerlessness of the masks—and hence his consciousness—to provide any satisfactory reason for living. Since the masks contain no intrinsic value, by logical extension nothing contains any intrinsic value. There is, in fact, "no ultimate 'reason' for valuing anything," no reason for preferring one mask over the other. This logic leads Todd to another syllogism: "Living is action in some form." No reason can ultimately validate action in any form. "There is, then, no 'reason' for living." From this conclusion Todd leaps to "the stance to end all stances," suicide. Values are satisfactory as reasons for existing, he implies, only if they are absolute, intrinsically worthy, and can be ultimately validated. If there is no reason for living, then one might as well die.

Todd does attempt to commit suicide, again assuming that it is desirable because it seems rational. He tries to blow up himself and the "Floating Opera," a showboat that has tied up at the dock of the small coastal Maryland town he lives in. But for unexplained reasons there is no explosion. Todd feels "neither relief nor disappointment" over his failure, but does come to the conclusion that there is no more reason to blow up the boat than not to. In his syllogism he adds a parenthesis: "There's no reason for living (or for suicide)." This does not dramatically change Todd. He expects to go on with his life as before, perhaps even try to blow up the show boat again. Yet, he does get the glimmer of a possibility: "I considered too whether, in the real absence of absolutes, values less than absolute mightn't be regarded as in no way inferior and even be lived by. But that's another inquiry, and another story."[2]

This ending is the one originally composed by Barth, but the publishers of the first edition ordered him to revise the manuscript. In the 1956 version of the story, the conclusion is considerably more positive and illuminating—at least for our purposes. In it, Todd merely tries to asphyxiate himself with gas in the *Floating Opera*'s galley. He is interrupted when little Jeannine Mack, the daughter of his best friends, Harrison and Jane Mack, is brought down below with convulsions. The activity of Life intervenes in Death. This experience brings about a "qualitative change" in Todd. He feels an intense concern for the child. The point is that, as Todd says, he has no "reason to be concerned." The intensity of that experience leads Todd to conclude that if there is no reason for living, there is no reason for dying either. If, furthermore, a value cannot be objectively and ultimately validated, "then a value is no less authentic, no less genuine, no less compelling, no less 'real,' for its being relative!" With this discovery, Todd finds himself "back in the game!" The meaning of all these discoveries can be clarified by Todd's previous dialogue with little Jeannine when he takes her, in the afternoon, to look at the *Floating Opera*. Todd tells her that it is a showboat where people go to "listen to music and watch actors dance and act funny."

> "Why?" [asks Jeannine.]
>
> "Why what?" I asked. "Why do the actors act funny or why do the people like to watch them?"
>
> "Why do the people?"
>
> "The people like to go to the show because it makes them laugh. They like to laugh at the actors."
>
> "Why?"
>
> "They like to laugh because laughing makes them happy. They like being happy, just like you."
>
> "Why?"
>
> . . . .
>
> "Why do they like being happy? That's the end of the line."

We can carry logic only so far before we hit the end of the line, where absolutes and ultimate reasons dissipate in what is simply and alogically there. It is precisely this that occurs to Todd when he is snapped out of his paralysis during his suicide attempt. The concern he feels for Jeannine at that time has no other warrant of its validity than that he feels it. He, as a feeling subject, is absolute; the values that he originates are relative. It is this recognition that puts him "back in the game."

In his second novel, *End of the Road,* a companion piece to *The Floating Opera,* Barth examines the possibility of basing action upon relative values. If, as he finds in *The Floating Opera,* no value is absolutely valid, what effects does this have upon the individual who must live in society? What he shows in *End of the Road* is the profound difficulty of getting along after we have lost our confidence in the objective absolute, and our tendency to find relief either in the abandonment of all guides or the substitution of objective values with other kinds of values just as absolute. Like Todd Andrews, who sits unable to move in the galley of the *Floating Opera* until he is brought around by concern for Jeannine, Jake Horner, the narrator of *End of the Road,* becomes paralyzed trying to decide which train to take out of Pennsylvania station. Jake begins at nearly the same point that Todd ends. It is not that Jake has so many alternatives, but that he can find no "reason" to prefer one alternative to another. Like Todd, Jake assumes that no action can be justified without a satisfactory intellectual explanation. Finding none, he has no reason to terminate his paralysis. A Negro "Doctor" who rescues Jake approaches the question from the opposite direction. It is true that one condition has no more intrinsic merit than another. No choice, ultimately, has a discoverable reason at its base. Action rises unexplainably from an enigmatic interior. What is important, therefore, is the choice, not its reason. By allowing the Doctor to bring him out of his paralysis, Jake has already chosen—though for no "reason"—the condition that would result from therapy. Jake's paralysis, says the Doctor, results from his demand that choices be logical.

The Doctor begins with no *a priori* values, either absolute or relative. His therapeutic method is wholly mechanical and pragmatic, designed to deal with the situation brought into being by a person's choice. He is not concerned with his patients as human beings, but simply with their problems. Once Jake has chosen to fight the paralysis, the Doctor can provide him with a therapeutic program. Jake should "act impulsively," not "get stuck between alternatives." Since the criteria of choice are not reasonable, they must be mechanical. The Doctor's criteria are "sinistrality" (choosing the alternative on the left), "antecedence" (the first in a series), and "alphabetical priority" ("the alternative whose name begins with the earlier letter of the alphabet"). The Doctor also advocates the assumption of "masks" for oneself and the assigning of them to others, the very thing that Todd Andrews found unsatisfactory. It is the Doctor's contention that the human personality contains no essential identity, but is instead a series of masks that each person puts on and takes off as they suit the situation. There is nothing behind these masks; the ego or self-center is each of them in turn. The Doctor is concerned with function, not with human being or identity. The donning of these masks is a game which the Doctor calls Mythotherapy. Immobility—"insincerity" or bad faith—occurs when one withdraws from the game or when one's masks are incompatible with each other or donned simultaneously: ". . . a man's integrity consists in being faithful to the script he's written for himself." The Doctor urges Jake to *be* his abstract masks. The weakness of this approach is that it assumes that the self is exhausted in the abstractness of the mask, that it does not allow for that great area of shadow and uncertainty that underlies all self-consciousness. The Doctor's view, moreover, is completely amoral. It does not take into consideration the intrusions of other life upon the subject, as Jeannine intrudes upon Todd. Furthermore, it assumes—while rejecting—that something is there that puts on and takes off the masks.

Joe Morgan, Jake's colleague at Wicomico State Teacher's College in Maryland, begins from a position similar to that of the Doctor. Every man, he says, is equipped with certain "psychological *givens*." These have no traceable source nor inherent value. But here Joe parts from the Doctor's philosophy. One's psychological givens constitute the core of one's identity and form the ground from which all other actions stem. They generate one's values and reasons for acting. Morality for Joe is acting consistently with the psychological givens, not with the masks one assumes like an actor. The highest good is being the same recognizable person in all situations, whether alone or with others. Joe assumes that we can know what our givens are and thus understand our identity. With this knowledge every choice not only can but must be explained in terms of the givens. The most repugnant of all phrases for Joe is "I don't know." For all the logicality of Joe's doctrine, he thinks, as does the Doctor, of consciousness as unambiguous and complete identity, insisting that the values that consciousness apprehends, in all their abstractness, are all that make life real and defensible.

Jake recoils from Joe's systematic consistency and the rigid distinctness of his values. He claims that far from being one person, he is one person one day, another person another day, and sometimes several simultaneously. He denies the argument that men always have a conscious explainable motive for acting: "There'll always be a few things in their autobiography that they can't account for." Jake, like the Doctor, postulates no intelligible values. But he cannot accept fully the Doctor's position, either, on the point of masks and assigning roles to other humans, for the better one comes to know a person the more contradictory will be his attitudes toward that person. "Existence," says Jake, "not only precedes essence: in the case of human beings it rather defies essence." Jake denies the possibility that consciousness, in its apprehension and creation of essences, can with its abstractions make complete sense out of existence. Existence and essence are irreconcilable because existence can never "be" essence.

All of these men assume that there are no absolute values. The way they act under that assumption and the morality of their action is the question of the novel. The sign that their behavior is unsatisfactory is that it has tragic consequences. The Doctor can think only of the mechanics of his "Mythotherapy." Joe lives only in his rigid system of values that replace such admonitions from God as the Ten Commandments. He ignores the "buzzing, blooming confusion" which goes beyond his rationalism. He educates his wife Rennie in this philosophy, and she refuses to admit that she is uncomfortable with it. Jake might give "notional" or intellectual assent to a particular set of values, but because he cannot acknowledge their validity in his living existence, he drifts along without subscribing to any at all. Jake has too little of Joe in himself and Joe has too little of Jake. Rennie is the victim of this clash. She is the most authentic human being of them all for, as Jake says, she has looked into herself and found nothingness. Afraid, she sought to fill it with the "being" constructed by Joe. When Jake arrives, she finds herself caught between the ultra-rationality of Joe and the negation of reason's validity by Jake, and she is destroyed.

Chance maneuvers Jake and Rennie into bed, and when Joe discovers his wife's infidelity, he begins immediately to look for a reason, to fit this act of existence into an intellectual category all fitted out with clear motives. But on this, Barth is careful to show that Jake is right. He takes pains to avoid suggesting any rational motive in Rennie's or Jake's behavior, even the motive of passion or lust. They have no reason for going to bed with each other—at least as Joe conceives of reason—and that is the point. Yet, Joe forces Rennie, against her will and temperament, to continue with the affair, claiming that only then can she understand her action and thereby save their marriage. He insists that she identify her nothingness as some recognizable mask, that she act in bad faith. Jake, refusing any kind of intellectual control, drifts along with the affair, mildly curious, allowing Rennie to come to his room and making love to her, while she slowly deteriorates.

Rennie becomes pregnant and vows that she will either commit suicide or abort the fetus, refusing to bear a child that might be Jake's. Joe acts according to the values he takes to be immutable. Rennie must consciously choose her own course. He furnishes her with a gun, insisting that he must honor as rational any act that she decides to perform, attaching more worth to his abstract system of values than to Rennie's life. Jake, on the other hand, wants only to be exonerated from any guilt in Rennie's death. He searches frantically for an abortionist, finally persuading the Doctor to perform the operation. Nor do the Doctor's values equip him to deal with the situation. He is more interested in Jake's paralysis than in Rennie's life. The preparations for the abortion are slipshod. Rennie vomits into the ether mask, aspires her vomit, and suffocates on the operating table.

The behavior of these three men is a wrong response to the conditions of our existence. That judgment follows from Rennie's tragic death. Their behavior is wrong because it does not acknowledge the character of human existence. But Barth is not saying that without absolute values there can be no moral behavior that works to preserve rather than destroy life. Todd Andrews is right. Values are no less satisfactory for being relative. In *End of the Road,* in spite of his own contributions to Rennie's death, Jake articulates a more valid position: "To turn experience into speech—that is, to classify, to categorize, to conceptualize, to grammarize, to syntactify it—is always a betrayal of experience, a falsification of it; but only so betrayed can it be dealt with at all, and only in so dealing with it did I ever feel a man, alive and kicking." Jake's statement recalls Whitehead's declaration that "no verbal statement is the adequate expression of a proposition." It reflects a high degree of consciousness: a recognition that there is an existence that must always elude our reason, but that part of our nature is to be rational. We impoverish our humanity by closing ourselves off from either factor of our being. More than that, we threaten our humanity by failing to embrace the entire range of human life. Because existence—experience—escapes our conscious statements about it does not mean that we do not consciously try to represent that existence to ourselves in meaningful abstractions. Because abstractions are the only thing we can "know" does not mean that we delude ourselves that they represent the whole of our existence. Moral behavior joins the abstract and the existential.

In *End of the Road,* Barth has worked out the question of whether relative values can be as authentic and as valid as absolute values. The answer is that they can, but they work only when they are the functions of an open consciousness that recognizes its own limits. In *The Sot-Weed Factor* and *Giles Goat-Boy* his central issue is the education of the hero to a high consciousness of the paradoxical "lack" in the human being, and the morality such a consciousness entails. These novels take off from the conclusions of *The Floating Opera* and *End of the Road.* Ebenezer Cook, of *The Sot-Weed Factor,* a young man in seventeenth-century London, begins with delusory dreams of abstract essences and absolutes. He decides to assume the identity of "virgin poet," an identity which will protect both his body and his spirit from contamination by existence, keeping him safe "From Life, from Time, from Death, from History." Without innocence, writes Eben, "I must breathe Man's mortal Breath: Commence a life—and thus commence my death!" Abstract values, he assumes, have a better and more real existence in a realm whose order of being is different from ours. Justice, Truth, Beauty—they "live not in the world, but as transcendent entities, noumenal and pure." The "world"—existence, death, disease, physical nature—is impure and hence without value. In his innocence, Eben repudiates this world and insists upon his superiority to it. He sees his life in it as a story—like Frankie Addams and Alma Boyd—distant from him but full of possibilities.

Eben's repudiation of the world takes the form, not of suicide or retirement, but of idealization. He falls in love with the London prostitute, Joan Toast, and would impose upon her, as Don Quixote does upon Dulcinea, an image of purity that is not in accord with reality. Later, Joan will call herself the "sign and emblem" of the world, so that in idealizing her, Eben is idealizing the world. He does the same thing in the long heroic poem he intends to write—*The Marylandiad.* The occasion of this piece is his journey to Maryland to take over his father's estate there, Malden, which Eben will one day inherit. In his poem, he says, before he leaves England and witnesses the colony firsthand, he plans to sing of Maryland's "peerless virtues—the graciousness of her inhabitants, their good breeding and excellent dwelling places, the majesty of her laws, the comfort of her inns and ordinaries, the richness and beauty of her fields, woods, and waters. . . ." Gradually, after he experiences the brutality, the cruelty, the greed, and the unfairness of the world, Eben's innocence undergoes a change. The critical incident is significant to Barth's theme. In Maryland, Eben observes a makeshift colonial court pass what he takes to be a patently unfair judgment. Absolute Justice has been violated and Eben ventures forth to restore its chastity. The judge, amused, reverses his decision. Eben, in his ignorance of the details and his quixotic reliance upon the purity of the abstraction, causes his own land to be awarded to one William Smith. Not only has Eben not served his abstract values; he contributes to the even greater corruption of the world, for Smith turns out to be a morally debased conniver who intends to use Eben's land for opium dens, whorehouses, and other means of degrading human beings. Not only does Eben's refusal of the world thwart his own individual satisfaction, it has deleterious social effects. It is immoral.

The unavoidable reality of his romantic mistake shocks Eben into the first stages of a higher consciousness, the loss of innocence. But his first reaction is to retreat from optimistic idealism into romantic despair. If the world does not conform to his idealized image of it, then it can be nothing but a sinkhole of corruption, incapable of redemption, unsupported by absolutes. Disappointed in his expectations, Eben refuses to see any good in existence. This is the reaction of Todd Andrews in his cynical stance, the reaction of many twentieth-century writers who turned to alienation and despair when they found their traditional values violated by modern science, philosophy, psychology. A signal of Eben's change is his revision of his poem. He changes it from a heroic epic to a satire, determining to express his bitterness that reality is not what he took it to be. He concludes that it deserves only ridicule and abuse. He assumes that, like Todd Andrews, if there are no absolutes, there can be no justification for living. He contemplates suicide. He sinks into apathy and indifference, allows himself to be married—at Smith's urging—to Susan Warren, who, unknown to Eben, is really Joan Toast. Joan has followed Eben to the colonies, fallen on bad luck, become a prostitute to the Indians, and contracted the pox and various venereal diseases. If Joan is the "sign and symbol" of the world, Eben is not marrying her as an act of affirmation. Hurt over the loss of his ideals, he can think of the world only as punishment. His marriage is a punitive action against himself taken as a disappointed romantic.

He cannot, however, bring himself to sleep with his disease-ridden wife, and take on the disease of her mortality. Nor can he bring himself to run away with her from Smith's domination, as she urges him to do. Instead, he turns back to his old identity as virgin poet, needing more fundamental education before he can be redeemed. He pledges his fidelity to Joan, but decides that the only pledge he is morally bound to honor is the one to his profession—virgin poet. Associated with both pledge and profession is his sister Anna, who represents for him the absolute ideal of beauty and purity. Thus, his cause as a poet is the cause of innocence, perfection, and detachment from the world of existence. Joan's cause is the cause of life, and Eben cannot yet take it up. Leaving Joan behind he runs off to find Anna, who has herself left England to come to America.

Eben seeks an impossible dream, identifying that dream with the only acceptable goal. But life is "lack" and change, not the clear, distinct, and permanent absolute he seeks in his image of Anna. His old tutor, Henry Burlingame III, tries to teach him this. Himself a metaphor of change, Burlingame takes various disguises throughout the novel. When Eben, demanding permanent, always-recognizable essences, is confused by these disguises, Henry says, "your true and constant Burlingame lives only in your fancy, as doth the pointed order of the world." Henry cautions Eben that his search for "whole understanding" is "fruitless, and there is no time for't." One's time is more fruitfully spent living in the world, for that is the proper sphere of individual satisfaction. "I love the world," Henry tells Eben, "and so make love to it!" If he is to confirm that he is alive, Eben too must grasp the world directly, not through illusory absolutes and a storybook life: "Time *passes* for the living . . . and alters things. Only for the dead do circumstances never change." Eben must also learn that to embrace the flux of existence does not require a surrender of value. Indeed, if we surrender the vision of the good and the true and the beautiful, we diminish our humanness. When the world appears to be, in itself, empty of such value, we ourselves must supply it, draw it from within ourselves. And Eben does come to see this. Perhaps the old ideals were "vain constructions," he muses, in that they are not embodied in the chaos of sheer existence, but they do express "all nobleness allowed to fallen men." When Eben arrives at this conclusion, he invests his virginity with different value. It is no longer a sign of his superiority to and his repudiation of the world, but an expression of his capacity as a man to create worth. He resolves not to dissipate his virginity in a pleasure "devoid of right *significance.*" By choosing to wait for the right moment, Eben will confer meaning upon that moment.

Significance comes with a fusion in one's consciousness of the abstract and the concrete, the real and the ideal, the form and the matter, a fusion that Joe Morgan and Jake Horner failed to execute. In *The Sot-Weed Factor*, the poles that must be joined in paradox are represented by Joan Toast and Anna. The force that moves Eben to join these extremes in the unit of his individual self is the force of life: Joan Toast. The setting up of this resolution occurs in a comically complicated conclusion to the novel's main plot. Burlingame, having searched his whole life for his origins, discovers that he is the grandson of Henry Burlingame I, who had accompanied John Smith's expedition into the Ahatchwoop Indian country and then been left there by Smith. He becomes the Indians' king, starting a "royal" line with his first son Chicamec, the father of Burlingame III. The present colony of Maryland is being threatened with extermination by the Indians. As the bridge between civilization and savagery—between plan and chaos, idea and existence, form and matter, thought and emotion—Henry is the only man in the province who can save the whites. He means to go into the Ahatchwoop country, proclaim himself the descendent of Burlingame I and heir to Chicamec's throne, and allay the natives' bloodthirstiness. The aim is to have the best of both worlds. The totally savage and the totally civilized are extremes which impoverish human potential when they exclude each other. Burlingame's effectiveness depends upon his virility. He must convince his father and his people that he can carry on the royal line. He has, however, inherited a genital deficiency from his grandfather which can be cured only with a secret "eggplant recipe," learned by Burlingame I from John Smith and duly recorded in his journal. That page of the journal is missing and on it hang the hopes of the survival of the colony and civilization. The abstractions of knowledge and plan do have a role in empowering physical existence to save itself.

At this point, Joan Toast appears as the pivotal character in the novel. She has stolen the important page and so possesses the key to Burlingame's manhood, civilization's survival, and even Eben's redemption. She offers the Governor of the colony the recipe in return for the disputed title of Eben's land. Eben realizes that, even though he has never claimed her as wife, she is trying to secure the property for him rather than for herself. The Governor consents to the trade, Burlingame goes off to make peace with the Indians, and Eben is put in the way of getting back the land which he had so naively surrendered earlier. But Joan has done more than save Eben's estate. She has saved him. Through a gesture of selfless love, she has taught him in a more than intellectual way that the world is not bereft of worthy values, even though they are not absolute. But now Eben goes farther than Todd Andrews. He recognizes that this is the situation of "right significance" which calls for the surrender of his virginity. It is time for him to embrace the world. Symbolically recuperating from a serious illness contracted when he ran away from Joan—when he tried to flee from the world—he takes her to the bridal chamber and commits himself to her mortally diseased body, completing his marriage to the world and losing, as he must, his innocence in the act.

The fusion this represents is conceptualized in a dream Eben has just before he comes out of his fever. As Eben sees it, his fever is a sojourn in hell, "penance for Lust and Pride," lust not for the world but for the abstract and wholly explainable; pride of being superior to the world in his role as virgin poet. In his dream he sees a healthy Joan Toast change into his sister Anna, who then becomes sick and herself turns into Joan Toast, who becomes healthy again and starts the cycle over. Here the world fuses with the dream of what the world might be, and in that fusion the original distinctions between the ideal and the real are broken down. Life is an interpenetration of the two, one contributing to the modification of the other. Eben sees with his highest consciousness that the dream is a punishment for his former innocence. Innocence, he says, is a crime "whereof the Knowledged must bear the burthen." Our original sin is innocence, ignorance of the world and rejection of it: "not that Adam *learned,* but that he *had* to learn—in short, he was innocent." The crime lies in the repudiation of the world implied in innocence, when the world is the only sphere we have in which to work out our special humanness. The destruction of that innocence may tarnish the illusory ideal, but it makes it possible to inject that ideal in its modified form into our existence, illuminating that existence which would otherwise remain dark and collective. We make our world human by giving it value, and value is a way of pointing to an individual, existing person. Innocence receives its values like a servant receiving instructions from a master. The human being—causally independent—makes his own values, not in the unthinking joy of innocence, but in the chastened, compassionate independence of human life. After Joan dies, Eben lives out his years with Anna, no longer exuberant with the old illusions, but matured into a gentle humor that recognizes the worth as well as the limitations of existence. Barth concludes, in this novel, that not only are reasons and values not satisfactory only when they are absolute, they cannot be satisfactory if one requires that they be absolute. Values are inventions of men that interpenetrate with existence and produce the uniqueness of human life. And only in the individual does that life appear. Once that is recognized, then man, with his newly learned compassion, can take up moral ties with his society.

Where Ebenezer Cook begins with civilized innocence, George Giles, in *Giles Goat-Boy,* begins with animal innocence, moves to the abstract distinctions of the rationalist, and ends in the higher consciousness that fuses the extremes of physical and mental existence. The problem George must overcome is the tendency to reify abstract categories by making distinctions. Barth's point, by now familiar, is not to avoid making distinctions, but to avoid using them as substitutes for rather than accompaniments to existence. George must learn to give distinctions their proper place, to realize they can, as Jake Horner says, "betray experience." George learns this in the context of a formal education that feeds upon distinctions to keep itself alive. The world of *Giles Goat-Boy* is a huge "University," divided into campuses—West Campus and East Campus—corresponding to the current major international factions. The Campuses are in turn made up of "Colleges." New Tammany College, for example, is the United States.

The operating principle of the University—the making of distinctions—is the main obstacle to the individual satisfaction of higher consciousness and freedom. The principle is administered by the huge computer WESCAC. It produces, by means of its punctured IBM cards, the values and the duties of West Campus. Its "AIM" is to "pass" or "fail" applicants for "Graduation." The implication is that a student "graduates" when he achieves essence, that state in which he is pure consciousness, absolutely free of the impediments of the worldly existence (the body). WESCAC is the intellectual faculty of the human mind that thinks of reality as a pattern of distinct entities. It is the "Mind-force," says George's old tutor, Max Spielman, "The thing that tells you there's a *you,* that's different from me." Without this mind-force we would not be men; but to attribute to it the power of rewarding us the highest accolades is to distort existence. Through WESCAC, George and the rest of the students of West Campus receive the tasks and directives that are supposed to carry them to graduation.

When the human tendency to make distinctions is carried to an extreme, it works adversely to the development of our humanness. Dr. Eierkopf (egghead) is completely intellectual, as suggested by his huge overdeveloped head and puny crippled body. Whatever deserves the verb *is,* he claims, can be empirically detected and rationally explained. For him, empirical investigation is discovering "the differentiation of *this* from *that.*" One of his most pressing enterprises is discovering the exact point at which tock becomes tick in the campus tower clock. Eierkopf has so ignored his physical part that he has no control over it and so is its virtual victim. This part of his existence is represented by a great simian creature called Croaker, whose life principle is the gratification of his prodigious sexual appetite. Eierkopf is incapable of sex. He resents Croaker's vital presence in the world, a presence which is tinged with death, complaining that the purity of his intellect is debauched by the fact that he must rely on Croaker to carry him around and perform for him the most mundane tasks to keep him alive.

According to the principles of WESCAC and Eierkopf, one graduates only by purifying the mind or the spirit of its contaminating "Croakerity." WESCAC supposedly passes or fails students according to their degree of success, though no one is known ever to have succeeded. After several experiences with these principles, George enthusiastically adopts them, convinced that "making clear distinctions must be the first step to Graduation: not confusing one thing with another, especially the passèd with the flunked." George thus allegorizes an oversimplified history of western man. Having just emerged from the relative unconsciousness of animality, George turns to its opposite, an Aristotelian compartmentalization of experience.

But George eventually breaks free of these traditional bonds.

He has an insight in which he sees that the "real" truth lies in the statement, "Passèd are the flunked." This statement is paradoxical only if one accepts WESCAC's definition of the terms. As a distinction-maker, WESCAC defines failure as being unable to rid oneself of "Croakerity"—of existence. Passage is successful purification. George finds that the old author of "*Taliped Decanus*" (Oedipus) realized that in this "University" there is only failure. Humans are humans by virtue of their "Croakerity," as well as of their power to distinguish. At this point of awareness, Todd Andrews and Eben Cook lapse into despair. George Giles makes an immediate leap by saying that the "original Sakhyan" (Buddha) and Enos Enoch (Christ) saw further, even, than *Taliped's* author: that "Failure is Passage." In this interpretation, *passage* retains the connotation of blessedness—even holiness—but loses the connotation of absolute and transcendent purity. Passage is not perfecting the ability to make distinctions or purify the mind of physical existence, but the affirmation of a life that, by definition, will always possess some Croakerity. In trying to fathom the meaning of the apparent paradox, George thinks his mind will "crack," for he is on the verge of breaking out of the old categories of consciousness set by WESCAC. He experiences a moment of panic. He is in the grip of life, that existence from which there is no escape. At that moment he hears a policeman order a prisoner, "Don't try to get loose!" Applying these words to himself in a clearly analogous situation, George relaxes: "I gave myself up utterly to that which bound, possessed, and bore me. I let go, I let all go; relief went through me like a purge." As when Eben Cook finally takes Joan to bed, George Giles chooses the world. It is not man's rebelliousness that Barth focuses upon. It is the satisfaction that accompanies the affirmation of the paradox and "lack" in human existence.

Having arrived at such an affirmation, George is ready to complete his education in the belly of WESCAC. There he repudiates the established grooves of the past and fuses all distinctions in the act of love with Anastasia Stoker. When the computer flashes the question of whether they are male or female, they press both buttons at once, simultaneously reaching orgasm. In this moment they arrive at the highest consciousness of which the human being is capable—the merging of the intellect and existence in an act of reproduction and fertility. With the sexual union of the male and female, the universe in both its abstract and existential aspect is joined: ". . . there was no East, no West, but an entire, single, seamless campus. . . . *Here* lay with *there, tick* clipped *tock, all* serviced *nothing*. . . ." In this act of fertility, the introduction of life into death, all that the mind differentiates merges. And in the lucid consciousness of the moment, George is *aware* of it. In this rare moment, when the nature of human life is directly experienced, WESCAC is shortcircuited. It is designed to make distinctions, not fusions.

But WESCAC, the "Mind-force," and the distinctions it makes are not to be abandoned completely. Thought is as necessary to human life as is Croakerity. George concludes that the function of WESCAC the distinction-maker is to stand between Failure and Passage in order to screen "from the general eye what only the few, Truth's lovers and tutees, might look on bare and not be blinded." This high consciousness, this vivid awareness of our condition, is a truth so powerful that even our existence works to censor it. Nor does this truth inaugurate a period of joy and bliss and ease, or bring any equilibrium or restful contentment. After his experience in WESCAC, George is unable to communicate his learning and he is held in considerable suspicion by West Campus's students and faculty. But this truth does affirm the human condition from which no one escapes, and in doing so confers value upon it. If the intellect does not carry with it the full knowledge of existence, it does produce values by which men know they are human beings and by which they put a premium on their existence. This is the muted satisfaction which maturity brings us and constitutes the final experience of Ebenezer Cook and George Giles.

By embracing the human condition, by adopting the "open decision" and learning to live the paradox of their own subjectivity, Eben and George lay the foundation of their moral being. That being is characterized by "moderation," Camus's word for the fusion of the conflicting forces that make up the human being's world and self. When they accept themselves and their mortality, they also accept other individual selves. And that acceptance is the basis of the most widely accepted of all twentieth-century moral codes. It is predicated upon the absolute value of the independent subject, no one of which can claim moral superiority to any other one. When that morality is prepared for by the assumption of the "open decision," the human being arrives at the highest possible intensity of individual satisfaction, for he affirms his own value both through himself and through others. And that is the overt and the implied significance of Barth's novels.

Kurt Vonnegut, Jr.,[3] is a much more obvious moralist than Barth. His novels have something of Swift in them—not merely in the canny pokes he takes at human weakness and the *status quo,* but a kind of fantasy that allows him, as it allowed Swift, to isolate the objects of his attack and praise. What Vonnegut praises, as we might expect in setting him against the background of the "open decision," is the human being—at least the human being as Vonnegut defines the phrase. The human being is most human—and most praiseworthy—when he lives wholeheartedly in his natural condition, working in the open, doing joyfully and spontaneously for his own support, loving other life, and being loved. Human worth—and hence significance—resides in the *being* of the human. The self is its own reason for being; its being is its own guarantee of its value. The more conscious one is of his being, the more individual he is and the firmer is his guarantee.

For Vonnegut, one of the defining characteristics of authentic human life is physical labor. In *God Bless You, Mr. Rosewater,* three people illustrate this value: Harry Pena and his two sons. A large robust fisherman, Harry daily sails out to his nets with his sons and hauls in the catch. Vonnegut is lyrical in his description of their work: it is "a magic time. Even the gulls fell silent as the three, purified of all thought, hauled net from the sea." And when they are through, "all three were as satisfied with life as man can ever be." Dr. Paul Proteus, in *Player Piano,* yearns to break away from his job as a manager of machines and go "outside of society" where he can "live heartily and blamelessly, *naturally,* by hands and wits." At the end of *The Sirens of Titan,* Malachi Constant, a former earthling, re-establishes his ties with nature on Titan, one of Saturn's nine moons as invented by Vonnegut: "He raised or gathered or made everything he needed. This satisfied him enormously." The significance or worth of such Thoreauvian values is not in the end of labor—profit—but in the act of labor itself, which is a confirmation of the individual experience. As Robert Frost says, "The fact is the sweetest dream that labor ever knew." From the standpoint of the "open decision," work establishes a high intensity of individual satisfaction simply because it is an individual act that supports itself. This, as Reverend Lasher says in *Player Piano*, provides "the feeling of participation, the feeling of being needed on earth—hell, *dignity*."

The act of loving also confers high value, both upon the lover and the loved. Such love is the basis of Vonnegut's conception of morality, and it rises from the metaphysical assumption in the "open decision" that there can be no individual identity or satisfaction without ties with others, without a relationship with other actual entities. In relativity, for example, there can be no motion—or entity—without other bodies. For Vonnegut, as for Fromm and Jaspers and others, love is the foundation of satisfaction. Talking with people in Homestead who have not had a productive job for years in their advanced computer society, Paul Proteus feels a "fresh, strong identity growing within him. It was a generalized love—particularly for the little people, the common people, God bless them." And when Paul is jailed for such subversive emotions, he discovers that a friend is in the next cell. That closeness produces in Paul an "exotic emotion." "For the first time in the whole of his orderly life he was sharing profound misfortune with another human being." Eliot Rosewater comes to feel it is his destiny to find a way "to love people who have no use." Those who are out of work have been rendered not only poor but useless. They are so unattractive that they cannot even care for themselves, and they become "ugly, stupid, boring." Eliot determines to make them useful by caring for them.

Love and work are, as Eric Fromm says too, the bases of human satisfaction; they are what the human being is uniquely capable of. His moral relationship to others—to society—is founded upon those attributes. They are virtues because they intensify the reality of the highest good—the individual. Yet, noble as man might be—and sometimes is—through love and work, he has his other side, his "lack." Vonnegut's reservation is subtly expressed in his comment upon Harry Pena and his two sons: they are "as satisfied with life *as man can ever be*." (My italics.) The old theme is struck once more. Human satisfaction must always fall short of its conception, and Vonnegut consistently undercuts the admirableness of human values and actions, introducing into his picture of experience moderation and ambiguity. It is not this inherent "lack," however, that Vonnegut attacks with his bitterest satire. It is the institutions that men have built which turn men aside from their proper activities to pursue the dehumanizing goals of empty material wealth and technological success. It is also the ignorance and the hatefulness of men that Vonnegut attacks, and he deals with these characteristics in their social aspect, for they are evil mainly as they thwart the valuable satisfactions of others. What excites his ire also is the impediments men set in their own way toward their own satisfaction and meaning, which exist only in the individual. What inhibits the full play of the individual must be attacked and pulled down.

The location of meaning and worth, as the prerequisite of moral behavior, is one of Vonnegut's main preoccupations. He deals with it most fully in *The Sirens of Titan.* Humans, says the narrator of that novel, assume that purpose is like some planet in the external world, to be searched for and discovered. They proceed, as Dewey would put it, on the "spectator theory of knowledge." The setting of *The Sirens of Titan* is the Solar System, and the time is the years between the Earth's Second World War and Third Great Depression. The significance of this period is that it occurs before anyone learned "how to find the meaning of life within himself." Winston Niles Rumfoord, an earthling who has inadvertently come upon the power to see into the future, looks outward for meaning and is frustrated. He attempts to discover what the "point" is of "this Solar System episode." In spite of the fact that Rumfoord declares that there is no meaning-giving deity, he cannot surrender the expectation that there is some "purpose" to his own activities and to the events in the future which he can predict but not control or determine.

The futility of Rumfoord's search is demonstrated through Salo, a creature from the planet Tralfamadore in another galaxy. Two hundred thousand years before Rumfoord first lands on Titan, Salo had developed spaceship trouble and landed on Saturn's ninth moon to await a replacement part. Unbeknownst to him, Rumfoord is instrumental in getting that part to Salo. But he is only a small element in a much larger plan, the last two thousand years of Solar System history. Rumfoord's "purpose" had thus been to make it possible for Salo to continue his journey. Learning this, Rumfoord decides that "the main point of this Solar System episode" must have been the message Salo was carrying from Tralfamadore. The message, however, is simply "Greetings." It reduces Rumfoord's expectations of meaning to an absurdity, but it contains the meaning that Vonnegut expressed in the novel. The purpose of life and the central force in the universe is the affirmation of that life, which comes with the communication between conscious creatures through the experience of love and work.

This purpose is expressed in two episodes. When the Negro Earthling Boaz goes to Mercury he concludes that "Not to be lonely, not to be scared" is what is important in life. He achieves this state through the curious "harmoniums," thin, spineless, diamond-shaped creatures that cling to the walls of Mercury's caves, "eating" the vibration the planet makes as it "sings." Their only sense is touch, and their only messages—which they send through touch—are: "Here I am, here I am, here I am," to which is answered, "So glad you are, so glad you are." In so communicating they affirm each other's existence and give each other a being. Boaz finds in the simple creatures a closeness he has never known, and he allows his favorites to feed off the vibrations of his heart and pulse, both reaffirming the existence of the other. Similarly, in his acquaintance with Rumfoord, Salo, originally a machine on Tralfamadore, becomes more human and thereby acquires a capacity for a higher intensity of satisfaction. He develops a mind which "fizzes and overheats with thoughts of love, honor, dignity, rights, accomplishments, integrity, independence."

What is most human and admirable about the human being leads to a kind of inefficiency—a fizzing and an overheating, threats of his own breakdown. Ironically, as Salo grows more human and becomes more capable of affirmation, Rumfoord, resentful at what he calls "being used" by Salo, grows more like the early Beatrice—distant, petulant, isolated, until he finally disappears altogether from this Solar System. In contrast, Salo ceases to be a machine when he defies the orders of his government and opens the sealed message at Rumfoord's request, moving out of his programmed circuits and making a gesture of human love. Salo grows the capacity to experience creature love, a growth which makes him a fit messenger for the words that he carries to no one in particular.

Ironically sent by machines who seem to recognize its significance before the human Earthlings do, the message demonstrates the desire to affirm life through contact with it, the desire to say, like Mercury's harmoniums, "Here I am," and wait for the meaning-giving answer: "So glad you are." The story that Vonnegut tells suggests that this message is the motive force of all human history, since human activity was utilized in making it possible for Salo to continue his journey. The symbol of the force of the message is the fuel which runs the Tralfamadorian space ship: UWTB, the Universal Will to Become, that "makes universes out of nothingness—that makes nothingness insist on becoming somethingness." It is the drive to overcome the "lack." In the affirmation of oneself and others, what was nothing becomes something. It is this will to become, captured in the simple Tralfamadorian message, which is the "point," as Rumfoord calls it, of "this Solar System episode."

Vonnegut reflects, here, the assumptions of the "open decision" about the nature of the human being. As a subject his life style is embodied in feeling, a feeling which, though he is "causally independent," is affected by the feelings of other subjects. That is, in his relationships with other human beings, the individual self can be modified internally. His own sense of being in the world is intensified as he opens himself to that world, consisting of things and creatures. When, Vonnegut suggests, one remains closed he commits a kind of sin against sacred life. Malachi Constant, for example, one of Earth's richest men, used his wealth in his young manhood simply to gratify trivial appetites. He devoted his life on Earth to demonstrating "that man is a pig," wallowing in "sycophants," "worthless women," "lascivious entertainments and alcohol and drugs." Not only did he do nothing to deserve his money; he used it selfishly and unimaginatively. So presented, he is a "central symbol of wrong-headedness." Beatrice Rumfoord, who becomes Malachi's mate and the mother of his child, sinned as an Earthling by fearing to live as a loving, participating human being. Her excesses, different from those of Malachi, were "excesses of reluctance. . . . As a younger woman, she felt so exquisitely bred as to do nothing and to allow nothing done to her, for fear of contamination. Life, for Beatrice as a younger woman, was too full of germs and vulgarity to be anything but intolerable." Like young Eben Cook, Beatrice refuses the world.

Beatrice, Malachi, and their son Chrono learn—as do Boaz and Salo—that a high intensity of satisfaction can be achieved only by exposing oneself to experience through love, and that love is an affirmation of the self through the affirmation of others. Malachi comes "to realize that a purpose of human life, no matter who is controlling it, is to love whoever is around to be loved." The search for objective purpose and external causes is not only futile, but irrelevant. Life has value simply in the living of it, and meaning simply in the loving of other life. Beatrice, who had as a girl recoiled from being used, writes a book—"The True Purpose of Life in the Solar System"—in which she concludes that "The worst thing that could possibly happen to anybody . . . would be to not be used for anything by anybody." Chrono's affirmation is less intellectual. He leaves his parents and takes up a primitive life among Titan's birds, and when his mother dies, he comes down to her new grave and shouts out thanks to his parents "for the gift of life." The implication is that a society whose ordering principle is love of others would be "living" in the highest sense of that word, as Whitehead uses it, producing an environment that would all but assure a high intensity of individual satisfaction for each citizen actual entity, because it would be composed of contrasting individuals and not conflict and selfishness. Below, I will deal with Vonnegut's attacks upon those societies whose ordering principle is the opposite of such love. Even in *The Sirens of Titan,* at the height of affirmation, Vonnegut must introduce a counterbalance that characterizes all his novels. He cannot ignore the pathos—the absurdity—of the human experience. Malachi Constant, as an old man, his wife dead, alone on Titan where he has been exiled, returns to Earth and there dies, still alone, sitting on a bus stop bench during a snowstorm. His only comfort is a vision of something better for him in the future, a vision which Salo has hypnotized him to see just before his death. That vision is "unreal." It is a myth. But it is human, one of our noble traits as well as one of our comforts. And Vonnegut is concerned to show that our myths, while childish retreats from harsh reality, are also the means by which we rationalize our otherwise meaningless existence.

But Vonnegut is seldom even as optimistic as he is in *The Sirens of Titan.* He spends most of his time attacking the impediments to human satisfaction and fulfillment. He is mainly preoccupied not with instances of affirmation, but with those factors that contribute to the human being's devaluation. In his first novel, *Player Piano,* and his most recent novel but one, *God Bless You, Mr. Rosewater,* his main target is the machine and the systems those machines spawn. *Player Piano* is something of a social protest novel. It is set in a fanciful future after World War III, when the engineers and managers have learned to get along without people. Machines do all the country's work and they are kept in working order by an elite corps of narrowly educated technologists. Production, marketing, and planning are carried on by the huge computer Epicac, buried deep in Carlsbad Caverns. The factories are eerily empty of workers. Material goods are abundant, but those who use them have no vital relationship with those goods, except as consumers. With the entire society organized into a huge corporation, the highest value is reduced to keeping the machines and the system running smoothly. The machines' caretakers are unattractive mutants of Whyte's organization man, fervidly patriotic and totally uncritical servants of the apparatus.

Such a society destroys what is best in the human being by wiping out the possibilities by which he identifies himself: his inventiveness, his spontaneity, his satisfaction in doing useful work. It is analogous to Whitehead's nonliving society, fixing every actual entity to a narrow range of alternatives. The machines classify every individual according to his I.Q. and aptitudes. Once he is fixed in a category he cannot ever break out and move to another one. His identity becomes the perforations in his IBM card. Even the managers are subject to these inflexible classifications, and if a machine is devised to do the work of one of the managerial classes, the human members of that class are suddenly stripped of their meaning and purpose. Those whose I.Q.'s do not qualify them to attend college and become an engineer or manager become wards of society, passing time in the make-work of the Reconstruction and Reclamation Corps. They feel frustrated, then surly, finally apathetic and indifferent. The members of this society lose their power of self-creativity and the opportunity for individual satisfaction.

One preserves the integrity of the individual self against such a system only through rebellion. Paul Proteus joins with his friend Ed Finnerty and the Reverend Lasher in a revolutionary organization designed to start civil war, overthrow the machines, and give the world back to the humans. Reverend Lasher does not expect the revolution to succeed. But that is not the point. Its value will lie in the opportunity it gives the people to activate their humanness, to say "no" to the system that would dehumanize them. Thus, though the revolt is crushed and its leaders are forced to surrender, Reverend Lasher can walk forward with his hands up "almost gaily." Yet, again Vonnegut qualifies the affirmation. Can we really accept as valuable an existence in which men are forced constantly to struggle for their identity and integrity and expect only defeat in the end? Vonnegut refuses to answer the question. For every value there is an antivalue.

Not all restrictive systems are quite so easy to rebel against as the obvious one in *Player Piano*. The automated society of contemporary America, depicted in *God Bless You, Mr. Rosewater*, is reinforced by a deep-rooted morality of capitalism and free enterprise. Vonnegut implies that this morality is a rhetorical construction built on false premises, premises he attacks in all of his novels and which are designed to justify the wealthy and indict the poor. The first premise is that wealth is a sign of industry and hence desert, and poverty a sign of laziness and hence deserved deprivation. Eliot Rosewater insists, to the contrary, that wealth is a matter of chance, an accident of birth: "I think it's a heartless government that will let one baby be born owning a big piece of the country, the way I was born, and let another baby be born without owning anything." By and large, says Eliot, the rich have had the luck to be born on the banks of the "Money River," regarding this not as fortuitous but as a sign of God's special favor. From the beginning they are trained to "slurp" from this river, even taking lessons from special teachers like lawyers and tax consultants on how to slurp more efficiently and profitably. And they spend much of their time keeping the poor from hearing them.

The second false premise of this morality is that free enterprise encourages incentive through competition, by which men better themselves. Eliot protests that competition neither ennobles nor dignifies. It degrades and shames. The real incentive that drives men to struggle for money, he says, is "fright," "fright about not getting enough to eat, about not being able to pay the doctor, about not being able to give your family nice clothes, a safe, cheerful, comfortable place to live, a decent education, and a few good times." Our system makes people ashamed for not having had the luck to be born by the Money River.

Not only is the premise of desert false; it actually contradicts the facts, as Vonnegut sees them. The rich, far from acquiring their wealth on their own hook, are almost all "beneficiaries of boodles and laws that had nothing to do with wisdom or work." The rich are feckless, weak, and personally corrupt. The small New England town where Eliot's distant cousin Fred Rosewater lives is a microcosm reflecting the general American dichotomy, for it is "populated by two hundred very wealthy families and by a thousand ordinary families whose breadwinners served, in one way and another, the rich." But for all the money the rich accumulate, their lives are "nearly all paltry, lacking in subtlety, wit or invention." Stewart Buntline, the heir of the town's richest family, sleeps most of the day and drinks when he is not asleep. His wife Aminta is a lesbian who buys the attentions of and then dominates the town's pretty but penniless housewives. And his daughter Lila sells racy books and pornographic pictures to her rich playmates. These people, writes the Buntline maid, an indigent orphan, think "that everything nice in the world is a gift to the poor people from them or their ancestors," including sunsets, "the ocean, the moon, the stars in the sky, and the United States Constitution."

This state of things is not only unfair and stultifying for the poor, it is dangerous to the authenticity of the human being. The good, represented by Harry Pena, the fisherman, is slowly being destroyed. Its destroyer is symbolized by The Weir restaurant, a place cluttered with worthless gingerbread and run at a huge profit by a sterile homosexual. From The Weir, the rich guests may gaze out at Henry Pena at work, witnessing his joy once removed as he works at his nets. The restaurateur, incapable of producing life himself, finds Harry's vitality distasteful. He declares with satisfaction that Harry's kind of life is "all over." Men working with their "hands and backs" are no longer needed. Harry, he explains, will soon go bankrupt and the system will destroy him.

It is in this context of disingenuousness and moral decay that Vonnegut places the basic irony of the novel. A greedy young lawyer, Norman Mushari, is attempting to have Eliot declared insane. The basis of his allegation is that Eliot has rejected the premises of the establishment. But of course what Mushari calls insanity is only an attempt to live by the humanitarian values to which a commercial society pays merely sanctimonious lip service. The real values that society lives by are economic, not human. Thus, when Eliot takes a small office in Rosewater, Indiana, and puts his huge fortune to work for America's poor instead of trying to keep it in the family, Mushari feels that he has a case. His plan is to shift control of the fortune to Fred Rosewater, who is penniless, with the expectation that in the transfer at the magic moment he will be able to scrape a goodly sum off the top. Mushari is thus motivated by the insane greed which our society moralizes as free enterprise. As Vonnegut conceives it, Eliot is a sane, moral man in an insane, immoral society.

However blameworthy our machines and systems are, a large obstacle to human fulfillment and meaning is the human himself, and Vonnegut reserves his most frustrated bitterness for that good-bad creature. As Reverend Lasher says, "It isn't the knowledge that's making the trouble, but the uses it's put to." In his two bitterest novels, *Mother Night* and *Cat's Cradle*, Vonnegut attacks human viciousness and stupidity, shifting the focus of his satire from a definition of the good in human life to an expression of despair that men can ever free their goodness. The title *Mother Night* comes from a passage in Goethe, in which Mother Night is that prevailing darkness with which light disputes "and yet cannot succeed." The darkness of this novel is the human capacity for hatred and prejudice, "that part of every man that wants to hate without limit, that wants to hate with God on its side."

The character who speaks these words is Howard W. Campbell. The novel is his journal, written in an Israeli prison in 1961 as he awaits trial as a war criminal. His experiences, which he chronicles in the journal, make him deeply pessimistic about the future of human life. An American writer in Germany during the 'thirties, Campbell consents to become an American agent when it appears that war is going to break out, even though he has sought to remain detached from politics during his stay in Germany. He masquerades as a convinced Nazi anti-Semite and becomes a propagandist for the Third Reich. Through his radio program he passes information out of the country. His position is so secret that even when the war is over he is publicly denounced as a war criminal.

The U.S., rather than reveal the truth, simply confuses the situation so that he goes free.

In a world powered by hate, however, freedom is an illusion. Campbell manages to live for several years in New York undetected and unknown, but he is finally discovered by an anti-Semitic group headed up by Dr. Lionel J. D. Jones, who remembers with approval Campbell's broadcasts during the war. Exposed, Campbell becomes the target of the world's spleen. West Germany and Israel vie for the right to try him. Russia shrills that such Fascists "should be squashed underfoot like a cockroach." And private citizens cry out for his destruction. Hatred requires that all offenses be *punished.* An ex-soldier savagely attacks him in twisted revenge for several buddies who died in the war. Bernard O'Hare, the officer who arrested him after the armistice, tracks him down intending to beat him mercilessly to a slow death. Vonnegut sees no appreciable difference between the anti-Semitism of Nazi Germany and Lionel Jones, and the virulent desire for revenge by Russia and O'Hare. The West's victory over Germany changed nothing. Driven by a snarling, hating self-righteousness, the victors claim to have the approval of God in their campaign to kill or mutilate those who are different. As one of Campbell's Israeli jailers declares, everyone who had been involved in the war, "no matter what side he was on, no matter what he did, is sure a good man could not have acted in any other way." Compassion meets a hostile environment in the darkness of the mind. Thus Adolph Eichmann, whom Campbell comes to know in prison, does not consider himself guilty of any crime. That he directed the extermination of hundreds of thousands of Jews is justified by his sacred obligation to protect the purity of Germany's Aryan blood line.

This human penchant for hatred is man's sick part, bad faith and false consciousness carried to an insane and destructive degree. Indeed, Campbell believes that Eichmann should be in a hospital rather than a prison. But this conclusion about Eichmann's sickness presents a puzzling contradiction, one that blunts the effectiveness of Vonnegut's attacks upon Jones, Eichmann, and O'Hare. Campbell implies that because they are sick, they are victims rather than criminals. If blame is to be put, it is to be put on the most sympathetic character of the novel—Campbell himself. In his Introduction to the 1966 edition of the novel, Vonnegut says that the moral of the story, if there be any, is that "We are what we pretend to be, so we must be careful about what we pretend to be." Campbell, playing the role of the Aryan hatemonger, convinced everyone he was what he pretended to be, and successfully hid "the honest me." In effect, that "honest me" had no existence. For all intents and purposes, Campbell *was* a hatemonger. By acting as he did, he provided the Germans with a justification for the atrocities against the Jews, thus contributing indirectly to those atrocities. Whatever small good he did as an American agent was more than offset by the evil he did in his pretense. As Camus argues in *The Rebel,* murder or its advocacy is never justifiable. Campbell's real crime was that he "served evil too openly and good too secretly." That crime is compounded by his own awareness: "I always know when I tell a lie, am capable of imagining the cruel consequences of anybody's believing my lies, know cruelty is wrong." He cannot even claim the justification of ignorance or insanity—which Jones and O'Hare and Eichmann can do. Nor is his job as an American agent an extenuating circumstance. His motive for becoming a spy is not all patriotic or humanitarian. As a born ham he gladly welcomes the chance to act a great part. Campbell sees that he is not sick in the same sense that Eichmann is sick. Where Eichmann should be in a hospital, he writes in his journal, "I am the sort of person for whom punishments by fair, just men were devised." The light of awareness and compassion is weak enough. It must not be further dimmed by pretending to be its enemy.

On the day before his trial, Campbell receives an affidavit testifying to his true role as an American agent. But the freedom that this promises is no longer attractive. The prospect of further life is "nauseating." Nor can he bear the thought of his "crimes against himself." Not only does he deserve to be punished, life is not worth living. Light cannot succeed against darkness. His answer is suicide. Life is no gift for Campbell, as it was for Chrono. The attitude of gloomy pessimism in this book is clear. Less clear is the object of that gloom. Is it the virulent hatred of the Joneses, the O'Hares, the Eichmanns? One would at first think so. Soon, however, these men seem to be exonerated and Campbell himself indicted for serving evil too openly. Vonnegut would rid us of both kinds of sin. He simply takes no great pains to make his novel logically consistent.

The prospects of finding life worthwhile are no brighter in *Cat's Cradle.* Its targets are human stupidity, greed, and detachment, which manifest themselves in the adulation given to science, the inhumane way in which scientists work, and the selfish way in which the results of science are misused. It illustrates that the good in human life, as defined in *The Sirens of Titan,* has almost impossibly tough going against its weaknesses. Science, suggests Vonnegut, is made to look attractive through the illusion that it is progress and that it contains the amelioration of human pain. Instead, human beings are only too eager to use it for what they take to be their own profit but turns out to be their destruction.

The symbol of this illusion is the cat's cradle, the angular figure made by looping a long piece of string around the fingers of both hands. On the day the atom bomb is dropped on Hiroshima, Dr. Felix Hoenikker, one of the fathers of the bomb, is sitting at home in his study playing with a piece of string. Making a cat's cradle, he shows it to his youngest child, Newton: "See? See? See? . . . Cat's cradle. See the cat's cradle? See where the nice pussycat sleeps? Meow. Meow." At this moment, perhaps, a hundred thousand people are being annihilated by an instrument he helped to create. The good of science is just as illusory as the cat's cradle. Later, Newton as a grown man pinpoints the deception. "No wonder kids grow up crazy. A cat's cradle is nothing but a bunch of X's between somebody's hands, and little kids look and look and look at all those X's. . . . *No damn cat, and no damn cradle.*"

Hoenikker, with his scientific ways of exterminating the human race, is not a malicious man. As Reverend Lasher says, it is not knowledge that destroys but the uses to which men put it. Hoenikker is quite innocent. He plays at science as he plays with a string, like a child. But his innocence is lethal. He gives no thought to the consequences of his play, for he has no sense of identity with other human beings. He is not "glad" about human life. With grotesque irony, Vonnegut has an undertaker acquaintance remark about Hoenikker: "Sometimes I wonder if he wasn't born dead. I never met a man who was less interested in the living. Sometimes I think that's the trouble with the world: too many people in high places who are stone-cold dead." Hoenikker is the prototypical scientist, who "receives honors and creature comforts while escaping human responsibilities." A doctor on the small Caribbean island of San Lorenzo, where most of the novel's action takes place, comments upon the scientist: "I am a very bad scientist. I will do anything to make a human being feel better, even if it's unscientific. No scientist worthy of the name could say such a thing."

Such indifference to human welfare is not only immoral, it encourages humans to show their very worst traits and it endangers all mankind. In one of his playful moments—his last—Hoenikker invents *ice-nine,* a substance which freezes all moist things into a marble-like hardness and which will thaw only at 114 degrees Fahrenheit, and a perfect symbol for Vonnegut's conception of the scientist. Hoenikker dies of his own invention, but his three children salvage a splinter of the stuff for themselves and use it for their own interest. Two of them put it into the hands of the world's two great powers, the U.S. and Russia, giving them the capability of freezing not only human but all life. The third child, Franklin, uses his portion to make himself heir of "Papa" Monzano, the military dictator of San Lorenzo. None of the children is any more thoughtful of his use of ice-nine than his father had been in inventing it. The narrator opines that there can be little hope for "mankind when there are such men as Felix Hoenikker to give such playthings as *ice-nine* to such short-sighted children as almost all men and women are."

The effects of the selfish misuses of ice-nine are exemplarily apocalyptic. In despair over the excruciating pain of incurable cancer, "Papa" commits suicide by swallowing the splinter which Franklin had given him. He instantly turns to solid ice and becomes a potential contaminant of everything moist around him. A natural catastrophe completes what human stupidity began. Part of "Papa's" castle falls into the sea, carrying the dictator with it. His ice-nined body turns the sea to ice. A series of violent tornadoes drives San Lorenzo's remaining population underground. When the survivors emerge after the storm they see a landscape of utter desolation. The sea is "hard and still"; all the trees are "broken" and the birds are dead; the sky is "sick and wormy." It is the end of the world and only the human's thoughtless misuse of his knowledge can be blamed.

In *Cat's Cradle,* a new aspect of Vonnegut's pessimism appears, an aspect that relates directly to the concept of ambiguity inherent in the "open decision." It comes not from the recognition that man aborts his possibilities through stupidity, as the ice-nine plot implies, but from the recognition that the condition into which man is born—and over which he has no control—tragically limits him. Human good and human possibilities are only dreams whose realization is inhibited by man's state. This proposition is expressed in *Cat's Cradle* through San Lorenzo's fugitive religious prophet, Bokonon. Maturity, writes Bokonon, "is a bitter disappointment for which no remedy exists, unless laughter can be said to remedy anything." But the concept of *homo ludens* for Bokonon does not introduce men to higher intensities of individual satisfaction. It is a sardonically pessimistic technique for staying sane. The disappointment of maturity arises from the great gap between man's appetite for knowledge and meaning and his ability to satisfy that appetite. It arises from the "absurd." Where in *The Sirens of Titan* Vonnegut identifies meaning with the affirmation of our individual experience, in *Cat's Cradle* he finds no ground for affirmation, nor any possibility of it. Humanity, while carrying out God's will, can never know what that will is, nor discover the direction of its destiny or the objective shape of its own development. Thus Bokonon cites the familiar problem of the absurd, the desire of man to find objective meaning in the world about him and the unwillingness of that world to yield up any such meaning. Bokonon expresses this notion in one of his "calypsoes," a kind of Caribbean psalm:

> Tiger got to hunt,
> Bird got to fly,
> Man got to sit and wonder, 'Why, why, why?'
> Tiger got to sleep,
> Bird got to land;
> Man got to tell himself he understand.

Man is defined by the fact that his most basic desires are doomed to frustration. Just so were Rumfoord's desires doomed, but in *The Sirens of Titan* Vonnegut found a way to resolve that doom affirmatively. In *Cat's Cradle* men are, as the narrator says, victims of a "cruel paradox": "the heartbreaking necessity of lying about reality, and the heartbreaking impossibility of lying about it." In our ignorance, "Each of us has to be what he or she is." If we are knowing creatures, as Bokonon suggests, we must "be" whatever we know. Since we cannot know God or reality, but only ourselves, we can be nothing other than ourselves. Because our knowledge is "cruelly" limited, we cannot ever be most of what we imagine. For Bokonon this conclusion can be met only with sardonic laughter, a kind of detached humor. When the San Lorenzan natives surface after the storm, Bokonon tells them that perhaps God meant to destroy them all because he had given up on them. In that case, they should all have the good grace to die. So useless, so stupid, so ignominious has man become that even God wants nothing more to do with him. And so the natives, thousands of them, commit suicide with ice-nine. Yet, Bokonon's advice to his worshippers was only tentative, charged with cosmic irony and cynicism. The despair, it might be said, was in the natives. Bokonon, significantly, does not commit suicide. Bokonon, indeed, is the last one we hear from in the novel and his words are typically cynical, rebellious, and tentative: "If I were a younger man, I would write a history of human stupidity. . . ." I would, he says, lie down at the top of Mt. McCabe, freeze myself with ice-nine into a horribly grinning statue "thumbing my nose at you know who."

These are both the concluding words to the novel and to Bokonon's "gospels." They are intentionally ambiguous—that "*If* I were a younger man" is a conditional clause, one of Bokonon's favorite tenses. They apply to the novel in the following way.

The narrator of the novel, Jonah, is one of a small band of survivors on San Lorenzo, all, but Bokonon, Americans. As they scratch ont an existence amidst the dead or dying countryside, Jonah spends his time writing his story, *Cat's Cradle*, in the same way Joseph Campbell wrote *Mother Night* in an Israeli prison. Jonah, typically human, would make sense out of his experience. He dreams, also, of climbing Mt. McCabe, the highest peak on the island, and planting at its summit "some magnificent symbol," which would represent the meaningful climax to half a million years of human existence upon earth. But what, Jonah asks, can that symbol be? Precisely at this point he comes upon Bokonon, and it is implied that Bokonon's final sentence says something about the nature of the symbol which might be placed atop Mt. McCabe—a man frozen into a position of eternal defiance of a condition which refuses to reveal to him what he most wants to know. It is in that image of the nose-thumbing rebel that the paradox of the human being as expressed in *Cat's Cradle* emerges.

Man for Vonnegut is a complex combination of nobility and meanness, knowledge and ignorance, grandeur and ignominy. There is something simultaneously admirable and ridiculous about that small band of Americans going on as if the world were not coming to an end. Thus, for all its tone of despair, *Cat's Cradle* is probably Vonnegut's most "mature" book—as Bokonon defines that word. It expresses man's tremendous need to make myths in explanation of his condition, and it shows as that need's companion the inescapable recognition that our explanations are only myths. This is the definition and the frustration of being human.

Still there remains in these novels an unanswered question. If man's perverseness, if his very nature works against his becoming a loving, accepting creature, how can we ever expect him to create a world in which his guiding principle of behavior is moral? How can man ever act morally? Vonnegut's problem lies in an unacknowledged assumption, one that Barth took up and dispensed with in his first novel. When Vonnegut despairs over man's absurdity he does so because he cannot quite let go of the hope for some ultimate set of rules conferred on us by a higher deity, even though in novel after novel he disavows such a possibility and a desire. Bokonon does not despair so much over the innocent evil of the world's Hoenikkers as he does over the enigma with which existence confronts him. And his last act of thumbing his nose at the forces that kept him from his heart's desire—absolute knowledge—is rather childish. Man does have "to sit and wonder, 'Why, why, why?' " But whom can we get angry with for that?

In his latest novel, *Slaughterhouse-Five; or the Children's Crusade,* Vonnegut identifies the main source of his pessimistic side—the unnecessary demolishment of Dresden by the U.S. Air Force just before the end of World War II, when the Germans had been defeated and all need of bombing any city has disappeared. That incident becomes, for Vonnegut, the example of the horror of war, the epitome of man's inhumanity to man, and the terrible pain with which life confronts the human being. The condition it exemplifies leads men to make myths that declare meaning and purpose. It is that condition with which Vonnegut deals in all his other novels. Indeed, *Slaughterhouse-Five* echoes Vonnegut's previous work like a kind of summary. The barren "moon-like" landscape of Dresden after the fire-storm, bereft of all life, is the model for the San Lorenzan landscape after the ice-nine catastrophe in *Cat's Cradle.* Characters from earlier novels appear and reappear: Howard Campbell, the masquerading Nazi of *Mother Night,* is mentioned for his comments about America, and are very similar to those of Eliot Rosewater. Eliot Rosewater and a relative of Winston Rumfoord, of *God Bless You Mr. Rosewater* and *The Sirens of Titan,* share hospital rooms with *Slaughterhouse-Five*'s protagonist Billy Pilgrim. Bernard O'Hare, the avenger of *Mother Night,* accompanies the narrator back to Dresden. Kilgore Trout, Eliot's favorite author, finally appears as more than a reference. And Tralfamadore becomes a focal point and Tralfamadorians are given their say on a great many subjects.

The trouble with *Slaughterhouse-Five* is that in its character as a summary novel it embodies most of the weaknesses of its predecessors and few of their strengths. Its basic weakness is a confusion of attitude, a failure to make clear the author's position. I have suggested that Vonnegut cites human stupidity and the human condition as the two chief obstacles to the achievement of the highest good. The human condition makes it impossible by definition to arrive at any completely satisfactory fulfillment. This is in keeping with the notions of the "open decision." Human stupidity leads men to kill and cheat and steal, impinging upon the freedom of men to work out their own novel ends. As I have said, for Vonnegut the symbol of human stupidity in *Slaughterhouse-Five* is war in general and Dresden in particular. War makes animals out of the defeated and cruel tyrants out of the triumphant. Devastated Dresden illustrates the lengths to which men will carry their victories over their victims. The horror of war brings Eliot Rosewater and Billy Pilgrim to the conviction that life is "meaningless," and both try "to reinvent themselves and their universe." This is what *Slaughterhouse-Five*—and Vonnegut's other novels—is about. The means for that reinvention is the myth embodied in the novel. It is partly in this myth that the main confusion lies.

How is that reinvention to be achieved? The question is never answered explicitly, and the implied answer is not clearly supported by evidence in the novel. It is difficult for any Earthling to reinvent his universe because he is severely limited by his conception of time. As one of the Tralfamadorians explains, the Earthling is like a man strapped to a railroad car in such a way that his vision is limited to what he can see through a long narrow pipe—a "little dot." The car goes up and down hills, across flatlands, around curves. But the Earthling knows nothing of this, only that "little dot" at the end of the pipe which he takes to be reality. Whatever the Earthling sees he has "no choice but to say to himself, 'That's life.'" The Tralfamadorian, on the other hand, can see the railroad car, the Earthling strapped on it, and the plains and mountains and curves over which the car travels. The reason for this is that Tralfamadorians understand that time does not exist as the Earthling sees it; they understand that time is not sequential, that cause and effect are Earthling misconstructions and distortions. Thus, when Billy asks the Tralfamadorians why they chose him rather than someone else to carry away in their flying saucer, they answer that his question is typical Earthling meaninglessness. There is no reason, they say, for the "moment simply *is*." Can Billy Pilgrim—or Eliot Rosewater—as an Earthling reinvent his universe trapped in his conception of time?

The answer, it seems at first glance, is No. In the midst of the Battle of the Bulge, when he is lost behind the German lines, cold and miserable, Billy Pilgrim becomes "unstuck" in time, and only then does it seem possible for him to transcend the war condition. After moving through several time events from his birth to the "present" of the novel, Billy tells the soldiers he is with to go on without him. He wants to opt out of the war. And in his Tralfamadorian time warp he occasionally manages to do just that, even though he has to return to the war from time to time. This is the Tralfamadorian way of doing it. They teach Billy that when "a Tralfamadorian sees a corpse, all he thinks is that the dead person is in bad condition in that particular moment, but that the same person is just fine in plenty of other moments." It is unnecessary to say anything more than "so it goes." Not that the corpse will come back to life. It is simply that death—which is "a violet light and a hum"—comes and goes in the pulse of one's total existence. Thus, the Tralfamadorians do not take war seriously, for it cannot be prevented: it is a "bad moment." One day there is peace, next day there is war. Since nothing can be done about the bad moments, the Tralfamadorians "ignore them," and advise Billy to ignore them, too. And in a way, the novel is precisely that: an ignoring of the war. After all, the narrator says, "there is nothing intelligent to say about a massacre." And so Billy travels through time, from one experience to another, unfettered by Earth's time concept, and never do we *see* Dresden or its horrors. The narrator, Vonnegut, returns in 1965 to Dresden, twenty years after the traumatic experience, and has a "million laughs"; just as Billy, Vonnegut's alter-ego, travels to Dresden two days after the city is destroyed to face the horror of digging for corpses and creating "corpse mines." One is a good moment and one is a bad. Neither, according to the Tralfamadorians, has any causal relationship to each other. Nor do Billy's experiences have any clear connection of causality with each other, except that he is the experiencer, and has some memory —of both past and future.

Eliot Rosewater and Billy Pilgrim find science fiction a "great help" in reinventing their universe, and for that reason are great fans of Vonnegut's inveterate science fiction author, Kilgore Trout. If Vonnegut finds science fiction a great help in myth-making, we must assume that he is using the Tralfamadorians with sardonic whimsy as one way of dealing with the horror of war. But apart from the obvious illogicalities of the Tralfamadorian view of time— it would require not only a kind of temporal simultaneity but also multiple presence (and science fiction would never make such a mistake)—this view reveals confusions and inconsistencies in Vonnegut's satiric picture. Even accepting the humor of his fantasy and his fun-poking at science fiction, we are left vague about his position. If the war in general and the horror of Dresden in particular are no more than bad moments in a cosmic simultaneity of time and events, how can we regard them with any particular seriousness or concern? If man's inhumanity to man is merely to be ignored, what power can Vonnegut's references to bleak and desolate landscapes have upon our moral senses? Billy's reinvention of the universe proceeds by diminishing the power of the reasons (the horrors of war) for wanting to reinvent it in the first place.

On the other hand, perhaps we are to regard the Tralfamadorian explanation as an example of the ultimate cop-out from the human condition—they "ignore" the bad moments. They do not consider death to be especially important. In this attitude they violate some of the basic assumptions of the "open decision," especially that assumption that says there is no appeal from death. They also violate the assumption of relativism that no one world view takes precedence over any other, that there is no meta-view, and that all observations are made from a limiting world-center. But if we do take the Tralfamadorian philosophy as the target of Vonnegut's satire, what are we left with? Is there any answer to Dresden other than despair?

On the basis of some evidence the answer seems to be Yes. After the firebombing, Billy and several of his fellow prisoners, captured during the Battle of the Bulge, march across the ruins of Dresden to the city's outskirts. There they find an old German and his family keeping their inn open even though they know Dresden has been destroyed and they expect no tourists. Like the small band of San Lorenzan survivors, these few—Germans and Americans—cling to life and seek to preserve its meaning by continuing to live. The citizens of Dresden, as the fires go out and the smoke settles, turn to scratching out their existence. The charred blackness of the ravaged city gives up its dead, but also brings new life: ". . . somewhere in there was springtime." Trees begin to leaf and birds begin to "talk." And one says to Billy questioningly, "*Poo-tee-weet?*"

Does this promise of new life counter despair? Does Vonnegut mean that life, in its insistent intensity, refuses to die? Does he mean that a good moment is coming? that it has not been so bad after all? or does he mean that the spring and the leaves and the birds represent the ignominious human who in his folly does not know when he is beaten, that the Tralfamadorian myth is a ridiculous and illusory alternative to what man has wrought and is given no other alternative than to face it? I find it impossible to tell from the novel which of these meanings—or others—Vonnegut expresses. He seems to be too much preoccupied with particular targets: one time war, another the Earthling concept of time, another the greed of American capitalism, another human folly. He seems less concerned that his view of the issues these things involve be consistent in the larger sense. And his failure to be so concerned diminishes the effectiveness of his outrage. I have suggested before that Vonnegut's thought reflects some of the ambivalence and contradictoriness of the "open decision." In *Slaughterhouse-Five*, however, that thought is so confused as virtually to defy interpretation.

Several things in it are clear: his conviction that though some men act according to admirable values, love others, and create lives of their own in the freshness of nature, the forces of cruelty and meaninglessness inevitably overpower them; and his compassion and admiration for men of good will like Eliot Rosewater and Harry Pena and even Billy Pilgrim. But this admiration is always deflated by the laughter of the gods, something that comes close to contempt for the puny strivings of a few weak creatures engaged in ignominious folly. And when Vonnegut softens the cruelty he is attacking, as he does in *Slaughterhouse-Five* through the Tralfamadorians, he either abandons the hope that he can touch our moral sensibilities or he so confuses us that we can find no place to stand.

In the end, Vonnegut's morality is most clearly stated in his first five novels. In his last novel, his picture of the human being as something simultaneously ignominious and noble becomes lost somewhere between the horns of the dilemma. The paradox of the "open decision" which is unified in the existing creature seems to pose a choice for Vonnegut which he cannot make. Instead he wavers between the poles, and, immobilized by the conflict between the horror of his vision and a rationalizing fantasy, he forfeits the possibility of expressing either with any persuasive clarity. The highest good—the free human being who lives the "open decision"—is aborted in Vonnegut's crucial attempt at examining its significance. And the formulation of a firm moral position, like that of Barth, is dissipated in superficial attacks on profound problems.

Bernard Malamud[4] has said that his writing is a defense of human life. The form of that defense is a full acknowledgment of the frustrating paradoxes and contradictions of the human condition, and the affirmation of others that acknowledgment imposes. At the core of that condition, as Malamud sees it, are human freedom and natural necessity. Absolute freedom is the limitless power to gratify every dream conceivable. Such power belongs only to the gods. The human being, by definition, is that creature whose freedom is qualified by natural necessity. The freedom that he does have, as I infer from Malamud's novels, arises from what Whitehead calls "causal independence." He is open to possibilities, and never absolutely compelled by some other force to choose one possibility over another. This freedom, however, also limits the human being. If, by natural necessity, he is causally independent, he must exist his own experience. He can enlist no stand-in for himself nor can he stand-in for others. Necessity compels each causally independent individual to be free and hence responsible not only for choosing and acting, but for the consequences of his choices and acts. His identity, incomplete until he perishes, is nevertheless inescapably founded on his past acts. In Malamud's version of the "open decision," the stress is upon limitation rather than freedom. The result of that limitation, placed by necessity upon the human power to realize all dreams, is suffering. It is for this reason—that the human condition is suffering within limits—that Malamud's protagonists regard themselves so frequently as prisoners. It is also for this reason that they feel a sense of guilt, of failing to come up to their promise, of making botches of their lives. Under the influence of this sense of failure they seek to escape their past and themselves. The human condition, however, does not permit such escape. More than that, in Malamud's eyes the attempt to flee is a rejection of life, a denial of the worth of human existence. Such rejection and such denial—manifestations of bad faith and false consciousness—thwart the real potential that the human being does have, the potential for love, for human commitment, for purpose and meaning. To affirm the human condition in the full knowledge of what that condition is, is to achieve a real intensity of individual satisfaction and harvest those pleasures that grow in this world. And a moral posture consistent with the metaphysics of the "open decision" must be preceded by this affirmation of the human condition.

The central situation in Malamud's four novels takes its form from this view of the world. The drama arises from one or more of his characters straining against his condition in bitterness, frustration, or despair. In the end, he is either destroyed by the futility of his rejection or he learns that his dream of escape is an irrelevant response to his existence. The dreamers think of the freedom they yearn for as the power to change the conditions of human life, to get out of themselves and cancel the debts they incur with their actions. The more relevant response is also a more positive one: it is to invoke one's true freedom, freedom of thought—consciousness, understanding, awareness. The more conscious one becomes of himself as a human being, the more willing he is to embrace the conditions that make him human and in doing so affirms himself as a participant in the human enterprise. Malamud educates his dreamer, sending him through experience to the reality of human freedom and the morality of human affirmation. The dreamer learns that suffering is inherent in the human condition, but that in accepting that suffering he bolsters human solidarity and gives his suffering purpose. He learns, as so many of Malamud's characters put it, to suffer for something. In the end, though luck, circumstance, necessity, and their own foolishness and pusillanimity seem to conspire to make men contemptible, Malamud finds that they possess astounding resources for making their suffering and hence their condition meaningful, for avoiding despair, and for achieving dignity. In his first two novels, Malamud limits his attention primarily to the education of the individual. In his next two he begins to look outward to the whole social context and the meaning individual experience has for the public good.

Malamud's first novel is an allegory of the view I have just tried to describe. *The Natural* is a baseball novel whose main character, Roy Hobbs, is a "natural" ball player. His skill is such that he is potentially one of the great baseball players of all time. Allegorically, this is man in his natural condition, willing to exploit what his existence gives him and showing promise in that willingness. But Roy Hobbs wants more than just to be a great player. The "more" that he wants constitutes that dream that is impatient with the given and which drives the self to search for the impossible. In *The Natural* this straining against one's condition is depicted symbolically. On the train to Chicago, where he is to have his first tryout with the majors, Roy meets Harriet Bird, a strange girl with whom Roy falls hopelessly in love, but who turns out to be his nemesis. Harriet is a representation of Roy's dream. Unknown to anyone on the train, she is the killer of two other young athletes, whom she shot down with a silver bullet at the beginning of promising careers. The reason for which she stalks these youngsters is only hinted at, but it seems she has sought to destroy that reality which can never reach perfection. When Roy tries to describe to Harriet how he expects his natural talent to enable him to live a full life, she speaks haltingly and inarticulately of "some more glorious meaning in life's activities." There is an air of regret about her, a sadness that reality is not nearer to the ideal. A sportswriter comments that the killer of the young athletes used a silver bullet for them because she had been "out after a ghost but couldn't find him." Harriet's ghost hunt is for a perfection that goes beyond the limits set by natural necessity. Those athletes, so steeped in physical life, must fall short of the ghostly purity for which Harriet futilely yearns.

In pursuing Harriet, Roy pursues the same ghostly dream. He eagerly hurries, at her invitation, to her hotel room where she shoots him, too. Like a siren she has lured him away from his nature, and though she only wounds him, she destroys his talent, preventing him from entering the major leagues at the height of his youthful strength. But Roy, unlike the other athletes, is given a second chance. Fifteen years later, after holding several kinds of jobs, Roy finally breaks into the major leagues when he joins the New York Knights. Here he meets another Harriet Bird—Memo Paris, the niece of the team's manager. Memo, too, becomes part of a ghostly chase, standing for Roy's tendency to abuse his natural condition and potential. When Roy falls in love with Memo, a "memorandum" of Harriet, he explicitly links the two women and their relationship with his baseball ambition. Though he is sensationally successful with the team as a batter and fielder, he "felt he had nothing of value yet to show for what he was accomplishing, and in his dreams he still sped over endless miles of monotonous rail toward something he desperately wanted. Memo, he sighed." It was on a train those many years ago that he had sped toward what he hoped was baseball fame and the winning of the ghostly Harriet.

Like Harriet, Memo saps Roy of his natural strength and dissipates his ability. When Roy arrives, Memo is in love with the team's best hitter, Bump Bailey. In the ensuing competition between the two players on the baseball diamond, Bump kills himself when he runs into a fence chasing a fly ball. Roy easily supplants him on the field, but his dream of taking Bump's place with Memo is less successful. Again like Harriet, Memo chases a ghost, clinging to Bump's memory and rejecting Roy's reality. In turn, Bump plagues Roy. Returning one evening to his room, Roy fancies he sees Bump's ghost flee into the bathroom, but discovers only his own image staring back at him from the mirror. In his pursuit of Memo, Roy rejects that which is most human in him: his "real" nature.

Memo's unattainability sends Roy into a hitting slump, his natural capacities weakened by his refusal to accept anything else but his dream. At this point, Roy is presented with a way to redeem those powers which he does possess, and fittingly the presentation is made in Chicago, where his career had been interrupted. Roy comes off the bench to pinch-hit in a critical spot. In the stands a mysterious dark-haired woman causes a commotion by standing up. Roy senses that she means to reassure him by making a gesture of human sympathy. He responds and hits a home run, winning the game for his team and starting them on another long winning streak. The woman turns out to be Iris Lemon, a mother (unwed) and a grandmother. Iris's sphere of existence is the human world of natural limitations, not dream. In this world men's achievements inevitably fall short of their dreams. The result is that their lives are charged with suffering. But what distinguishes this experience as true is its purposefulness. Suffering, Iris gently urges, teaches us "to want the right things." The right thing is to want to do for and give to other people, rather than to retreat into the isolation of self-gratifying and ultimately futile dreaming. Doing the right thing requires sacrifice, "giving up something of your own." When she stood for Roy in Chicago, Iris gave up her "privacy among all those people." Iris teaches Roy what neither Harriet nor Memo understood: the need to affirm the natural condition by reaching out to the realities of other people.

In *The Natural,* as in his subsequent novels, Malamud identifies the choice of one's humanity—one's natural condition—with the moral and the good, the rejection of that condition with the destructive and the bad. Memo pretends to make herself accessible to Roy, but only if he acquires enough money to provide her with the comforts she has become used to. Roy, in turn, discovers that, because of high blood pressure, another season of baseball would kill him. Thus, his source of income for sustaining Memo's high living is cut off. In order to get the money necessary for winning Memo, Roy agrees to take a bribe for batting poorly in a crucial playoff game. This agreement violates and rejects his authentic self. The destructiveness of the conflict between his natural self and the ghostly vision of winning Memo is symbolized when, on the night of the game, Roy hits a foul ball and splits his old bat Wonderboy, his companion of the real world by which he expresses his potential. Without Wonderboy, Roy cannot hit. Even when he decides to repudiate his bribe agreement, it is too late. His last time at bat he strikes out. Nor can the reappearance of Iris succeed in restoring Roy to himself. When she rises in the stands, Roy accidentally hits her with another foul ball. Yet, in the end, Roy has learned something. Apparently turning away from Memo, he throws his money into the face of the man who bribed him, with whom Memo has conspired. And earlier, the possibility of redemption and rebirth is suggested when Iris tells him that in their one close human encounter he had impregnated her.

The vision that Roy Hobbs pursues is not the vision of the rebellious man, conscious of the contradictions in his existence and determined to assert his spirit against the injustice and chaos of his condition. It is the vision of false consciousness, the closing of one's possibilities. By pursuing Harriet and Memo, Roy shows that the dream of the impossible, far from investing one with the power to actualize it, turns one away from fulfilling the natural potential he does have. Harriet and Memo are unwilling to accept the limitations existence places upon that potential, and in turning to them Roy shows himself to be unwilling also. Only in the end, with his bat Wonderboy destroyed and his baseball career at an end, does Roy recover something of his humanity by angrily but reluctantly—fully sensible of what he has lost—repudiating Memo.

In *The Assistant,* the escapee is Frank Alpine, an Italian of Catholic parentage, who all his life has been running away from the mistakes he seems chronically to make. Hating himself both for his missed chances and for running from situations of his own making, he yearns for that freedom that would give him the power to revise the past, to escape the consequences of his acts, and to keep all options open even when a choice has irrevocably closed some of them. "I always think about the different kinds of chances I have," he says. "This has stuck in my mind—don't get yourself trapped in one thing, because maybe you can do something else a whole lot better." Failing to find that freedom, he thinks of himself as a prisoner of his past and lives in "a climate of regret that he had turned a good thing into a bad. . . ."

The novel depicts, on the one hand, Frank's attempts to evade the consequences of his own existence and, on the other, his gradual education into affirmation. Frank enters the scene with a mistake. He helps Ward Minogue rob Morris Bober, a destitute Jew who runs a failing grocery store in Brooklyn. Full of remorse, Frank determines, as he had so often in the past, to start a "new life." "Would he ever get what he wanted?" he thinks in self-pity. This question is a key to his instability, for it reflects his obsession with himself and with his futile dream that he might wipe away his record. To do this he plans to make amends. Because he was masked at the time of the robbery, he knows that Morris does not recognize him some days later when he returns to the store. He persuades Morris to let him work in the store as an assistant, with no pay but a place to sleep and meals. As an assistant, Frank expects it will be easier to confess his part in the robbery. By these means he hopes to cancel his mistake, to revoke the irrevocable. He wants "to jump free of what he had done." Jumping free involves not only paying the debt Frank feels he owes Morris, but also winning the favor of Morris's daughter, Helen. In her he sees his new life, free of all past mistakes. He courts her with a pathetic desperateness.

But those mistakes prevent him from revising the past. He begins to steal small sums from Morris, rationalizing that he is getting only a tiny recompense while helping greatly to increase the store's business. He has been seeing Helen in secret and finally she asks him to meet her in the park, planning to tell him that she loves him. This same day, Frank has decided to mend his past wrongs by starting to pay back the money he has stolen. On this day, Frank's fortunes seem on the rise. But he cannot be anyone but Frank Alpine. The whole web of his past deceits—his thievery and his secret wooing of Helen—entangle him inextricably. When Frank finds he must meet Helen, he takes a dollar for spending money from the register out of the five he had put back earlier. Trying to jump free, Frank only activates his nemesis, for Morris catches him taking the dollar. This confirms Morris's suspicion that Frank had been stealing regularly, and he orders the assistant to leave the store. Feeling more desperate than ever, fearful that he is going to be imprisoned rather than freed, Frank completes the destruction of his hopes. Arriving in the park that night just in time to save Helen from being raped by Ward Minogue, he in turn forces her to make love to him, frantic that he might lose her forever without ever experiencing the pleasure of her body. In wishing to escape, Frank has denied his condition and succeeded only in bringing purposeless suffering upon himself.

If one's condition cannot be evaded, if one cannot escape that self which is the accumulation of past acts and choices, the only means for avoiding the destructive split between desired freedom and necessary limitation are in attitude. Frank learns to change his attitude through Morris. Morris, too, has made mistakes but unlike Frank he does not try to run from them. He surrounds himself with them, bitter trophies of his failures. Their symbol is the grocery store. When he resents his bad fortune, the store is a "prison," a "graveyard," a "tomb." It is the source of bitterness, suffering, and frustration—evidence of our condition's limitations. At the same time, it is Morris's existence, the source of his strength, his humanity. He has a soft-hearted, open, and unsuspicious nature: he allows himself to be swindled by almost everyone who will take the trouble; he gives credit when he cannot afford to; he refuses to be dishonest with his customers. His character limits his power to succeed. As his daughter Helen says, "He was Morris Bober and could be nobody more fortunate."

Frank concludes that as a Jew Morris lives in order to suffer. But Morris explains that because we live we suffer; it is one of the conditions of life. If we affirm life and regard it as something else than a cruel curse, we must also affirm suffering. But suffering for its own sake is not human. A Jew, says Morris, suffers for the Law, and the Law is "to do what is right, to be honest, to be good." Like Iris Lemon, Morris declares that to help other people we need to sacrifice something. The Law teaches us to sacrifice our isolated self-interest. Part of our suffering comes from that sacrifice, but its purpose is the affirmation of other human beings: "Our life is hard enough," says Morris. "Why should we hurt somebody else? . . . We ain't animals."

It is this positive view that Frank Alpine finally substitutes for his negative dream of escape and restitution. That substitution does not take place until Morris dies. After the funeral, Frank returns to the store, from which Morris had earlier banned him. Frank's aim is to win back Helen by working so hard that she will eventually forgive him and allow him to send her to college. But Frank has subtly changed. He does not run from his mistakes as he once did, nor does he seek some suspension of the rules of his condition.

He acquires a "staying power" that mystifies and frightens Helen. He works himself to exhaustion and seems to revel in his suffering. Now he is living according to the Law, suffering for someone. He carefully avoids any overtures to Helen, but he is eager to suffer for her, finding in that the foundation of a "new life" for which he had never bargained. To send Helen to school, he reflects, "would be a rocky load on his head, but he *had* to do it, it was his only hope; he could think of no other." Frank "becomes" Morris Bober. He takes over the grocery store; he follows Morris's old routine; and in the spring he has himself circumcised and becomes a Jew. He embraces the Law, accepts suffering as a token of purpose in human experience. He is aware of the seeming futility of winning back Helen, but he is now willing to risk himself in life for his hope. If life is suffering, it is at least suffering for something. Frank Alpine achieves a more acute consciousness of what that suffering and that meaning entail. Thus conscious, he transforms his attitude, and makes what was once his prison his home. More than that, he adopts a morality based upon his condition, a morality which can act as a guide for his behavior with others.

Seymour Levin, in *A New Life,* closely resembles Frank Alpine. Like Frank, Seymour complains to himself that his life has been a series of mistakes, which he wants to set right. His father was a thief, his mother a suicide, and he a bum for a while. He wants to improve his life. More than that, he wants to cancel out some of his past and move into a more predictable future. He wants, like Frank, to jump free of himself, to "win freedom in and from the self." Levin tries to secure the future with a plan that is analogous to the dreams of Roy Hobbs and Frank Alpine. The plan is to start a "new life" as a college teacher, away from New York, where he has been so unsuccessful. His logic is that freedom is a matter of the spirit and that the liberal arts best nourish the spirit. Therefore, he will teach English literature, which, as he sees it, is at the center of the liberal arts. He wins a master's degree from NYU and stumbles into a job in the English Department at Cascadia College, a technical institution in the state of "Cascadia" in the Northwest United States. His plan requires that he spend two successful years at Cascadia so that, with good recommendations, he can return to the university for his Ph.D.

Levin's dream, then, is much clearer and more logically designed than are the dreams of Hobbs and Alpine. It is also more realistic. But given Levin as the man he is, it is no more realizable. He falls in love with Pauline Gilley, the wife of the English Department's director of composition. It is precisely the kind of choice that will work most effectively against his plans for a new life. In the conservative community of Cascadia College, adultery would never be tolerated. Levin is explicit in linking the man who falls in love with Pauline with the man who was a drunkard and a bum, always seeming to act against his own best interests and then having to face the consequences of those actions. Levin has come to Cascadia to escape that man, only to find him appearing at the most inopportune time.

There are new forces in *A New Life* which were not present in the first two novels. Not only can Levin not escape himself, he cannot escape his social context. The English Department at Cascadia reflects the entire community's social, political, and academic conservatism, a conservatism that finds values in work and the acquisition of money. College, for this conservatism, is merely a technical training ground for entering the labor market with good credentials, not a generator of ideas and spirit. The prestige goes to the departments teaching technical and vocational subjects and to the athletic teams. The influential members of the English Department enthusiastically contribute to this atmosphere and remain vaguely hostile to the humanities. Cascadia College is a microcosm of America in the early 1950's, when Levin is there. In its resistance to change and the liberating forces of the liberal arts, it reflects the fear of the rest of the country, which was "frightened silly of Alger Hiss and Whittaker Chambers, Communist spies and Congressional Committees, flying saucers and fellow travelers, their friends and associates, and those who asked them for a match or the time of day." Levin's plans are thus doubly jeopardized: by himself and by his society.

The policy of the English Department, Levin decides, must be changed. It must play down the emphasis on the mechanical "service" courses, classes in composition and grammar, and lay more stress on literature, the teaching of spiritual values. In his campaign to force such a change, however, Levin is hampered by his sense of guilt over his affair with Pauline. He feels morally vulnerable, that he is trespassing upon the rights of Gerald Gilley. Like Morris

Bober, Levin takes morality to be honoring the rights of other people. We are alone, reasons Levin, with each other in a "remorseless" universe. "We have no certain understanding of Nature's intentions, nor God's if he intends." In our ignorance we can protect the human only if moral people band together and do right. Feeling morally inferior to Gilley, he cannot wage as strong a campaign in favor of the humanities as he might have done were he not engaged in a deception. At a crucial time, however, he and Pauline break off. At least temporarily free of the guilt produced by the affair, Levin feels the strength to push his own program for reform in the department. Unable to support either Gilley or Gilley's opponent in the coming election of a department chairman, he offers himself as a candidate and campaigns on a platform calling for increased emphasis upon the liberal arts.

For the first time, Malamud has explicitly raised the issue of the social implications of the individual's behavior. Necessity decrees that no one may jump free of what he has done. It does not insist that the individual "be" what society tells him to be or that the individual accept those institutions that can be changed. Levin's efficacy, however, in modifying the social situation is vitiated by his inability to escape what he is—"How to be," he says, "not Levin? How to live loveless or not live? Once more he paid for who he was, a dirty deal." His work to change the department is undercut by the fact that he is Levin. A bearded bachelor, a New York Jew, and liberal to boot, Levin has never been quite free of the suspicion of the other department members, especially the older ones. When he decides to run for the chairmanship, his aggressiveness antagonizes most of the department; his defeat is almost certain. By his active promotion of his values he has all but insured the defeat of his plan for a new life. Even if he is kept on as a teacher for the next year, the new chairman—Gilley—will be so hostile that Levin could not expect any kind of satisfactory recommendation for graduate school.

Levin's "old" self reemerges in another form and administers the *coup de grace* to whatever hope he had left of salvaging some shreds of his new life. Pauline, feeling that she cannot go on with Gerald, wants to come back to Levin. Although he does not love her as he once did, he decides to accept her. When it becomes known that they are going to go off together, the College summarily dismisses Levin. Worse than this, in return for custody of the Gilley children, Levin agrees to Gilley's demand that he never teach college again. His new life lies in shambles about him. Yet, like Frank Alpine, Levin does come to a new life, though it is not the one for which he had so carefully planned. His prospects are dim. He has allowed himself to be talked into taking a wife—whom he no longer loves—and her children—whom he has never been close to. He has given his word that he will never again seek to do what he has always wanted to do, teach college. Levin has got Levin into this. He dreams of flight, of freedom, but he does not run, as he has run before. Why does he want to do it? asks Gerald Gilley. Levin replies, "Because I can, you son of a bitch!"

Levin affirms that which cannot be escaped. He does not receive the key to the celestial city for that affirmation, but he does enter into his own humanity. He loved Pauline once. He must now accept the consequences of that choice. And, like Frank Alpine, he accepts the risk of an unpredictable future while at the same time sneaking fugitive thoughts of abandoning Pauline and starting back to school. What Levin has found is not a different self, but a more acute consciousness of his present self and its predicament. The sun does not sink slowly in the west and the protagonists do not live happily ever after. Levin's status at the end of the novel recalls an earlier episode. Walking into the country on a late day in January, Levin is pleased by the unseasonable warmth in the middle of winter. At the same time he is saddened by the evidence of "the relentless rhythm of nature." The changes that occur in nature are simply repetitious cycles, each cycle containing the seed of its death. He is a part of these natural cycles. How, then, can he win his freedom, change himself? "Was this why his life, despite his determined effort to break away from what he had already lived, remained so much the same?" In the end, Levin remains Levin, but a Levin changed in the lucidity of his awareness. Moreover, in the natural cycle there is life even in winter. This is what Levin learns when, during his walk, he sees the bright green spears of wheat shooting up out of a January ground.

Levin comes consciously to embrace, and hence to affirm, that subjective self which is his identity, which is vexed by its own paradoxes, which is inescapable, but which is finally the vehicle of human satisfaction. In the course of this, he has strengthened his own power to act morally in his social context. Whatever the contradictions between his own character and his ability to effect reforms in the stiflingly conservative Cascadia College English Department, he was moved by the same moral impulse as that described by Iris Lemon and Morris Bober: that one suffers for others, and, as a corollary, one is concerned about the ordering principle in his own society. Levin seeks to change that ordering principle at Cascadia, and his efforts are at least partially successful. Several of his liberalizing suggestions have been accepted. Because of him, Cascadia College will not be, hereafter, quite so conservative.

Yet the issue of the affirmation of the self and its condition and its relation to virtuous action is not clearly stated or resolved in *A New Life.* The morality is clear, as it is in all Malamud's novels. Moral behavior—love and compassion toward others—is founded upon individual freedom and self-respect, where these qualities represent liberation from bad faith and the recognition that personal value arises in the self. But the way that morality emerges in social action is blurred. In *The Fixer,* Malamud brings this issue into a much sharper focus. That is, what does the individual actually *do* to preserve his own integrity and help other people in a world governed by natural necessity and the social apparatus? *The Fixer* is a story about Yakov Bok, a Russian Jew, who in the years 1911 to 1913 is arrested in Kiev and held for a year and a half on false charges before he is brought to trial. More explicitly than ever before, Malamud examines the question of the human condition as a prison, the function of suffering, and the effectiveness of rebellion.

The design of *The Fixer* repeats in clearer form that of Malamud's previous novels. Born a Jew in anti-Semitic Russia, a failure forced to live in the Jewish shtetls, Yakov is bitterly resentful of the condition he was born into, feeling he has "been cheated from the start." He regards the shtetl, like Bober's grocery store a symbol of his condition, as a "prison." Like Frank Alpine and Seymour Levin he dreams of escape, and like them also he tries to run from his prison. He goes to Kiev and there tries to make his escape complete by keeping his Jewish origins secret, taking a job that requires him to live in an area prohibited to Jews. He blames politics for the suffering he goes through, and claims that politics have nothing to do with him. Yakov would forget the identity he is born to as well as the hostility of the Russian government and people. What Levin's past was to him, Yakov's Jewishness is to him; what conservative Cascadia College was to Levin, Russian government is to Yakov.

In trying to escape, Yakov entangles himself even more tightly in the net of life. First, he is arrested and charged with living illegally in a gentile area, and loses what freedom he had sought to gain when he is imprisoned. At this time a frenzied anti-Semitism prevails in Russia, and this hostility leads the Russian government to try to make Yakov a scapegoat. It accuses him of the ritual murder of a Russian gentile boy. Fantastic charges are made and evidence against him is shamelessly manufactured by an ambitious prosecutor with the help of corrupt politicians and shady underworld characters. Because he is a Jew, he is condemned by all of Russia even before he is brought to trial. He refuses to say he is guilty. His trial is therefore delayed, and for more than a year he languishes in a filthy jail cell, suffering increased pain and humiliation and decreased freedom.

At first Yakov reacts to this injustice as though it were the result of the accident of his birth, as though it were one of those natural limitations placed upon his freedom. "His fate nauseated him. Escaping from the Pale he had at once been entrapped in prison. From birth a black horse had followed him, a Jewish nightmare. What was being a Jew but an everlasting curse? He was sick of their history, destiny, blood guilt." Yakov, like Levin, regards his existence as a "dirty deal," reflecting, by analogy, one of the principal twentieth-century reactions to the "new" world without the escape of God and transcendent absolutes. Now he is not free. He has only his existence left, he says, and existence without freedom of choice is not living. As in *A New Life,* there are two limitations here: necessity (he is Yakov Bok, Jew) and society (Russian society controls Jews). Yakov has not yet clearly distinguished between the two kinds of limitation, regarding them both as inescapable absolutes. And when he thinks of freedom, in this context, he means what other of Malamud's escapees mean by it, the power to change his condition. The last sign of that power is suicide, and Yakov reasons that if he were to commit suicide he would relieve himself of his suffering and demonstrate that there is always "one last choice." If being a Jew is a curse, however, which one can escape only through suicide, then life is a curse and suicide a rejection of it.

But there are some forces against which man can freely assert himself, and in doing so maintain his integrity and achieve a high degree of individual satisfaction. This is what Yakov eventually comes to learn. At the nadir of his despair over the imprisonment of being who he is, the direction of his thought takes an upward turn. He has been imprisoned because he tried to escape his original condition as a Jew. Men as men are also restricted in their power. But because the human being lacks the absolute freedom to actualize every dream—to escape his condition—is the logical and relevant response suicide, the analogy to running? What, he asks himself, would be gained by his death? Only a release from suffering. In contrast, the probable consequences of his death are horrifying to consider. If he implies his guilt by committing suicide, he would jeopardize all of his people. The Russians, assuming that what one Jew is all of them are, would accuse the rest of the tribe of the same crime of which they have accused Yakov. This could result in a pogrom: pain, suffering, death for anyone who is a Jew.

The logic of this possibility generates a change in Yakov. Where once he repudiated his Jewish origins he now affirms them. He is "half Jew himself." Instead of being sickened by Jewish destiny, he now "pities" his people in their hardships. It is not a curse to be a Jew, though it entails suffering; it is not a curse to be alive, though it entails suffering. In accepting his natural condition he learns how to be a human being. But this does not dispose of another source of limitation—Russian anti-Semitism. This is not part of natural necessity; it is an artificial atmosphere that imposes *un*necessary suffering upon a people because of an accident of birth. Yakov comes to see that it is these artificial conditions of life that must be resisted. And in having Yakov recognize this, Malamud expresses with persuasive clarity what he has referred to in all his novels. Moral behavior is the according of respect and freedom to other men as our condition allows us. As his philosophical guide, Spinoza, might say, Yakov affirms the Jews' right to "live in the world like men." Life grants a certain form of freedom, withholds another form. No society or government has the right to limit the freedom of being a man. And every man who has found his own freedom—who has achieved the "open decision"—has an obligation to achieve that freedom for all. Yakov learns something more than what Frank Alpine and Seymour Levin learned. That is, he goes beyond the mere acceptance of the consequences of being alive: suffering. He takes up an attitude that is implicit with a kind of political action. "He is against those who are against them [the Jews]. He will protect them to the extent that he can. This is his covenant with himself." It is precisely here that Malamud reflects the intellectual construct of the "open decision." First, freedom is not illimitable power, but independence of cynicism, despair, prejudice, tradition. Second, thus free, men enjoy the highest intensity of individual satisfaction available to them. Third, in their freedom, men affirm themselves and others. Men, moreover, have only themselves to trust and cling to. "If God's not a man," says Yakov, "he has to be. Therefore he must endure to the trial and let them confirm his innocence by their lies. He has no future to hold on, wait it out."

His imprisonment teaches Yakov that his suffering might win something for his people. At least if he will not say he is guilty, he will help protect the Jews in one way. He learns, in other words, that he is free to be a man, which is to refuse the artificial limitations upon his inherent freedom even while he embraces the natural ones. He says, along with Camus's rebel, "this far and no farther." But can such learning, he wonders, open the door of his cell and turn him out into the world again? The fact that requires the full measure of human courage is that learning—understanding, awareness, freedom—can not do that, certainly not in his case. It can only illuminate the nature of his situation, not unlock the physical doors of his cell or change the minds of millions of Russians. "Still," thinks Yakov, that is "better than not knowing," for learning to know is part of man's nature, part of that freedom by which he is defined as a human being. When a government tries to limit that freedom, it is tyranny and must be challenged. Thus Yakov lacks the physical freedom to escape the struggle and the strength to bring forth a victory. But he does still possess the human freedom to resist being turned into a puppet, of acting according to what Ken Kesey might call the "things" installed in his head by the "Combine." Instead of confessing a crime he did not commit and implicating millions of other innocent people, instead of feeding social tyranny, instead of committing suicide, Yakov decides to fight by enduring and protesting his innocence. After having tried to escape the human condition, he concludes that "there's no such thing as an unpolitical man, especially a Jew." To be political is not simply to take an active part in one's society, though that is an important factor. To be political, as Spinoza says, is to think. This, explains one of the characters, is the one freedom that Spinoza concedes in the face of necessity. The possession of that freedom helps to define the human being. And Yakov concludes that to possess it is to fight for it: "Where there's no fight for it there's no freedom. What is it Spinoza says? If the state acts in ways that are abhorrent to human nature, it's the lesser evil to destroy it. Death to the anti-Semites! Long live revolution! Long live liberty!"

The Fixer suggests that Malamud has gained a firmer grasp of the human questions—and some of their answers—that he has examined in all of his previous novels. In it Malamud shows the possibility of a heightened effectiveness of the human will. It is true that our natural condition imposes limits upon us which we cannot challenge—that is to say, we cannot "jump free" of ourselves. To these limits we must bow gracefully, affirmatively, with dignity. We must suffer the thwarting of our desires, the destruction of our dreams. It is in the nature of things that we cannot escape from our lives by rejecting them in suicide. It is upon these limits and the need to suffer them that Malamud's attention has been fixed in his previous novels. *The Fixer* says that such sufferance is not retreat and rejection. When artificial limits are invented and then imposed on the individual by a tyrannical state or a prejudiced society, we must mobilize the freedom we do have and resist, for to accept those limitations is not to affirm the human condition, but to cooperate in its destruction. Yakov is free not to *be* what the Russian government would have him be. The human being invests his life with meaning by affirming his natural limitations and by asserting the freedom of his consciousness against artificially imposed limitations. As he makes this investment he becomes more human, for it is by this that we define him. So long as he is free in his own mind and soul he is human. And his humanness is intensified when he recognizes his obligations to help others to their own freedom, for to do so is to affirm his solidarity with all humans.

In that solidarity, as emphasized in the "open decision," lies a high intensity of individual satisfaction.

The issues Saul Bellow[5] takes up in his novels are very much like those with which Malamud is concerned, but Bellow is less attentive to the social obligations of the free individual. In this world men must deal with suffering and humiliation. Our condition is an absurd dialectic between human hopes and the resistance of nature to those hopes. Bellow sees two extreme reactions that one might make to this dialectic. Finding that the world makes it impossible for the human being to fulfill his hopes completely, the individual may become what Herzog calls a "snarling realist," concluding that human life is mean and ignoble, full of degenerate prostitutes whose selfishness and cruelty must be returned in kind. The other extreme reaction is that of the man who cleaves to his hope and rejects the world. In his dissatisfaction with the condition as given, he cultivates a sense of grievance which becomes the center of his moral position. Like Malamud's escapees, he looks for a way out of his world and himself, feeling unjustly treated by a reality which denies him his fondest hopes, seeking to evade the responsibility that is thrust upon him by life.

Bellow examines the machinery of this dilemma and attempts to work out the "best solution" to it. In the seven novels he has written to date, his conclusion is that the solution lies somewhere in the middle ground between the two extremes. The "whole man" neither abandons hope nor seeks to resist nature. He arrives at a higher consciousness similar to that achieved by Yakov Bok. To be human, Bellow might argue, is to attempt to give order and value to life even while we recognize that nature itself will never yield to such order and value. We can neither resist that condition nor repudiate our need for order and value and expect to remain human. Augie March says that you "try out what of human you can live first. And if the highest should come in that empty overheated tavern with its flies and the hot radio buzzing between the plays and plugged beer from Sox Park, what are you supposed to do but take the mixture and say imperfection is always the condition as found; all great beauty too, my scratched eyeballs will always see scratched. And there may gods turn up anywhere." The "highest," as suggested in the "open decision," is human, and human is the paradox of order and chaos. One must make his peace with that paradox. He must accept the responsibility for being what he is, for only each self is its creator, sufferer, enjoyer. It is only in the self that the "highest" appears.

The salient pattern of Bellow's novels is comprised of the main character's attempt, like Malamud's, to free himself from the limits of his condition in order to achieve a "superior" life, some "higher fate" or "grand synthesis." He is then confronted with the impossibility of that achievement. In the confrontation, the issue becomes a question of whether the protagonist will reach that higher consciousness which will illumine the paradox and show him the way toward accepting and affirming it. This pattern turns up in Bellow's first novel, *Dangling Man,* a story written in the form of a diary by Joseph (whose last name we never learn) while he waits suspended for several months to be called into the service during World War II. Joseph has always regarded the "world" as an encumbrance, threatening his importance as an individual and endangering the values that give him that importance. He convinces himself that he can maintain his own personal significance only by preserving his independence from the world. Independence for Joseph is a matter of rejection or evasion of the world, not its affirmation. He conforms outwardly by wearing the "uniform of the times" and doing his job competently, but inwardly cultivating differences. Assigning low value to his world, he treats it with amused tolerance, remaining detached, like a spectator at a comedy. As Joseph sees it, for a man to be truly human he must exist in a "colony of the spirit," to be inhabited by friends who are free from hatred, cruelty, animality—who barricade themselves against the world and its crudeness. From behind such ramparts, Joseph thinks he will find the answer to his basic moral question: "How should a good man live; what ought he to do?" This is the approach to reality that Joseph would take, for he is, like Seymour Levin, a "creature of plans." Joseph's question expresses his central attitude: he looks for the preexistent, abstract imperative, some code to be discovered and lived by.

The general metaphor of the world that Joseph rejects is the war, which is bloody and cruel, and the Army, which would regiment him and deprive him of his freedom. When he is called by the draft, the bureaucracy postpones his final induction, which gives him a chance to work at his "superior" life of reading, writing, and thinking. His wife enthusiastically supports his enterprise, urging him to take advantage of his new "liberty." After a few half-hearted attempts at getting a job—suggesting some anxiety about actually attempting to realize his dream—he isolates himself in his room while Iva works. Now he is all but completely free of the world, but instead of finding his way to the truth or an answer to his question, he simply grows more dispirited. He "dangles."

Joseph has assumed that the world is a drag upon one's better part, and that, freed from the drag, one can find fulfillment. There is, however, no freedom in isolation, and no fulfillment apart from the human condition "as found." Like Ebenezer Cook's concept of ideal Truth and Beauty, the "old" Joseph's plans for a "colony of the spirit" cannot work because they do not "take into account all that was natural, including corruptness." The ground of our existence is the world. It imposes limits upon our hopes—what Joseph calls "suffering and humiliation." But no one can "plead for exception" from these limits; "that was not a human privilege." The colony of the spirit is such a plea. But if one cannot be excepted, how does he meet the suffering and humiliation? Joseph's answer: "with grace, without meanness." In his state of "dangling" Joseph has not acquired these virtues. Detaching himself from the flow of life has not taught him to face his condition on his own. The freedom he thought he would have turns out to be chaos and disorder. After nearly a year, he finds it "impossible to resist any longer." He has been evading what he thinks of as the "leash" of the world. Now he turns and slips that leash about his neck, doing so with relief. He asks the draft board to call up his number, and within a fortnight he has submitted himself to regimentation, to the world, to the war: "Perhaps the war could teach me, by violence, what I had been unable to learn during those months in the room. Perhaps I could sound creation through other means. Perhaps. But things were now out of my hands. The next move was the world's. I could not bring myself to regret it."

Joseph moves from one extreme to the other, from the assumption that in complete freedom from the world he can generate his own values and meaning, to the assumption that order can only be given to him by some agent that deprives him of his freedom. But neither extreme carries the "best solution." That would be, writes Joseph, "to live as if the ordinary expectations had not been removed, not from day to day, blindly." That is, the best solution is to be a "creature of plans," but to maintain awareness of the ambivalence and contradictoriness of the real world. Plans must be made, the "ideal construction" must be envisioned, innocence and dreams must be maintained. But one must also keep his "natural shrewdness," a wariness of the world and its suffering and humiliation. A reconciliation of these opposites would free the self from its imprisoning inwardness to participate in the whole world, not just the world that innocence or shrewdness sees. In other words, the subjective values of the "open decision," which are implied in all of Bellow's fiction, do not lead to isolation of the self. Though the highest good is considered to lie in the individual intensity of satisfaction, that satisfaction is not accessible to creatures seeking to exist entirely alone. The achievement of one's "novel aim," as Whitehead puts it, depends largely upon the recognition of the nature of the self—its contradictoriness, its freedom, its limitations, its subjectivity. But it also depends upon a recognition of one's environment, upon which the self relies for the quality of his existence. As one gains confidence in his own individual authenticity and independence, he becomes a better contributor to his society. And as his society is strengthened by his own contribution of freedom and awareness, so is his own capacity expanded to create himself out of ever-widening possibilities. Bellow does not formulate this syllogism explicitly. It lies unstated, however, in all his work. Joseph is an example of one who fails to find the middle ground, for he tries to do it in isolation. He puts himself at last into someone else's hands, unable to achieve the "self-mastery" required for the reconciliation between his desire for order and the world that refuses him what he considers to be his individuality. He fails to find an acceptable moral position because he refuses to accept the conditions of the "open decision."

To a degree, Asa Leventhal, in *The Victim*, fails in the same manner. He resists a world that is analogous to that from which Joseph tries to withdraw, a world—in Asa's words—of "the lost, the outcast, the overcome, the effaced, the ruined." Like Joseph,

Asa is afraid of falling into this world and losing his self-importance, being subjected to its suffering and humiliation. Asa wants to be more than his condition will permit him to be; he wants to confine himself only to the pleasant and the self-aggrandizing. A phrase that Joseph used to describe his "old" self applies to Asa: "a person greatly concerned with keeping intact and free of encumbrance a sense of his own being, its importance." The world of the outcast, like the war and the service for Joseph, would negate that freedom and diminish that importance. Asa sees that world as a kind of "Mother Night," a ubiquitous threat to his own wavering flame. He is horrified by it, frightened of its meaninglessness and purposelessness. He recalls it in vivid terms: "images of men wearily sitting on mission benches waiting for their coffee in a smeared and bleary winter sun; of flophouse sheets and filthy pillows: hideous cardboard cubicles painted to resemble wood. . . . And if it were *his* flesh on those sheets, *his* lips drinking that coffee, *his* back and thighs in that winter sun, *his* eyes looking at the boards of the floor . . . ?" It is not the principle of that world Asa fears, it is the immediate felt presence of himself experiencing it.

Fearing ignominy, Asa always seeks for the "advantage" over people, is quick to take offense, to feel he is not being given his due respect. To preserve his self-importance he frequently takes on a disagreeable pugnacity. This characteristic, the result of his fear of the "outcast" world, leads to the episode that brings about the crisis chronicled by the novel. Out of a job and feeling self-conscious about it, Asa is on the verge of entering the world he so dreads. Kirby Allbee, a superficial acquaintance, sets up an interview with Mr. Rudiger, Allbee's employer, It is clear to Asa, however, that Rudiger wants no part of him. In the ensuing discussion Asa interprets the other man's remarks as insults, causing him to believe what he was afraid of believing: that he is worthless. To compensate for his feeling of inadequacy—to avoid being humiliated—Asa strikes back, will not "let his nose be pulled." He enrages Rudiger by insulting him. In turn, Rudiger fires Allbee, convinced that the two had planned the course the interview takes. Several years later, Allbee re-enters Asa's life, having lost his most recent job, his wife, and what little money he had. Now he is destitute and he blames Asa for it.

Allbee is the symbol of Asa's outcast world turning now to lay the guilt upon Asa for, as he often feels, having "got away" with not serving his time in that world, for luckily and through no effort of his own escaping "that part of humanity of which he was frequently mindful. . . ." Asa has always avoided this world, making "things easier for himself, toning down, softening, looking aside." Another symbol of that world is the fatal illness of his nephew Mickey. At the same time Allbee appears, Mickey becomes sick. Asa is now confronted with a "showdown," a "crisis" on two fronts, forcing him to face the world he has so long sought to evade.

This confrontation is most effectively forced by Allbee. When Asa returns to his apartment one evening to find Allbee with a whore he becomes infuriated and throws them out. It is not the moral issue that upsets him. They represent, in their destitute sordidness, the world he is trying to escape: they appear to him "out of a depth of life in which he himself would be lost, choked, ended. There lay the horror, evil, all that he had kept himself from." The key phrase here is "depth of life." The deep life is the full life of the whole spectrum of existence, embracing the outcast as well as the rich man, and all human beings are exposed to that life. It is this fullness and depth that Asa fears. It shows itself to him as a suffocating, destructive power. At times when that life is too close to him, he comes up short of breath, feels his heart beat painfully in his chest, and finds it necessary to get into the open for fresh air. As it was for Joseph, so for Asa: life is a drag upon what he takes to be his best self and he seeks to escape that drag. He does so, as Allbee says, by keeping his "spirit under lock and key," never taking risks. "Nothing dangerous and nothing glorious. Nothing ever tempts you," says Allbee, "to dissolve yourself."

But why should Asa feel guilty about not spending any time as an outcast? Why should it be a "fault" to resist that world? The answers come indirectly from old Mr. Schlossberg, the drama critic, who articulates Bellow's basic moral position. To want to be more than human, says Schlossberg in a familiar vein, is to want to be a god, free of diseases, of sweat, of dying. To be less than human is to be bereft of feelings, hopes, plans. "It's bad to be less than human and it's bad to be more than human." Human existence is good in itself, needs no art to make it more than it is. "Good acting," says the old man, thinking of the theater, "is what is exactly human. And if you say I am a tough critic, you mean I have a high opinion of what is human. This is my whole idea. More than human, can you have any use for life? Less than human, you don't either." Life, he goes on, implies death. Human life is defined by the bounds of birth and death. A person is what he exists between these bounds. If he wants to be free of death like a god, he wants exemption from life. "I was born once and I will die once," says Schlossberg. "You want to be two people? More than human? Maybe it's because you don't know how to be one." It is knowing how to be one human being that must precede all moral action.

Though Schlossberg's words are not addressed to Asa, they apply to him. Asa does not know how to be one person, for he wants to be excepted from much of what life entails—suffering and humiliation, the analogies to death. As Joseph says, the human being cannot plead for exception from these things. The irony in Asa's case is that the only way one achieves fulfillment is by risking the self in life. Asa himself sees this, and likens the situation to wrapping a mirror in a blanket. It is less likely to get broken but it will never flash either: ". . . nothing really good was safe." Life is by definition the endangerment of its most fragile beauties. Endangerment entails responsibility; that is, risk means that you are responsible for your actions. Mickey's illness and death are examples. They come about "because" his parents got married and gave him life. Though they did not intend this result, nevertheless they have to pay the suffering for it. It might be "unfair" to hold a person accountable for a situation not intended in the original act, but human existence is such that a debt must be paid. One cannot decline to pay. To ask exemption from that debt is to ask suspension of our humanness. Asa "liked to think 'human' meant accountable in spite of many weaknesses—at the last moment, tough enough to hold," tough enough to accept the responsibility that we do not ask for.

Allbee delivers Asa his bill for that interview with Rudiger specifically, and for his condition as a human being in general. To be himself to the full, to become whole, Asa must take up an attitude of willingness to accept the responsibility. He must assimilate what Allbee stands for—"all being." This does not mean that one courts misfortune or that paying the debt is joyous. Life hurts. Asa does admit the fact that his interview with Rudiger had the effect, whatever Asa's intention, of causing Allbee to lose his job. And he does loan Allbee money, even takes him into his apartment for a time. But one's responsibility extends to only so many acts. Allbee must do a little paying himself. Instead, he abuses Asa's hospitality, refuses to assume any of the responsibility, continues to blame Asa, and keeps breaking his many promises to "change."

The Victim contains no firm resolution. In a sense, Asa is "tough enough to hold." When Allbee returns later in the evening after the episode with the whore, he attempts to commit suicide with the gas from the stove, oblivious to the danger to Asa asleep in the bedroom. Assuming that Allbee wanted to kill him, too, Asa throws him out again and this time he does not return. In the years following this crisis, Asa loses "the feeling that he had 'got away with it,' his guilty relief, and the accompanying sense of infringement." Though he does not become "affable," he dismisses much of his old pugnacity. He seems reconciled to the possibilities of life that he so long fled. But at this point in his career, Bellow has not quite seen through to the clear affirmation of the paradox. He does in his next novel, *The Adventures of Augie March.* I shall, however, delay discussion of that work in order to take up now *Seize the Day,* a short novel which fits better with *Dangling Man* and *The Victim* than with *Augie March, Henderson the Rain King, Herzog,* and *Mr. Sammler's Planet.*

Seize the Day is a portrait of Tommy Wilhelm, a man who is not tough enough to hold, who demands exemption from his payments and, when that exemption is refused, surrenders himself to tears. A chronic maker of mistakes, he always looks to someone else to pay his debts. A failure at nearly everything he has tried, including marriage, he arrives broke and over forty to put up at the retirement hotel where his widowered father stays. He pleads unsuccessfully for money, needing funds for his getaway. The world he attempts to escape from is the world of his own character, and once more the central issue is self-importance. Perhaps, thinks Tommy, his "business of life" might be "to carry his peculiar burden, to feel shame and impotence, to taste these quelled tears." "Maybe the making of mistakes expressed the very purpose of his life and the essence of his being here." If this is so, he cannot face it. He tries to withdraw from the pain of his own making into the "pure" and the "beautiful," seeking respite either in "those marvelous, foolish wasted days" of the past, when he thought he could escape the average, or in some future in which he will be freed from his mistakes by a lucky windfall.

Hoping for just such a windfall, he puts his last cash in the hands of the dubious Dr. Tamkin, who promises him a killing on the stock market that will give him financial security for the rest of his life. Part of Tamkin's dubiousness comes from his own philosophy. He advises Tommy to "seize the day," uncritically to accept nature, which knows only the present: "You must go along with the actual, the Here-and-Now, the glory." While this might be a provocative antidote for Tommy, who refuses to face the present, it is of questionable value in the long run, and suggests a kind of existentialism for which Bellow finds no sympathy. Unconditional acceptance of the present leaves no room for values, no way for the human being to create his own identity. Some resistance to one's condition, as Camus says, is necessary. Unconditional acceptance is not shouldering responsibility, but escaping from it; not an affirmation of the human condition, but a debasement of it. Tamkin confirms this judgment by turning out to be nothing but a thief. Tommy gives him his last reserves for a questionable stock deal, and Tamkin runs off with it, leaving Tommy destitute and helpless.

Tommy does not deny his mistake, but he does deny that he should suffer for it more than he already has. Though it tortures him to turn to his unsympathetic father again for help, he justifies doing so by saying that once he admits his mistakes, he should no longer be blamed for them. If, he reasons, making mistakes is his character, then he cannot change it. And anything he cannot change he ought not be held responsible for. But life does not understand the human meaning of "ought." Rewards and punishments for good and bad acts do not figure into nature's ways. It demands payment of debts incurred and Tommy is caught inexorably in that demand. In wanting to be exempt from the debt, he yearns to escape what he is. He feels trapped, like Yakov Bok and Seymour Levin, by his own being.

Pursuing Dr. Tamkin through the crowds on New York's streets, he is shouldered into a synagogue where a funeral is taking place. Now he is confronted with the ultimate evidence of the inescapability of the human condition. Propelled by the line of mourners past the casket, in a rush of sentiment Tommy identifies himself with the corpse. He begins to weep, at first for the dead man—"a human creature"—then for himself and his plight: "What'll I do? I'm stripped and kicked out. . . . Oh, Father, what do I ask of you? . . . Why, why, why—you must protect me against that devil [Tommy's wife] who wants my life. If you want it, then kill me. Take, take it, take it from me." Tommy's "prayer" is a metaphor of the unwillingness of the twentieth-century man to surrender his conviction that God might suspend His rules and confer grace, relieving the human being of having to live "without appeal." Tommy is like Rabbit Angstrom, but instead of running he weeps. Also like Rabbit, Tommy experiences an exhilaration in surrendering to the easiest thing. Melodramatically, consumed with self-pity, Tommy sinks deeper into weeping, like a child hiding "himself in the center of a crowd by the great and happy oblivion of tears," sinking "toward the consummation of his heart's ultimate need." That need is the surrender to the overwhelming sense of being unjustly victimized, of being called upon to pay a debt which he "ought" not have to pay. Tommy Wilhelm is the picture of a man unable to transcend his condition into a higher consciousness, totally frustrated by being denied his escape.

The main issue in these three novels is the way the human being *feels* about his inescapable condition, the attitude he takes up toward it. Joseph gladly puts himself into someone else's hands. Asa Leventhal, confronted with his debt even while trying to escape it, at least partially acquires the strength for affirmation. Tommy Wilhelm crumbles into tears, unable to bear not escaping. In all of these characters there is a defect of consciousness which blocks the "best solution" to living in the world. And in none of them do we get a sense of improved understanding of the self's relationship to others, to his society. *The Adventures of Augie March* is given over to an examination of removing the defect of consciousness and discovering the appropriate solution, through which the individual may accept his condition and take up more satisfactory ties with others. One side of Augie is very much like Joseph, Asa, and Tommy. His "adventures" are a search for "consummation," for, as Tommy might say it, his "special business," for a " 'higher' independent fate." The ideal Augie seeks is a state of equilibrium, of what Sartre calls "repose," freedom from striving and searching. ". . . my hope," says Augie, "is based upon getting to be still. . . . When striving stops, the truth comes as a gift—bounty, harmony, love, and so forth." In search of consummation, Augie spends his time "trying various things on," looking for his fate to reveal itself.

On the face of it, Augie tries to escape the given condition—Joseph's and Asa's "world." And many of his self-appointed teachers are not slow to admonish him. His brother Simon attempts to persuade him to be more practical. In always "looking for the best there is," says Simon, "everything else gets lost." Sophie Geratis, one of Augie's girl friends, comments: "Nothing is ever good enough for you to stick to." Manny Padilla tries to persuade him that he thinks too much of purity, that he is "too ambitious." If he does not get what he wants he blames himself "too hard" rather than admitting that it is simply not there in the world to get. Clem Tambow jokes about Augie's search for a "worth-while fate," claiming that he has a "nobility syndrome. You can't adjust to the reality situation." The main gist of this criticism is that Augie is naively "trying to cheer up the dirty scene." Mimi Villars, whom Augie helps to get an abortion, tells him that he refuses to see reality accurately because he cannot love it as it exists. The "challenge," she says, is not to try to make that reality better in your mind through fantasy, but to put everything into the picture, as Joseph admonishes himself to do in *Dangling Man*—in Mimi's words: "the bad, the criminal, sick, envious, scavenging, wolfish, the living-on-the-dying."

This advice has a limited amount of validity, but Augie is not really the one who needs it. Thea Fenchel, whom he accompanies to Mexico, is a better example of the character who seeks to escape from a world she does not like. She is certain "that there must be something better than what people call reality," some "better, nobler reality." For Thea that higher reality exists in the courage she finds to be inherent in nature. She spends much of her time trying to harness that courage, trapping snakes and training the great eagle, Caligula, to hunt giant lizards. She is unable to tolerate any violations of her expectations. When Caligula displays more discretion than courage in his first encounters with the wild lizards, Thea is enraged and will have nothing more to do with the bird. If nature does not fit the construction she puts upon it, she does not modify her construction; she simply rejects the offender. When Augie, like the eagle, fails her expectations, she rejects him, too.

Augie does not resist reality. He recognizes, with Asa, that the ideal "is harmed by what it suffers on the way to proof." But this is no reason either to abandon the ideal, which his friends apparently want him to do, or reject the world, like Thea does. The human being is condemned to live in the world. In order to do so he needs some construction to make his life meaningful, even possible: "External life being so mighty, the instruments so huge and terrible, the performances so great, the thoughts so great and threatening, you produce someone who can exist before it. You invent a man who can stand before the terrible appearances." In Augie's scheme of things, that strength comes from the ground of the individual's being, the permanent but frequently obscured grid of "axial lines": "Truth, love, peace, bounty, usefulness, harmony!" Once a man uncovers these lines, thinks Augie, "He will live with true joy. Even his pains will be joy if they are true, even his helplessness will not take away his power, even wandering will not take him away from himself, even the big social jokes and hozes need not make him ridiculous, even disappointment after disappointment need not take away his love. Death will not be terrible to him if life is not." This is the equilibrium that Augie seeks.

Augie's ideal is not a means of escaping the world, but of finding a way to live in it affirmatively and richly. But the ideal contains a defect, which Augie sees all too clearly. The irony is that the axial lines can be found only if the person is "still," and Augie cannot be still. "Maybe," he thinks, "I can't take these very things I want." If character is fate, as Augie maintains, then his fate is not simplicity and equilibrium, but complexity and striving. Augie's situation at the end of the novel reflects just this irony. He and his wife Stella have taken up residence in Paris, Stella working in second rate French films as an actress. Augie is still "a person of hope, and now my hopes have settled themselves upon children and a settled life." The fulfillment of his hope requires that he and Stella return to America and make their home. But Stella will have nothing to do with this. She has her own "special business" to find. They will stay in Paris and Augie will continue his "striving," harming his ideal of simplicity and rest in the search for it.

There is a way to unify this typically human situation and avoid despair or cynicism—through humor. Though nature, says Augie, might think "it can win over us and the power of hope," we generally "refuse to lead a disappointed life." This insight provokes in Augie the "*animal ridens*." But what exactly is the laughter about? The futility of either nature or the human being? There is no answer; it "is an enigma which includes both." The human being laughs and in laughing embraces his condition, affirming it in good nature, recognizing its limits and striving to go beyond them. Hope, plans, details—they are as much a part of the human condition as the world's negation of them. Their value lies not in their promise to transform the world, but in what they are, in the attitude they create, in their power to make the world human without mistaking it for something other than it is.

Augie arrives at the "open decision," at a higher state of consciousness than do Joseph, Asa, or Tommy, and because of that he lives more richly, though perhaps no more comfortably, with the ambiguity of the conflict between his hopes and the world he lives in. His consciousness savors the humor of the human condition and relishes the variety it presents at the same time he looks for simplicity. Moreover, he has acquired a foundation for moral action —that is, the "open decision." But there is no real conclusion to his story. It does not end; it stops. His adventures, like his life, are open—as Augie calls his existence, "free-style." *Henderson the Rain King* and *Herzog* bring human consciousness one more step toward the fusion of order and chaos in the mind and provide the resolved conclusion that *Augie March* does not.

Henderson, like Augie, is a restless striver, full of energy and strength. Yet, for all his ebullience, he is impatient with and frightened of the world, calling it a "mighty oppressor." He has spent his life trying to evade it. His evasion, he says, has taken the form of trying to remain a child (very much like Tommy Wilhelm), for children stay free of the world by making life "strange," by looking at it as a fairly tale in which secret forces are in control and relieve them of responsibility. Henderson dreads the world "because of death," and tries to keep it mysterious, as a child does. Says Henderson, "I have never been at home in life. All my decay has taken place upon a child." King Dahfu, the African king of the Wariris, tells him, "You did not believe you had to perish." And he himself realizes that he guided himself by "unreality," a "scheme for a troubled but eternal life." Henderson's spirit is asleep in strangeness, unreality. He rejects that higher consciousness that would put him in touch with reality—with pain, violence, death. But like all of Bellow's protagonists so far discussed, he suffers in his evasion. By the time Bellow writes *Henderson the Rain King*, he sees more explicitly what his characters must do to achieve a high intensity of satisfaction. Henderson is driven by a voice that cries, "*I want*," but does not tell him what it "wants." To learn that, he must, as his voice urges him to do, "burst the spirit's sleep."

The first stage of his education comes when he journeys to Africa and meets the gentle cow-worshippers, the Arnewi. From them Henderson learns "grun-tu-molani," the desire to live. This is not the desire for immortality, but for life as it is given, with all its limits and disappointments. His teacher is Queen Willatale, whose wisdom embraces all things: male and female, life and death, joy and sorrow. She is the female principle whose serenity is a kind of animal being: around her plenteous body is draped, symbolically, a lion skin. But there is a defect in Willatale's animal power, suggested by a cataract in her eye that blurs her vision. Her essence is quietude, not action. She makes no attempt, for example, to rid the village's water supply of the frogs infesting it. The tribe cannot allow the sacred cattle to drink impure water and the animals are rapidly dying off. The village suffers sorrow and tears. Willatale merely smiles. In quietude, she accepts all states unconditionally. But without action, which for a human being implies plan, value, and goal, her existence is its own victim. Where humans typically feel compelled to move to sustain themselves and their values, Willatale sits contentedly at rest. She has "no anxious care." What Willatale can teach Henderson is too limited to serve him, much as Dr. Tamkin's advice to Tommy Wilhelm is defective though not irrelevant. The sign that Willatale's serenity is not altogether valid for Henderson is his own impulsive action. Without taking into account important details, and still wanting, childishly, to be a savior, Henderson attempts to rid the cistern of its frogs, but in the attempt destroys the cistern itself. If Willatale refuses to act, Henderson acts impetuously. His education is far from complete.

The desire to live, which Henderson begins to learn from the Arnewi, entails the imperative of learning to face the most terrible of all realities: death, the end of the self. Upon the acceptance of this lies the hope for moral action. Henderson's lesson in this is taught him by King Dahfu through the lioness Atti that Dahfu keeps in an underground den. Like all of Bellow's characters, Henderson has always attempted to insulate himself from the full experience of existence, from being-in-the-world and all the dangers that condition implies. Such insulation is a form of bad faith, a deficiency of consciousness. Atti, says Dahfu, "will make consciousness shine. She will burnish you." Her power lies in the immediate, the throb of life at this second. She sharpens consciousness by forcing "the present moment upon you." Atti is unavoidable reality —the world—a power so tremendous that Henderson is almost prostrated with fear of it. He sees there are no "practical alternatives" to her presence, which he had heretofore always sought, looking for "salvation" from his condition. But Atti—and by analogy his condition—is "unavoidable." Nor does Atti herself try to avoid. She "Does not take issue with the inherent. Is one hundred per cent within the given." Atti is "still," filling her being completely, planning no changes and looking to no future, a kind of Sartrean "in-itself." In urging Henderson to imitate Atti, to "be" the lion, Dahfu demonstrates his similarity to Willatale. Atti, like Willatale, has no "anxious care." And Dahfu, who seeks the repose of the animal, lies among his many naked wives "sumptuously at rest."

Like Willatale and Atti, Dahfu accepts his situation unconditionally. But, as with Willatale, however much he has to teach Henderson, his lesson contains what for Henderson is a defect. Before he can be confirmed fully as king of the tribe, Dahfu must go into the bush to capture a grown lion said to be the soul of his predecessor. This is one of the traditional rigid conditions of the tribe's system. Dahfu has not yet done this. Moreover, he has angered the tribe's priests by insisting upon keeping Atti, a violation of the system. As a result, the priests are engaged in a plot to take Dahfu's life. Getting wind of this conspiracy, Henderson rushes to inform Dahfu. Dahfu's response to Henderson's excited warning is to introduce him to Atti in order to illustrate how one may protect himself from fear. Like Willatale, who neglects to act against the frogs, Dahfu neglects to act against the priests' plot. In his philosophy the plot is not something one takes precautions against, any more than one takes precautions against reality and the death it presupposes. Thus, when Dahfu goes into the bush after Gmilo, the lion in which his father's soul supposedly lives, he refuses to take steps to protect himself against the conspiracy. The priests fix the trap; it fails to hold; Dahfu is killed by Gmilo.

But Henderson has more to learn than the unconditional acceptance urged on him by Dahfu, and he learns it through Gmilo rather than Atti. Compared with the great beast Gmilo, Atti is a pale copy of reality, reality under control. Accompanying Dahfu in his last encounter with Gmilo, Henderson is at last brought face to face with the staggering power of the wild male lion in the bush, and its tremendous force batters "at the very doors of [Henderson's] consciousness." Henderson sees now that his search for reality has been only pretense. That is why his voice cried "I want." His spirit was asleep. Confronted with the lion's roar, he is "blasted away" from his former avoidance. He bursts his spirit's sleep. But does this mean that he must place himself on the altar of that reality like a sacrificial victim? Dahfu, too much confined by the pampered feminineness of Atti, did. Having been awakened by the roar of Gmilo, Henderson arrives at a higher consciousness. As Rain King, Henderson will succeed Dahfu, but he does not accept the inheritance of that danger nor the enmity of the priests. He rejects the assumption that his death at this point and at this time is inevitable, threatened as he is by the still plotting priests. Ironically, he attributes his rejection to his own deficiency—that he has burst his spirit's sleep too late to be able to face death as Dahfu has. For Henderson, however, this is no deficiency. His fate lies in America. He has stilled the voice, seen reality, faced death. He is reborn. He engineers his escape, carrying away with him the lion cub that was supposed to be presented to the tribe as Dahfu's soul, taking back with him a knowledge of animality that helped him burst the spirit's sleep, but does not dominate him.

Mere knowledge and acceptance of the human condition are not the foundations of the higher consciousness and a more intense individual satisfaction. Henderson, like Augie, had sought to become a "Be-er," to find repose and stillness. But for the human being there is no state of absolute rest. Existence is defined as openness and possibility—action of some kind. As Joseph writes in *Dangling Man*, "Continued life means expectation. Death means abolition of choice." Death is an inescapable factor in life, but before death, life is becoming, not being, and becoming is a mixture of the power of animality and the vision of the intellect which looks to the future, which says that one has other possibilities than those already realized. The human being, at the very moment he accepts the inherent, does take issue with it. Death may be the inescapable boundary of life, but there is no need to avoid using hopes and plans to widen that boundary—as Willatale and Dahfu do not. Death need not be courted. Dahfu is altogether too comfortable with the inherent. The human being is restless and seeking. He must not try to run, but at the same time, he must not abjectly submit. His animality must be energized by thought.

Henderson's experience illustrates the relationship between the values disclosed by the metaphysics of the "open decision" and the society in which those values are to be guides. Before he left America, Henderson was "asleep," unconscious, outside of the "open decision." He felt caught in the stifling embrace of the American social apparatus, unable either to fulfill himself or to contribute to the fulfillment of others. He went away from that America, bracketed it, and located the core of his own authenticity, which lay in his acceptance of the elements of his condition as defined by the "open decision"—that is, death, violence, chance, ignorance. That discovery, however, though it does bring with it a degree of satisfaction, is not the novel aim of Henderson as an individual entity. That aim, Bellow suggests, cannot be achieved outside of America and the society from which Henderson first fled. The possibility for moral action, the possibility of self-fulfillment, and the possibility of contributing to the value of that society are now increased for Henderson through his affirmation of himself and his condition. He returns to America with a "saner relation" to it.

Herzog comes closer than Bellow's previous characters to the "best solution" for living in the world, and perhaps is his best representative of the "open decision." In the familiar pattern, Herzog has spent most of his life as an avoider, possessed of an "infantile fear of death" that sent him for refuge in the "child-man," hiding from a nasty world in abstractions like "truth, friendship, devotion to children." He seeks explanations that will soften the harshness of life, refuses to accept pain and death and sorrow as necessary to the human condition. He is bedeviled by emotions that he tries to escape, complains of his "throb-heartedness," his vulnerability to being hurt. He deplores the confusion he is thrown into by his feelings. Outside of himself the world, too, disturbs and confuses him. In a courtroom he sees that world in its most sordid aspects. It is a scene that recalls the vivid visions of skid row that plagued Asa Leventhal. Coming before the bar of justice are outcasts wholly alien to Herzog's world—two drunk Negroes involved in robbing each other, a respectable laboratory worker caught in immoral practices in a men's toilet, a male prostitute apprehended trying to rob a department store counter, and a sullen stupid woman accused of beating her child to death. The tragedy of these people is that, as Herzog says, they have fallen asleep in the "thick embrace" of "Reality." They are overwhelmed by its mightiness and have become either totally cynical and hopeless or quite unconscious and helpless. In Henderson's words, the world for Herzog—both internal and external—is a "mighty oppressor." But at least he has not lost his consciousness.

Herzog the "child-man" erects a protective order about himself, claiming an innocence too delicate to be exposed to the coarse world unsupported and unprotected. He receives assistance from those who are willing to protect him by telling him softening lies. He is always on the lookout for advice and help, seeking to put himself into other people's hands, as Joseph finally does. Examined by a doctor and given a clean bill of health, he is disappointed, for he had hoped to go to a hospital so that he "would not have to look after himself." Besides other people's protective lies, Herzog's order is made up of intellectual abstractions, formed in the process of thinking and used to cushion him against the pained confusion of his feelings and the frightening violations of civilized intelligence found on the streets of any city. He sees his book on Romanticism as a "grand synthesis," an "example of order." As the architect of that synthesis, he childishly thinks of himself as a savior, perhaps a little more than human. He fancies himself as "the man on whom the world depended for certain intellectual work to change history, to influence the development of civilization." He believes he has been chosen to do "the work of the future. . . . The progress of civilization . . . depended upon the successes of Moses E. Herzog." Herzog has not achieved that higher consciousness that takes "moderation" as its good, that sees the inherent contradiction between the abstract explanation and the "buzzing, blooming confusion" of the experiencing subject.

The novel is about a crisis which virtually compels Herzog to take the final step toward that consciousness. The occasion of that crisis is his divorce from his second wife, Madeleine. His behavior has been typical. For most of the time they are married, Madeleine carries on an affair with the pretentiously emotional Valentine Gersbach, Herzog's best friend and next-door neighbor. Herzog knows nothing of the affair and is stunned when Madeleine orders him to leave and begins divorce proceedings. Months later, as he comes out of his shock, Herzog is seized "by the need to explain, to have it out, to justify, to put in perspective, to clarify, to make amends." To perform this work, he undertakes a series of "letters"—written to famous people and familiar, living and dead, composed in his mind and notebook but never sent. These letters are analogous to the "grand synthesis" his book was to be. Smarting over his failure with Madeleine, he seeks to establish himself as an innocent unjustly pained by a cruel world, to confirm his own guiltlessness, and to explain how others are guilty. His letters are intended to construct a significant order of right and wrong, to pinpoint with unequivocal sharpness truth and falsehood. But that order is a linguistic order, not an existential one. He goes "after reality with language." Through language he means to give himself certain rights to punish those who have wronged him, "to force Madeleine and Gersbach to have a *Conscience*." He conceives a vague plan to shoot both Madeleine and Gersbach, convinced that no one has ever had a more obvious "right" to kill, for they have forced sorrow, pain, humiliation upon him. At the last moment, however, he cannot go through with it, and the reason is significant to the values implied in the "open decision."

By means of his linguistic constructs, Herzog sought to protect himself from any confusion and pain, and to put the blame for things upon the "right" people. In the course of the novel, he learns that no individual can be completely "excepted" from pain. Nor can fault or blame be assigned for this state of things. To wish to punish someone for his own confusions and emotions is childish theatricality. To insist upon absolutely ordering through linguistic abstractions that which is inherently impossible to order—as are his own emotions—is a violation of man's wholeness. He has rejected the human condition and its corollary—human solidarity. Thus, in his search for a grand synthesis, says Herzog, he "committed a sin against his heart." His attempt to explain away his emotions suggests that he thinks their unruliness threatened his existence, as if his existence depended upon complete explanation. Thinking has been his métier and feeling his humiliation. Flooded by emotions, he has always tried to "restore order by turning to his habit of thoughtfulness." But he discovers that even thought can turn into confusion if it becomes "the delusion of total *explanations*." Nor is it a catastrophe that his feelings must always elude thought: He realizes "that he did not need to perform elaborate abstract intellectual work—work he had always thrown himself into as if it were the struggle for survival." He does not need intellectual justification to guarantee his existence.

This conclusion is, for Herzog, "the start of true consciousness," the beginning of a state of "simple, free, intense realization," a high intensity of individual satisfaction through awareness. It is only a start because it is an explanation, and no explanation can be total. Explanations—"grand syntheses"—are "comprehensible," and man is more than can be comprehended. Sounding now like a spokesman for the "open decision's" moderation, Herzog says that man is "more subtle than his models," so much more so that "only the incomprehensible [seems to] give any light." There is something incomprehensible that the heart accepts—that is realizable, subject to awareness—but that cannot be programmed for the intellect. Herzog has spent his life precisely in attempting to program the heart for the intellect, assuming that whatever the intellect could not account for threatened his existence. In looking for merely an intellectual rather than an existential synthesis, Herzog has refused to pay the debt of being human and has lost out on much richness because of it.

As a "victim," Herzog nursed a "sense of grievance" that has been, as he says, the disaster of the present generation. Robbed of its comfortable explanations, subjected to doubting the old grand synthesis of Classical-Judeo-Christian tradition, the present generation, implies Herzog, obviously referring to what he takes to be the hurt pessimism of such literary existentialists as Sartre, feels it has been undeservedly pained. It was just this sense of grievance that

Herzog sought to redress in his revenge against Madeleine and Gersbach, that moved him to look for the grand synthesis in a world which refuses to yield up everything to the intellect. That sense of grievance shatters, however, when Herzog sees himself with a gun in his hand, skulking outside his ex-wife's house, contemplating a melodramatically self-justifying murder. Disgusted with himself, he wonders how those two people could have "broken" his heart. In his new awareness, he says, "No more of that!" No more nursing of grievances, no more complaints of being unjustly hurt.

He retires to his home in the New England Berkshires and there he reaches his most vivid consciousness, which is not simply intellectual. He abandons the melodramatic struggle against his own being and the human condition. Perhaps, he thinks, he can do it only by playing "the instrument I've got." He cannot escape what he is, can expect no one else to take the punishment for his "throb-heartedness." If he is to be human he must accept the conditions imposed, acknowledging his responsibility without trying to destroy or escape. Now he no longer seeks the protection of others nor of his explanations: "I am pretty well satisfied to be, to be just as it is willed, and for as long as I remain in occupancy." Full being —wholeness—is incomprehensible and unexplainable, but it is existable. Having decided to exist it, Herzog diminishes the need for explanation, and in the end he finds, not only that he is in no one's hands but his own, but that he has no messages for anyone. "Nothing. Not a single word."

The break out of the need for total explanation is made by means of that enigmatic laughter pointed to by Augie March. Herzog remembers that his mother had tried to shield him from the pain of living, but showed in her face the sadness that living brings. Her sadness revealed her "submission to the fate of being human," the response of her "finest nerves to the greatness of life, rich in sorrow, in death." The ambivalence expressed in this picture is at the heart of the "open decision." It affirms the value of life without ignoring what life inevitably does to its occupants. What is poignant about his mother's attitude is that there is no melodramatic breastbeating in it, no cries of *mea culpa,* none of the "canned sauerkraut of Spengler's 'Prussian Socialism,' the commonplaces of the Wasteland outlook, the cheap mental stimulants of Alienation, the cant and rant of pipsqueaks of Inauthenticity and Forlornless" that Herzog mentions in another context. His mother fondly regards the human plight with wry humor, not the cry of the victim. To demonstrate the origin of mankind, she does not go to the Bible, does not make its creation heroic. She rubs her palms together until a slight line of dirt gathers. Such is man, springing from that smudge. "Maybe," says Herzog, "she offered me this proof in a spirit of comedy. The wit you can have only when you consider death very plainly, when you consider what a human being really is."

Essentially, Herzog's solution turns out to be just this wit—not the wit that degrades but that that affirms. Consciousness, the central ingredient of wit, when it "doesn't clearly understand what to live for, what to die for, can only abuse and ridicule itself." This is what the snarling realist does, and the "child-man." But abuse and ridicule are beneath the "civilized intelligence." It laughs, but without cynicism or despair. Wit knows what it lives for, looks with fondness upon man sprung from the dirt, involves the whole person in the whole range of experience: sadness, joy, humiliation. It is Huizinga's play, simultaneous commitment and detachment. It is Camus's absurd. It is the hallmark of the highest consciousness and the highest intensity of satisfaction. It is the ability to say that the heart is "contemptibly aching"—as Herzog does—without feeling contempt as the final judgment. It recognizes the desire to be rid of the aching heart at the same time it embraces the heart. It chooses to be, to experience, to exist the condition as given. In *Herzog*, much more than in *Henderson the Rain King*, the emphasis is upon affirmation through acceptance. The Herzog of the novel is the beginning of a new Herzog, who analyzes his old self through the lens of the present, and the judgments he makes are accompanied with laughter. His tone is ironic, occasionally self-effacing; accusatory but not pious or sermonizing. He is never blind to the humor in his pretenses of having been chosen to do "the work of the future," of suffering the injustices of a cruel world. Yet, at the same time he sees the comedy of his seriousness, he can take himself seriously, maintain some self-respect. His final victory is the victory over the theatricality of his former pretensions, his sense of grievance, his "victim bit." More than any other Bellow protagonist, Herzog manages to reconcile himself to an existence he sought to escape. In that reconciliation, he affirms life by accepting its conditions, and opens up the way for a more intense satisfaction through the data of this existence.

Bellow does not make an explicit issue in his novels of the moral relationship between the individual and others. He is more concerned with the success of his characters in "bursting their spirit's sleep" as preparation for a more intensely satisfying and, by implication, a more moral life. But as it does for most of his contemporaries, such an achievement comes with a higher consciousness made up of the paradoxes of "moderation" and a freedom from fears of the human condition. And the desire of both Henderson and Herzog for a life of "service" suggests the direction in which Bellow's moral sensibilities tend—toward an identification of a "generality of outlook" (that is to say, service) with a "morality of outlook."

The question of that service and that outlook is taken up again in Bellow's most recent novel, *Mr. Sammler's Planet.* We can place it in the context of Bellow's first novel, *Dangling Man.* "How should a good man live; what ought he to do?" asks Joseph. Twenty-six years later, Bellow's protagonist, grown to an old man in his seventies, a Jew who has miraculously escaped from death at the hands of the Germans and virtually come back from the dead, a commentator on the human condition who has experienced that condition stripped of its adornments in the moment of death, answers: A good man ought to live by "Feeling, outgoingness, expressiveness, kindness, heart." The "service" of *Henderson* and *Herzog* is this: being human toward other human beings, loving them, being kind to them, showing affection, compassion, and understanding. This simple knowledge is what the higher consciousness, the civilized sensibility, the human *being,* after facing the "oppressive world" that is the hallmark terror of Bellow's people, finally and vividly identifies as the ground of a high intensity of individual satisfaction and the moral basis of behavior.

This uncomplicated moral outlook, which other ages have called charity and which is so explicitly formulated by Artur Sammler, has lain implicit in all of Bellow's novels. The nature of man, pictured as a restless questing creature in a constant search for the repose of total explanation, has been Bellow's most explicit theme. Mr. Sammler, like his predecessors, rejects total explanation as neither possible nor desirable. Instead, he seizes upon service. There is, in Mr. Sammler, the same horror of the world as Bellow's other people feel, of death, of the end of himself. But, now a septuagenarian, he has put this aside. His attention is focused upon more basic, simpler things. His "planet" is the world of the United States, to which he has come as a displaced person from the hell of war-time and post-war Europe. But he feels a stranger here, always wondering if his reactions are normal, or even valid. His world ended in 1939, and his escape from being buried alive by the Nazis literally puts him on borrowed time. This strangeness makes him an appropriate judge of the modern scene, an appropriate asker of the question originally posed by Joseph. It is also right that he come from another period of time, one we associate with a calmer atmosphere and a more stable sense of right and wrong.

The world that Mr. Sammler sees about him is one in which a cult of individuality holds sway, characterized by "a fever of originality," "a strange desire for originality, distinction, *interest*." Mr. Sammler is most disappointing when he deals with the modern scene. Perhaps his being an old man justifies the old-man crotchetiness of his attacks upon mini-skirts and free love. Wanting to be an individual is fine, but, he cries, "In these poor forms? Dear God! With hair, with clothes, with drugs and cosmetics, with genitalia, with round trips through evil, monstrosity, and orgy, with even God approached through obscenities?" Wherever one's sympathies lie in this matter, there is something too topical and too superficial about these trivial and ephemeral symbols of a particular culture. And Mr. Sammler's reflections are not worthy of the universality of his basic outlook. Are we to take seriously his request that his cousin Angela not wear her mini-skirt into her dying father's hospital room? Are not mini-skirts, long hair, genitalia, even a certain sexual monstrosity simply part of that world-weight that shows itself with such comic intensity to so many of Bellow's characters? Indeed, Bellow is never without this comic sense. Mr. Sammler's daughter, Shula, forty years old and separated from her husband, is so obsessed with her illusion of her father's supposed memoir of H. G. Wells that she steals an invaluable manuscript thinking it indispensable to her father's work. His young nephew, Wallace Gruner, with plenty of money and brains, undertakes zany schemes in an atmosphere of indulgent permissiveness. His young friend

Feffer is one of those many con men that delightfully people Bellow's world. This may be a crazy world, but it is not evil, only comic. Why must Bellow bring his biggest guns to bear upon such specific transgressions as long hair and short skirts?

What is important about his criticism is his contention that an excessive individualism can lead to evil. In Mr. Sammler's example, we can see how close Herzog came to this evil. To head up their extermination camp at Lodz, the Germans appointed a Jew, Rumkowski, a failure as a man and possessed of a grotesque sense of fun and his own importance. He made a macabre comedy out of the camp. He was like "a mad Jewish king presiding over the death of half a million people." He was poisoned by a destructive "theatricality," the very motive that drove Herzog to plan on killing Madeleine and Gersbach. Sammler finds in Rumkowski an early example "of our modern individuality boom." He killed people in a hideous comic game as an accent to his own personality. How are we to explain this boom? As Sammler sees it, the forms of behavior available to modern humanity are weak, and there is a "pitiable lack of confidence" in those that are available. Without stronger forms, people, in their impotence, assert their personality ever more loudly and wildly. It is just that sense of impotence that leads Asa Leventhal to play the game of self-importance, which for Sammler leads, in this modern age of exaggerated individuality, to the most brutal and cruel consequences. The extreme acts of a Rumkowski, figured forth in less lethal forms in long hair, "shit" philosophy, and the trading of sex partners, reflect a quality of the human being that for Bellow is most inhibiting to the growth toward a higher consciousness—the desire to drop out, to divorce oneself from life. Such extreme behavior, as illustrated in the deadly theatricality of Rumkowski, is anti-life. This Mr. Sammler rejects. To counter it, he would employ an "ethical life," echoing, again, Joseph. "As long as there is no ethical life," says Mr. Sammler, "and everything is poured so barbarously and recklessly into personal gesture this must be endured."

Asa Leventhal describes the ethical life as the one which is, in the eye of crisis, "strong enough to hold." Herzog decides, finally, after freeing himself from the "delusion of total explanation," that he is content merely to be "as it is willed." Both of these phrases are relevant to Mr. Sammler's conception of the ethical life. But he carries the definition farther, to its simplest and most profound form. The ethical life is that which embraces the human condition, which is made up of "longing, suffering, mourning," which "come from need, affection, and love—the needs of the living creature, because it *is* a living creature." It does not divorce itself from the human in excessive individuality or absolute explanation. It also recognizes that, though "All is not flatly knowable," yet there are "adumbrations" that send it inquiring into the future, into other states of being. The ethical life is made up of this paradox. At its heart is a duty to being an individual in the correct and untheatrical way, an acceptance of the conditions of the human state. Every man has a capacity to fulfill this duty, but not every man is capable of doing so. Perhaps the most important point of all is the fact that every man knows that duty which is the essence of the ethical life.

This point is made in the final words of the novel, to which its actions lead. But the force of those words rests on what happens before they appear. In a flashback, Mr. Sammler kills a man, when he himself, a Polish partisan fighting against the Germans, was "nearly a corpse," and "not entirely human." He killed a German soldier when that soldier had begged for his life. Unexplainably, Sammler had felt an ecstasy in that action and had himself received life, both literally and symbolically. The knowledge of one's duty to the human condition cannot obscure the sad fact that there is no unity in human society, no splash of God, as Sammler puts it, that we all share as our most precious birthright. The fact that when it comes to our life or someone else's, we will choose our own life—that, indeed, such choices are part of the terms of our existence—makes our pursuit of the ethical life terribly difficult and our knowledge of that duty doubly painful.

What is the reader to make of the black pickpocket Sammler inadvertently observes plying his trade on a bus? How does he contribute to the force of the novel's final words? Sammler is fascinated. Secretly even to himself he seeks out the man again, this time drawing the huge thief's attention. Dressed in bright colors and the most recent fashion, the black man has the audacious air of a confident aristocrat, scorning, in his skill, not only the laws that prohibit his life style, but also detection in violating those laws. Seeing Sammler seeing him, he follows the old man home, and there crowds Sammler into a corner and silently, wordlessly, displays his penis, parades as a warning that great phallic power. Sammler understands and takes the warning. The pickpocket occupies the combined roles of Dahfu and the great lion Gmilo in *Henderson.* Later, Feffer, the salesman of "interest" and "individuality," tries to photograph the pickpocket at work. He gets two shots, but the black man pins him against the bus and tries to force the camera out of his hand. Sammler is disgusted with Feffer's theatricality, which is related to that of Rumkowski but here less noxious. As for the black man, he is magnificent. That huge strong man, like Gmilo in the bush, is irresistibly there in tremendous physical vividness. Like Henderson, Sammler thinks, "How consciousness was lashed by such a fact!" Sammler sees him as a prince: "The clothing, the shades, the sumptuous colors, the barbarous-majestical manner. He was probably a mad spirit. But mad with an idea of *noblesse.* And how Sammler sympathized with him. . . ."

One might say, recalling Dahfu's advice to Henderson, that the form imitated by the pickpocket is stronger than that imitated by Rumkowski. While he is lawless, his individuality has a majesty about it that transcends the foolish personality cult that Sammler finds so odious. It is as if this black pickpocket, in a princely way, defies singlehandedly the unreality of every person that gathers to watch him struggle with Feffer. These people passively bask in the black's presence rather than act in the crisis. Only Sammler is there to act, and he, he finds, is too old to do something by himself. He has the sensation of being on the verge of death, of being a powerless person, a "*past* person," between being and non-being, between the state of fullness and plenitude of this world and the emptiness and nothingness of no world. He must turn to his son-in-law Eisen, just arrived from Israel and speaking no English. Eisen is mad, too, off in his own orbit, but his is not the noble madness of the pickpocket. Eisen's madness is vicious, lacking the cosmic audacity of that of the black man. But Eisen, in madness, stuns the huge thief and frees Sammler.

As in *Henderson,* this bout with consciousness and reality does not bring either the reader or Bellow's protagonist to the final resolution. It only prepares for the last words. The incident with the pickpocket occurs as Sammler is on his way to the hospital. His nephew, Elya Gruner, is dying. Elya has been generous and helpful to Sammler from the beginning, having been instrumental in bringing him to this country after the war and providing both Sammler and Shula with a modest income to sustain themselves. Even more than Mickey's death in *The Victim,* Elya's illness hangs oppressively over the entire novel. The business with the pickpocket delays Sammler's arriving at the hospital at a time when Elya is on the brink of death. From that intense experience of life and reality, marked by crime and violence, by the passiveness of the crowd and the majesty of the black criminal, Sammler races on to the hospital, to that quiet place where the basic principles of the ethical life, isolated from the mad world, are put in their clearest form. Sammler, who has faced death and killed, who has been not quite human, who is a stranger on this strange planet, who has had his consciousness lashed in this recent encounter on the streets—this Sammler boils the entire moral question down into its simplest components. Elya has been a success in life, not because he has piled up a material fortune—though he has—but because in the center of existence he has cared and has shown it. Now he is sick and dying. His son, Wallace, is in the sky in an airplane shooting pictures on a hare-brained scheme to make money. His daughter, Angela, worries only about whether her father will forgive her for her sexual behavior and leave her enough money to continue to live self-indulgently. Elya, says Sammler, like all humans needs a "sign," and Sammler, failing in trying to persuade either Angela or Wallace to give Elya that sign, tries to do it himself. But the world intervenes on that New York street corner and Sammler is prevented from giving the symbolic sign of love to Elya. He dies before Sammler can see him. Elya dies, however, as a model of the ethical life. Sammler's last words—and, to date, Bellow's—are a prayer for Elya which sums up the nature of the ethical life and the central thesis of Bellow's moral outlook:

> Remember, God, the soul of Elya Gruner, who, as willingly as possible and as well as he was able, and even to an intolerable point, and even in suffocation and even as death was coming was eager, even childishly perhaps (may I be forgiven for this), even with a certain servility, to do what was required of him. At his best this man was much kinder than at my very best I have ever been or could ever be. He was aware that he must meet, and he did meet—

through all the confusion and degraded clowning of this life through which we are speeding—he did meet the terms of his contract. The terms which, in his inmost heart, each man knows. As I know mine. As all know. For that is the truth of it—that we all know, God, that we know, that we know, we know, we know.

This is the "open decision," this consciousness of the unavoidable conditions of our existence, the terms of our contract, calling for a duty to live life as it is given, in spite of its madness and confusion, its absurdity, its contrary way of separating the real and the ideal. One does what one can. The ideal—rest, repose, total explanation—cannot by definition replace the real, which is the negation of those prizes. But one can behave decently and lovingly to others who are caught in the same glorious pathos. And when one does, that novel end, grounded on such service, will return the highest of all *possible* intensities of individual satisfaction.

For Norman Mailer[6] morality is much more a matter of personal power than of "generality of outlook." This does not mean that he would disregard all social structures in favor of anarchy or that he would absolve the individual of any moral responsibility to the society in which he lives. It is simply that, on the one hand, he regards as much more important than "generality of outlook" the fact that social structures thwart individual intensity, and on the other, he sees the crucial human drama to be played in the conflict between man's thrust for omnipotence—god-like freedom and power—and the limitations of his condition which prevent him from activating that omnipotence. Both of these themes pervade Mailer's fiction. As a writer, he is caught between the rebel's recognition of limits and the revolutionary's claim upon absolute power. The omnipotence that Mailer's characters pursue is analogous to what Sartre describes as the identification of the for-itself with the in-itself. In the impossibility of that identification man is, for Sartre, a "useless passion." Mailer recognizes a similar impossibility as the radical character of the human being, but finds in it a pathos which he has never quite elevated to tragedy. Where other novelists find this paradox and this pathos something their characters must reconcile themselves to, Mailer makes them the sources of unresolved tension. Mailer's novels resound with moral "shoulds" and "oughts," with instructions on how to achieve omnipotence. But the tension is never broken; his people never become gods.

As one might expect, placing him against the construct of thought expressed in the "open decision," Mailer tacitly assumes that the highest good is individual life: growth, feeling, vision, the exercise of that part of the self which is most unique. It is valid to say that, in terms of the "open decision," this good presupposes a satisfactory society in which the individual achieves some of his growth by his concern for others. But Mailer focuses his attention upon the way in which the individual works out such exercise. As Mailer says in *The White Negro,* the self must open up its own nervous "circuits" in response to the world, that the self stand constantly on new thresholds. If one is to exist intensely as his individual self, he must not rely on other people's values or some preexistent social pattern to determine his own choices for action. The most individual person—what Mailer calls the "hipster" or the "American existentialist"—abandons the old circuits and well-traveled roads, and without charts or maps or assurances of safety explores "the rebellious imperatives of the self."[7] Like Husserl, he brackets the world. Because he travels his own new territory, he cannot know what to expect; every act, therefore, is a gamble. Because they imply an affirmation of what is most true of the human condition, they are moral acts.

Mailer expresses these principles in his novels. William McLeod, the Stalinist revolutionary in *Barbary Shore,* refers to "the potentiality of the human" as an "open question," a comment that comes so close to Scheler's phrase—the "open decision"—as almost to suggest a direct debt. Because his potential is open, says McLeod, the human being is "impossible to determine philosophically," a sentiment that not only echoes the construct of thought described in Part I, but recalls the attitude of almost every writer I have discussed. In his highest form, the human being is an individual who stands open to his unique possibilities, unable to see the future because it is not yet realized in his own experiences, unsusceptible to total explanation and free of social or psychological compulsion. The authentic center of the human being thus contains an element of mystery and irrationality. Charles Francis Eitel, the once successful movie director in *The Deer Park,* thinks of the individual's genuine self as a "buried nature," which he characterizes as a "noble savage," that spontaneous core whose reasons for acting are hidden from the explainable and predictable patterns of civilized logic. Sergius O'Shaughnessy, *The Deer Park*'s narrator, suggests that this self acts most effectively when it abandons reason. Recalling a time when he had been stunned in a boxing match and had lashed out instinctively, knocking his opponent unconscious, he says that "sometimes a fighter is dangerous when all that's left is his instinct sort of, because he can't think his fight any more. It seems to come from way inside. . . ."

In *The White Negro,* Mailer describes this self as an "inner unconscious life," existing in the "senses of the body." It is "God"—not the God of the churches, but the "God who is It, who is energy, life, sex, force."[8] This God—or "It,"—when free of fear and totalitarian restrictions, moves us to our most individual and therefore "life-giving" actions, and invests our existence with "grace." As a soldier in Italy, Stephen Rojack, the narrator of *An American Dream,* experiences the power that comes from "It." When his platoon is pinned down by two German machine gun nests, he attacks them alone and destroys them both with hand grenades. His courage comes from his "buried nature," whose instinctual vitality frees him from the caution of fearing death, the caution that results from thinking and intellectualizing, that makes one pull back from the gamble of unconditional commitment to an act: "*it* threw them [the hand grenades]," thinks Rojack some years after the event, "and *it* did a near-perfect job."

This "God who is It" is "the unachievable whisper of mystery within the sex, the paradise of limitless energy and perception just beyond the next wave of orgasm."[9] It is that self that has broken free of tradition and prejudice, that has "bracketed" the world and penetrated its own depths. It is there in the darkness, in that free and spontaneous indeterminacy, where truth and reality lie. Mailer's relationship to the intellectual background of the twentieth century is demonstrated in this concept of God. Speaking of Heidegger, Werner Brock explains that the "self" is "called" by the conscience to *be* in the world. "The 'call' discloses something which is unambiguous, despite the apparent vagueness of its content, namely a sure direction of drive in which the Dasein of the 'self' is to move." "This call is not planned nor prepared nor voluntarily carried out by ourselves. 'It' calls against one's own expectation and even one's own wishes."[10] The "call" is the word of the gods, and their word is named by poetry. The poet plumbs the darkness and emerges with the gods' powerful words. The poet—or the artist in general—must brave the dreadful seat of power and grasp the guides for action. Heidegger cites Hölderlin for the poetic expression of this point:

> Yet it behoves us, under the storms of God,
> Ye poets! with uncovered head to stand,
> With our hand to grasp the very lightning-flash
> Paternal, and to pass, wrapped in song,
> The divine gift to the people.
>
> . . . the bold spirit like an eagle
> Before the tempests, flies prophesying
> In the path of his advancing gods.[11]

For both Heidegger and Mailer, the human being's authentic core contains a power that is godlike. But at the very point at which he defines that power—calling it "the unachievable whisper of mystery within the sex, the paradise of limitless energy and perception just beyond the next wave of orgasm"—Mailer establishes the bounds of the human condition. By his own definition, the inner mystery of sex is "unachievable." By any definition, the real world cannot host a "paradise of limitless energy and perception." Man, suggests Mailer, is a paradox that by definition cannot be resolved. If man does contain godlike potential, that potential also threatens his condition as a man, for the very word *man* denotes limitation. All attempts to release that potential must invoke the ambivalent feelings of ambition and dread: ambition to become godlike and dread of offending the gods. Rojack says that the savage accepted dread as "the natural result of any invasion of the supernatural: if man wished to steal the secrets of the gods, it was only to be supposed that the gods would defend themselves and destroy whichever man came too close. By this logic, civilization is the successful if imperfect theft of some cluster of these secrets, and the price we have paid is to accelerate our private sense of some enormous if not quite definable disaster which awaits us." The vision of a "paradise of limitless energy," which can be realized by stealing all the gods' secrets, is at once tantalizing and fearsome. When men commit murder, continues Rojack, they do not fear being brought to justice by other men, but attracting "the attention of the gods." Murder is a godly power; for mortals to seize it is to commit the ultimate sin, even though it might promise godly paradise.

Deep in the heart of the human condition is a built-in obstacle to the consummation of godly power, an innate fear that ceaselessly impedes the liberation of the real self. Joined with that internal impediment, as I have already suggested, are the external blocks to the development of a high intensity of individual satisfaction. I have discussed the way in which society blocks that development in *The Naked and the Dead.* Not one character in that novel is free of circuits laid out in him by the structure of his past and his society. The opening passage of the novel establishes the atmosphere of glut and check and drag. A soldier arises from his bunk aboard a troop ship bound for the invasion of Anopopei. The air is stifling, permeated with the odor of sweat and vomit and urine. The bunks press down on the men lying in them. Duffel bags and rifles make a jungle out of the deck. Here one is caught, his freedom diminished, his perspective blurred, his limbs detained. The jungle, too, exerts its steaming, clammy controls upon the men who would challenge it. Sergeant Croft's I & R Platoon beats its way through the jungle, but the men are exhausted by rain, muddy ground, the thick tendrils and vines; their muscles ache and their jungle sores torment them. The world thwarts the development of the godlike: Cummings is thwarted by his men, Croft by hornets and fatigue, the men by their officers and the jungle.

All of the characters in *The Naked and the Dead* have their moments. They lean forward eagerly, feeling as if they are on the verge of some great discovery, some insight into themselves and the nature of truth, some illumination that will disclose the precise nature of the "call" and permit them to transcend the drag of themselves, of their society, and of the natural world. But always words just escape them; the vision disappears. The conflict between the hoped-for revelation and the obstacles to its realization embodies Mailer's central theme. We can fulfill ourselves as human beings only in this world, but that world more or less stifles us, drags us down. Yet, the obstacles elicit what is best in men. Even the complaining Jew, Roth, has his moment of glory when he rebels against the society of his platoon. After suffering insult after insult because of his Jewishness, Roth becomes, "for the first time in his life . . . genuinely furious." Though his "magnificent anger" is pitifully ineffective, yet, as he marches along with the other exhausted men, "there was something different in him, something more impressive." And the promise of a symbolic victory over the limitations of existence drives Croft up Mt. Anaka, a climb which, though they do not complete it, strikes pride in all the men as they look back at what they did accomplish. This is what men can do, and for some it is enough. But for others, the failure of consummation produces a painful and frustrating ambivalence. Croft—an early embodiment of Mailer's hipster—is both relieved and hurt "vitally" by his failure to reach the summit of the mountain. Yet, in looking back, he re-experiences the "anxiety and terror" he had felt during the climb, that same dread which Mailer later says comes with the human intrusion upon the gods' secrets. Croft is a man, and must find his victories among men. Had he tried the climb alone, he would not have been slowed down by the other men. On the other hand, ". . . he realized suddenly that he could not have gone without them. The empty hills would have eroded any man's courage." The emphasis should be placed upon *man's* courage. He is not a god. In this moment of reflection, Croft expresses the frustration of the human being that will characterize most of the protagonists that Mailer will draw in his subsequent novels. He may not have been able to make it alone among those rare heights, yet Croft laments that he had "lost" the mountain. More than that, he

> had missed some tantalizing revelation of himself.
>
> Of himself and much more. Of life.
> Everything.

He failed to seize the words of the gods.

In *Barbary Shore* and *The Deer Park*, Mailer presents two characters who achieve a qualified liberation. In each novel, the situation is similar to that of *The Naked and the Dead*. The individual —what McLeod calls the "open question"—is hindered from achieving absolute consummation by himself and the external world. In *Barbary Shore*, the main hindrance is the political totalitarianism as represented by the United States and Russia. Their capitalistic economies, differing only slightly, both lead toward the exploitation of the worker and eventually to the restraints of the concentration camp. These systems generate enormous power which is concentrated in the hands of a few officials, who use it to create still more power for themselves and to curb the freedom of their people. As a high "Party" official in an unnamed Balkan country, McLeod resorts to murder to protect the power he has gained. And because Trotsky, in his fidelity to the original aims of the revolution, threatens that power, McLeod makes no attempt to stop his assassination. McLeod's U.S. counterpart is Leroy Hollingsworth, a secret agent wielding the Government's power, violating individual rights. In their political capacities, these two men are, as one character speaks of them, simply guards of two huge social prisons.

Whatever shape the totalitarian society takes, it dams up individual potential, thwarts growth, and makes one vulnerable to death by conformity. A theoretical solution to such a society comes from McLeod, who, unlike Hollingsworth, abandons his brutality and returns to the purer motives of his revolutionary days by fleeing to America. His answer to totalitarianism is "revolutionary socialism," a scheme that recalls Whitehead and Mannheim, and the moral posture that self-discovery must precede the establishment of satisfactory societies. Revolutionary socialism postulates an open system which will be created when enough individuals choose to be free in themselves, and act on their own motives to break out of the rigid classifications of the conformist society: "marriage, family, and the spirit vapor of love and God." A new era will be ushered in, one in which the individual will be granted the wide alternatives of "extraordinary contrasts," words nearly identical to those used by Whitehead when he speaks of the "living society" and its contrasts.

Barbary Shore gives no reason to hope that such an era is imminent, but if there is hope—as I have already suggested—it lies neither in McLeod nor Hollingsworth, but in Michael Lovett, the story's narrator. Lovett is, significantly, not a political theoretician, but a writer, a man for whom the "It" is immediately important. He has lost his memory in World War II and, unsure of his identity, exemplifies McLeod's description of the human as an "open question." His nervous system has not been conditioned by a past to respond in rigidly predetermined ways, so his potential for change and growth is almost unlimited. It is true that at first he seeks to avoid the actions that would implement his possibilities by retiring from society to a rooming house to write a novel. But he cannot for long avoid becoming deeply involved in the lives of the other people in the house, a fact which demonstrates Mailer's commitment to one of the basic assumptions of the "open decision." McLeod calls Lovett a romantic and an innocent, but chooses him as heir to "the remnants of my socialist culture," implying that he must carry the hope of "revolutionary socialism" into the future. In the character of Lovett, then, Mailer expresses a qualified optimism that rests upon the formation of a society favorable to the free exercise of the individual self. It is true that Lovett must go temporarily underground at the end of the novel—like the narrator of *Invisible Man*—to protect himself from the rampant forces of totalitarianism. There he will wait "for the signs which tell me I must move on again." But at least there is a promise of "signs." And Mailer implies, at least in this novel, that a discovery of the self is not the last step to a high intensity of individual satisfaction. When one emerges from that self-discovery, he returns to society.

A more explicit representation of hope for consummation of the individual is Sergius O'Shaughnessy, in *The Deer Park*. Where the solution to individual freedom in *Barbary Shore* is largely political, in *The Deer Park* it is expressed as the strength of the individual to hold out against society and insist on living on his own terms. The sign of that strength is the achievement of the "artistic mind," whose integrity produces the ability to triumph over social obstacles. Sergius is an orphan, a state analogous to Lovett's amnesia. The uncertainty and homelessness of his early years turn him toward the search for a home, stability, predictability. He refuses to gamble his life in adventurous acts. He wants to be a member of that society whose conformism protects one from the danger of the unknown. He thinks he finds such a home in the Air Force, developing a warm feeling for his fellow fliers and, like them, remaining essentially untouched by the fact that in their World War II raids they are killing real people. In the society he has found, its citizens experience in the abstract, insulate themselves from the actual pain of torn flesh and mutilated bodies. Combat is merely a game; its victims have no humanness or immediacy for the fliers. But when

Sergius suddenly realizes that in his fire bomb raids he is burning real people, whose flesh smells and whose screams pierce the air, he is plunged into life, and it hurts. He abandons his secure home.

Out of the comfortable grooves of Air Force life, Sergius feels adrift and disoriented. He begins to shape the notion that he will one day be a writer, but the prime requisite for that is the ability to face himself, to break completely free of the influence of what Eitel calls the "snob soul," the antithesis of the authentic buried nature. Sergius, however, is not ready to do that. Though he has fled from the Air Force, he wants for a while to draw back from the real world in which "orphans burned orphans," to take up residence in the "imaginary world . . . in which almost everybody lived." And so he comes to the resort town of Desert D'Or. It is the externalization of the snob soul, that element of the self which takes the safe way, refuses to gamble, follows the grooves already cut deep by others. In Desert D'Or the snob soul is most comfortable and the buried nature the most inhibited. The character of Desert D'Or is expressed in its correspondence to the "deer park," the name of Louis XV's retreat where young virgins were brought to satisfy the debauched appetites of the French aristocracy. Mailer's deer park is the favorite spot of certain Hollywood celebrities and their hangers-on. Its corruptness lies in its violation, not of innocent virgins, but of the spontaneous self. It is a large theater in which the actors are expected to stay faithful to the script laid out by those in control. Departures from that script are greeted with dismay and anger. One casts his acquaintances in certain roles in order to empty them of troublesome ambiguity and unpredictability and to protect oneself from the pain of hitting too near the buried nature. This social tyranny is also expressed in the political sphere, for the script calls for unquestioning allegiance to some vague entity "America," an awed and mystical respect for the flag, and unceasing vigilance against Communist subversion.

It is to this "imaginary world" that Sergius escapes, but in doing so he jeopardizes his chances of becoming a writer. First, he meets Lulu Meyers, the beautiful Hollywood actress who is between husbands. Though she is vital and fascinating, she is still part of that society that approaches life as a movie. She is a game-player who avoids the uniquely individual action. She loves to act out stereotyped situations with Sergius: the photographer and the model, the movie star and the bell hop, the queen and the slave. For all her charm, Lulu is Sergius's experience with the imaginary world. But true art does not grow in an atmosphere of make-believe. So long as he continues his affair with Lulu, Sergius can neither write nor begin to train his mind in the open circuits of the artist. The stifling, imaginary world of Desert D'Or threatens Sergius from another quarter. Collie Munshin, the ambitious son-in-law of the head of Supreme Pictures, offers Sergius a large sum of money and a possible starring role in the story of his life. This would require that he surrender his artistic integrity to the cheapening process of commercial picture-making. Just as he is attracted to Lulu, he is attracted by the offer, and Lulu predictably urges him to accept it. But at this point Sergius's buried nature begins to assert itself. He decides to rely on his instincts and his instincts tell him that he must be free of Hollywood's desire to falsify his life, that he must reject the offer. "I don't want somebody else to tell me how to express myself." In coming to this decision, Sergius has changed from the home-seeker he was when he went into the Air Force. He has become a gambler: ". . . if I passed this chance by, it was because I had the deeper idea that I was meant to gamble on better things than money or a quick career."

One of those "better things," of course, is becoming a writer, and one decision does not make him that. When he rejects Munshin's offer, however, he creates a situation which forces him to grow towards his goal. Refusing to sell his life story means that he has chosen to write. That choice is a gamble that frightens him and he is struck, as he was when he left the shelter of the Air Force, with sexual impotency. In both cases he fears the uncharted individuality into which he has chosen to plunge. He recounts his Air Force experiences to Lulu and his confession of this most intimate memory restores his potency. But their relationship has reached the point where they must separate. Lulu's life is a play. She operates in that snob world once removed from reality. She must return to the surface, to the frivolity of the film capital. Sergius must probe deeper into himself and become a writer. As Heidegger might say, his conscience has called him to be in the world. But that call presupposes a painful and difficult struggle, and Sergius does not embrace that struggle joyously. But with Lulu gone his alternative is gone, and "there was no other choice than to sit down and begin the apprenticeship of learning to be a writer."

To be fully liberated from the totalitarian society and his own snob soul, Sergius must face the political threat to his individual existence. He is visited by two tough investigators from the Congressional "Subversive Committee," who, with all the power of the Government behind them, try to intimidate him, insinuating Communist associations, subversion, and moral degeneracy. For a few moments he is afraid, feeling his snob soul tyrannizing over his buried nature, responding with a nervous system trained to work through only certain circuits. But soon the "It" asserts itself and, as it did momentarily for Roth in *The Naked and the Dead,* anger replaces fear. If he refuses to let anyone tell him how to express himself, he also refuses to consent to being what these men insinuate. The control that he exerts over his snob soul throughout the interview prepares him for his final revelation. After the investigators leave, he embarks upon an exploration of himself. In his thoroughness, he touches "bottom," and what once was so frightening he now finds less terrifying and more understandable. At this point, he begins to try to shape a new "nervous system," as Mailer calls it in *The White Negro.* This new system will be composed of new responses resolving themselves into "the most elusive habit of all, the mind of the writer." The "habit" of the writer's mind is elusive because it is the habit of the true gambler. It acts, as all men must, in ignorance, with no assurance of the efficacy of its action, but finding validity simply in the fact that it is acting. When that act is a gamble based on faith in one's self, it is the act of individual life. Sergius acts, then, as a writer, composing a few pages of manuscript, knowing those pages are bad, but that he will "try again."

The optimism in Sergius's conclusion is the optimism inherent in all gambling, in all trying. Sergius imagines Eitel saying, "One cannot look for a good time, for pleasure must end as love or cruelty . . . or obligation." But Sergius declares that "one must invariably look for a good time since a good time is what gives us the strength to try again." Eitel's advice is based on the conviction that in this world fulfillment is impossible and therefore integrity and effort are futile. Sergius concludes that the artist must take the world as his sphere of good and stand open before it. The artist, the prototype of the individual, finds his good to be in the unique way in which he lives in the world and says that uniqueness is heightened through "the connection of new circuits," the constant tolerance of and search for new responses. From Sergius's point of view, the theatrical role-playing of Desert D'Or—the symbol of Hollywood and America—fixes the human being in inflexible categories, which, however many times they are changed, possess no capacity for growth, the root quality of the individual. Victory over the death of conformity is keeping the circuits open for new connections. The essential human being is not an entity at rest, complete in itself. Nor is it an abstract image. It is the "open decision," eager in life, earnest in action. The human hero, as Sergius sees it, is an artist embracing the world with no illusions, finding in the actual his province of value. Art is not the expression of a good superior to the real world, but an articulation of the world's reality. It is impossible to think that Mailer does not share Sergius's attitude.

The optimism in the discovery of courage by Lovett and Sergius, however, is overshadowed by that other human emotion, fear. And this takes us back to the scheme I have already described. The "It's" energy is life in this world. Thus, to activate that energy one must, like Nietzsche's superman, accept the world, seize upon it, revel in it. This is no more than Sergius implies. Fear of one's godlike potential, therefore, is also fear of existence. Those who fear their inner "God" avoid new responses, take sanctuary in the sterility of abstractions and images, cautiously moving along other people's circuits. Mailer does not ridicule or satirize these people; he anatomizes their moves toward success and depicts the pathos of their inevitable failure. Like Croft, Charles Eitel and Stephen Rojack are portraits of such failure.

As a young director in Hollywood, Eitel tapped his buried nature for the creative energy needed to turn out several artistically admirable films. They were good because he had had the courage of his "hunger and anger" to challenge the static patterns of social expectation. But his hunger is fed by success and his anger dissipates. He loses "the energy of his talent." As he betrays his artistic integrity, he tries to succeed commercially. That, however, is impossible. He has closed his own circuits, so to speak, for nothing.

Another demand upon his integrity comes at this time from the Subversive Committee, investigating Communist associations in Hollywood. He is asked to inform upon colleagues and acquaintances, but in this instance he stands on his principles and refuses to testify. Hollywood's producers, refusing to tolerate unorthodoxy, blacklist him.

Eitel's ideal is to direct only those films he thinks are worthy and to ignore politics altogether. But he lives in and is dependent upon a society that grants the realization of such an ideal only to the strong. Eitel is too weak to carve a place for himself on his own terms. He begins a script that he hopes will transform his life into an "imperishable" work of art and gain him reentry into the inner circle of influential directors. But he lacks his old vitality. Too much the creature of his society, he turns out a manuscript that is immature and sentimental. Reversing all of his good intentions, he puts it into the hands of Collie Munshin, who turns it into something commercial and "beautifully false." The kind of art he hopes to produce demands that the artist touch the "bottom" of himself, as Sergius does. For Eitel that has become impossible.

Giving in to Collie Munshin—as Sergius does not give in to him—leads Eitel to acknowledge that "he was not an artist." He is a commercial man, one who sharply rearranges the cinematic clichés but does not strike out into new territory of his own. To be what he can be he needs to be in Hollywood, and to be in Hollywood he must give in to the Subversive Committee. The concomitant of his giving up on the script is his agreement to testify before the Committee. If he wants to exercise his trade, he must betray both his artistic and his political principles, and unless he is ready to commit suicide—he reasons—he must learn not to resist what seems inevitable and inescapable. Though he feels like a prostitute in testifying, he claims that "In the end that's the only kind of self-respect you have. To be able to say to yourself you're disgusting."

Eitel's fear of risk is also expressed in his affair with Elena Esposito. After the first flush of artistic success as a young man, Eitel loses his taste for the world. He refuses to gamble in his art, and then finds that he cannot gamble even when he wants to. He demands the certainty of being in control. Just so with Elena. He regards her as a work of art, wanting complete control over her in order to shape her to his desires. He wants the power of a god, but cannot take the necessary risks—in Elena's case the risk is to love. He sees her, not as a human being with whose buried nature his own might communicate, but as an "image in his mind." Elena is too much of the earth and the earth encumbers Eitel's vision of limitless freedom. Her body in bed beside him "only hindered his limbs, he could not really believe in the painful existence of that body." Eitel thinks that to stay with Elena and to love her would inhibit the freedom he needs for his art, for then "he would be obliged to travel in *her* directions."

What Eitel is attempting to preserve here is not his individual freedom, but a certainty of the future which his timidity requires. He himself recognizes his weakness. In his world "morality and caution were identical," and the cautious person lives at a low intensity, less individually. Needing safety, he retreats from the world and the life one lives in it. For the artist, this is death. A passage in "The Homosexual Villain" applies precisely to Eitel:

> A writer has his talent, and for all one knows he is born with it, but whether his talent develops is to some degree responsive to his use of it. He can grow as a person or he can shrink, and by this I don't intend any facile parallel between moral and artistic growth. The writer can become a bigger hoodlum, if need be, but his alertness, his curiosity, his reaction to life must not diminish. The fatal thing is to shrink, to be interested in less, sympathetic to less, desiccating to the point where life loses its flavor, and one's passion for human understanding changes to weariness and distaste.[12]

Eitel surrenders to the power of his society and in doing so loses his taste for life. His life becomes a "dreary compromise."[13] As Sergius says, Eitel drifts into the "sad frustration of his middle age." Caution for Mailer is death. Even Eitel sees that "the essence of spirit . . . was to choose the thing which did not better one's position but made it more perilous." To fear peril is to fear life. The irony that Mailer emphasizes is that in trying to save one's life through caution and withdrawal into the protection of the conforming "they," one loses it. The real life-giving answer comes, writes Mailer in *The White Negro,* only when we do that which seems most dangerous, when we agree

> to accept the terms of death, to live with death as immediate danger, to divorce oneself from society, to exist without roots . . . to explore

that domain of experience where security is boredom and therefore sickness, and one exists in the present, in that enormous present which is without past or future, memory or planned intention, the life where a man must go until he is beat, where he must gamble with his energies through all those small or large crises of courage and unforeseen situations which beset his day, where he must be with it or doomed not to swing.[14]

An American Dream is an even closer examination of the possibility of winning life by facing death, and the way that fear impedes such possibility. Rojack, like Eitel, fails to break through the barrier of fear surrounding his buried nature, though he comes closer to that "unachievable whisper of mystery" than does Eitel. When Rojack charges the machine gun nests he performs an operation of high individual intensity. That intensity comes from the paradox of the gamble: in going out to meet death, in refusing the low and diffuse intensity of timidity and caution, he also goes out to meet life. He displays that courage in a moment of crisis which Mailer calls the "heart of hip." The condition that makes an act courageous, as Mailer sees it, is violence, danger to one's own life and the expression of one's deepest and most infantile desires. Violence "prepares growth," activating the authentic self, realizing the most potent possibilities, and putting one in a new and lively relationship with himself and his surroundings. Rojack, by acting courageous—by exposing himself to violent death—embarks upon the first step of forming a new nervous system which will allow him new and original responses.

But such courage, as I have pointed out, encroaches upon the domain of the gods, giving the individual a power in life that transforms his order of being. *An American Dream* implies that to be free of fear is beyond human capacity. Still operating under the impulsive courage of "It," Rojack shoots three of the four Germans manning the machine gun nests. But when the fourth one stands, mortally wounded and weakly brandishing his bayonet, Rojack's courage deserts him. Honor—what Rojack calls his "contract" with the German—requires that he charge the dying soldier's bayonet, that he place himself in peril. But he hesitates. He, too, has been wounded and he is unwilling to risk that wound further. In that instant he loses a part of his life by trying to save it: "the clean presence of *it,* the grace, *it* had deserted me." In the young German's eyes is a knowledge which Rojack can no longer face, a knowledge of "what was waiting on the other side," that "death was a creation more dangerous than lies." From then on the fear of death imprisons him. He associates it with the full moon, which was out on that fateful night; that is, death has a "lunacy" about it, a mystery and a magic which frightened him by their irrationality. Death is thus inextricably bound in unexplainable ways to the "It."

Rojack attempts to deal with his fear in two ways. First, as a professor of existential psychology, he writes books and gives lectures on savagery, magic, and mysticism and their relationship with death, trying by this means to empty them of their danger by reducing them to the certainties of abstractions—very much in the same way that Eitel thought of Elena as an "image." Second, he marries Deborah Kelly, a rich and beautiful member of the international set, as a support for his ego. When he feels he is a failure, he can point to the fact that he is, of all her many suitors, the man she married. But the most effective kind of protection she gives him is really a kind of death. She does not call on him to assert the "It." Indeed, she seeks to drain him of his strength, to make him a coward, requiring from him in their sexual relations "unconditional surrender." She is possessed by "demons." She seeks to exert power and emasculate, not give life. She is one aspect of the dark circumference which, like the jungle and society and government in Mailer's previous novels, act as drags upon the straining hipster. The same agencies turn up in *An American Dream,* all related in some way to Deborah—the mob controlled by her father, Barney Kelly; the C.I.A., with which Deborah herself is said to have had some vague connections; the Mafia, which is in the past of Deborah's Sicilian family. Benignly, these are limiting forces; malignantly, they threaten Rojack with death. In this atmosphere, married to Deborah, Rojack has become the cautious man who fears to gamble.

One of the symbols of Rojack's rejection of life and his refusal to gamble is his sterility. Sex with Deborah is torrid, sometimes orgiastic, but unproductive. In their eight years of marriage, Deborah is childless, though she did have one miscarriage. Rojack's fear of death is expressed in this symbol as a fear of life: ". . . when I was in bed with a woman, I rarely felt as if I were making life, but rather as if I were a pirate sharpening up a raid on life, and so somewhere inside myself—yes, *there* was a large part of the fear—I had dread of the judgment which must rest behind the womb of a woman." To plant a seed in a woman's womb is to gamble on new life, and Rojack, fearing the death that inevitably brings, is unwilling to make the gamble.

In the thirty hours or so that constitute the present of *An American Dream,* Rojack oscillates between courage and fear. The crucial episodes are couched in terms of birth and death, fertility and sterility, old life and new. His first move toward a new life of courage and fertility is his murder of Deborah. Finally driven to the point of outrage by Deborah's attempt to unman him, Rojack strangles her in her own bed after a violent physical struggle with her. That act of violence establishes new relationships for him. He puts his own life in jeopardy and at the same time penetrates "as far into myself as I had ever been." His murder of Deborah also suggests sexual fertility. In the act he feels a sensation similar to that when one makes the choice in sexual intercourse to climax even though the woman cries "that she is without protection." That choice plants the seed of life; Rojack impregnates his own situation with new life.

This move toward liberating himself from the caution of his old life is followed by another decision: to leave the choice of confessing the murder or making it look like suicide up to "the buried gaming rooms of the unconscious." In the process of making that choice, his unconscious produces a magnetic pull toward a fierce desire for pleasure. He descends from Deborah's bedroom to the maid's quarters and there, with Ruta, engages in something of an orgy. His orgasm, however, occurs in Ruta's "Devil" (rectum) rather than her "Lord" (vagina), carrying with it no chance for the conception of new life. He is afraid of the judgment of her womb. As Rojack says, however, with ironic humor, "from the end to the beginning" there are only "a crucial few centimeters of distance." He has momentarily betrayed the beginning of his new life by taking Ruta's "end." And he senses that betrayal, for in the aftermath of their lovemaking, he feels a great oppressiveness. For a moment, Ruta becomes a Deborah, a prison, a hindrance—as Elena was to Eitel—to his limbs, an extension of his own renewed fear of life symbolized by the sterility of the recently concluded sexual act. He asks himself whether his oppression had been "That the seed was expiring in the wrong field."

But the gamble for pleasure has somehow brought him to a decision for life. Were he to be jailed for killing Deborah, he would remain her prisoner, and his reproductive organs would continue to be a "charnel house." The "buried gaming rooms of his unconscious" decide to make her death look like a suicide, and in acting upon that decision, Rojack throws her body out of the window into the busy street below, creating the appearance that she had jumped. That this is a choice for life is demonstrated in his next encounter with Ruta. When she weeps at the news of Deborah's "suicide," Rojack embraces her, feeling like a woman who has killed her brutal and tyrannical lover. Deborah may have sought to unearth the weak, feminine part of Rojack, but Ruta's femininity wants no part of that. She needs his manhood "to pull in a life" for herself. She does not require the unconditional surrender of his manhood, but its assertion. Moreover, in receiving life from Rojack, she can give life to him. He takes her in the hall before the police come, dispensing "one hot fierce streak of fierce bright murder, fierce as a demon in the eyes of a bright golden child." In this act, Rojack unites two of Mailer's keys to liberation: the "good" orgasm and the violence of murder. In risking the creation of new life, he is indirectly a murderer, since once life is conceived, death is inescapable. In murdering Deborah and sending his seed into Ruta, he demonstrates his willingness to gamble on the unpredictable: new life.

His new life is further nourished at the nightclub where he goes to meet the singer Cherry after the police interrogation. He breathes "fine new breaths" and vomits up in the men's room "all the biles of habit and the horrors of pretense" that had marked his past. Later, he makes love with Cherry, "alive in some deeper water below sex," now ready deliberately to take the chance of making new life. He removes the diaphragm she has installed and the two of them perform the act of life. The shield of his old fears and restraints breaks and his life mixes with Cherry's, his new existence now in the wombs of both Ruta and Cherry.

What Mailer would call Rojack's courage brings him love, and for Rojack, God is courage whose reward is love. Love cannot last, however, unless courage is constantly renewed by continuing the gamble of his life. But just as he fails to press the gamble with the fourth German soldier, so he fails to press it in his relationship with Cherry. When her ex-lover, the Negro singer Shago Martin, appears, the two men argue. Shago disdainfully shoves Rojack and Rojack leaps on the Negro from behind. Lacking the nerve to fight him face to face, Rojack beats him bloody and pushes him down the stairway. Afterwards, he bitterly regrets his dishonorable behavior. His body, so alive when loving Cherry, has now become "like a cavern where deaths are stored." The fight sours the mood with Cherry. The ascent up love's mountain, thinks Rojack, "was not yet begun, and I had been ready to betray."

Rojack can redeem himself by choosing a situation which will put him in danger, show him capable of finally accepting the terms of death and thus affirming life and receiving the reward of love. He chooses to answer a summons by Barney Kelly to his hotel suite high above the city. Their discussion eventually turns to the subject of courage. Kelly dares Rojack to walk around the balcony parapet and Rojack accepts the dare. By walking the parapet, he thinks, he will deliberately imperil his life, and by doing so, advance growth, affirm his individual existence. The first trip, Rojack's inner voice tells him, means liberation for himself; the second will win a new life for him and Cherry. At the end of the first round, Rojack has succeeded for himself, and he is confident that he can return for Cherry. But Kelly, diabolically playful, pokes an umbrella at Rojack's chest, causing him to teeter and almost fall. The umbrella belongs to Shago Martin. Rojack has carried it with him as a kind of talisman to Barney's apartment. Now the umbrella takes on the aspect of a totem instrument possessing a power of its own. In the hands of Kelly it becomes a grave threat to Rojack. Here, Kelly is the dark world of the underground, that part of existence which, as he tells Rojack, does not want Rojack to succeed. He is now the symbol of the kind of violence and death which has both frightened and attracted Rojack. But at this point, for all his momentary conviction that he can face it, Rojack cannot continue the return trip along the parapet. Furious that Kelly has frightened him, Rojack leaps from the parapet and beats the older man to the ground. Though his voice warns him that he must go around once more for Cherry, he rushes out of the apartment, his fear and dread renewed.

The consequences of his refusal to face death both in his encounter with Shago Martin and his failure to go twice around the parapet is the death of Cherry and the seed of himself he has planted in her. When he returns to her room, he finds her being carried to an ambulance, dying from a beating by one of Shago's friends. Her death is both a direct result of and a symbol of his failure. Instead of seizing the opportunity to grow, Rojack shrinks, falling short of the Hip ideal that Mailer outlines in *The White Negro*. In the abstract context of exposition, Mailer seems to find it easy to be optimistic about individual consummation. But in the more concrete sphere of the novel, his honesty dims that optimism. Human life can promise no "paradise of limitless energy." Yet, Rojack has not been destroyed. His possibilities remain open. First he goes to Las Vegas, exposing himself to the revenge of Barney's gambling hoodlums. Then he departs for the jungles of Guatemala and Yucatan, suggesting that there in the primitive surroundings of uncivilized Indians, he might regain some of the spontaneous "It" which will let him be himself in the face of physical and institutional death.

Why Are We in Vietnam? is an addendum to *An American Dream* and a summary of all Mailer's other novels, ranging from social criticism to man's individual revelations and his own struggles against the cosmos. What Rojack expects to find in the primitive interiors of Yucatan and Guatemala is made explicit in *Why Are We in Vietnam?*, except that the setting of the latter novel is the frozen wilderness of the Arctic Circle rather than the tropical jungles of Central America. The common feature of the two locations is their distance from America, at whose heart, as suggested in *An American Dream,* eats a malignancy of inhibition and conformity.

Why Are We in Vietnam? is the story of a bear hunt in the far North. Its narrator is Ranald Jethroe, an eighteen-year-old Texan who calls himself D.J., the "disc jockey of the world." His story is both an answer to the question posed in the title, though its action and setting have nothing directly to do with Vietnam or our conflict there, and an attack upon the American presence in that country. The answer and the attack are expressed partly through the language of the novel. Except for one fairly long passage at the end, D.J.'s language is deliberately and jubilantly obscene. His strings of four-letter words are, perhaps, appropriate to his age, his home, and his viewpoint (sardonic detachment masking passionate involvement). But for Mailer, the obscenity has a more special function. In a now notorious performance as master of ceremonies for a program of speakers before the 1967 March on the Pentagon, Mailer offended many by grunting and growling obscene epithets covering a wide variety of subjects. In his later account of the episode, he explains that he uses obscenity because he loves America, the America of the democratic, common man. That man, says Mailer, is "obscene as an old goat." The common man's obscenity works to help him keep his sanity. In the midst of a country inflated by self-important men who seek to stifle and thwart the helpless, the common man stays sane through an obscene humor by which he deflates the pretentious. Obscenity, as Lenny Bruce has also used it, is a satiric device which may be used to establish new circuits for the writer, to create new nervous systems. Speaking of himself in the third person, Mailer says that "he had kicked goodbye in his novel *Why Are We in Vietnam?* to the old literary corset of good taste, letting his sense of language play on obscenity as freely as it wished, so discovering that everything he knew about the American language (with its incommensurable resources) went flying in and out of the line of his prose with the happiest beating of wings—it was the first time his style seemed at once very American to him and very literary in the best way, at least as he saw the best way."[15]

In the sense that Mailer uses the word *obscenity* to apply to his language in *Why Are We in Vietnam?*, it means offensive to conventional good taste. But its offensiveness also calls attention to another meaning of the word: offensive to human life. *Obscenity* in this latter sense applies to the war America has waged in Vietnam. The true obscenity of that engagement is America's willingness to countenance killing, but to rise up in righteous indignation against the public use of four-letter words. One moment, says Mailer, in the mind of an army general directing the operations in Vietnam is more obscene than all the "obscene" words in the English language put together. Still thinking of the similarity between the army general and the businessman, Mailer writes, "The

American corporation executive, who was after all the most representative of Man in the world today, was perfectly capable of burning unseen women and children in the Vietnamese jungles, yet felt a large displeasure and fairly final disapproval at the generous use of obscenity in literature and in public."

In *Why Are We in Vietnam?* Rusty Jethroe, father of the young narrator, is a symbol of the corporation executive who might bear these sentiments, though Mailer never puts them in his mouth. Nevertheless, he has a kind of sanctimonious pride in his own two-fisted strength that characterizes the premise of many Americans who argue for the justness of our action in Vietnam. Rusty's main concern is to kill a grizzly bear in Alaska to bring back as a trophy to his colleagues. His expedition into the Northern wilderness and his obsession with victory over the bear is analogous to the American expedition in Vietnam and its insistence upon victory. The men in Rusty's group carry an astonishing arsenal of guns; the guide thinks like a general when placing the men in the hunt; and Rusty considers shooting a charging grizzly in terms of the principles of aerial bombardment. To complete the analogy, the guide employs a helicopter to transport the party from place to place and in extreme cases to protect them from dangerous animals. Rusty—as Mailer's corporation executive who supports the war in Vietnam—regards himself as the "fulcrum of the universe." If he misses getting a bear, he will fail, and his failure will be the "world's doom." This, Mailer would say, is the same self-important pretentiousness that accounts for the American involvement in Southeast Asia, the notion that upon American righteousness the world stands or falls. In this way the novel answers the question of its title. And in D.J.'s use of obscenities, he suggests that the analogous bear hunt implies the obscenity of the Vietnam war and at the same time deflates what Mailer would call the empty and pompous rhetoric that justifies that war.

But Rusty as corporation executive—and his representation of the attitudes that underlie American foreign policy—has a more direct and personal meaning in *Why Are We in Vietnam?* than just as an object of satire and criticism vis-à-vis Vietnam, a meaning that clearly links the novel with Mailer's previous work. Rusty is a General Cummings, a Leroy Hollingsworth, a subversive Committee of Congress, and a Barney Kelly all wrapped up in one. He is a straight-line American: a big businessman who is part of the establishment that operates as a kind of gestapo to the American common man. D.J. half-jokingly says that Rusty is "an unlisted agent for Luce Publications, American Airlines Overseas Division, and the I.I.R.—the Institute for International Research." Says D.J., "Spy Heaven they ought to call it." When D.J. looks into his eyes, he sees a "mysterious hidden mastermind" that runs America, a "chasm and a tomb." Mailer is not contemptuous of the power Rusty runs a tap line to, just as he is not contemptuous of his other power characters. As D.J. says of him, "He's a pig with a wild snouty mouth, but he's got good blood." He has courage and a tremendous selfishness and determination. But he represents a destructive and debasing force. The company he works for manufactures plastic cigarette filters that sterilize and destroy the natural. The "Pure Pores" filter can, says D.J., also be used as a contraceptive for women. But not only does it prevent life; it corrupts it as well, for it is said to cause cancer of the lip. The filter and the men who produce it represent that feature of American business which dams up all impulses and healthy spontaneity, straining out all but the conforming, and produces cancerous knobs of unexpressed desires which turn into "knots of hatred."

A society so dominated is, as D.J. characterizes it, "mixed shit." When Rusty takes credit for killing a grizzly bear that D.J. actually downed, D.J. wants no more of that society. He sneaks out of camp with his teen-age friend, Tex Hyde, and they hike toward the summit of a neighboring peak in order to "clean their pipes," leaving the sign of their civilization's destructiveness—their rifles and knives—behind them. Out in the wilderness the "boys [get] their powers," for the forest is a-hum with a God that is not a man. Alone, away from the wraps of muffling civilization they are "charged with magnetism in electric cells," feel "the clean in them free of mixed shit . . . lying without a gun or a knife. . . ." This is the antidote to the obscenity of the mechanized bear hunt, and, allegorically, to the obscenity of napalm and bombing and defoliation in Vietnam. The point is driven home indirectly by D.J.'s language. In the long lyrical passage describing the boys' first day alone in the forest, fifteen or twenty miles from the nearest human being, the four-letter words are absent. D.J. and Tex are driven to take refuge in a tree when a grizzly appears. They watch it eat berries, belch contentedly, sleep, awaken with the passage of a caribou herd, and bring down a young caribou calf with the insensitive power of the beast. Later, a lone moose, grazing near their camp, raises his head, regards their fire—consciousness in that vastly powerful and frightening wilderness—and gives "a deep caw." In the animal's voice there is "a sound somewhere . . . which spoke beneath all else to Ranald Jethroe Jellicoe Jethroe and his friend . . . 'Texas' Hyde." To describe this, D.J. needs no obscenities, for Nature is not obscene and does not require deflation.

In the center of this idyll there is violence, killing, death—as the merciless bear's slaughter of the caribou lamb suggests. And, too, as the boys lie close together in human friendship listening to "something up here" saying to them, "come to me," murder springs up between them, for the God in that wilderness "was a beast, not a man, and God said, 'Go out and kill—fulfill my will, go and kill.' " They are near to their primordial selves, the beast in them, the seat of godly power. But the death they would bring about in their killing is a spiritual rather than a physical one. Each would own the other—subdue him—by being the first to take the other in pederasty. But each in turn, in the familiar contradiction, is afraid that the other will kill him, and neither wants to die. Through the night they have a psychological struggle, and then "something of the radiance of the North went into them," some indefinable communication that turns them away from pederasty. They reach their consummation. Liberated from the insulation of the civilized, they communicate in that "magnetic-electro fief of the dream" of the North, and they become "killer brothers, owned by something, prince of darkness, lord of light, they did not know. . . ." They have come as close as possible to the simultaneous experience of the animal's instinctual strength and the human's self-awareness.

The killer instinct that draws them together is a metaphor of the human rebel's fundamental stand in the protection of his life and his integrity. The point is illustrated in an earlier passage. As D.J. and Rusty are walking through the forest on the trail of a grizzly, D.J. suddenly discovers the "hole of his center"—that "It," perhaps, that Rojack speaks of, or the "hole in being" described by Sartre. He wants to kill his father, in the same way that Rojack wants to kill Barney Kelly. With his desire comes a memory. He sees his father beating him when he was five years old, and his father's face has the look of a madman, reflecting "a power which wishes to beat him to death." The fear of extinction arouses a murderous rage to protect oneself by destroying that which would destroy him. One says, with Camus's rebel, this far and no farther: it is *I* you would smother. It is in the rare openness of the North, where the "messages" of the gods are transmitted freely, that Tex and D.J. discover this elixir of consciousness, this sense of self. During these few hours they are free of the murk and drag of the American corporation, which kills, not in the defense of its life integrity, but in the attempt to justify its pride and self-importance.

In the end, the issue of Vietnam reappears. Consummation can only be momentary. Their second morning out, the boys are sucked back into the corporation, for "as morning comes on, one hour before dawn, they are scheming in their sleep, getting practical, getting ready to get up." The intimacy of the wilderness leaves them and civilization returns: ". . . the ionization layer (first cousin to static telepathic affairs) comes down again like a cloud, and intercranial communication is muffled. . . ." They hike back to camp and return to their home state of Texas, where two years later D.J. recalls all of this while seated at the dinner table. The occasion is a party to celebrate his departure the next day for Vietnam. The American atmosphere has been reinstated; the obscenities have returned to D.J.'s style.

D.J.'s time in the forest in the Arctic Circle is as close to consummation as Mailer has allowed any of his characters to get. But Mailer, with the same premises as the "open decision," affirms that we are human and must always return to the human, and that is the sphere of the limited and the muffled. In the end, Mailer restates one of the principal themes: the failure inherent in the human being to realize his total strength. Yet, though he dramatizes the ultimate limitations of the human state, he also sees the moment of glory, when the life of limiting order and rationality is charged with magic, power, and the inexpressible. This is the ambivalence of the "open decision," which finds reality in the individual, inherently free and open to possibility, but surrounded by time, chance, death, nature, and a society that would own or thwart him.

For Mailer, then, the highest good occurs when the human being plunges to the core of his authentic self, opening his own unique circuits of perception and experience, gambling courageously against life and death. There are times—for example, in *The White Negro* —when that good might entail violence directed against others when violence means a liberation from fear and conformity. And certainly neither Sergius O'Shaughnessey nor Stephen Rojack is concerned with the kind of "service" we find in the desires of Bellow's Eugene Henderson of Moses Herzog. Yet, Mailer, whose vision of the impossible contradiction between man's desire for omnipotence and the forces that thwart that power is one of the most vital in contemporary fiction, is not immoral from the standpoint of the "open decision." As I have pointed out, the ideal society referred to in *Barbary Shore* depends upon the willingness of individuals to come to terms with their own open condition. And Mailer's contempt for and attacks against suffocating social structures expresses a concern for an auspicious environment which shows a "generality of outlook." Nor is this merely ingenious maneuvering of a recalcitrant attitude. The obscenity Mailer uses in *Why Are We in Vietnam?* is a weapon used in an attack against an immoral social apparatus. His use of that weapon is a moral act. Its goal is the disclosure of an environment more hospitable to the crucial exploration of the "rebellious imperatives of the self." But the point to be made here is that such exploration does not result in self-isolation and hedonistic self-indulgence. If it is valuable for one, *Why Are We in Vietnam?* implies, it must be valuable for all. The exposure of the forces that thwart such exploration is the work of one who has already explored his own imperatives and been led to affirm the right of others to do the same. By such affirmation does the human being demonstrate his own "morality of outlook" and confirm his solidarity with others. It is that affirmation which is the tacit assumption of *Why Are We in Vietnam?* and that may be logically deduced from all of Mailer's novels. The very attention he devotes to the struggle of the individual to realize himself testifies to his own certainty that this is the moral problem of all of us who live in the human condition by the values of the "open decision."

CONCLUSION

I HAVE TRIED to show that the contemporary American novel embodies a world view that is formulated in the science, the social science, and the philosophy of our time. That view is characterized by the "open decision" and influences the way we perceive both our physical world and our human world, and stands at the basis of our modern morality. It assumes that reality lies in the individual, that the individual is subjective and ambiguous, that the preferred state is to be as much an individual as possible, that such individuality requires "true consciousness," that from true consciousness emerges a concern for others and a sense of human solidarity. These metaphysical and moral assumptions reflect some of the main preoccupations of our age. Men, bereft of their old explanations, feel themselves adrift; condemned to freedom, find themselves terrified to choose; confronted with inescapable responsibility for their actions, draw back from the risk it entails; deprived of total explanation, continue their frustrated search for it; limited in their strength, are vulnerable to the social apparatus; isolated in their own individual skins seek for love and community.

The contemporary American novelist frames his action in terms of this world view and its attendant morality. The individual—the highest good—is constantly endangered by suffocating social institutions and by his own shortcomings: his tendency toward bad faith, his vulnerability to chance and death, his fear of exposing himself to the human condition. The means of achieving the highest good and the highest good itself are essentially the same. One avoids being stifled by the apparatus, escapes bad faith, transcends chance and death, and learns to affirm the human condition through the very characteristics that define the human being —"true consciousness," independence, commitment, love, the willingness to risk oneself. The novels I have discussed in this book do not express a uniform attitude toward these concerns. Some, especially the early war novels, display a profound hopelessness, dramatizing the destruction of admirable men by an inhuman, "non-living" society. But for the most part, the report of the contemporary American novelist is positive. He finds in the human condition the proper theater for the acting out of human value, and he emphasizes the intrinsic worth of the individual human being. The pain of his characters rises principally from their difficulty in finding themselves and the consequent ground of their worth.

This has been a book about contemporary ideas and contemporary novelists. I have omitted any systematic references to previous history. However, the values I have noted above and throughout are not unique to our age. The "open decision" is the modern way of expressing values long cherished in the western philosophical and literary tradition. What is new is the metaphysical basis for these values. For the modern, the individual is valuable because he is ultimate reality, not because some more ultimate good has created him and conferred value upon him. The values of love, human compassion, and independence arise from the notion that they constitute the vivid awareness that is the center of individual satisfaction. For the modern, the human being is *causa sui*, causally independent, deprived of any appeal to some higher authority. He is alone in the universe except for other awarenesses, with nothing to fall back upon except himself. It is this conviction that gives new urgency to the ethics of human solidarity and new meaning to a modern vocabulary that expresses long-held values. If meaning comes only from ourselves, if death is the absolute conclusion to our life, what comfort can we take in supporting any abstract principles that call for the death or the pain or the coercion of any human being? The sad fact is that some argument can always be adduced precisely in support of just such principles. It is a pleasure to note, however, that such arguments have not yet appeared in the contemporary American novel. Perhaps it presents no romantic optimism for some imminent utopia or for the imminent regeneration of the human race. But our novelists do look at the world honestly, as their twentieth-century world picture allows them to. And they do ultimately celebrate the intrinsic value—even worth—of the human being. This is not a trivial thing to do.

NOTES

Part One

INTRODUCTION

1. Max Scheler, *Philosophical Perspectives,* trans. Hans Meyerhoff (Boston: Beacon Press, 1961) p. 101.
2. *Man in the Modern Age,* trans. Eden and Cedar Paul (London: Routledge & Kegan Paul Ltd., 1959) p. 143.
3. *Philosophical Investigations,* trans. G. E. M. Anscome (Oxford: Basil Blackwell, 1958) p. 167e.

CHAPTER 1

1. *Turning Points in Physics* (New York: Harper & Row, 1961) p. 13.
2. *Science and the Modern World* (New York: New American Library, 1962) p. 88.
3. Quoted by David Park, *Contemporary Physics* (New York: Harcourt, Brace & World, 1964) p. 13.
4. *The Quest for Certainty, A Study of the Relation of Knowledge and Action* (London: George Allen & Unwin, 1930) p. 115.
5. Quoted by E. N. da C. Andrade, *Rutherford and the Nature of the Atom* (Garden City, New York: Doubleday, 1964) p. 73.
6. cf. Werner Heisenberg, *Physics and Philosophy* (New York: Harper & Row, 1962) pp. 30–31.
7. George Gamow, *Biography of Physics* (New York: Harper & Row, 1961) p. 243.
8. *Contemporary Physics,* pp. 38–39.
9. Albert Einstein and Leopold Infeld, *The Evolution of Physics* (New York: Simon and Schuster, 1961) p. 275.
10. *Nuclear Physics* (New York: Philosophical Library, 1953) p. 30.
11. *Physics and Philosophy,* p. 56.
12. *The Evolution of Physics,* p. 280.
13. *Physics and Philosophy,* p. 45.
14. *Contemporary Physics,* p. 45.
15. Ira Freeman and Arthur March, *The New World of Physics* (New York: Vintage Books, n.d.) p. 169.
16. (Princeton, New Jersey: Princeton University Press, 1960) p. 749.
17. *The Quest for Certainty,* p. 196.
18. *The ABC of Relativity* (London: Kegan Paul, Trench, Trubner, 1925) pp. 215, 214.

19. *Ibid.*, pp. 209, 150.
20. *Ibid.*, p. 191.
21. *Ibid.*
22. *Ibid.*, p. 190.
23. *Einstein's Theory of Relativity*, revised edition (New York: Dover, 1962) p. 3.
24. Quoted by R. G. Collingwood from the *Scholium*, *The Idea of Nature* (New York: Oxford University Press, 1960) p. 108.
25. Sir James Jeans, *The Growth of Physical Science* (Greenwich, Connecticut: Fawcett, 1961) pp. 258–259.
26. *Evolution of Physics*, pp. 177, 186.
27. *The ABC of Relativity*, pp. 52, 50.
28. *Relativity*, trans. Robert W. Lawson (New York: Henry Holt, 1920) p. 86.
29. *Evolution of Physics*, p. 237.
30. *Relativity*, p. 118.
31. *The ABC of Relativity*, p. 118.
32. *Space, Time and Gravitation* (New York: Harper & Row, 1959) pp. 180, 182.
33. *Evolution of Physics*, p. 31.
34. *Causality and Chance in Modern Physics* (New York: Harper & Row, 1961) p. 31.
35. *Anatomy of Criticism* (Princeton, New Jersey: Princeton University Press, 1957) pp. 348, 62.
36. *Quanta and Reality; A Symposium* (New York: World Publishing Co., 1964) pp. 56–57.

CHAPTER 2

1. Alfred North Whitehead, *Process and Reality* (New York: Harper & Row, 1960) p. 4; original edition (New York: Macmillan, 1929).
2. This is the term he uses most frequently in *Process and Reality;* elsewhere he uses *actual occasion, natural occasion, occasion of experience,* and the like.
3. *Process and Reality*, pp. 178, 177.
4. *Ibid.*, p. ix.
5. *Ibid.*, p. 8.
6. *Adventures of Ideas* (New York: New American Library, n.d.) p. 187.
7. *Man's Place in Nature*, p. 74.
8. *Process and Reality*, pp. 20, 19, x.
9. *Ibid.*, p. 23.
10. *Ibid.*, p. 121.
11. *Ibid.*, pp. 10, 11.
12. *Ibid.*, p. 122.
13. *Adventures of Ideas*, p. 178.
14. *Process and Reality*, p. 65.
15. *Ibid.*, p. 133.
16. (New York: Dover Publications, 1962) p. 21.
17. *Adventures of Ideas*, pp. 186, 183.
18. *Ibid.*, p. 200.
19. *Process and Reality*, p. 135.
20. *Adventures of Ideas*, p. 185.
21. *Process and Reality*, p. 129.

22. *Ethics,* trans. J. A. K. Thomson (Baltimore: Penguin Books, 1955) p. 25.
23. Ivor Leclerc, *Whitehead's Metaphysics: An Introductory Exposition* (New York: Macmillan, 1958) p. 214.
24. *Process and Reality,* pp. 137, 127.
25. *Adventures of Ideas,* pp. 208–209.
26. *Ibid.,* pp. 238–239.
27. *Process and Reality,* p. 23.
28. *Adventures of Ideas,* p. 209.
29. *Process and Reality,* p. 160.
30. *Adventures of Ideas,* p. 179.
31. *Process and Reality,* p. 143.
32. *Ibid.,* p. 254.
33. *Ideas: A General Introduction to Pure Phenomenology,* trans. W. R. Boyce Gibson (New York: Macmillan, 1958) p. 182.
34. "Philosophy as a Strict Science," trans. Quentin Lauer, S.J., *Cross Currents,* VI (Summer, 1956), p. 236.
35. *Ibid.,* p. 244.
36. *Science and the Modern World* (New York: New American Library, 1962) p. 80.
37. *Ideas,* pp. 43, 129, 375, 135.
38. *Ibid.,* pp. 130, 138.
39. *Ibid.,* p. 17.
40. *Ibid.,* pp. 145, 169.
41. Pierre Thevenaz, *What Is Phenomenology?,* trans. James M. Edie, *et al.* (Chicago: Quadrangle Books, 1962) p. 121.
42. *Ideas,* p. 222.
43. *Being and Time,* trans. John Macquarrie and Edward Robinson (London: SCM Press, 1962) p. 32.
44. *Adventures of Ideas,* p. 178.
45. *Existentialism from Within* (New York: Macmillan, 1953) p. 30.
46. Examples of inauthentic existence can be found in the stereotypes of the present age formulated by other authors: Ortega y Gasset's mass-man, W. H. Whyte's Organization Man, Riesman's "other-directed" man.
47. Werner Brock, *Existence and Being* (Chicago: Henry Regnery, 1949) p. 58.
48. *Invitation to Sociology: A Humanistic Perspective* (Garden City, N.Y.: Doubleday, 1963) p. 146.
49. *Existence and Being,* p. 71.
50. *Ideas,* p. 119.
51. Wilfrid Desan, *The Tragic Finale: An Essay on the Philosophy of Jean-Paul Sartre* (Cambridge, Mass.: Harvard University Press, 1954) p. 10.
52. *Being and Nothingness,* trans. Hazel Barnes (New York: Philosophical Library, 1956) p. lxii.
53. *Ibid.,* pp. 565–566.
54. *Ibid.,* p. 90.
55. *Nausea,* trans. Lloyd Alexander (New York: New Directions, 1959) pp. 211, 162.
56. *Being and Nothingness,* p. 70.
57. "Existentialism as Humanism" in William V. Spanos, *A Casebook on Existentialism* (New York: Crowell, 1966) p. 294.

CHAPTER 3

1. *Two Major Works of Charles H. Cooley* (New York: The Free Press, 1956) p. 68.
2. *Ibid.*, p. 37.
3. *Reconstruction in Philosophy* (Boston: The Beacon Press, 1962) pp. 208–209.
4. *Methodology of the Social Sciences,* trans. Edward A. Shils and Henry A. Finch (New York: The Free Press, 1949) pp. 52, 53, 7.
5. With this phrase, Mannheim links himself with Scheler, for Scheler invented it: *Man's Place in Nature,* trans. Hans Meyerhoff (Boston: Beacon Press, 1961) p. xxii.
6. *Ideology and Utopia,* trans. Louis Wirth and Edward Shils (New York: Harcourt, Brace and World, 1959) p. 190.
7. *Man and Society* (London: K. Paul, Trench, Trubner, 1949) p. 369.
8. *Ibid.*, p. 352.
9. *Ibid.*, pp. 377, 315.
10. Reinhold Niebuhr, *Moral Man and Immoral Society* (New York: Charles Scribner's Sons, 1960) pp. xvi, 257.
11. *Man in the Modern Age,* pp. 178, 182–183.
12. *The Web of Government* (New York: Macmillan, 1947) p. 409.
13. Calvin Hall, *A Primer of Freudian Psychology* (New York: New American Library, 1959) p. 26.
14. *Interpretation of Dreams,* trans. A. A. Brill (New York: Random House, 1950) p. 465.
15. *The Ego and the Id,* trans. Joan Riviere (New York: Norton, 1962) p. 15.
16. *Ibid.*, pp. 42, 2.
17. *Totem and Taboo,* trans. James Strachey (New York: Norton, 1950) p. 30.
18. *General Introduction to Psychoanalysis,* trans. Joan Riviere (New York: Washington Square Press, 1960) p. 289.
19. *The Ego and the Id,* p. 7.
20. *General Introduction to Psychoanalysis,* pp. 290–292.
21. *Ibid.*, p. 112.
22. *Ibid.*
23. *Ibid.*
24. *Escape from Freedom* (New York: Rinehart, 1941) pp. 257, 260, 261.
25. *Ibid.*, p. 273.
26. *New Ways in Psychoanalysis* (New York: W. W. Norton, 1939) p. 11.
27. *Childhood and Society* (New York: W. W. Norton, 1950) p. 233, *et passim.*
28. *Two Essays in Analytical Psychology,* ed. G. Alder, *et al.*, trans. R. F. Hull, Collected Works, VII (New York: Pantheon, 1966) p. 238.
29. *The Structure and Dynamics of the Psyche, in Collected Works,* VIII (New York: Pantheon, 1960) pp. 185, 279.
30. *The Practice of Psychotherapy, Collected Works* (2nd edition), XVI (New York: Pantheon, 1966) p. 34.
31. cf. Erikson, *Childhood and Society:* ego integrity "is a comradeship with the ordering ways of distant times and pursuits," p. 233.
32. *The Structure and Dynamics of the Psyche,* p. 205.
33. *Ibid.*
34. *Ibid.*, p. 210.

35. *The Archetypes and the Collective Unconscious, Collected Works* (2nd edition), IX, Part I (New York, Pantheon, 1968) pp. 284–285.
36. *The Structure and Dynamics of the Psyche,* p. 213.
37. *Ibid.,* p. 208.
38. *Ibid.,* p. 210.
39. *Two Essays,* p. 185.
40. *Ibid.,* p. 238.
41. *The Structure and Dynamics of the Psyche,* p. 189.
42. *Two Essays,* p. 192.
43. *The Archetypes of the Collective Unconscious,* p. 282.
44. *Two Essays,* p. 171.
45. *The Structure and Dynamics of the Psyche,* p. 83.
46. *The Archetypes and the Collective Unconscious,* p. 288.
47. *Two Essays,* p. 176.
48. *The Structure and Dynamics of the Psyche,* p. 72.
49. *Two Essays,* pp. 235, 234.
50. *Modern Man in Search of A Soul,* trans. W. S. Dell and Cary F. Baynes (New York: Harcourt, Brace, n.d.) pp. 237, 238.
51. *The Quest for Identity* (New York. W. W. Norton, 1958) pp. 127–128.
52. *The Mystery of Being* (Chicago, Illinois: Henry Regnery, 1960) I, p. 164.
53. *Being and Nothingness,* pp. 599, 626.
54. *Homo Ludens: A Study of the Play-Element in Culture* (Boston: Beacon Press, 1960) pp. 5, 3.
55. *Ibid.,* pp. 14, 24.
56. *Ibid.,* pp. 211, 212.
57. *The True Believer: Thoughts on the Nature of Mass Movements* (New York: Harper & Row, 1951) pp. 79, 80, 31.
58. *Homo Ludens,* p. 213.
59. *Erasmus and the Age of the Reformation* (New York: Harper, 1957) p. 104.
60. *Reconstruction in Philosophy,* pp. 168, 162–163.
61. Spanos, ed., *A Casebook on Existentialism,* p. 289.
62. *The Myth of Sisyphus* (New York: Random House, 1959) p. 38.
63. *Ibid.*
64. *The Rebel* (New York: Random House, 1960) p. 6.
65. *Ibid.,* p. 22, 281, 138, 284.
66. *Ibid.,* pp. 295, 67.
67. *Ibid.,* p. 302.

Part Two

INTRODUCTION

1. cf. Basil Willey, *The Seventeenth-Century Background* (Garden City, N.Y.: Doubleday, 1953) pp. 13–14.

CHAPTER 4

1. *Fiction of the Forties* (Chicago: University of Chicago Press, 1963) p. 21.
2. In the following list I cite the original edition of the novels discussed. If I also list a paperback edition, that is the copy from which I quote in the text.

Fred Booth, *Victory Also Ends* (New York: Rinehart, 1952).
Ned Calmer, *The Strange Land* (New York: Charles Scribner's Sons, 1950).
Paper: (New York: New American Library, 1951).
John Cobb, *The Gesture* (New York: Harper & Row, 1948).
James Gould Cozzens, *Guard of Honor* (New York: Harcourt, Brace & World, 1948).
Stefan Haym, *The Crusaders* (Boston: Little, Brown, 1948).
James Jones, *From Here to Eternity* (New York: Charles Scribner's Sons, 1951).
Paper: (New York: New American Library, 1953).
Dan Levin, *Mask of Glory* (New York: McGraw-Hill, 1948).
Paper: (New York: Popular Library, 1952).
Norman Mailer, *The Naked and the Dead* (New York: Rinehart, 1948).
Paper: (New York: New American Library, 1951).
Irwin Shaw, *The Young Lions* (New York: Random House, 1948).
Paper: (New York: New American Library, 1950).
Herman Wouk, *The Caine Mutiny* (Garden City, N.Y.: Doubleday, 1951).

3. Ned Calmer, a news analyst and a war correspondent, has written other novels, such as *Beyond the Street* (1934) and *All the Summer Days* (1961).

4. Heym, who is German-born, was in the U.S. Army during World War II, first as a private, then as a lieutenant in psychological warfare. He wrote two other books about the war: *Hostages* (1942) and *Of Smiling Peace* (1944).

5. *Escape From Freedom*, pp. 162–164.

6. *The Radical Novel in the United States, 1900–1954* (Cambridge, Mass.: Harvard University Press, 1956) p. 218.

7. *Advertisements for Myself* (New York: The New American Library, 1960) p. 200.

8. This is a pseudonym for John C. Cooper III.

9. Joseph Waldmeir, "Novelists of Two Wars," *Nation*, CLXXXVII, no. 14, 306.

10. Dan Levin has also written *The Dream of Flesh* (1953), *The Son of Judah* (1961), and *Stormy Petrel: The Life and Work of Maxim Gorky* (1965).

11. (New York: New American Library, 1948) p. 10.

12. cf. Malcolm Cowley, *The Literary Situation* (New York: Viking, 1958) pp. 23–42.

13. In this list, if a paperback is included, that is the text I cite.
Mitchell Goodman, *The End of It* (New York: Horizon Press, 1961).
Joseph Heller, *Catch-22* (New York: Simon and Schuster, 1961).
Paper: (New York: Dell, 1962).
James Jones, *The Thin Red Line* (New York: Charles Scribner's Sons, 1962).
Stephen Linakis, *The Spring the War Ended* (New York: Putnam, 1965).
George Mandel, *The Wax Boom* (New York: Random House, 1962).
Paper: (New York: Bantam Books, 1963).
James E. Ross, *The Dead Are Mine* (New York: David McKay, 1963).

14. Goodman is the husband of poetess Denise Levertov, and has been writing since 1948.

15. Mandel has sometimes been associated with the Beat Generation. A prolific writer, he has published, besides *The Wax Boom, Flee the Angry Strangers* (1952), *Beatville, U.S.A.* (1961), *Borderline Cases* (1962), and other books. Linakis, like his hero, deserted from the Army, was court-martialed and imprisoned, and learned to write while serving his prison term.

Ross was convicted of murder in 1950 and was sentenced to a term in Washington State Penitentiary. There he finished his high school education.

CHAPTER 5

1. *The Organization Man* (Garden City, N.Y.: Doubleday, 1957) pp. 147, 7.

2. Review of Alan Harrington's *Life in the Crystal Palace, Saturday Review,* XLIII (Jan. 2, 1960), p. 35.

3. "To Whom and for What Ends Is Corporate Management Responsible?" in *The Corporation in Modern Society,* ed. Edward S. Mason (Cambridge, Mass.: Harvard University Press, 1960) p. 59.

4. Following is a list of novels dealt with in this chapter. If I list the paperback, that is the edition from which I quote.

John Brooks, *The Big Wheel* (New York: Harper & Brothers, 1949).
———, *The Man Who Broke Things* (New York: Harper & Brothers, 1958).
George de Mare, *The Empire* (New York: G. P. Putnam's Sons, 1956).
Seymour Epstein, *The Successor* (New York: Charles Scribner's Sons, 1961).
Garth Hale (pseud.), *Legacy for Our Sons* (New York: E. P. Dutton, 1952).
Cameron Hawley, *Executive Suite* (Boston: Houghton Mifflin, 1952).
Paper (Boston: Ballantine Books), 1952.
Stanley Kaufmann, *A Change of Climate* (New York: Rinehart, 1954).
Frederick Laing, *The Giant's House* (New York: Dial, 1955).
Ralph Maloney, *Daily Bread* (Boston: Houghton Mifflin, 1960).
Robert Molloy, *The Other Side of the Hill* (Garden City, N.Y.: Doubleday, 1962).
Theodore Morrison, *The Whole Creation* (New York: Viking, 1962).
W. H. Prosser, *Nine To Five* (Boston: Little, Brown, 1953).
Ayn Rand, *Atlas Shrugged* (New York: Random House, 1957).
Howard Swiggett, *The Power and the Prize* (New York: Ballantine Books, 1954).
———, *The Durable Fire* (Boston: Houghton Mifflin, 1957).
Amelia Elizabeth Walden, *The Bradford Story* (New York: Appleton-Century-Crofts, 1956).
Sloan Wilson, *The Man in the Gray Flannel Suit* (New York: Simon and Schuster, 1955).

5. Garth Hale is the pseudonym of Albert Benjamin Cunningham, born in 1888, teacher and author of some twelve other novels under his real name and two others, *Substance of A Dream* (1951) and *That Love Hath an End* (1951), under Garth Hale.

6. Howard Swiggett is the author of several other books, including *War Out of Niagara* (1933) and *The Extraordinary Mr. Morris* (1952). Amelia Elizabeth Walden, once a teacher, has devoted most of her time to writing books for young people, such as *Gateway* (1946), and *Palomino Girl* (1957).

7. Prosser worked as a cub reporter before he went to Harvard. He joined an advertising agency after graduation from college, then turned to full-time writing.

8. Joe Morgan, a newspaperman, has also written *Amy Go Home* (1964).

9. Frederick Laing has also written *Why Heimdall Blew His Horn* (1968), and several children's books.

10. Stanley Kaufmann is a *New York Times* critic and the author of many other novels, including *The Hidden Hero* (1949), *The Tightrope* (1952), and *If It Be Love* (1960).

11. George de Mare was once an executive for A.T. & T.

12. Epstein is the author of several other novels, among them the excellent *Leah* (1964).

13. Robert Molloy was born in 1906 and has also written *Pride's Way* (1946), *A Multitude of Sins* (1953), and *The Reunion* (1959).

14. Ralph Maloney spent several years in public relations and is the author of several other books, including *Manbait* (1960) and *The Great Bonacker Whiskey War* (1966).

CHAPTER 6

1. Trocchi is a Britisher, but *Cain's Book* was written about America in America and so I take him to be a legitimate part of this study.

2. Following is a list of the novels dealt with in this chapter. If I list the paperback, that is the edition from which I quote.

Elliott Baker, *A Fine Madness* (New York: Putnam, 1964).
Chandler Brossard, *The Bold Saboteurs* (New York: Farrar, Straus & Young), 1953).
Paper: (New York: Lancer Books, 1962).
William Burroughs, *Naked Lunch* (Paris: Olympia Press, 1959).
———, *The Soft Machine* (Paris: Olympia Press, 1964).
———, *Nova Express* (New York: Grove Press, 1964).
J. P. Donleavy, *The Ginger Man* (Paris: Olympia Press, 1955).
Alfred Grossman, *Acrobat Admits* (New York: Braziller, 1959).
———, *Many Slippery Errors* (London: Heinemann, 1963).
John Clellon Holmes, *The Horn* (New York: Random House, 1958).
———, *Get Home Free* (New York: Dutton, 1964).
Jack Kerouac, *On The Road* (New York: Viking, 1957).
Paper: (New York: New American Library, 1959).
———, *The Subterraneans* (New York: Grove Press, 1958).
Alexander Trocchi, *Cain's Book* (New York: Grove Press, 1960).

3. *Advertisements for Myself* (New York, New American Library, 1960), p. 313.

4. *Evergreen Review,* II, no. 5, pp. 72–73.

Part Three

CHAPTER 7

1. *The Quest for Identity* (New York: Norton, 1958), p. 189.

2. Following is a list of novels dealt with in this chapter. If I list the paperback, that is the edition from which I quote.

Ralph Ellison, *Invisible Man* (New York: Random House, 1952).
Paper: (New York: New American Library, n.d.).
Ken Kesey, *One Flew Over The Cuckoo's Nest* (New York: Viking, 1962).
Paper: (New York: New American Library, 1963).
Carson McCullers, *Member of the Wedding* (Boston: Houghton Mifflin, 1946).
Paper: (New York: Bantam Books, 1958).
Flannery O'Connor, *Wise Blood* (New York: Harcourt, Brace, 1952).
Paper: (New York: New American Library, 1962), in *Three.*
Walker Percy, *The Moviegoer* (New York: Knopf, 1961).
Paper: (New York: Popular Library, 1962).

James Purdy, *The Nephew* (New York: Farrar, Strauss & Cudahy, 1960).
Paper: (New York: Avon, n.d.).
Thomas Pynchon, *V.* (New York: Lippincott, 1963).
Paper: (New York: Bantam Books, 1964).
J. D. Salinger, *The Catcher in the Rye* (Boston: Little, Brown, 1951).
Paper: (New York: New American Library).
William Styron, *Set This House On Fire* (New York: Random House, 1960).
John Updike, *Rabbit, Run* (New York: Knopf, 1960).
Paper: (New York: Fawcett, 1962).

3. *Modern Man in Search of a Soul,* p. 197.

4. *The Rebel,* p. 261.

5. *Preparation for a Christian Life,* in *Selections From the Writings of Kierkegaard,* trans. Lee M. Hollander (Garden City, N.Y.: Doubleday, 1960), p. 169.

6. I deliberately use the word *technology* here rather than *science,* because modern science is founded essentially upon the principles of relativity and indeterminacy, which acknowledge the limits of rational empiricism in accounting for reality in itself. The antagonists of these novelists are the engineers and technologists whose approach to experience is allegedly materialistic and simplistic.

7. *Preparation for a Christian Life,* pp. 175–177.

8. trans. Walter Lowrie (Garden City, N.Y.: Doubleday, 1954), pp. 142–143.

9. *Ibid.,* p. 142.

10. It is surely unnecessary to belabor here the obvious connections with blind Teiresias, the blinding of Oedipus, and the blinding of Paul on the road to Damascus, all of whom found truth in darkness.

11. (New York: Harcourt, Brace, 1956), p. 169.

CHAPTER 8

1. John Barth's novels are as follows (the paperback listing means I cite that edition in my text):
The Floating Opera (New York: Appleton-Century-Crofts, 1956).
Paper: (New York: Avon, 1965).
End of the Road (Garden City, N.Y.: Doubleday, 1958).
Paper: (New York: Avon, 1960).
The Sot-Weed Factor (Garden City, N.Y.: Doubleday, 1960).
Paper: (New York: Grossett and Dunlap, 1966).
Giles Goat-Boy (Garden City, N.Y.: Doubleday, 1966).
Paper: (Greenwich, Connecticut: Fawcett, 1968).

2. (Garden City, N.Y.: Doubleday, 1967). This is the original version, predating the versions published in 1956 and 1965.

3. Kurt Vonnegut's novels are as follows (the paperback listing means I cite that edition in my text):
Player Piano (New York: Scribner's, 1952).
Paper: (New York: Avon, 1967).
The Sirens of Titan (Boston: Houghton Mifflin, 1959).
Paper: (New York: Dell, 1966).
Mother Night (Greenwich, Connecticut: Gold Medal Books, 1961).
Paper: (New York: Avon, 1967).
Cat's Cradle (New York: Holt, Rinehart & Winston, 1963).
Paper: (New York: Dell, 1965).

God Bless You, Mr. Rosewater (New York: Holt, Rinehart & Winston, 1965).
Paper: (New York: Dell, 1966).
Slaughterhouse-Five; or The Children's Crusade (New York: Holt, Rinehart & Winston, 1969).

4. Bernard Malamud's novels are as follows (the paperback listing means that I cite that edition in my text):
The Natural (New York: Harcourt, Brace, 1952); (New York: Farrar, Straus & Giroux, 1966) (this is edition cited).
The Assistant (New York: Farrar, Straus & Cudahy, 1957).
Paper: (New York: New American Library, 1964).
A New Life (London: Eyre & Spottiswoode, 1961).
Paper: (New York: Dell, 1963).
The Fixer (New York: Farrar, Straus & Giroux, 1966).
Paper: (New York: Dell, 1967).

5. Saul Bellow's novels are as follows (the paperback listing means I cite that edition in my text):
Dangling Man (New York: Vanguard, 1944).
Paper: (New York: Meridian Books, 1960).
The Victim (New York: Vanguard, 1947).
Paper: (New York: New American Library, 1965).
The Adventures of Augie March (New York: Viking, 1953).
Paper: (Greenwich, Connecticut: Fawcett, 1965).
Seize The Day (New York: Viking, 1956).
Paper: (New York: Viking, n.d.).
Henderson The Rain King (New York: Viking, 1959).
Paper: (New York: Popular Library, 1960).
Herzog (New York: Viking, 1964).
Paper: (Greenwich, Connecticut: Fawcett, 1965).
Mr. Sammler's Planet (New York: Viking), 1970.

6. Norman Mailer's novels are as follows (the paperback listing means I cite that edition in my text):
The Naked and the Dead, loc. cit., Chapter 4.
Barbary Shore (New York: Rinehart, 1951).
Paper: (New York: New American Library, n.d.).
The Deer Park (New York: Putnam, 1955).
Paper: (New York: New American Library, 1959).
An American Dream (New York: Dial, 1965).
Paper: (New York: Dell, 1966).
Why Are We in Vietnam? (New York: Putnam, 1967).
Paper: (New York: Putnam, 1968).

7. in *Advertisements for Myself* (New York: New American Library, 1960) p. 304.

8. *Ibid.*, p. 316.

9. *Ibid.*

10. *Existence and Being, loc. cit.*, Chapter 2; pp. 66–67.

11. "Hölderlin and the Essence of Poetry," in *Existence and Being*, pp. 285, 287.

12. in *Advertisements for Myself*, p. 202.

13. "The Man Who Studied Yoga," in *Advertisements for Myself*, p. 169.

14. *Ibid.*, p. 304.

15. "The Steps of the Pentagon," *Harper's* (March, 1968), p. 65.

INDEX